Handbook
of
Korean
Vocabulary

Handbook

of

Korean

Vocabulary

A Resource for
Word Recognition and Comprehension

Miho Choo & William O'Grady

University of Hawai'i Press

Honolulu

01 00 99   5 4 3 2

A Study from the Center for Korean Studies, University of Hawai'i

The Center for Korean Studies was established in 1972 to
coordinate and develop the resources for the study of Korea at the
University of Hawai'i. Its goals are to enhance faculty quality and
performance in Korean studies; to develop comprehensive,
balanced academic programs; to stimulate research and
publications; and to coordinate the resources of the University of
Hawai'i with those of other institutions, organizations, and
individual scholars engaged in the study of Korea. Reflecting the
diversity of the academic disciplines represented by affiliated
members of the University faculty, the Center seeks especially to
promote interdisciplinary and intercultural studies.

Library of Congress Cataloging-in-Publication Data
Choo, Miho, 1959–
    Handbook of Korean vocabulary : a resource for word
recognition and comprehension / Miho Choo & William O'Grady.
        p.   cm.
    Includes bibliographical references and index.
    ISBN 0–8248–1738–9 (cloth) ISBN 0–8248–1815–6 (pbk.)
    1. Korean language—Glossaries, vocabularies, etc. I. O'Grady,
William D. (William Delaney), 1952– . II. Title.
PL939.C517 1996
495.7'82421—dc20   95–38076
                                                CIP

Camera-ready copy for this book was prepared by the authors.

Contents

Acknowledgments

We have benefited from the insightful comments and suggestions of several colleagues during our preparation of the *Handbook*. We would like to express our gratitude to Dong-Jae Lee for his detailed commentary on parts of an earlier version of the *Handbook*. We also acknowledge with gratitude the feedback received from the anonymous reviewers commissioned by the University of Hawai'i Press as well as the helpful comments provided by Joel Bradshaw, Seongchan Kim, and the late Marshall Pihl.

We are grateful to Patricia Crosby and the editorial team at the University of Hawai'i Press for expertly guiding the manuscript through the review and production process. Special thanks are also due to the proofreaders and production specialists led by Cheri Dunn who helped us with preparation of the final manuscript. We also owe an enormous debt of gratitude to Seok-Hoon You for his invaluable advice and assistance with the computer hardware and software used to produce the *Handbook*.

Work on the *Handbook* was supported by grants from the Research Relations Fund, the Dean's Research Support Fund, and the National Resource Center at the University of Hawai'i as well as by a publication grant from the Center for Korean Studies. We are most grateful for this assistance.

Introduction: How to Use This Book

1. Background

Vocabulary learning is arguably the single most important component of second language acquisition. In cases where the second language is unrelated to one's native language, this task presents special challenges since there are typically few clues in a word's form to assist in learning and remembering its meaning. Whereas English-speakers learning Spanish can easily guess the meaning of *automovíl* and can remember that *libro* means 'book' thanks to its similarity to words in their native language (cf. English *library*), the student of Korean finds no such help in dealing with 자동차 and 책.

However, this does not mean that Korean vocabulary must be acquired by endless rote memorization. To better understand this point, it is necessary to consider some facts about how words are formed in Korean.

Word structure and word formation

The vocabulary of Korean has two principal sources. Approximately forty-five percent of its words can be traced back to Middle and Old Korean. These so-called 'native Korean' words tend to denote things and concepts central to everyday life—body parts, traditional foods and cultural practices, kinship relations, basic actions, native plants and animals, and so forth.

Over half of all Korean words are of Chinese origin. These 'Sino-Korean' words are especially common in vocabulary areas pertaining to science, government, and society—a fact that can be traced to the extensive influence of Chinese culture and learning on Korea over a period of many centuries. A distinguishing feature of 'Sino-Korean' vocabulary items is that they are sometimes written in newspapers and scientific publications with Chinese characters (한자) rather than the traditional Korean alphabet, *hangul* (한글).

Both native Korean and Sino-Korean words are often built from smaller meaning-bearing units called *morphemes*. Of special interest to us are so-called *roots*, morphemes with wordlike meanings. This is because a particularly common strategy for word formation in Korean involves combining two or more roots to create a *compound* or other multipart expression. For example, the word 눈물 'tears' is built from the native Korean roots 눈 (meaning 'eye') and 물 ('water') while the word 학기 'semester' is built from the Chinese roots 학 ('study') and 기 ('period'). (Of course, English too has many compounds— *notebook*, *front porch*, *law school*, and so on.)

A very sizable portion of Korean vocabulary consists of compounds, and many of these are like 눈물 and 학기 in that their meaning can be at least partially determined from the meaning of their component roots. Herein lies the key to systematic and efficient vocabulary building for the student of Korean.

Each time you learn a new word, there is a very good chance that you have also learned part of several other words. For example, when you learn the word 학기, you have learned not only the Korean word for 'semester', but also half of many additional vocabulary items. This is because the root 기 'period' can be found in various words pertaining to time (such as 기한 'time limit' and 장기 'long-term') while the root 학 'study' forms part of several other words whose meaning pertains to studying (for example, 학교 'school' and 대학 'college'). And in learning the word for 'school' (학교), you are also learning half of the word for 'principal' (교장), half of the word for 'school uniform' (교복), and so on.

The *Handbook of Korean Vocabulary* is a type of 'root dictionary'. It is designed to provide the information necessary to increase the size of your vocabulary. In this way, a relatively small effort on your part can multiply to yield impressive dividends.

2. Organization

As you can see by looking ahead, the *Handbook* consists of a series of lists (more than fifteen hundred in all) divided into two parts. The first and larger section provides the lists for roots of Chinese origin while the second section contains lists of words that are built from native Korean morphemes.

Within each section, lists are arranged with respect to one another in alphabetical order, as determined by the Korean spelling of the root morpheme. The alphabetical order of the *hangul* consonant symbols is as follows.

ㄱ ㄲ ㄴ ㄷ ㄸ ㄹ ㅁ ㅂ ㅃ ㅅ ㅆ ㅇ ㅈ ㅉ ㅊ ㅋ ㅌ ㅍ ㅎ

(The symbol ㅇ has a dual status in the Korean alphabet: when it occurs in syllable-final position, it stands for a sound similar to the one at the end of the English word *sing*; however, when it occurs syllable-initially, it has no pronunciation.)

The alphabetical ordering employed for the vowel symbols is as follows.

ㅏ ㅐ ㅑ ㅒ ㅓ ㅔ ㅕ ㅖ ㅗ ㅘ ㅙ ㅚ ㅛ ㅜ ㅝ ㅞ ㅟ ㅠ ㅡ ㅢ ㅣ

Thus, combining the consonant and vowel orders, you can see that 가 will precede 개, which in turn will precede 고, and so forth. Similarly, a word beginning with

아 will precede one beginning with 애, which in turn will precede one commencing with 오 , and so forth.

Quite often you will find that distinct roots have an identical pronunciation and spelling. For example, there are several 가 morphemes in Korean, including one that means 'song', one that means 'add', another that means 'street', yet another that means 'specialist', and so on. Such *homophony* (different morphemes with the same pronunciation) is widespread in Korean. It is common to distinguish among Sino-Korean homophones by using the appropriate Chinese characters in addition to or in place of the *hangul* spelling. For example, each of the different 가 morphemes has its own Chinese character.

가 (歌)	song; sing		가 (可)	alright
가 (加)	add; apply		가 (假)	temporary; false
가 (街)	street		가 (家)	house; specialist

Because these Chinese characters are understood and used by educated speakers of Korean, especially in newspapers and scientific writing, each root of Chinese origin is accompanied by the appropriate character at the beginning of its list in the *Handbook*.

Within the lists

Each list is organized around a particular root morpheme and presents a set of (mostly) noun compounds formed from that root. In the case of longer lists and lists whose members have diverse meanings, we have tried to group the lexical items along semantic lines, with entries arranged in rough descending order of transparency within each group.

At the head of each list you will find the relevant root written in *hangul* together with its Chinese character (if there is one) and its English translation. So as to highlight the role of the root in word formation, it is written in boldface each time it appears in an item in its list.

Each entry in a list consists of a lexical item written in *hangul* followed by its colloquial interpretation and, wherever possible, a literal meaning (in square brackets). Thus, the list for the native Korean root 물 'water' includes the following entries. (The symbol '~' is used to stand for the literal meaning of the root from which the compounds in a particular list are formed.)

물   **water**
눈물   tears [eye~]
물개   otter [~dog]
물고기   live fish [~fish]

The first of these entries indicates that 눈물 has the colloquial meaning 'tears' and the literal meaning 'eye water'. Subsequent entries provide additional examples of words built from the root 물.

In the case of words containing a Sino-Korean root, entries also provide information about the Chinese character used to write individual compounds. (This information is for the sake of advanced students and those who are already familiar with Chinese characters; it can be ignored by others.) The character for the key morpheme, which is indicated at the head of the list, is not repeated in each entry; instead, the symbol '~' is used to mark its place. Consider in this regard some of the items in the list for the Sino-Korean root 물 (物) 'thing', which has the same pronunciation as the native Korean root exemplified above.

물 (物)   **thing**
보물   treasure [precious~] 寶 ~
동물   animal [move~] 動 ~
괴물   monster [strange~] 怪 ~

In the entry for 보물 'treasure', for example, information about the word's literal meaning ('precious thing') is followed by 寶 ~, with 寶 corresponding to the character for the root 보 'precious' and the tilde standing for the character associated with 물 'thing'. The entire compound can thus be written in Chinese characters as 寶物. Subsequent entries follow a similar pattern.

How to use the lists

It is anticipated that the *Handbook* will be employed as a supplement to whatever textbooks you are using. Because of the nature of Korean word formation, potentially any new vocabulary item that you encounter will occur in whole or in part in other words. Let's say, for example, that you are a beginning student and that you have just learned the word 책 'book'. By looking up that form in the *Handbook,* you will find a list of words that include many other useful items, including 공책 'notebook', 책방 'bookstore', and 책장 'bookcase'.

Or let's say that you have just encountered the word 한국 'Korea' for the first time. Since each syllable in a Korean word often corresponds to a separate root, you decide to look up both 한 and 국 in the *Handbook.* As you will quickly discover, both 한 (with the meaning 'Korea') and 국 ('country') serve as the building blocks for a large number of other words. For example, 한 shows up in the words 한복 'Korean dress', 북한 'North Korea', and 한식 'Korean food', while 국 is found in the words 국기 'national flag' and 외국 'foreign country' – to name just a few of the items offered by the *Handbook*.

Of course, you probably will not want to learn all the items in a particular list right away. But by looking through a list, you should see some useful words, given your current level of proficiency and particular communicative goals. Because you have already learned 'half' of each of these words just by learning the meaning of the root at the head of the list, you will probably find it relatively easy to acquire some additional items.

Not every morpheme that occurs in a particular compound will have its own list elsewhere in the *Handbook*. Normally, a root morpheme is given its own list only if it appears in at least three commonly used relatively transparent compounds. As it turns out, more Sino-Korean roots pass this 'productivity test' than do native Korean roots. This is why even some very basic native Korean roots have no list in the *Handbook* and why the set of Sino-Korean lists is much larger than its native Korean counterpart.

3. Types of Compounds

The vast majority of words listed in the *Handbook* are noun-noun compounds (i.e., compounds whose component parts are both nouns), although the section on native Korean presents a significant number of verb-verb compounds as well. Compounds of these types can be analyzed and classified in various ways. You will probably find it easier to use the *Handbook* if you are familiar with some of these distinctions.

Transparent vs. opaque compounds

For most Korean compounds, it is relatively easy to see how the meanings of the component morphemes contribute to the meaning of the entire word. (Such compounds are said to be *transparent* or *compositional*.) For example, given that 수 means 'number' and that 학 means 'study', it is not surprising that 수학 means 'mathematics'. Similarly, given that 군 denotes 'military' and 인 means 'person', it is not hard to remember that the word 군인 means 'soldier'.

Although transparent compounds are very common in Korean, there are also many *opaque* or *noncompositional* compounds, in which the meaning of the whole is not clearly related to the meaning of its parts. Consider, for example, the morpheme 사 'sand'. This morpheme appears in compounds such as 사막 'desert' and 백사장 'sandy beach', where its contribution to the meaning of the whole word is fairly transparent. However, it is also found in the far less transparent 사과 'apple' and 사공 'boatman', where its contribution to the meaning of the compound is much harder to discern.

While an educated native speaker familiar with the history of Korean might be able to explain how the meaning of an opaque compound is related to the meaning of its parts, this type of analysis cannot be expected of second language learners. We therefore anticipate that the *Handbook* will be most useful in the case of transparent compounds, whose component morphemes recur with roughly the same meaning in at least several words.

Long compounds

Most of the words in each list consist of two component parts—the key morpheme for the list in question and one other morpheme. For example, the following two-part or *binary* compounds appear in the list for the morpheme 가 (假) 'false':

> 가면　mask [~face] ~ 面
> 가발　wig [~hair] ~ 髪
> 가명　pseudonym; alias [~name] ~ 名

Not all compounds are binary, however. In fact, a very large number of Korean words consist of more than two roots. We can call such items *long compounds.*

Many long compounds are formed by combining an already existing binary compound with one or more other elements. You will often find such compounds treated as subentries that are indented and written in smaller type right below the binary compound from which they are built. Thus, the long compound 타자기 'typewriter' occurs immediately beneath the compound 타자 'typing'.

> 타자　typing [hit letter]
> 　타자기　typewriter

In the interests of economy, long compounds are not given a morpheme-by-morpheme translation; they are generally recorded once in the list for their final morpheme (which usually names the general class to which their referent belongs) and once in the list for the most semantically informative and productive of the other morphemes. Thus 타자기 in the example above appears in the list for 기 (機) 'machine' (since a typewriter is a type of machine) and in the list for 자 (字) 'letter'.

xiv

Idiom compounds

Many Korean idioms are actually a type of long compound. Although they are not in and of themselves grammatically complete sentences, they nonetheless express a complete thought or proposition—not unlike English sayings such as 'finders keepers, losers weepers' or 'first done, worst done'. One popular idiom of this sort is 견물생심 [see thing be born mind], which might be freely translated into English as 'seeing is wanting'.

By their very nature, idioms are relatively opaque and their precise meaning often cannot be determined from the literal meaning of their component parts. Nonetheless, we have included some popular idioms of this type to illustrate this special use of compounding.

Truncated compounds

Sometimes, Korean permits compounds whose component parts are themselves shortened or *truncated* versions of longer words. For example, the compound 사대, with the meaning 'college of education' consists of two truncated elements: 사 (from 사범 'teacher/master') and 대 (from 대학 'college'). In cases such as these, the *Handbook* records the compound in its truncated form, placing it in the lists of only those morphemes from which it is actually composed. Information about the morphemes that have been deleted is provided in parentheses. Thus 사대 appears in the lists for 사 and 대 as follows:

> 사대　　college of education [teacher college] 師大
> 　　　　(＜사범대학)

Hybrid compounds

A relatively small number of Korean compounds consist of roots of different origins—for example, one Sino-Korean root and one native Korean root or (much less commonly) a native Korean root and a root borrowed from English. Such *hybrid* compounds can be recognized in the list for a Sino-Korean root by the symbol 'K' (for Korean) or 'E' (for English) that appears in the lexical entry to indicate the origin of the other root. Hybrid compounds in the native Korean lists can be identified by the presence of a Chinese character or the symbol 'E' in the lexical entry. Thus, the hybrid compound 노래방 'karaoke room', which consists of the native Korean root 노래 'song' and the Sino-Korean root 방 'room' is given the following entry under the list for 방.

xv

노래**방** karaoke room [song~] K~

The hybrid expression 종이컵 'paper cup' receives the following entry under 종이, the native Korean root meaning 'paper'.

종이컵 paper cup [~cup] ~E

4. Other Things That You Need to Know

There are a few other facts about Korean word formation that may be helpful to you in using this book.

하다 *and verb formation*

The vast majority of Korean compounds are nouns. This is especially so in the case of Sino-Korean compounds, whose component parts were almost all borrowed into Korean from Chinese as nouns. In many cases, however, it is possible to convert these nouns into verbs by adding the special verb 하다 ('be', 'do', or 'make') or, less frequently, 스럽다 or 롭다. For example, 편리 by itself means 'convenience' while 편리하다 has the meaning 'be convenient'. Similarly, 연구 means 'research' while 연구하다 means 'conduct research'.

Because a very large number of nouns can be converted into verbs in this way, it would be uneconomical to include the verb 하다 in our lists each and every time this word formation strategy is possible. We will therefore use an asterisk (*) right after an element to indicate that it can be commonly converted into a verb by adding 하다. (Some words can occur with a semantically different 하다, which can have the sense of 'run' or 'manage' as in 식당하다 'run a restaurant' or 'wear' as in 목걸이하다 'wear a necklace'; an asterisk is not used in such cases.)

Bound roots

The majority of roots in Korean as well as some compounds are *bound* in the sense that they normally do not stand alone as independent words. For example, 매 'every' is found only with a following noun (e.g., 매일 'everyday', 매주 'every week', etc.) while 무 'duty' appears only with a preceding noun (e.g., 사무 'office work', 의무 'duty', etc.). Even more common is the pattern illustrated by 묵 'silence', which can occur with either a preceding noun (침묵 'silence') or a following noun (묵인 'tacit approval'), but cannot stand alone. Another common class of roots is exemplified by 급 'urgent', 전 'transmit', and 묘 'exquisite, strange', which are generally not used as independent words themselves but can occur with 하다 or some other special verb (see above).

Since only a minority of roots can be words on their own, it is more economical to indicate these elements than to mark all the bound roots that occur in Korean compounds. The *Handbook* uses the superscripted symbol ^W (for 'word') to indicate that a particular root is commonly used as an independent word in the relevant sense. Unless you see this symbol after the root at the head of a list, you can assume that it cannot normally be used by itself as a word.

There are also some binary compounds that are normally not used as independent words, although they can occur in a larger compound or with an appropriate verb (e.g., 경솔, which typically must occur with 하다 giving the meaning 'be frivolous'). We indicate this type of bound element by including in its entry the verb with which it must normally appear.

Untranslated morphemes

Some of the words in our lists consist of a root and a second element that is either a semantically empty root or an affix. These second elements include the 'nominalizers' 음/ㅁ and 이, which convert a verb into a noun (as in 싸움 'a fight', from 싸우다 'to fight', and 넓이 'width', from 넓다 'be wide'); the adjectivalizer 적 (的), which converts a noun into an adjective (as in 일반적 'general' and 일시적 'transient'); the adverb marker 게 (as in 늦게 'late'); the location marker 에 (as in 밖에 'outside'); markers of adjectival modification such as 은/ㄴ and 을/ㄹ (as in 단것 'sweet things'); the 'connectors' 아 and 어 found in verb-verb compounds (as in 돌아가다 'go back'); and so forth. No attempt is made to provide a literal translation for these special elements. When such an element occurs as part of the item at the head of a list, it is written in a regular font rather than boldface.

Uncertain etymologies

In some cases, it is not possible to be certain of the identity of a word's component morphemes. For example, there are several homophonous roots with the spelling 한 in Korean, and there is some uncertainty over which of these occurs in the word 한글 '*hangul*': some dictionaries say that it can be either the root meaning 'great' or the root meaning 'Korea'. It is likewise unclear whether the 비 in 비싸다 'be expensive' is the morpheme used elsewhere in the language to mean 'not'.

In cases such as these, we opt for the analysis that is most likely to be helpful to language learners. Thus, we translate 한 as 'Korea' in 한글 since this is the name of the Korean writing system and we take advantage of the fact that 싸다

means 'be cheap' to analyze 비싸다 as 'be not cheap' since this provides an easy way to remember that it means 'be expensive'.

Roots with more than one spelling

In a small number of cases, Korean roots can be spelled in more than one way. For example, there are a number of Sino-Korean morphemes whose initial letter alternates between ㄴ and ㄹ. A case in point is the morpheme meaning 'difficult(y)', which is sometimes written as 난 (as in 피난 'refuge') and sometimes as 란 (as in 곤란 'trouble'). When this happens, we list all compounds formed from the root in question under the more common spelling (even if this is not the historically original spelling), but we indicate the alternative in parentheses at the head of the list. The list for the less common spelling of the root is left empty, with a note referring the reader to the other spelling.

Thus, in the case of the example just mentioned, all compounds are listed under 난 'difficult(y)', which is the more common spelling, and the alternative spelling 란 is indicated in parentheses at the head of the list. The list for 란 itself is empty, except for the note 'see 난'.

5. Some Limitations of the *Handbook*

The *Handbook of Korean Vocabulary* is not a conventional dictionary. It does not try to include all the words in the language, or even all the 'common' words. Rather, it seeks to record and present words built from roots that appear with some frequency. If we were preparing a similar handbook for students learning English, there would be a list for *vision* (because of *television, envision, visionary, super-vision, revision,* etc.), but probably not for the more common word *rather*, from which no other words are derived.

In selecting the items that appear in the *Handbook,* we have tried to focus on words and expressions that are most likely to be encountered in everyday situations, ranging from conversation to reading to watching television. We have deliberately chosen to emphasize items that, in our judgment, are common and useful enough to have a place in the vocabulary of beginning and intermediate students of Korean. However, even advanced students will find much to occupy their attention.

You will probably find that the *Handbook* is far more useful for recognizing and interpreting words that you see and hear than for deciding which word to use in your own speech. This is because learning the meaning of a new word in a second language involves several layers of information. For example, someone learning the English word *sight* must learn not only that it has a particular meaning and that it can appear in various compounds (*eyesight, insight, foresight, sightsee,* etc.), but also that it contrasts in subtle ways with the word *vision* (there is a big difference between 'seeing visions' and 'seeing the sights'!), that it has special idiomatic uses (as in 'That idea is out of sight'), and so on. Much of the information about how to use a particular word is highly idiosyncratic and must be learned over a period of years through experience with how the language is used in a multitude of different situations. No book (and certainly not a root dictionary) is able to provide the type of encyclopedic information that is needed to know precisely which word from among various alternatives 'sounds right' in a particular context.

Our goal in the *Handbook* is to provide a first 'layer' of lexical knowledge— essentially, information about the literal meaning of useful roots and examples of the compounds in which they appear. Where feasible, we have also included information about a word's idiomatic uses as well as an indication of whether it is honorific or vulgar. This may not allow you to use each and every new word in exactly the right way, but it can at least provide a way to analyze and decode new words that you encounter in the speech and writing of others.

We hope that all students of Korean will find the *Handbook* helpful as they strive to improve their proficiency in this challenging language.

Bibliography

In researching the Chinese characters and literal meanings of the roots appearing in the *Handbook*, we have made use of the following bibliographic resources.

Daniels, Michael. *Chinese-Korean-English Dictionary.* 2d ed. Seoul: Kwang Il Printing Co., 1981.
Essence Korean-English Dictionary. Seoul: Minjungseorim, 1990.
Martin, Samuel, Yang Ha Lee, and Sung-Un Chang. *A Korean-English Dictionary.* New Haven: Yale University Press, 1967.

List of Abbreviations

~	stands for the meaning and/or Chinese character associated with the root morpheme around which the items in a particular list are built
*	indicates that a particular word can occur with 하다 to form a verb
<	indicates the form from which a word originated
·	indicates that the following consonant is tensed (see the Pronunciation Guide)
derog	derogatory
E	English
hon	honorific
K	Korean
pron	pronunciation
w	superscripted w indicates that a particular root can be used as an independent word

Pronunciation Guide

Since the *Handbook* is intended to serve as a supplement to regular textbooks and classroom instruction, we will not attempt to provide a comprehensive guide to the pronunciation of Korean. However, it is worthwhile to note a set of phenomena that are especially common in compounds and other multipart words, the predominant type of entry in the *Handbook*. These phenomena affect the pronunciation of consonants in very important ways and must be mastered by anyone who wishes to speak and understand Korean.

Except for ㅇ and ㅎ , a consonant that appears at the end of a syllable in Korean orthography is pronounced at the beginning of the next syllable if that syllable begins with a vowel. Thus, 앞에 'in front' is pronounced as [a-pʰe] and 넓이 'width' as [nəl-bi]. In contrast, ㅇ does not shift (영어 'English' is pronounced [yəŋ-ə]) and ㅎ is silent (좋아 'is good' is pronounced [čo-a]).

The *hangul* consonant symbols and their most common pronunciations at the beginning and end of syllables are outlined below.

Symbol	syllable-initial		syllable-final
ㄱ	[k]		[k]
ㄲ	[kk]	(tense)	[k]
ㄴ	[n]		[n]
ㄷ	[t]		[t]
ㄸ	[tt]	(tense)	n/a
ㄹ	[r]		[l]
ㅁ	[m]		[m]
ㅂ	[p]		[p]
ㅃ	[pp]	(tense)	n/a
ㅅ	[s]		[t]
ㅆ	[ss]	(tense)	[t]
ㅇ	n/a		[ŋ] (as in *sing*)
ㅈ	[č]		[t]
ㅉ	[čč]	(tense)	n/a
ㅊ	[čʰ]	(aspirated)	[t]
ㅋ	[kʰ]	(aspirated)	[k]
ㅌ	[tʰ]	(aspirated)	[t]
ㅍ	[pʰ]	(aspirated)	[p]
ㅎ	[h]		see change F on p. xxv

Two types of phonetic modification are especially common in Korean. The first involves what linguists call *assimilation*, a process that makes a sound more like (or even identical to) a neighboring sound. The table on the next page presents examples of assimilation in Korean compounds. (As noted above, the symbol [ŋ] stands for the final sound in *sing*; [š] represents the sound heard at the beginning of the English word *shy* and [ʰ] marks aspiration. The symbol [æ] represents a vowel similar to the one in the English word *cat* while [ə] stands for a vowel close to the one in unstressed *the*.

Sometimes more than one process can apply to the same consonant. As shown in the table on the next page, for example, ㅌ is pronounced as [n] (as if it were ㄴ) in front of a nasal (see the second example under *D*). At the same time, ㄴ can be pronounced as [m] in front of a labial consonant (see the first example under *C*). What happens, then, when ㅌ occurs in front of the nasal labial consonant ㅁ ? Under such circumstances, the ㅌ is converted to [n], which in turn can optionally be changed to [m]. Thus, the word 낱말 'word' can be pronounced as either [naṉmal] or [naṃmal].

> 낱말　naṯʰmal
> 　　　↓　　　　　　[tʰ] changes to [n] because of the following nasal
> 　　naṉmal
> 　　　↓　　　　　　[n] changes to [m] because of the following labial
> 　　naṃmal

A more intricate case involves ㄹ . This consonant is pronounced as [n] when the preceding consonant is neither ㄷ nor ㄴ (see the second example under *A*). In addition, ㄱ is pronounced as [ŋ] in front of a nasal consonant (see the third example under *D*). This leads to an intriguing result in words such as 식량 'provisions', in which the ㄹ is pronounced as [n] because of the preceding ㄱ and the ㄱ is pronounced as [ŋ] because of the newly created nasal that follows it— giving the pronunciation [šiṉnyaŋ]!

> 식량　šikṟyaŋ
> 　　　↓　　　　　　[r] changes to [n] because of the preceding [k]
> 　　šikṉyaŋ
> 　　　↓　　　　　　[k] changes to [ŋ] because of the following [n]
> 　　šiṉnyaŋ

Change	Example		Pronunciation

A: Changes affecting [n] and [l]

Pronounce ㄴ as [l] when it is next to ㄹ — 월남 'Vietnam' [wəllam]

단련 'training' [tallyən]

Pronounce ㄹ as [n] if the preceding consonant is neither ㄹ nor ㄴ — 공룡 'dinosaur' [konnyoŋ]

삼류 'third rate' [samnyu]

B: Palatalization (Note: the palatal sounds are [š], [č], [ǰ], and [čʰ].)

Pronounce ㅅ as [š] in front of 이 — 맛있다 'be tasty' [mašitta]

Pronounce ㄷ as [ǰ] in front of 이 — 해돋이 'sunrise' [hædoǰi]

Pronounce ㅌ as [čʰ] in front of 이 — 같이 'together' [kačʰi]

C: Changes in place of articulation (Note: labial sounds are produced with the lips; all *p*- and *m*-type sounds are labial. Velar sounds are produced on the roof of the mouth; all *k*- and *ng*-type sounds are velar.)

ㄴ can be pronounced [m] in front of a labial sound — 신부 'bride' [šinbu] or [šimbu]

ㄴ can be pronounced [ŋ] in front of a velar sound — 한국 'Korea' [hanguk] or [haŋguk]

D: Nasalization (Note: the nasal sounds are [m], [n] and [ŋ].)

Change [p] or [pʰ] to [m] in front of a nasal — 앞문 'front door' [ammun]

Change [t] or [tʰ] to [n] in front of a nasal — 낱낱이 'each and every' [nannačʰi]

Change [k] or [kʰ] to [ŋ] in front of a nasal — 작년 'last year' [čaŋnyən]

E: Voicing (Note: voiced sounds are produced with vibrating vocal cords; all vowels are voiced (vd), as are the nasals and [l].)

Pronounce ㅂ as [b] bet. vd sounds — 바보 'fool' [pabo]

Pronounce ㄷ as [d] bet. vd sounds — 도둑 'thief' [toduk]

Pronounce ㅈ as [ǰ] bet. vd sounds — 재주 'talent' [čæǰu]

Pronounce ㄱ as [g] bet. vd sounds — 가구 'furniture' [kagu]

F: Aspiration (Note: aspiration involves a puff of air at the end of the consonant.)

Pronounce ㅂ + ㅎ or ㅎ + ㅂ as [pʰ] — 집합 'gathering' [čipʰap]

Pronounce ㄷ + ㅎ or ㅎ + ㄷ as [tʰ] — 놓다 'put' [notʰa]

Pronounce ㄱ + ㅎ or ㅎ + ㄱ as [kʰ] — 국화 'chrysanthemum' [kukʰwa]

The second major phenomenon that is observed when consonants come into contact is *tensification*. The most straightforward examples of this involve two occurrences of the same consonant, as in the following examples.

Tensification	Example	Pronunciation
ㄱ + ㄱ is pronounced [kk]	학교 'school'	[ha<u>kk</u>yo]
ㄷ + ㄷ is pronounced [tt]	닫다 'to close'	[ta<u>tt</u>a]
ㅂ + ㅂ is pronounced [pp]	압박 'oppression'	[a<u>pp</u>ak]

However, tensification is not restricted to these contexts. As the next examples illustrate, tensification can also occur after an *obstruent* (any consonant other than [l], [r], [m], [n] or [ŋ]).

Tensification	Example	Pronunciation
ㄱ is pronounced [kk]	덮개 'a cover'	[təp<u>kk</u>æ]
ㄷ is pronounced [tt]	각도 'angle'	[kak<u>tt</u>o]
ㅂ is pronounced [pp]	숙박 'lodging'	[suk<u>pp</u>ak]
ㅅ is pronounced [ss]	각성 'awakening'	[kak<u>ss</u>əŋ]

Tensification comes about in a different way when the preceding sound is [t]. Under such cirmustances, [t] undergoes complete assimilation, resulting in a serie of two identical consonants. This can be seen in the word 옷장 'closet', pronounced [oččaŋ], in which the [t] of 옷 (recall that a final ㅅ is pronounced as [t]) becomes [č] under the influence of the neighboring consonant.

Matters are further complicated by the fact that consonants are *sometimes* tensed even when the preceding sound is not an obstruent. For example, ㅂ is tensed after ㅇ in 상법 'business law' (pronounced [saŋppəp]), but not in 방법 'method' (pronounced [paŋbəp]). Similarly, ㄱ is tensed after a vowel in 주가 'stock price' (pronounced [čukka]), but not in 추가 'addition' (pronounced [čʰuga]). Unfortunately, there is no simple rule to predict whether tensification will occur in these contexts: the form 장기 can be pronounced [čaŋkki], with the meaning 'special talent', or [čaŋgi], with the meaning 'long-term' or 'chess'. Our practice in the *Handbook* is to place a dot (.) in front of a consonant that undergoe tensification even though the preceding sound is not an obstruent (thus, 주·가 vs 추가).

Tensification of a consonant that follows a vowel within words containing a native Korean root is associated with the spelling convention known as 사이 ㅅ

(*sai siot*—literally 'in-between ㅅ'), the addition of ㅅ between the vowel and the consonant. This newly added consonant then behaves just like a regular ㅅ does in this context: it undergoes complete assimilation, becoming identical to the following consonant (see the discussion of 옷장 above).

Before *sai siot*	**After *sai siot***		**Pronunciation**
바다 + 가	바닷가	'seaside'	[padakka]
고기 + 배	고깃배	'fishing boat'	[kogippæ]
차 + 집	찻집	'tea house'	[čʰaččip]

When it occurs in front of a nasal consonant, the ㅅ undergoes nasalization and is pronounced as [n] in front of another [n] and as either [n] or [m] in front of an [m].

Before *sai siot*	**After *sai siot***		**Pronunciation**
코 + 노래	콧노래	'humming'	[kʰonnoræ]
바다 + 물	바닷물	'seawater'	[padanmul] or [padammul]

    The preceding is a very general overview of some of the major phenomena affecting the pronunciation of consonants in Korean compounds and other multi-part words. There are some well-known cases that require reference to additional principles, however. Perhaps the most notorious pattern of this type is found in words such as 꽃잎 'petal', in which the final consonant of the first morpheme is pronounced as [n]. In cases such as these, where the pronunciation is dramatically different from what the orthography would lead one to expect and where there is no general rule suitable for beginning students, we resort to indicating the pronunciation as part of the word's entry in the *Handbook*. Thus, the entry for 꽃잎 is accompanied by the notation 'pron. = 꼰닙'.

Roots

of

Chinese

Origin

ㄱ

가 (家) house; specialist

가정   home; family [~yard] ~ 庭
가정환경 home environment
결손가정 dysfunctional family

처갓집 one's wife's house/family [wife~house] 妻 ~ K

가출* running away from home [~come out] ~ 出

귀가* returning home [return~] 歸~

가사 housekeeping [~matter] ~ 事

가계부 housekeeping book [~count book] ~ 計簿

가구 furniture [~tool] ~ 具

가족 family [~clan] ~ 族

가문 family; clan [~door] ~ 門

외갓집 mother's family/house [outside~house] 外 ~ K

가장 head of a family [~boss] ~長

애처가 devoted husband [love wife~] 愛妻~

공처가 henpecked husband [fear wife~] 恐妻~

가축 domestic animals [~livestock] ~ 畜

국가 country; nation [country~] 國 ~

정치가 politician [politics~] 政治~

법률가 lawyer [law~] 法律~

작가 writer [compose~] 作~

화가 painter; artist [picture~] 畵 ~

만화가 cartoonist [cartoon~] 漫畵~

전문가 expert [specialty~] 專門~

대식가 big eater [big eat~] 大食 ~

애주가 alcohol lover [love liquor~] 愛酒~

자가용 one's own car [self~use] 自~用

가 (價) price; value

가격 price [~rank] ~ 格

대·가 price; cost [substitute~] 代~
대·가를 치르다 pay the price

정·가 fixed price [fix~] 定~

원·가 cost price [origin~] 原~

시·가 market price [market~] 市 ~

물·가 price of things [things~] 物 ~

염·가 low price [moderate~] 廉~
염·가대매출* bargain sale

최저·가 lowest price [lowest~] 最低~

주·가 stock price; (a person's) public reputation [stock~] 株~

가치 value; worth [~value] ~ 値

영양·가 nutritive value [nutrition~] 營養~

진·가 true value [true~] 眞~

평·가* evaluation; estimation [comment on~] 評~

가 (假) false; temporary

가면 mask [~face] ~ 面
가면쓰다 wear a mask

가장* disguise; camouflage [~costume] ~ 裝

가명 false name; alias [~name] ~ 名

3

가발 wig [~hair] ~ 髮
가발쓰다 wear a wig

가성 falsetto [~voice] ~ 聲

가짜 imitation; spurious article [~thing] ~ K

가식 hypocrisy; dissimulation [~decorate] ~ 飾
가식이 없다 be unpretentious

가설 hypothesis [~theory] ~ 說

가령 hypothetically; suppose that; even though [~tell] ~令

가정* assumption [~decide] ~ 定

가불* salary advance [~pay] ~ 拂

가량 approximately [~amount] ~ 量
한달·가량 걸린다
It takes about a month.

가 (歌) song; sing

가요 song [~song] ~ 謠
대중가요 folksong
최신가요 most recent songs

가곡 (classical) song [~tune] ~ 曲

유행가 pop song [fashion~] 流行~

찬송가 hymn; psalm [praise~] 讚頌~

축가 song of congratulation [congratulate~] 祝~

자장가 lullaby [rockabye~] K~

가사 lyrics [~words] ~ 辭

애국가 national anthem [love country~] 愛國~

군가 military song [military~] 軍~

가수 singer [~means] ~ 手

가 (加) add; apply

첨가* adding; addition [add~] 添~

추가* adding; addition [follow~] 追~

증가* an increase [increase~] 增~

가열* heating [~heat] ~ 熱

가속도 degree of acceleration [~speed] ~ 速度

가공* processing; manufacturing [~labor] ~ 工

가입* joining (an association) [~enter] ~ 入

참가* participation [participate~] 參~

가 (街) street

중심가 main street [center~] 中心~

가로수 trees bordering the street [~road tree] ~ 路樹

가로등 street light [~road lamp] ~ 路燈

상가 shopping mall [trade~] 商~

번화가 prosperous area; busy street [bustle~] 繁華~

유흥가 amusement center [pleasure-seeking~] 遊興~

가 (可) alright

가망 hope; possibility [~hope] ~ 望

가능하다 be possible [~able] ~ 能
가능한 한 as far as possible
가능성 possibility
불가능* impossibility

가급적 as far as possible [~extend] ~ 及的

가부간 whether yes or no [~not alright between] ~ 否間

허가* permission; license [permit~] 許~

ㄱ

가소롭다   be laughable [~laugh] ~ 笑

가 (暇)   leisure

여가   spare time; leisure [surplus~] 餘~

한가하다   have leisure time [leisure~] 閑~

휴가   (worker's) vacation; time off [rest~] 休~

각 (各)   each; every; all

각각   each; separately [~~]

제각기   each; respectively [one's own~that] K ~ 其
제각기 이유가 있다
Each has her/his own reason.

각국   each nation [~nation] ~ 國

각개인   each individual [~individual] ~ 個人

각자   each person [~self] ~ 自
각자 주문하다
Each orders her/his own dish.

각가지   various kinds [~kinds] ~ K

각종   all kinds [~kinds] ~ 種

각처   all places [~place] ~ 處
세계 각처에서
from all parts of the country

각지   all places [~place] ~ 地
전국각지   all parts of the country

각계각층   all walks of life [~field~layer] ~ 界 ~ 層

각별하다   be special; be particular [~special] ~ 別
각별히 조심하다
take special care

각 (覺)   perceive; conscious

감각   sense; perception [feel~] 感 ~

시청각   the visual and auditory senses [see hear~] 視聽 ~

미각   sense of taste [taste~] 味 ~

착각*   (optical) illusion; hallucination [mistaken~] 錯 ~

환각제   hallucinogen [illusion~medicine] 幻 ~ 劑

각성*   awakening [~sober up] ~ 醒

각오*   preparedness; resolution [~realize] ~ 悟
어려움을 각오하다
be prepared for difficulties
새해의 각오
New Year's resolution

각 (刻)   water clock; engrave

시각   the hour and minute; time [time~] 時 ~

정각   exact time [right~] 正 ~
정각 아홉시 9 o'clock sharp

즉각   immediately [immediate~] 卽 ~

지각*   (a person) being late [late~] 遲 ~

조각*   carving; sculpture [carve~] 彫 ~

심각하다   be serious [deep~] 深 ~

각 ʷ(角)   angle; horn

각도   angle [~degree] ~ 度
각도기   graduated protractor

직각   right angle [straight~] 直 ~

삼각   triangular [three~] 三 ~
삼각형   triangle
삼각관계   love triangle

사각형	quadrangle [four~shape] 四~形 정사각형 square 직사각형 rectangle
각설탕	cube of sugar [~sugar] ~ 雪糖
촉각	feeler; antenna [touch~] 觸 ~
총각	unmarried man; bachelor [all~] 總~

간 (間) interval; (space) between

기간	period; term [period~] 期~
당분간	for the time being [suitable minute~] 當分~
막간	interval between acts or scenes [curtain~] 幕~ 막간을 이용하다 make use of an intervening time
간격	space; interval [~partition] ~ 隔 간격을 두다 leave spaces 오분 간격으로 at an interval of five minutes
중간	the middle; midway [middle~] 中 ~ 중간고사 midterm exam 어중간하다 be about halfway
공간	space [empty~] 空~
간식*	eating between meals; snack [~eat] ~ 食
시간	time [time~] 時~
순간	an instant [wink~] 瞬 ~ 순간적 instantaneous 순식간에 in a blink
조만간	sooner or later [early late~] 早晚~
간혹	occasionally [~perhaps] ~ 或
형제간	sibling relation [sibling~] 兄弟~

좌우간	at any rate; anyway [left right~] 左右~
하여간	anyway [how similar~] 何如~
간첩	spy; secret agent [~spy] ~ 諜
간접	indirect [~touch~] ~ 接 간접적으로 indirectly
인간	human being [person~] 人~

간 (刊) publish

간행*	publication [~act] ~行 정기간행물 periodicals
일간	daily publication [day~] 日~ 일간신문 daily newspaper
주간	weekly publication [week~] 週~ 주간지 a weekly (magazine)
월간	monthly publication [month~] 月~ 월간지 monthly magazine
창간*	first publication [beginning~] 創~ 창간호 first issue
발간*	first edition [depart~] 發~
석간(신문)	evening paper [evening~ newspaper] 夕~新聞
조간(신문)	morning paper [morning~ newspaper] 朝~新聞

간 (簡) simple; abridge

간.단하다	be simple; be brief [~single] ~ 單
간소하다	be simple; be plain [~simple] ~ 素 간소화 simplification
간략하다	be brief; be informal [~abbreviated] ~ 略
간편하다	be handy; be convenient [~convenient] ~ 便

ㄱ

간 (看) **watch; take care of**

간판 signboard; credentials [~board] ~ 板

간주하다 regard (as) [~make] ~ 做

간호* nursing; tending [~protect] ~ 護
간호원 nurse

간 (姦) **adultery**

간통* adultery [~communicate] ~ 通

강간* rape [force~] 強 ~

간 (奸) **crafty**

간사하다 be cunning [~evil] ~ 詐

농간 machination; trickery [play with~] 弄 ~

간 (懇) **earnest; beseech**

간절하다 be earnest; be eager [~earnest] ~ 切

간청* entreaty [~request] ~ 請

갈 (渴) **thirst(y)**

갈.증 thirst [~symptom] ~ 症
갈.증나다 be thirsty

기갈 hunger and thirst [starve~] 飢 ~

해갈* relief from drought [solve~] 解 ~

갈망* earnest desire [~hope] ~ 望

감 ᵂ(感) **feel(ing)**

감정 emotion [~feeling] ~ 情
감정적 emotional

감개무량* be full of deep emotion [~deep no measure] ~ 慨無量

감격* being deeply touched [~intense] ~ 激
감격적 deeply impressive

감촉 the feel; the touch [~touch] ~ 觸

촉감 the touch; the feel [touch~] 觸 ~

쾌감 pleasant feeling [pleasant~] 快 ~

호감 good feeling; favorable impression [good~] 好 ~
호감이 가다 be amiable; be pleasing
호감을 주다 impress one favorably

실감* actual feeling [real~] 實 ~
실감나다 appeal to one's sense of reality

동감* same feeling; same opinion [same~] 同 ~
동감이다 (I) agree.

친근감 feeling of closeness [friendliness~] 親近 ~

거리감 feeling of distance [distance~] 距離 ~

승차감 feeling of riding a car [riding a car~]

거부감 repulsive feeling [refusal~] 拒否 ~

배신감 betrayed feeling [betrayal~] 背信 ~

자신감 feeling of self-confidence [confidence~] 自信 ~

책임감 sense of responsibility [responsibility~] 責任 ~

우월감 sense of superiority [superiority~] 優越 ~

열.등감 sense of inferiority [inferiority~] 劣等 ~

소외감 sense of alienation [alienation~] 疎外 ~

7

감각	sense; perception [~perceive] ~ 覺 무감각* insensitivity 방향감각 sense of direction
감수.성	sensitivity; susceptibility [~receive nature] ~ 受性 감수.성이 예민하다 be susceptible (to)
민감하다	be sensitive; be susceptible [sharp~] 敏 ~
감명	impression [~impress] ~ 銘 감명깊다 be deeply impressive 감명을 주다 to impress
감상	thoughts; impressions [~think] ~ 想 감상문 description of one's impressions
독후감	impressions of a book [read after~] 讀後 ~
소감	one's impression; opinion [whatsoever~] 所 ~
감동*	being impressed [~move] ~ 動 감동적 impressive
예감*	premonition; hunch [beforehand~] 豫 ~ ...한 예감이 들다 have a hunch that ...
감탄하다	be struck with admiration [~exclaim] ~ 歎 감탄사 exclamation
직감	immediate perception; intuition [straight~] 直 ~
육감	sixth sense [six~] 六 ~
죄책감	guilty conscience [guilt reprove~] 罪責 ~
감염	infection [~infect] ~ 染
감기	a cold [~air] ~ 氣 감기걸리다 catch a cold 감기약 cold medicine
독감	flu; bad cold [poison~] 毒 ~
감사하다	thank; feel grateful [~thank] ~ 謝
감전*	receiving an electrical shock [~electricity] ~ 電

감 (減) decrease; subtract

감소*	decrease [~little] ~ 少
감퇴*	decrease; loss [~retreat] ~ 退 식욕감퇴 loss of appetite
감하다	reduce; subtract
감속*	reducing speed [~speed] ~速 감속운전* Reduce speed.
감.점*	demerit mark [~point] ~ 點
절감*	curtailment (of expenses) [moderation~] 節 ~

감 (甘) sweet

감주	sweet drink (made from rice) [~liquor]
감미롭다	be sweet [~taste] ~ 味 인공감미료 artificial sweetener
고진감래	sweet after bitter [bitter exhaust~come] 苦盡~來
감초	licorice root [~grass] ~ 草
감수하다	be ready to suffer; willingly submit [~receive] ~ 受

감 (敢) daring; venturing

감히	daringly; boldly [~-ly] ~ K
용감하다	be brave [brave~] 勇 ~
과감하다	be courageous; be daring [result~] 果 ~

감 (監) **supervise**

감독* supervision; supervisor [~direct] ~ 督
시험감독* supervision of an examination
영화감독* film director

감시* watch; vigil [~look] ~ 視

감옥 prison [~prison] ~ 獄

감금* imprisonment; confinement [~prohibit] ~ 禁

감.방 cell; ward [~room] ~ 房

갑 (匣) **case; box**

비눗갑 soap case [soap~] K~

성냥갑 match box [match~] K~

장갑 gloves [palm~] 掌~
벙어리장갑 mittens
고무장갑 rubber gloves

수갑 handcuffs [hand~] 手~

지갑 purse; wallet [paper~] 紙~
동전·지갑 coin purse

강 (強) **strong; force**

강하다 be strong; be powerful

막강하다 be very strong [extreme~] 莫~

강자 the strong [~person] ~ 者
강자와 약자 the strong and the weak

강.점 one's strength; strong point [~point] ~ 點

강화* strengthening [~change] ~ 化

강력하다 be powerful [~power] ~ 力

강적 formidable rival [~enemy] ~ 敵

강대국 superpower [~big country] ~ 大國

강도 intensity [~degree] ~ 度

강렬하다 be intense [~vehement] ~ 烈

강조* emphasizing [~control] ~ 調

약육강식 law of the jungle [weak meat~eat] 弱肉~食

강요* forcible demand [~demand] ~ 要

강제* compulsion; coercion [~suppress] ~ 制
강제로 by force

강압적 coercive; oppressive [~repress] ~ 壓的

강간* rape [~adultery] ~ 姦

강도 armed robber [~thievery] ~盜

강탈* extortion; robbery [~deprive] ~ 奪

강행군* forced march; tight-scheduled travel [~go military] ~ 行軍

강박관념 obsession; persecution complex [~oppress idea] ~ 迫觀念

강 (講) **lecture; discuss**

강의* a lecture [~meaning] ~ 義
강의실 lecture room

강사 lecturer [~teacher] ~ 師

강연* lecture; speech [~perform] ~ 演

강당 auditorium [~hall] ~ 堂

휴강* (professor's) skipping a lecture [rest~] 休~

종강* finishing a lecture at the end of a semester (in college) [finish~] 終 ~
종강파티* semester-end party

개강* beginning of lectures (in college) [begin~] 開~

강좌	course; lecture [~seat] ~ 座 특별강좌 special course
강습*	(short) training course [~practice] ~ 習 요리강습* cooking class
수강*	taking a course [receive~] 受~
청강*	auditing (a course) [listen~] 聽~

강 ʷ(江) **river**

강물	river water [~water] ~K
강·가	riverside [~edge] ~K
강변	riverside [~side] ~ 邊 강변도로 riverside road
강촌	riverside village [~village] ~ 村
강산	rivers and mountains; native land [~mountain] ~ 山
한강	the Han River 漢~

개 (開) **begin; open**

개학*	beginning of school [~study] ~ 學
개강*	beginning of lectures (in college) [~lecture] ~ 講
개막식*	opening ceremony (for a sporting event) [~curtain ceremony] ~ 幕式
개관*	opening of a hall, museum [~building] ~ 館
개장*	opening (a place) [~place] ~ 場
개점*	opening of a store [~store] ~ 店
개업*	opening of a business [~business] ~ 業

개시*	first sale (of the day) [~market] ~ 市
개통*	opening to traffic [~go through] ~ 通
개방*	opening; lifting the ban [~release] ~ 放 개방적 open-hearted; liberal
공개*	opening to the public [public~] 公~
개봉*	opening (a letter); releasing (a movie) [~seal] ~ 封
개최*	holding (a meeting) [~urge] ~ 催
절개*	incision; section [cut~] 切~
전개*	unfolding; development [spread~] 展~
개척*	development; reclamation [~land development] ~ 拓
개발*	development [~rise] ~ 發
미개하다	be uncivilized [not~] 未~ 미개인 primitive people
개표*	ballot counting [~ticket] ~ 票
개천절	National Founding Day [~sky festival] ~ 天節

개 (個) **individual; unit**

개인	an individual [~person] ~ 人
개성	individuality [~nature] ~ 性
개별	individuation [~different] ~ 別 개별.적으로 individually
낱개	each piece [each piece~] 낱개로 팔다 sell by the piece
별개	different one [different~] 別~ 별개의 문제 another question
개중에는	among others [~among] ~ 中K

ㄱ

(일)개월   (one) month
[one~month] 一 ~ 月

개 (改)   amend

개정*   amendment; revision
[~right] ~ 正
헌.법개정 constitutional
amendment

개조*   remodeling; reconstruct
[~make] ~ 造

개선*   improvement; betterment
[~good] ~ 善

개혁*   reformation [~revolt] ~ 革

개정판   revised edition
[~correct printing] ~ 訂版

개 (槪)   outline

개론   survey; introduction
[~discuss] ~ 論

개념   concept [~thought] ~ 念

대개   in general [big~] 大 ~

개 (介)   mediate

개입*   intervention
[~enter] ~ 入

개의하다   care about; mind
[~intention] ~ 意
개의치않다 do not care

소개*   introduction [introduce~] 紹~
자기소개* self-introduction

객 w (客)   guest

불청객   uninvited guest; gate
crasher [not invite~] 不請~

관객   audience; spectator
[see~] 觀~

방청객   audience; hearer
[hearing~] 傍聽~

고객   customer [care for~] 顧~

승객   passenger [to board~] 乘~

관광객   tourist [tour~] 觀光~

객지   strange land (where
one is staying on a trip)
[~land] ~ 地

주객이 바뀌다 the cart is put before
the horse; the tables are
turned [host~switched] 主 ~ K

객관적   objective [~observe] ~ 觀的
객관성 objectivity

거 (巨)   big

거대하다   be huge; be gigantic
[~big] ~ 大

거금   big money [~money] ~ 金

거액   huge amount of money
[~amount of money] ~ 額

거인   gigantic person
[~person] ~ 人

거구   huge body
[~human body] ~ 軀

거물   big shot [~thing] ~ 物

거창하다   be on a large scale
[~beginning] ~ 創

거 (擧)   lift

거수경례*   military salute
[~hand salute] ~ 手敬禮

거동   conduct; behavior
[~move] ~ 動

거행*   carrying out; performing
(a ceremony) [~act] ~ 行

열거*   enumeration [line~] 列~

거 (居) dwell

거처* one's place of residence [~place] ~ 處

거주* dwelling; residence [~reside] ~ 住

거실 living room [~room] ~ 室

동거* living together [together~] 同 ~

거 (去) go away

과거 past [pass~] 過 ~

제거* removal [remove~] 除 ~

철거* removal (of a building) [remove~] 撤 ~

건 (建) build; establish

건물 building [~thing] ~ 物

건축* construction; architecture [~build] ~ 築
건축가 architect

건설* construction [~establish] ~ 設

건평 floor space [~land measure] ~ 坪

건의* proposal; suggestion [~discuss] ~ 議

건 (乾) dry

건조* dryness [~dry] ~ 燥

건성피부 dry skin [~nature skin] ~ 性皮膚

건전지 dry cell [~battery] ~ 電池

건배* making a toast [~glass] ~ 杯

건포도 raisin [~grape] ~ 葡萄

건빵 a type of biscuit [~bread] ~K

건 (健) healthy; strong

건강* health [~comfortable] ~ 康

건전하다 be healthy; be sound [~whole] ~ 全

건장하다 be robust [~robust] ~ 壯

보건 preservation of health [protect~] 保 ~
보건소 health center
보건사회부 Ministry of Health and Social Affairs

건투를 빌다 hope one will do one's best [~fight pray] ~ 鬪 K

건 (件) thing; object

물건 article; goods [thing~] 物 ~

용.건 important matter; business matter [use~] 用 ~

사.건 event; happening [matter~] 事 ~

조.건 condition; stipulation [clause~] 條 ~

여.건 given condition; circumstances [give~] 與 ~

검 (檢) inspect

검사* inspection [~inspect] ~ 査
신체검사* physical checkup

점검* checking one by one; close inspection [spot~] 点 ~

검열* inspection; censorship [~inspect] ~ 閱

검토* examination; scrutiny [~discuss] ~ 討

검문* a check; inspection [~ask] ~ 問
검문소 checkpoint

검진* medical checkup [~medical examination] ~ 診

검안*	eye examination [~eye] ~ 眼		파격적	exceptional [break~] 破 ~ 的

검안* — eye examination [~eye] ~ 眼

검정고시 — qualification exam [~decide exam] ~定考試

검산* — checking calculations [~calculation] ~ 算

검찰 — investigation and prosecution [~observe] ~ 察

검사 — public prosecutor [~matters] ~ 事

검출* — (chemical) detection [~come out] ~ 出

검인 — seal of approval [~seal] ~印

겁 ᵂ(怯) **cowardice; fear**

겁많다 — be cowardly [~much] ~K

겁쟁이 — coward [~habitual doer] ~K

겁먹다 — be scared; lose one's nerve [~eat] ~K

겁주다 — scare (a person) [~give] ~K

겁없다 — be fearless; be bold [~not exist] ~ K

게 (揭) **raise**

게시* — a notice; bulletin [~manifest] ~ 示

게양* — hoisting (a national flag) [~raise] ~ 揚

격 ᵂ(格) **rule; frame; category**

격식 — rule; formality [~ceremony] ~ 式
격식을 차리다 stick to formality

규격 — a standard; a norm [regulation~] 規 ~

엄.격하다 — be strict; be stern [strict~] 嚴 ~

파격적 — exceptional [break~] 破 ~ 的

격언 — proverb; maxim [~words] ~ 言

합격* — passing (an examination) [unite~] 合 ~

자격 — qualification [property~] 資 ~

적격이다 — have proper qualification; be fit (for) [suitable~be] 適 ~ K

성.격 — character; personality [nature~] 性 ~
성격차이 incompatibility in character

인.격 — character; personality [person~] 人 ~

격조높다 — be refined; be high-toned [~harmonize high] ~ 調 K

체격 — physique [body~] 體 ~

격 (撃) **attack; strike**

공격* — an attack; an offense [attack~] 攻 ~

폭격* — bomb attack [explode~] 爆 ~

습격* — an attack; a raid [attack~] 襲 ~

반격* — a counterattack [opposite~] 反 ~

사격* — firing; shooting [shoot~] 射 ~

충격 — a shock [pierce~] 衝 ~
충격적 shocking
충격을 주다 to shock
충격을 받다 be shocked

타격 — a shock; a blow [hit~] 打 ~

격파* — defeat; smash up [~break] ~ 破

목격* — witnessing [eye~] 目 ~

격 (激) **violent; intense**

격하다   be enraged

격전*   hot fight; fierce battle
[~fight] ~ 戰

격투*   grapple; fight [~fight] ~鬪

격렬하다   be severe; be intense
[~vehement] ~ 烈

감**격***   being deeply touched
[feel~] 感 ~

격려*   encouragement
[~encourage] ~ 勵

격 (隔) **partition; isolate(d)**

간**격**   space; distance
[space between~] 間 ~

격리*   isolating (a patient)
[~separate] ~ 離

격차   difference (in quality); gap
[~difference] ~ 差

격주   every other week [~week]

견 (見) **opinion; see**

의**견**   opinion; view
[intention~] 意~

견해   opinion; view [~explain] ~解

참**견***   meddling; minding
(others') business
[participate~] 參~
말참견* verbal interference

예**견**하다   foresee [beforehand~] 豫~

선입**견**   preconception; prejudice
[first enter~] 先入~

편**견**   biased view; prejudice
[lean toward~] 偏 ~

꼴불**견**   ugliness; unsightliness
[shape no~] K 不~

견학*   field trip [~study] ~ 學

견본   sample [~sample] ~ 本

발**견***   discovery [depart~] 發~

결 (結) **tie; result**

단**결***   unity; solidarity
[group~] 團 ~

집**결***   gathering [gather~] 集~

연**결***   connection; linking
[connect~] 連~

결합*   union; cohesion [~unite] ~合

결부   linking; involving
[~attach] ~ 付
결부시키다 link; connect

결혼*   marriage; wedding
[~marriage] ~ 婚

자매**결**연   sisterhood relationship
[sister~affinity] 姉妹~ 緣

결과   result [~result] ~ 果

결국   eventually
[~circumstances] ~ 局

결론   conclusion [~discuss] ~ 論

결말   conclusion; an end
[~end] ~ 末

결.실*   bearing fruit; fruition
[~fruit] ~ 實

결핵   tuberculosis [~nucleus] ~ 核
폐결핵 pulmonary
tuberculosis

결 (決) **decide**

결.정*   decision [~decide] ~ 定

결.단*   determination [~cut off] ~ 斷
결.단력 decisiveness
결.단을 내리다 reach
a definite decision

결.심*   making up one's mind;
resolution [~mind] ~ 心

14

ㄱ

판**결*** judgment; decision of the court [judge~] 判~

다수**결** majority vote [large number~] 多數~

결.승(전) championship game [~win fighting] ~ 勝戰
준**결**.승(전) a semifinal

결·재* sanction; approval [~judge] ~ 裁

해**결*** settlement (of a problem) [solve~] 解~

결·산* settlement of accounts [~calculate] ~ 算

대**결*** confrontation; showdown [opposite~]

결코 absolutely... not
그는 결코 바보가 아니다
He is by no means a fool.

결·사적으로 desperately [~death] ~ 死 的K

결 (缺) defect; deficient

결.점 defect; shortcoming [~point] ~ 點

결함 defect; shortcoming [~fall into] ~ 陷

결핍* deficiency [~lack] ~ 乏
애정결핍 lack of affection

결근* absence from work [~work] ~ 勤

결.석* absence (from school) [~seat] ~ 席

출**결** attendance and absence [appear~] 出~

결 (潔) clean; pure

청**결*** cleanliness [clear~] 淸~

불**결*** uncleanliness [not~] 不~

결백* innocence; being not guilty [~white] ~ 白

순**결*** purity; chastity [pure~] 純~

결벽 fastidiousness [~bad habit] ~ 癖

겸 (兼) combine

겸하다 serve both as
주택과 사무실을 겸하다
serve as both a house and an office
아침겸 점심 brunch

겸용* combined use [~use] ~ 用
밥솥 밥통 겸용 combined use for rice cooking and warming

겸비* combine (one thing with another); have both [~equip] ~ 備
재색을 겸비하다
have both wit and beauty

경 (輕) light

경공업 light industry [~industry] ~ 工業

경유 light oil; gasoline [~oil] ~ 油

경양식 light western food [~western food] ~ 洋食

경음악 light (instrumental) music [~music] ~ 音樂

경범죄 minor offense [~violate crime] ~ 犯罪

경쾌하다 be light-hearted; be cheerful [~refreshing] ~ 快

경시하다 make light of [~look] ~ 視

경솔하다 be thoughtless; be frivolous [~to lead] ~ 率

경박하다 be flippant [~superficial] ~ 薄

경멸하다 despise [~despise] ~ 蔑

15

경 (經)	pass through; govern; scripture
경로	course; channel; route [~road] ~ 路
경과*	passage; progress [~pass] ~ 過 시간이 경과함에 따라 as time goes by 경과보고* progress report
경유*	passing through; via [~from] ~ 由
경력	career record; experience [~pass] ~ 歷
경험*	experience [~examine] ~ 驗
신경	nerve [spirit~] 神~
경영*	management [~manage] ~ 營
경리	accounting [~manage] ~ 理
경비	expenses [~expense] ~ 費
경제	economics; finances [~relief] ~ 濟 경제적 economical
성경	the Holy Bible [holy~] 聖~

경 (景)	scenery
경치	scenery [~bring about] ~ 致
풍경	landscape [scenery~] 風~ 풍경화 landscape painting
설경	snowscape [snow~] 雪~
배경	background scenery [a back~] 背~ 무대배경 background scenery (stage)
광경	spectacular sight [brightness~] 光~
야경	night lights [night~] 夜~
경기	the times; the state of the market [~spirit] ~ 氣

경황	situation [~moreover] ~ 況 경황이 없다 have no time for

경 (競)	compete
경쟁*	competition [~fight] ~ 爭 경쟁자 competitor 경쟁률 amount of competition 경쟁심/의식 competitive spirit
경연대회	contest [~practice large meeting] ~ 演大會
경기*	(sports) game [~skill] ~ 技 경기장 stadium
경보*	walking race [~walk] ~ 步
경주*	(foot) race; running match [~run] ~ 走
경마*	horse racing [~horse] ~ 馬 경마장 race track
경매*	auction [~sell] ~ 賣

경 (警)	warn
경고*	warning [~notify] ~ 告
경보*	alarm; warning [~report] ~ 報 경계경보 air-defense alarm 공습경보 air-raid alarm 화재경보기 fire alarm 폭풍경보 storm warning
경계*	precaution; vigilance [~warn] ~ 戒
경비*	defense; guard [~prepare] ~ 備 경비원 security guard
경찰	the police [~observe] ~ 察 경찰차 police car
전경	combat police [combat~] 戰~ (<전투경찰)
순경	patrolman; cop [patrol~] 巡~

경 (境)   **boundary; circumstances**

경계   land boundary
[~boundary] ~ 界
경계선   boundary line

국경   national border
[nation~] 國~

경우   circumstances; case
[~happen] ~ 遇
경우에 따라서   depending
on the circumstances
최악의 경우에
in the worst case

역경   adverse circumstances
[contrary~] 逆~

곤경   predicament [hardship~] 困~

지경   (bad) situation [place~] 地~
죽을 ·지경이다   be in a bad fix

환경   environment;
surroundings [round~] 環~

경 (敬)   **respect**

존경*   respect; looking up to
[honor~] 尊~

공경*   respect (for elders,
parents) [respect~] 恭~

경로   respect for elderly people
[~old] ~ 老

경의   respect; homage
[~intention] ~ 意
경의를 표하다
show one's respect

경례*   salutation [~etiquette] ~ 禮

경건하다   be pious [~devote] ~ 虔

경 (鏡)   **mirror**

안경   glasses [eye~] 眼~
물안경 goggles

현미경   microscope
[manifest tiny~] 顯微~

망원경   binoculars
[observe far~] 望遠~

요지경   magic glass 瑤池~

경 (傾)   **incline; lean**

경사   slant; slope [~inclined] ~ 斜
경사지다 incline; slope
급경사 steep slope

경향   tendency; inclination
[~to face] ~ 向
...한 경향이 있다
have a tendency to...

경청*   listening attentively
[~listen] ~ 聽

경 (慶)   **congratulate**

경사   happy event [~matters] ~ 事

경축*   celebration
[~congratulate] ~ 祝

국경일   national holiday
[nation~day] 國~日

계 (計)   **calculate; plan**

계산*   calculation [~calculate] ~ 算
계산기 calculator

통계*   statistics [govern~] 統~

시계   watch; clock [time~] 時~

온도계   thermometer
[temperature~] 溫度~

합계*   the total (sum) [unite~] 合~

총계*   the total (sum) [all~] 總~

회계   finance; treasurer
[gather~] 會~
회계학 accounting

계획*   plan [~mark] ~ 劃

설계*   plan; design [establish~] 設~

흉계   wicked scheme [evil~] 凶~

계 (繼) **continue; adopt**

계속*   continuation [~continue] ~續

계승*   succession [~succession] ~承

후계자   successor
[after~person] 後~者

중계*   relay; rebroadcasting
[middle~] 中~
중계방송*   relay broadcasting

계모   stepmother [~mother] ~母

계 (階) **rank; stairs**

계급   rank; class [~grade] ~級

계층   social stratum [~layer] ~層

단계   stage of development
[step~] 段~

계단   stairs [~step] ~段

층계   stairs [layer~] 層~

계 (界) **world; circle; boundary**

세계   world [world~] 世~

연예계   entertainment world
[performance~] 演藝~

경계   demarcation [boundary~] 境~

한계   boundary; limit [limit~] 限~

화류계   pleasure quarters; geisha
world [flower willow~] 花柳~

계 (系) **connection; lineage**

계통   system; genealogy
[~govern] ~統
한국계(통)미국인
Korean American
신경계통   the nervous system

체계   system; organization
[body~] 體~
체계적   systematic

인문계   humanities
[humanities~] 人文~

자연계   natural sciences
[nature~] 自然~

직계   direct line (family)
[direct~] 直~
직계가족   family members
in a direct line

계 (鷄) **chicken**

계란   egg [~egg] ~卵
날계란   raw egg
삶은계란   hard-boiled egg
계란후라이*   fried egg

양계장   poultry (chicken) farm
[raise~place] 養~場

영계   spring chicken [tender~]
영계백숙   boiled chicken
with rice

고 (告) **tell; inform; accuse**

고자질*   tale-telling; informing

예고*   advance notice
[beforehand~] 豫~
예고편   a (movie) preview
예고없이   without notice

공고*   public notice [public~] 公~

통고*   notification [circulate~] 通~

고지서   written notice
[~know writing] ~知書

보고*   report [report~] 報~
보고서   written report
경과보고*   progress report

신고*   (legal) report [petition~] 申~
경찰에 신고하다
report to the police

이실직고*   reporting the truth
[with reality straight~] 以實直~

경고*   warning [warn~] 警~

충고*   advice [loyal~] 忠~

ㄱ

고백*	confession [~tell] ~ 白
선전포고*	declaration of war [proclaim war notify~] 宣戰布~
선고*	pronouncement; a sentence [proclaim~] 宣~
광고*	advertisement [broad~] 廣~ 구인광고 a help-wanted ad 구직광고 a want ad for a job
고발*	accusation; complaint [~shoot] ~ 發
고소*	(legal) accusation; (filing) complaint [~accuse] ~ 訴 고소당하다 be accused
원고	plaintiff [origin~] 原~
피고	defendant [suffer~] 被 ~
고사	offering to the spirits [~offering] ~ 祀 고사지내다 offer a sacrifice to spirits 고사떡 rice cake offered to spirits

고 (高) high

최고	the highest; the best [the most~] 最~
고급	high quality; advanced level [~grade] ~ 級 고급품 high-grade goods
고등	high; advanced [~grade] ~等 고등학교 high school
고층	a high-rise [~story] ~ 層 고층건물 high-rise building
고속	high speed [~speed] ~ 速 고속도로 freeway 고속버스 express bus
고온	high temperature [~temperature] ~ 溫
고기압	high atmospheric pressure [~atmospheric pressure] ~氣壓
고혈압	high blood pressure [~blood pressure] ~ 血壓
고음	high tone [~sound] ~ 音
고함	a shout; yell [~shout] ~ 喊 고함치다 to shout
고위층	persons holding high positions [~rank layer] ~位 層
고하	the upper and lower classes; rank [~below] ~ 下 지위의 고하를 막론하고 regardless of rank
고졸	high school graduate [~graduation] ~ 卒 (<고등학교졸업)
여고	girls' high school [female~] 女~ (< 여자고등학교)
고상하다	be refined; be high-toned [~noble] ~ 尙
고귀하다	be noble; be precious [~precious] ~ 貴
잔고	the balance (in an account) [remainder~] 殘~

고 (苦) suffering; bitter

고생*	hardship [~living] ~ 生
고난	hardship; ordeal [~difficulty] ~ 難
고통	pain; agony [~pain] ~ 痛
고민*	anguish [~anxiety] ~ 悶
고충	difficulties; predicament [~sincerity] ~ 衷
고역	hard work; drudgery [~serve] ~ 役
고전*	hard fight; tough going [~fight] ~ 戰
고심하다	take pains; make every possible effort [~mind] ~ 心
노고	labor; pains [toil~] 勞~

19

수고*	trouble; efforts 헛수고* vain effort
고대하다	wait eagerly for [~wait] ~ 待
고진감래	sweet after bitter [~exhaust sweet come] ~盡甘來

고 (固) firm

고체	a solid [~body] ~ 體 고체연료 solid fuel
고정*	fixing; fixation [~decide] ~ 定 고정관념 fixed idea 고정시키다 to fix
고수하다	hold fast to [~guard] ~ 守 입장을 고수하다 hold fast to one's stance
고집	stubbornness [~grasp] ~ 執 고집쟁이 stubborn person 고집불통 extreme obstinacy 고집세다 be stubborn 고집하다 stick to; insist upon
확고하다	be firm; be adamant [certain~] 確 ~
완고하다	be conservative; be bigoted [obstinate~] 頑 ~
고유하다	be peculiar; be native (to) [~exist] ~ 有 고유명사 proper noun

고 (考) think; examine

사고*	thinking [consider~] 思~ 사고방식 way of thinking
고려*	consideration [~think] ~ 慮
재고*	reconsideration [again~] 再~
심사숙고*	thorough consideration [deep consider mature~] 深思熟~
고안*	devising; contrivance [~plan] ~ 案

고사	examination [~examine] ~ 査 학기말고사 final exam
고시	examination [~test] ~ 試 사법고시 state law exam
참고*	reference; consultation [consult~] 參~
비고	note; remarks (for reference) [provided~] 備 ~

고 (古) old; ancient

고대	ancient times [~generation] ~ 代
자고로	from ancient times; traditionally [from~-ly] 自 ~K
고적	historic remains [~traces] ~ 蹟
고전	old book; classic [~codes] ~ 典
고참	old-timer; senior [~participate] ~ 參
복고풍	revival of old fashions [restore~custom] 復 ~ 風
중고	second-hand (article) [middle~] 中 ~ 중고차 used car

고 (故) the past; cause

고국	homeland [~country] ~ 國
고향	one's hometown [~province] ~ 鄕
죽마고우	bosom buddy [bamboo horse~friend] 竹馬~友
고인	the deceased [~person] ~ 人
고장	breakdown; out of order [~obstacle] ~ 障
사고	accident [matter~] 事~ 교통사고 traffic accident 사고나다 An accident happens

별고없다 be well [special~not exist] 別 ~ K

고로 accordingly; therefore [~-ly] ~ K

고의 willfulness; intentionality [~intention] ~ 意

고 (庫) storehouse

창·고 warehouse [storehouse~] 倉~

재고 stock; stockpile [exist~] 在~
재고정리세일* clearance sale

차고 garage [vehicle~] 車~

금고 strongbox [money~] 金~

냉장고 refrigerator [refrigerating~] 冷藏~

고 (孤) orphan; alone

고아 orphan [~child] ~ 兒
고아원 orphanage

고립* isolation [~stand] ~ 立
고립되다 get isolated
고립시키다 isolate

고독* solitude [~alone] ~ 獨

곡 ʷ(曲) tune; bend

가곡 (classical) song [song~] 歌~

신곡 new song [new~] 新~
최신곡 most recent songs

곡조 a tune; melody [~harmonize] ~ 調

명곡 famous music [fame~] 名~

편곡* (music) arrangement [weave~] 編~

작곡* composing (music) [make~] 作~

곡선 curved line [~line] ~ 線

굴곡 a bend; a curve [bend~] 屈~

곡예사 acrobat [~art master] 曲 ~ 師

왜곡 distortion [twist~] 歪~
왜곡되다 get distorted
왜곡시키다 distort

곡절 hows and whys; twists and turns [~break] ~ 折

곤 (困) tired; hardship

피곤하다 be tired [tired~] 疲~

노곤하다 be languid [toil~] 勞~

식곤.증 after-meal fatigue [eat~symptom] 食~症

곤란* difficulty; trouble [~difficulty] ~ 難

곤경 predicament [~circumstances] ~ 境
곤경에 처하다 be in a predicament

골 ʷ(骨) head; bone

골통 skull; noggin [~bulk] ~ K

골아프다 have a headache [~ache] ~ K
골치아프다 have a headache

해골 skeleton [skeleton~] 骸~

골반 pelvis [~tray] ~ 盤

약골 weakling [weak~] 弱~

골·자 the pith and marrow; the essentials [~thing] ~ 子

골·수분자 hard core [~marrow element] ~ 髓分子

노골.적 outspoken; plain [reveal~] 露 ~ 的

골.동품 antiques; curios [~correct article] ~ 董品

골때리다 be ridiculous; be preposterous (slang) [~hit] ~ K

공 (公)	public; official
공.적	public; official ~ 的
공금	public money [~money] ~ 金
공해	public hazard; pollution [~harm] ~ 害
공개*	opening to the public [~open] ~ 開
공고*	public notice [~inform] ~ 告
공중	public [~multitude] ~ 衆 공중전화 public phone 공중도덕 public morals
공립	public establishment [~establish] ~ 立 공립학교 public school
공약*	public promise [~promise] ~ 約
공연*	public performance [~perform] ~ 演
공무원	public service personnel [~affairs member] ~ 務員
공청회	public hearing [~hear meeting] ~ 聽會
관공서	government and public offices [official~office] 官~署
공직	official position [~post] ~ 職
공휴일	official holiday [~holiday] ~ 休日
공식	formula; official ceremony [~ceremony] ~ 式 공식적 official
공원	park [~garden] ~ 園
공정*	fairness [~right] ~ 正
공평하다	be fair; be just [~even] ~ 平
공증*	notary [~testify] ~ 證
공주	princess [~host] ~ 主
주인공	protagonist; main character [host~] 主人~

공 (空)	sky; empty
공기	air [~atmosphere] ~ 氣
공중	midair [~middle] ~ 中
공군	air force [~military] ~ 軍
공습*	air raid [~surprise attack] ~ 襲
공항	airport [~port] ~ 港
항공	aviation [navigate~] 航 ~ 항공우편 airmail 대한항공 Korean Air
공간	space [~space] ~ 間
허공	a void [empty~] 虛 ~
진공	vacuum [true~] 眞 ~ 진공청소기 vacuum cleaner
공책	notebook [~book] ~ 冊
공백	blank; blank space [~white] ~ 白
공복	empty stomach [~stomach] ~ 腹
공일	holiday; Sunday [~day] ~ 日
공짜	a thing obtained without cost; free (of charge) [~thing] ~ K

공 (工)	industry; labor(er)
공업	industry [~business] ~ 業
공대	engineering college [~college] ~ 大 (<공·과대학)
공장	factory [~place] ~ 場
공원	factory worker [~member] ~ 員
직공	factory worker [post~] 職~
여공	female factory worker [female~] 女~

ㄱ

인공 human work; artificiality
[person~] 人 ~
인공위성 man-made satellite

수공 manual work; handiwork
[hand~] 手 ~
수공이 들다
take much handiwork

가공 processing; manufacturing
[add~] 加 ~
가공식품 processed food

공예 industrial arts [~art] ~ 藝

공사* construction work
[~matter] ~ 事
공사중 under construction

착공* starting (construction)
work [reach~] 着 ~

완공* completion (of
construction)
[complete~] 完 ~

사공 boatman [sand~] 沙 ~

공부* study; learning
[~artisan] ~ 夫
공부·방 study room
시험·공부* study for an exam
과외·공부* taking private
lessons (tutoring)

공교롭게 coincidentally;
as ithappened
[~opportune] ~ 巧 K

공 (共) together; cooperate

공범 accomplice [~offence] ~ 犯

공저 joint work; coauthorship
[~write] ~ 著

공학 coeducation [~study] ~ 學
남녀공학 coed

공통 common; mutual
[~communicate] ~ 通
공통·점 something in common

공동 cooperation; collaboration;
union [~together] ~ 同
공동묘지 public cemetary
공동책임 joint liability

공감* sympathy [~feeling] ~ 感

공산 common property
[~produce] ~ 産
공산군 the Communist army
공산당 the Communist Party
공산주의 Communism

반공 anti-Communism
[opposite~] 反 ~
반공정신
anti-Communist spirit

공화 republic [~harmony] ~ 和
공화국 a republic
공화당 the Republican Party

공 w(功) merit; achievement

공로 meritorious deed [~toil] ~ 勞

공치사* self-praise; admiration of
one's own merit
[~achieve speech] ~ 致辭

성공* success [to complete~] 成 ~

공들다 require much labor or
trouble [~take] ~ K
공들이다 take trouble;
put in efforts
공든 탑이 무너지랴
Hard work is never wasted.

공 (恐) fear(ful)

공포 fear; terror [~fear] ~ 怖

공갈* threatening; blackmail
[~rebuke] ~ 喝

황공하다 be awestruck [fear~] 惶 ~

공처가 henpecked husband
[~wife person] ~ 妻家

23

공 (攻)   **attack**

공격*   an attack; an offence
[~attack] ~ 擊

전공*   major study; specializaion
[exclusive~] 專~

과 (過)   **exceed; excessive; pass;
to err**

과하다   be too much

과히   too much [~-ly] ~ K
과히 좋아하지 않다
do not like so much

초과*   exceeding; excess
[excel~] 超~
예산초과*   amount
above the estimate
정원초과*   exceeding
capacity; overcrowding

과잉   excess [~surplus] ~ 剩
과잉인구
excessive population

과음*   excessive drinking
[~drink] ~ 飮

과식*   overeating [~eat] ~ 食

과로*   overwork [~toil] ~ 勞

과속*   excessive speed
[~speed] ~ 速
과속운전   driving
over the speed limit

과신*   overconfidence
[~believe] ~ 信

과대평·가*   overestimation
[~big estimation] ~ 大評價

과소평·가*   underestimation
[~small estimation] ~ 小評價

과언   saying too much;
exaggeration [~talk] ~ 言
과언이 아니다
It is no exaggeration.

과찬*   excessive praise
[~praise] ~ 讚

과용*   spending too much money
[~use] ~ 用

과민하다   be oversensitive
[~sharp] ~ 敏

과분하다   be more than one deserves
[~share] ~ 分

과중하다   (burden) be too heavy
[~weighty] ~ 重

불과*   no more than; only
[not~] 不~
불과 일주일 밖에 안되었다
It has only been a week.
소문에 불과하다
It is just a rumor.

과반·수   majority
[~half number] ~ 半數

과거   past [~go] ~ 去

통과*   passing; passage
[go through~] 通~

경과*   passage; progress
[pass~] 經~

과도기   transition period
[~crossover period] ~ 渡期

과정   process; course [~route] ~程

사과*   apology [apologize~] 謝~

과 ʷ(科)   **department; course;
science**

영어·과   English department
[English~] 英語~

내·과   dept. of internal medicine
[inside~] 內~

외·과   dept. of external medicine
[outside~] 外~

치·과   dental office [teeth~] 齒~

소아·과   pediatrics
[small child~] 小兒~

산부인·과   obstetrics and gynecology
[produce married woman~]
産婦人~

ㄱ

이비인후·과 ear, nose, and throat department [ear nose throat~] 耳鼻咽喉~

과장 (department) chairperson [~superior] ~ 長

과목 course (subject) of study [~item] ~ 目

과학 science [~study] ~ 學

과 (果) fruit; result

과일 fruit

과수원 orchard [~tree garden] ~ 樹園

사과 apple [sand~] 沙~

약과 a type of Korean cake; nothing (compared to) [medicine~] 藥~

결과 result [result~] 結~

성·과 result; outcome [to complete~] 成~

효·과 effect [effect~] 效~

과연 as expected; sure enough [~as such] ~ 然

과감하다 be courageous; be daring [~daring] ~ 敢

과 (課) lesson; task; section

제일과 lesson one [order one~] 第一~

과외(·공부)* taking private lessons (tutoring) [~outside study] ~外工夫

과정 course of study; curriculum [~route] ~ 程 박사과정 Ph. D. program

과제 assignment; question [~subject] ~ 題

일과 daily task; schedule [day~] 日 ~

부과* levy; imposition [tax~] 賦 ~

과장 head of a section [~superior] ~ 長

과 (菓) sweets; fruit

제과 confectionery [make~] 製 ~ 제과점 bakery

과자 cookie; confectionery [~thing] ~ 子

다과 tea and cookies [tea~] 茶 ~ 다과회 tea party; reception

관 (觀) see; view

관찰* observation [~observe] ~ 察

관광* sightseeing; touring [~brightness] ~ 光 관광객 tourist

관람* (movie) watching [~view] ~ 覽

관객 audience; spectator [~guest] ~ 客

관중 (sports) onlookers; audience [~crowd] ~ 衆

방관* looking on as a spectator [side~] 傍~

미관 beautiful view [beautiful~] 美~

관·점 viewpoint [~point] ~ 點

관념 concept; idea [~think] ~ 念

인생관 view of life [life~] 人生~

가치관 values in life [value~] 價值~

가관 sight; something to see (sarcastic) [alright~] 可 ~

관상 physiognomy [~face] ~ 相

25

주관	subjectivity [host~] 主~	상관*	connection; meddling; concern [mutual~] 相~ 상관없다 have nothing to do with; not matter
객관적	objective [guest~] 客~的		

관 (館) building; house

본관	main building [origin~] 本~
신관	new building; extension [new~] 新~
별관	annex [separate~] 別~
여관	hotel; inn [traveler~] 旅~
대사관	embassy [ambassador~] 大使~ 미대사관 American Embassy
영사관	consulate [consul~] 領事~
도서관	library (building) [books~] 圖書~
박물관	museum [extensive things~] 博物~
회관	assembly hall [meeting~] 會~ 시민회관 city hall 세종문화회관 Sejong Cultural Center
영화관	movie theater [movie~] 映畵~
체육관	gymnasium [physical training~] 體育~
사진관	photo shop [photo~] 寫眞~
개관*	opening of a hall, museum [open~] 開~

관 (關) concern; locked; customhouse

관하다	concern; be related to ...에 관하여 concerning...
관련*	connection; correlation [~relation] ~聯
연관*	connection; correlation [relation~] 聯~
관계*	relation [~connection] ~係

관심	concern; interest [~mind] ~心
관여*	participation; involvement [~give] ~與
기관	engine; organization; organ [machine~] 機~ 기관총 machine gun
관절	joint (bones) [~joint] ~節 관절염 arthritis
난관	difficult situation; obstacle [difficulty~] 難~
현관	entrance; porch [obscure ~] 玄~
세관	custom house [tax~] 稅~
통관*	customs clearance [go through~] 通~

관 (官) official

관사	official residence [~house] ~舍
관청	government office [~government office] ~廳
관공서	government and public offices [~public office] ~公署
관직	government job [~post] ~職
장관	cabinet minister [superior~] 長~
외교관	diplomat [diplomacy~] 外交~
상관	superior official [above~] 上~
관료	bureaucracy [~fellow] ~僚 관료주의 bureaucratism
법관	a judge; the judiciary [law~] 法~

ㄱ

관 ^w(管) **tube; govern**

시험관   test tube [test~] 試驗~

혈관   blood vessel [blood~] 血~

기관지염   bronchitis [air~branch inflammation] 氣~支炎

관현악   orchestral music [~string music] ~絃樂

관리*   administration; management [~manage] ~理

관할*   jurisdiction; control [~control] ~轄

관 (慣) **habit**

습관*   habit [practice~] 習~

관습   custom; convention [~practice] ~習

광 ^w(光) **shine; brightness**

광택   luster; gloss [~glossy] ~澤

광나다   be shiny [~come out] ~K

광내다   polish [~bring out] ~K

전광판   electric sign board [electric~board] 電~板

형광등   fluorescent lamp [firefly~lamp] 螢~燈

야광   shining in the dark [night~] 夜~

광선   ray of light [~line] ~線
   직사광선   direct ray of light

광명   light; hope [~bright] ~明

영광   glory; honor [glory~] 榮~

광경   spectacular sight [~scenery] ~景

관광*   sightseeing; touring [see~] 觀~

광복절   Independence Day [~restore festival] ~復節

광 (狂) **mad; crazy**

광.적   mad; fanatic ~的

열광*   wild enthusiasm [heat~] 熱~

발광하다   act crazily [arise~] 發~

광신   religious fanaticism [~believe] ~信
   광신자   religious fanatic

광견.병   rabies [~dog disease] ~犬病

광 (廣) **wide; broad**

광야   wide plain [~field] ~野

광범위*   wide scope [~scope] ~範圍

광장   open ground; plaza [~place] ~場
   역전광장   station square

광고*   advertisement [~inform] ~告

광 (鑛) **mine; mining**

광산   a mine [~mountain] ~山

광부   mine worker [~man] ~夫

탄광   coal mine [coal~] 炭~

괴 (怪) **strange**

괴상하다   be strange; be odd [~usual] ~常

괴물   monster [~thing] ~物

괴짜   odd/eccentric person [~person] ~K

괴한   suspicious fellow [~base person] ~漢

27

교 (教) **teach(ing); religion**

교직 teaching profession
[~post] ~ 職

교육* education [~raise] ~ 育

교사 school teacher
[~teacher] ~ 師

교수님 professor [~give
respected person] ~ 授 K
조교수 assistant professor
부교수 associate professor

조교 teaching assistant
[assist~] 助 ~

교대 teachers' college [~college]
~ 大 (<교육대학)

교실 classroom [~room] ~ 室

교단 teacher's platform
[~altar] ~ 壇

교재 teaching material; text
[~material] ~ 材
부교재 supplementary
textbook

교·과서 textbook
[~course book] ~ 科書

교본 manual; textbook
[~base] ~ 本

교훈 precept; lesson
[~admonish] ~ 訓

교양 culture; refinement
[~nourish] ~ 養
교양있다 be cultured
교양없다 be uncultured

태교* prenatal care; fetal
education [pregnant~] 胎~

교련* military drill [~to train] ~ 鍊

교회 church [~meeting] ~ 會

종교 religion [sect~] 宗~

불교 Buddhism [Buddha~] 佛~

기독교 Christianity
[foundation direct~] 基督~

교인 believer; Christian
[~person] ~ 人

천주교 Catholicism [God~] 天主~

교황 the pope [~emperor] ~ 皇

설교* sermon; preach [talk~] 說~

선교* missionary work
[spread~] 宣~
선교사 missionary

교 (校) **school; revise; field officer**

학교 school [study~] 學~
국민학교 elementary school
중학교 middle school
고등학교 high school
대학교 university

모교 alma mater [mother~] 母~

교내 intramural; on-campus
[~inside] ~ 內

교정 school campus [~yard] ~ 庭

본교 main campus (of a school)
[original~] 本~

분교 branch campus
[divide~] 分~

교문 school gate [~door] ~ 門

휴교* (temporary) closure
of a school [rest~] 休~

교장 school principal; director
[~superior] ~ 長

교복 school uniform
[~clothes] ~ 服

개교기념일 school anniversary
[open~anniversary]
開~紀念日

교정* proofreading [~right] ~ 正

장교 military officer
[military officer~] 將~

28

교 (交) **exchange**

교환* exchange [~exchange] ~ 換
교환교수 visiting professor
교환(수) telephone operator

교류* interchange [~flow] ~ 流
문화교류* cultural exchange

교대* taking turns; shift
[~substitute] ~ 代

교통 traffic [~go through] ~ 通

교차* crossing; intersection
[~crossing] ~ 叉
교차로 crossroads

외교 diplomacy [outside~] 外 ~
외교관 diplomat

절교* breaking off friendship
[cut~] 絶 ~

교섭* negotiation [~crossover] ~ 涉

교제* dating [~occasion] ~ 際

성교* sexual intercourse
[sex~] 性 ~

교 (巧) **clever**

교묘하다 be clever; be dexterous
[~exquisite] ~ 妙

기교 art; technique [skill~] 技 ~

정교하다 be elaborate; be exquisite
[fine~] 精 ~

교 (橋) **bridge**

육교 overpass [land~] 陸 ~

대교 grand bridge [big~] 大 ~

구 (口) **mouth; opening**

구두로 orally; verbally
[~head -ly] ~ 頭 K

구어 colloquial speech
[~language] ~ 語

구령* verbal order
[~command] ~ 令

구호 slogan; catchword
[~title] ~ 號

구실 an excuse; pretext
[~reality] ~ 實

이구동성 (with) one voice; (in)
chorus [different~same
voice] 異 ~ 同聲

일구이언* being double-tongued
[one~two talk] 一 ~ 二言

구미 appetite; taste [~taste] ~ 味
구미가 당기다
appeal to one's appetite

식구 family members [eat~] 食 ~

인구 population [person~] 人 ~

출구 an exit [exit~] 出 ~

입구 entrance [enter~] 入 ~
출입구 exit and entrance

비상구 emergency exit
[emergency~] 非常 ~

하수구 gutter; drain
[descend water~] 下水 ~

항구 port; harbor
[harbor~] 港 ~

구 (具) **tool; implement**

용구 tool; instrument [use~] 用 ~

도구 tool; implement [way~] 道 ~
청소도구 cleaning tools

기구 appliance; tool
[utensil~] 器 ~
전기기구 electric appliance
운동기구 sporting goods

완구 toy [play~] 玩 ~
완구점 toy store

가구 furniture [house~] 家 ~

문(방)구 stationery
[literature room~] 文房 ~

29

구비하다 have all; be fully equipped [~prepare] ~ 備

구체적 concrete [~body] ~ 體的

불구 deformity [no~] 不~

표구* mounting; framing [manifest~] 表~

구 (球) sphere; ball

탁구* table tennis [table~] 卓~

농구* basketball [basket~] 籠~

야구* baseball [field~] 野~
발야구* foot baseball

축구* soccer [kick~] 蹴~

배구* volleyball [push out~] 排~

당구* billiards [hit~] 撞~
당구장 billiard hall

송구* handball [send~] 送~

전구 light bulb [electricity~] 電~

지구 the earth; the globe [earth~] 地~

구슬 glass beads

구 (求) request; seek

요구* a request; a demand [demand~] 要~

청구* a demand; a claim [request~] 請~

구걸* begging [~beg] ~ 乞

구하다 look for; seek

욕구* desires; wants [desire~] 欲/慾~

추구* pursuit [pursue~] 追~

구 (救) save; rescue

구하다 save

구조* rescuing; saving (a life) [~assist] ~ 助
구조원 lifeguard

구출* helping out; rescuing (a life) [~come out] ~ 出

구제* relief; salvation [~relief] ~ 濟
구제불능 being incorrigible

구원* relief; rescue [~help] ~ 援

구세주 the savior (of the world) [~world lord] ~ 世主

구세군 the Salvation Army [~world military] ~ 世軍

구 (區) district; distinguish

종로구 Jong-ro district

구청 district office [~government office] ~ 廳

구역 district; zone [~boundary] ~ 域

구별* differentiation [~separate] ~ 別

구분* division; classification [~divide] ~ 分

구구하다 be diverse (in opinions)

구 (構) compose; structure

구성* composition; organization [~to complete] ~ 成

구상* visualization; plan; idea [~thought] ~ 想

허구 fiction [unreal~] 虛~

구조 structure [~make] ~ 造

기구 organization [mechanism~] 機~

구내 a compound; (on) the campus [~inside] ~ 內

구 (舊)　old(-time)

구식　old style [~style] ~ 式

구형　old-fashioned model [~model] ~ 型

구면　old acquaintance [~face] ~面

복구*　restoration; repair [restore~] 復 ~
원상복구*　restoring to the original state

구정　New Year's Day by lunar calendar [~January] ~ 正

친구　friend [friendly~] 親 ~

구 ᵂ (九)　nine

십중팔구　nine out of ten; most likely [ten among eight~] 十中八~

구구단　multiplication table

구 ᵂ (句)　phrase

구절　phrase [~joint] ~ 節

구두.점　punctuation mark [~start point] ~ 讀点

국 (國)　country; nation

국가　country; nation [~house] ~ 家

미국　U.S.A. [America~] 美 ~

영국　England [England~] 英 ~

중국　China [middle~] 中 ~

한국　Korea [Korea~] 韓 ~

전국　the whole country [whole~] 全 ~

외국　foreign country [outside~] 外 ~

타국　foreign country; alien land [others~] 他 ~

출국*　departure from a country [exit~] 出 ~

입국*　entry into a country [enter~] 入 ~

귀국*　returning to one's country [return~] 歸 ~

선진국　developed country [first advance~] 先進 ~

후진국　backward country [back advance~] 後進 ~

강대국　superpower [strong big~] 强大 ~

국민　a nation; a people [~people] ~ 民

국토　national land [~land] ~ 土

국어　national language; native language [~language] ~ 語

국기　national flag [~flag] ~ 旗

국화　national flower [~flower] ~ 花

국군　national army [~military] ~ 軍

국방　national defense [~defend] ~ 防

국력　national power [~power] ~ 力

국경　national border [~boundary] ~ 境

국립　national establishment [~establish] ~ 立
국립공원　national park

국전　National Art Exhibition [~exhibition] ~展
(<국립전시회)

국적　nationality [~a record] ~ 籍

국보　national treasure [~treasure] ~ 寶

국회　Congress [~meeting] ~ 會

국무총리	prime minister [~affairs minister] ~ 務總理		판국	state of affairs; situation [situation~] K~
조국	one's fatherland [ancestor~] 祖~		결국	eventually [result~] 結~
모국	mother country [mother~] 母~			

군 ʷ(軍) **military**

국무총리	prime minister [~affairs minister] ~ 務總理
조국	one's fatherland [ancestor~] 祖~
모국	mother country [mother~] 母~
애국*	love of one's country [love~] 愛~ 애국가 national anthem 애국자 patriot 애국심 patriotism
국내	domestic [~inside] ~ 內
국산	domestic production [~produce] ~ 産 국산품 domestic products
국제	international [~internation] ~ 際 국제전화* international call
이국적	exotic [different~] 異~的
천국	heaven; paradise [heaven~] 天~

국 (局) **office; position;
circumstances**

우체국	post office [mail post~] 郵遞~
전화국	telephone company [telephone~] 電話~
방송국	broadcasting station [broadcasting~] 放送~
약국	pharmacy [medicine~] 藥~
당국	the authorities concerned [suitable~] 當~ 정부당국 government authorities
국한*	localization; limitation [~limit] ~ 限 국한시키다 localize
국번	area code [~number] ~ 番
시국	situation; the times [time~] 時~

군인	a soldier [~person] ~ 人
여군	female soldier [female~] 女~
군사	soldiers [~soldier] ~ 士 군사정.권 military regime
장군	a general; commander in chief [military officer~] 將~
군대	army; troops [~army] ~ 隊
육군	army [land~] 陸~
공군	air force [air~] 空~
해군	navy [ocean~] 海~
예비군	reserve army [preparation~] 豫備~
국군	national army [nation~] 國~
미군	U. S. Armed Forces [America~] 美~
적군	enemy force [red~] 赤~
공산군	the Communist army [common property~] 共産~
구세군	the Salvation Army [save world~] 救世~
군복	military uniform [~clothes] ~ 服

굴 (屈) **bend**

굴곡	a bend; a curve [~bend] ~ 曲
굴.절*	refraction [~break] ~ 折
굴복*	submission; surrender [~submit] ~ 服
비굴하다	be servile; be obsequious [low~] 卑~

ㄱ

굴하다	give in	권한	rights; power [~limit] ~ 限
굴욕	humiliation [~insult] ~ 辱	여·권	women's rights [woman~] 女~

굴 ʷ(窟) **tunnel; cave**

땅·굴	tunnel [ground~] K~
소굴	den; hotbed [nest~] 巢~
동굴	cave [cave~] 洞~
굴뚝	chimney

발언·권 — the right to speak [shoot words~] 發言~

기·권* — renunciation of one's rights [abandon~] 棄~

특권 — privilege [special~] 特~

권력 — authority; power [~power] ~ 力

궁(窮) **poor; used up**

궁색하다	be poor [~block] ~ 塞
궁하다	be in want
궁상	extreme straits [~shape] ~ 狀 궁상떨다 act poor 궁상맞다 have a poor and miserable look
궁지	sad plight; hot seat [~place] ~ 地 궁지에 몰리다 get into a scrape
궁리*	deliberation; thinking over [~reasoning] ~ 理

주·권 — sovereign power [host~] 主~

정·권 — political power [politics~] 政~

주도·권 — leadership; initiative [leading~] 主導~ 주도·권을 잡다 take the initiative

소유·권 — ownership [possession~] 所有~

권위 — dignity; prestige [~dignity] ~ 威

유·권자 — eligible voter [exist~person] 有~者

궁(宮) **palace; zodiac**

궁궐	royal palace [~palace] ~ 闕
경복궁	Kyongpok Palace 景福~
덕수궁	Tokswu Palace 德壽~
궁합	marital harmony as predicted by a fortune-teller [~unite] ~ 合 궁합을 보다 predict marital harmony 궁합이 맞다 the horoscopes of a couple agree

권(券) **ticket; document**

초대·권	invitation ticket [invitation~] 招待~
입장·권	admission ticket [admission~] 入場~
승차·권	passenger ticket [getting in a car~] 乘車~
식권	meal ticket [food~] 食~
복권	lottery ticket [blessing~] 福~
회원·권	membership card [member~] 會員~
회수·권	commuter's ticket; coupon ticket [frequency~] 回數~

권(權) **rights; authority**

권리 — rights [~benefit] ~ 利

여.권 passport [travel~] 旅~
증.권 stock; bond [evidence~] 證~

권 (勸) encourage
권장* encouragement; exhortation [~encourage] ~ 奬
권유* inducement; exhortation [~induce] ~ 誘
권하다 recommend; offer

권 (拳) fist
권투* boxing [~fight] ~ 鬪
태.권도* taekwondo [kick~principle] 跆 ~ 道
권총 pistol [~gun] ~ 銃

귀 (貴) precious; honorable
귀중하다 be valuable; be precious [~important] ~重
귀중품 valuables
귀금속 jewelry [~metal] ~ 金屬
희귀하다 be rare [rare~] 稀~
품귀 shortage of goods [article~] 品~
귀하다 be noble; be precious
고귀하다 be noble; be precious [high~] 高~
귀족 nobles [~clan] ~ 族
귀하 esquire (used on envelopes) [~below] ~ 下

귀 (歸) return
복귀* a return; making a comeback [return~] 復~

귀국* returning to one's country [~country] ~ 國
귀가* returning home [~house] 歸~

귀 (鬼) ghost
귀신 ghost; demon [~spirit] ~ 神
귀신이 곡할 일 something disagreeably surprising
마귀 devil [demon~] 魔~

규 (規) regulation; scale
규율 rule; regulation [~rule] ~ 律
규칙 rule; regulation [~rule] ~ 則
규칙적으로 regularly
규정* rules; regulations [~decide] ~ 定
규제* regulation; restriction [~govern] ~ 制
정규 regular; formal [right~] 正~
정규교육 regular school education
규격 a standard; a norm [~frame] ~ 格
규모 scale; scope [~shape] ~ 模
대규모 large scale
소규모 small scale

균 (菌) germ
세균 germ; microbe [minute~] 細~
병균 (disease) germ [disease~] 病~
대장균 colitis germs [large intestine~] 大腸~
살균* sterilization [kill~] 殺~
멸균* pasteurization [destroy~] 滅~
멸균우유 pasteurized milk

ㄱ

균 (均)　equal; level

균일하다　be uniform; be even
[~one] ~ 一
균일가　uniform price

균등하다　be equal; be even
[~equal] ~ 等
기회균등*　equal opportunity

평균*　average [even~] 平~
평균내다　find a mean

균형　balance [~balance] ~ 衡
균형잡히다　be balanced

극 (極)　pole; extreme

북극　the North Pole [north~] 北 ~

남극　the South Pole [south~] 南 ~

적극적　positive; active
[positive~] 積 ~ 的

소극적　negative; passive
[negative~] 消 ~ 的

극히　extremely [~-ly] ~K

극도로　extremely
[~degree -ly] ~ 度 K

극단적　extreme [~end] ~ 端 的

지극하다　be extreme; be utmost
[extreme~] 至 ~
지극히　extremely; very

극치　zenith; culmination
[~reach] ~ 致

극비　top secret [~secret] ~ 秘

극진하다　be very kind; be utterly
devoted [~entirely] ~ 盡
극진한 대접
heart-warming hospitality

극소수　small minority
[~small number] ~ 少數

극 ᵂ(劇)　drama

극적　dramatic ~ 的

사극　historical drama
[history~] 史~

연극*　play; drama [perform~] 演 ~

극장　theater [~place] ~ 場

연속극　soap opera [serial~] 連續 ~

희극　comedy [pleasure~] 喜 ~

비극　tragedy [sad~] 悲~

근 (近)　near; recent

친근하다　be close; be familiar
[friendly~] 親 ~

접근*　approaching [contact~] 接 ~

근처　neighborhood; vicinity
[~place] ~ 處

근방　neighborhood; vicinity
[~direction] ~ 方

부근　neighborhood; vicinity
[append~] 附 ~

근교　suburbs [~suburb] ~ 郊
서울근교　suburbs of Seoul

근시　nearsightedness [~see] ~ 視

최근　the latest; the most recent
[the most~] 最~

근래　recent times; these days
[~coming] ~ 來

근대　modern times
[~generation] ~ 代
근대문명　modern civilization

근황　present situation
[~situation] ~ 況

근 (勤)　diligent; work

근면*　diligence [~effort] ~ 勉

근무*　service; work [~duty] ~ 務
근무시간　office hours

개근*　good attendance [all~] 皆 ~

35

통근*	commuting to work [go through~] 通 ~	금.방	goldsmith's shop; jewelry store [~room] ~ 房
출근*	going to work [come out~] 出 ~	금반지	gold ring [~ring] ~ 班指
퇴근*	getting off work [leave~] 退 ~	금목걸이	gold necklace [~necklace] ~K
결근*	absence from work [deficient~] 缺 ~	금메달	gold medal [~medal] ~ E
전근*	transfer (to another office) [transfer~] 轉 ~	금테안경	gold-rimmed glasses [~rim glasses] ~ K 眼鏡
야근*	night duty [night~] 夜 ~	금니	gold tooth [~tooth] ~ K
		금발	blond hair [~hair] ~ 髮

근 (根) root

근붕어 goldfish [~carp] ~K

근본	root; foundation [~origin] ~ 本 근본적 fundamental
근원	root; origin [~origin] ~ 源
근거	basis; ground [~depend on] ~ 據
근성	fundamental nature [~nature] ~ 性
당근	carrot

근 (筋) muscle

근육	muscle [~flesh] ~ 肉
철근	iron reinforcing rod [iron~] 鐵 ~

금 ʷ(金) gold; metal; money

순금	pure gold [pure~] 純 ~
십팔금	18 carat gold [eighteen~] 十八 ~
십사금	14 carat gold [fourteen~] 十四 ~
황금	gold; money [yellow~] 黃 ~ 황금만능시대 money-worshipping era

도금*	gilt; gilding [gold plating~] 鍍 ~
합금*	alloy; compound metal [unite~] 合 ~
금속	metal [~class] ~ 屬 귀금속 jewelry
금고	strongbox [~storehouse] ~庫
금전	money [~money] ~ 錢 금전출납기 teller machine
금액	amount of money [~amount] ~ 額
거금	big money [big~] 巨~
현금	cash [current~] 現 ~
금품	money and goods [~article] ~ 品
원금	principal sum [principal~] 元 ~
금융	finance; money market [~blend] ~ 融
공금	public money [public~] 公 ~
상금	prize money [prize~] 賞 ~
임금	wage [wages~] 賃 ~
저금*	saving money; deposit [save~] 貯 ~
적금	installment savings [accumulate~] 積 ~

비상금	emergency money [emergency~] 非常~
잔금	balance; rest of the money [remainder~] 殘~
송금*	remittance [send~] 送~
자금	funds [fund~] 資~
기금	fund; endowment [foundation~] 基~
성금	donation (of money) [sincerity~] 誠~
모금*	fund raising [collect~] 募~
장학금	scholarship [encourage study~] 獎學~
축의금	congratulatory money [congratulate rite~] 祝儀~
퇴직금	retirement allowance [retirement~] 退職~
연금	annuity; pension [year~] 年~
세금	tax [tax~] 稅~
요금	fee; fare [estimate~] 料~ 전기요금 electricity bill 전화요금 telephone bill
벌금	a fine [punish~] 罰~
등록금	registration fee; tuition [registration~] 登錄~
지참금	dowry [bringing~] 持參~
현상금	bounty; reward [prize~] 懸賞~

금 (禁) prohibit

금지*	prohibition [~stop] ~止
금하다	forbid
엄금*	strict prohibition [strict~] 嚴~
금연*	prohibition against smoking [~smoke] ~煙

금주*	abstinence from alcohol [~liquor] ~酒
금욕*	self-restraint; stoicism [~desire] ~慾
금물	prohibited thing [~thing] ~物
금기	taboo [~shun] ~忌
통금	curfew [go through~] 通~
감금*	imprisonment; confinement [inspect~] 監~

금 (今) now

지금	right now [only~] 只~
금방	a moment ago; just now [~just now] ~方
방금	just now; just a moment ago [just now~] 方~
금일	today [~day] ~日 금일휴업 closed today
금주	this week [~week] ~週
금년	this year [~year] ~年
금시초문	hearing (something) for the first time [~time first hear] ~時初聞

급 (急) urgent; fast

급하다	be urgent 급히 hastily
시급하다	be urgent [time~] 時~
긴급하다	be urgent [tense~] 緊~
급선무	the most urgent business [~first duty] ~先務
지급	utmost urgency (telegram) [extreme~] 至~ 지급전보 urgent telegram
위급하다	be critical; be an emergency [dangerous~] 危~

응급	emergency [reply~] 應~ 응급실 emergency room		봉급	salary [salary~] 俸~
구급약	first-aid medicine [save~medicine] 救~藥		월급	monthly salary [month~] 月~

급성   acute form of a disease [~nature] ~性
급성맹장염 acute appendicitis

기 ᵂ (氣) air; atmosphere; energy; spirit

성급하다	be hasty [nature~] 性~
조급하다	be hasty; be impatient [hasty~] 躁~
급행	an express (train) [~go] ~行
특급	special express (train) [special~] 特~
급강하*	sudden drop (in temp.) [~drop] ~降下
급정거*	sudden stop (of a vehicle) [~stopping a vehicle] ~停車

공기	air [sky~] 空~
기압	air pressure [~pressure] ~壓
연기	smoke [smoke~] 煙~ 담배연기 cigarette smoke
증기	steam; vapor [steam~] 蒸~
향기	fragrance [fragrant~] 香~
환기*	ventilation [exchange~] 換~
기후	climate [~weather] ~候
기온	temperature [~warm] ~溫
일기예보*	weather forecast [day~forecast] 日~豫報
기상대	meteorological observatory [~shape tower] ~象臺
감기	a cold [feel~] 感~
분위기	atmosphere; ambience [fog circumference~] 雰圍~
전기	electricity [electricity~] 電~
기력	energy [~strength] ~力
기운	energy [~transport] ~運
생기	animation; vitality [living~] 生~
활기	vigor; vitality [lively~] 活~
용기	courage [brave~] 勇~
사기	morale; spirit [soldier~] 士~
오기	unyielding spirit; obstinacy [arrogant~] 傲~
기질	temperament; nature [~disposition] ~質

급 ᵂ (級) class; grade

고급	high-class; advanced [high~] 高~
중급	intermediate level [middle~] 中~
초급	elementary level [beginning~] 初~
등급	a grade; a rank [rank~] 等~ 등급을 매기다 to rank
진급*	promotion [advance~] 進~
최상.급	superlative (degree) [the best~] 最上~

급 (給) give; pay

공급*	supply [offer~] 供~
발급*	issuing (a passport, license, etc.) [issue~] 發~ 재발급* reissuance
지급*	payment; supply [pay~] 支~

ㄱ

혈기	hot blood; vitality [blood~] 血~
열기	heat; heated atmosphere [heat~] 熱~
숫기	innocent openness [innocent~] K~ 숫기가 없다 be shy
장난·기	mischievousness; playfulness [play~] K~
바람·기	philandering spirit; wantonness [wind~] K~
끈기	tenacity; patience [sticky~] K~
윤·기	luster; shine [luster~] 潤~
습기	moisture; dampness [damp~] 濕~
물·기	moisture; dampness [water~] K~
기절*	fainting [~cut] 絶
현기.증	dizziness; vertigo [dizzy~symptom] 眩~症
기분	feeling [~share] ~分 기분좋다/나쁘다 be in a good/bad humor 기분전환* diversion; change
기합	concentration of spirit; disciplinary punishment [~unite] ~合 단체기합 group punishment
인·기	popularity [person~] 人~
경기	economic conditions [scenery~] 景~ 불경기 (business) depression 호경기 business boom
기 (機)	**machine; mechanism; opportunity**
기계	machine [~machine] ~械
비행기	airplane [flying~] 飛行~

사진·기	camera [picture~] 寫眞~
청소기	vacuum cleaner [cleaning~] 淸掃~
세탁기	washing machine [washing~] 洗濯~
탈수기	machine for extracting water from clothes [dehydration~] 脫水~
계산기	calculator [calculation~] 計算~
자판기	vending machine [auto selling~] 自販~ (<자동판매기)
전화기	telephone (instrument) [phone call~] 電話~
수화기	telephone receiver [receive talk~] 受話~
응답기	answering machine [answer~] 應答~
타자기	typewriter [typing~] 打字~
선풍기	mechanical fan [fan wind~] 扇風~
환풍기	ventilation fan [ventilation~] 換風~
가습기	humidifier [add moisture~] 加濕~
정수기	water purifier [clean water~] 淨水~
기능	function [~ability] ~能
기구	organization [~compose] ~構 세계보건기구 World Health Organization
기관	engine; organization; organ [~concern] ~關
동기	motive; incentive [move~] 動~
기회	opportunity; chance [~meeting] ~會

39

시기	opportunity; the (right) time [time~] 時~ 시기를 놓치다 miss an opportunity	환절기	transition between two seasons [exchange season~] 換節~
위기	critical moment; crisis [dangerous~] 危~	권태기	stage of weariness [boredom~] 倦怠~
대기*	waiting (for a chance) [wait for~] 待~	기약*	pledge; promise [~promise] ~ 約
투기*	speculation (in real estate) [throw~] 投~	기대*	expectation; anticipation [~wait for] ~ 待

기 (期) period; term

기 (器) vessel; utensil

기간	period; term [~interval] ~ 間
조기	early period; stage [early~] 早~
초기	early period; stage [early~] 初~
말기	the last period [end~] 末~
주기	period; cycle [revolve~] 週~ 주기적 periodical; recurrent
정기적	periodic; regular [fix~] 定~
장기	long term [long~] 長~
기한	time limit [~limit] ~ 限
임기	one's term of office [be in charge~] 任~
전성기	golden period; one's best days [all prosper~] 全盛~
사춘기	adolescence; puberty [think spring~] 思春~
연기*	postponement; deferment [extend~] 延~
학기	school semester [study~] 學~
기말	end of semester [~end] ~末
동기	graduates of the same year [same~] 同~

용기	receptacle; container [permit~] 容~ 플라스틱 용기 plastic container
식기	table ware [food~] 食~
사기	earthenware; porcelain [sand~] 沙~ 사기그릇 porcelain dishes
도자기	ceramic ware [earthen~] 陶磁~
뚝배기	unglazed earthenware bowl
세면기	wash bowl [wash face~] 洗面~
변기	toilet bowl [excretion~] 便~
청진기	stethoscope [listen medical examination~] 聽診~
녹음기	tape recorder [sound recording~] 錄音 ~
소화기	fire extinguisher [dissolve fire~] 消火 ~
계량기	meter; gauge [calculate measure~] 計量~
악기	musical instrument [music~] 樂~
기구	appliance; tool [~tool] ~ 具
무기	weapon [military~] 武~

흉기   lethal weapon [evil~] 凶~

성기   sexual organ [sex~] 性~

기 (記)   record

기록*   putting on record;
a record [~record] ~ 錄

필기*   note taking [pen~] 筆~

속기*   shorthand; quick writing
[speedy~] 速~

표기*   transcribing [manifest~] 表~

표기*   marking [mark~] 標~

기입*   writing in; entering
[~enter] ~ 入

일기   diary [day~] 日~

수기   memoirs [hand~] 手~

기억*   memory [~remember] ~ 憶
기억력   memory power

전기   biography [transmit~] 傳~

기자   journalist; reporter
[~person] ~ 者
기자회견*   press interview

기사   (newspaper) article
[~matters] ~ 事

기호   a sign; symbol
[~number] ~ 號

등기(우편)   registered mail
[advance~mail] 登~郵便

기 (技)   skill

기술   skill; technique [~skill] ~ 術
기술·자   technician

특기   special skill; specialty
[special~] 特~

묘기   exquisite skill
[exquisite~] 妙~

장·기   special skill; talent
[superior~] 長~
장·기자랑*   talent show

실기   practical skill [real~] 實~
실기시험   (practical) skill test

연기*   performance; acting
[perform~] 演~

기교   art; technique
[~clever] ~ 巧

기사   engineer; technician
[~master] ~ 師
운전기사   driver

경기   (sports) game
[compete~] 競~
운동경기   sporting event
육상경기   track and field
events

기 (奇)   strange; mysterious

신기하다   be marvelous; be
supernatural [god~] 神~

기묘하다   be strange; be queer
[~exquisite] ~ 妙

기적   miracle [~footprints] ~ 蹟

호기심   curiosity; inquisitiveness
[like~mind] 好~心

기발하다   be extraordinary; be novel;
be striking [~pull out] ~ 拔
기발한 생각   striking idea

기형   deformity [~shape] ~ 形

기습*   surprise attack [~attack] ~ 襲

기 (紀)   century; record

세기   century [world~] 世~
이십세기
the twentieth century

기원전   B. C. [~the first before]
~元前

서기   A. D. [west~] 西~

41

기념* commemoration
[~think] ~ 念
기념품 souvenir
기념일 anniversary

기행문 travel description
[~go writing] ~ 行文

기 (起) rise; begin

기상* rising from bed [~bed] ~ 床

재기* rising again; recovery
[again~] 再 ~

발기* erection [sudden anger~] 勃 ~

기.점 starting point [~point] ~ 點

칠.전팔기* never giving in to
adversity [seven upset
eight~] 七顚八 ~

제기* instituting (a lawsuit);
bringing up (a problem)
[suggest~] 提~

기 (基) foundation

기반 foundation [~plate] ~ 盤

기금 fund; endowment
[~money] ~ 金

기초 basis; foundation
[~foundation] ~ 礎

기본 basis [~base] ~ 本
기본적 basic

기준 a standard; criterion
[~measure] ~ 準

기독교 Christianity
[~direct religion] ~ 督教

기 (寄) entrust; lodge at

기증* donation; contribution
[~give a present] ~ 贈

기여* contribution; services
[~give] ~ 與

기부* donation [~append] ~ 附

기숙사 dormitory
[~lodge house] ~ 宿舍

기생충 parasitic worm
[~live insect] ~ 生蟲

기 (旣) already

기성복 ready-made clothes
[~complete clothes] ~ 成服

기정사실 established fact
[~decide fact] ~ 定事實

기혼 married [~marriage] ~ 婚

기 ʷ (旗) flag

깃발 flag ~ K

국기 national flag [nation ~] 國 ~

태극기 Korean flag
[the Great Absolute~] 太極 ~

기 (棄) abandon

자포자기* self-abandonment
[self abandon self~] 自暴自 ~

포기* giving up [abandon~] 抛 ~

기.권* renunciation of
one's rights [~rights] ~ 權

긴 (緊) important; tense

긴요하다 be important; be essential
[~essential] ~ 要

요긴하다 be essentially important
[essential~] 要 ~

긴급하다 be urgent [~urgent] ~ 急

긴장* tension; tenseness
[~extend] ~ 張

ㄴ

길 (吉) lucky

길몽 lucky dream [~dream] ~ 夢

불길하다 be ill-omened; be inauspicious [not~] 不~

ㄴ

낙 (諾) **consent** (/락)

응낙* consent [reply~] 應~

승낙* approval [consent~] 承~

허락* permission; consent [permit~] 許~

수락* acceptance [receive~] 受~

낙 ʷ(樂) **pleasant** (see 락)

낙 (落) **fall; omit; scatter** (see 락)

난 (難) **difficult(y)** (/란)

곤란* difficulty; trouble [hardship~] 困~

고난 hardship; difficulty [bitter~] 苦~

난관 difficult situation; obstacle [~locked] 關

험난하다 be rough and difficult [rough~] 險~

무난하다 be not difficult; be easily passable [not~] 無~

수난* sufferings; ordeal [receive~] 受~

진퇴양난 being in a dilemma; being driven to the wall [advance retreat both~] 進退兩~

난처하다 be in a difficult situation [~place] ~ 處

논란* negative criticism [discuss~] 論~

재난 calamity [calamity~] 災~

비난* criticism; blame [wrong~] 非~

다사다난하다 be eventful [many matters much~] 多事多~

피난* refuge; evacuation [avoid~] 避~

도난 robbery; burglary [steal~] 盜~

난 (煖) **warm**

난로 stove [~stove] ~ 爐

난방 heating (a room); heated room [~room] ~ 房
난방시설 heating facilities

난 (亂) **chaotic** (see 란)

남 (男) **male; man**

남자 male; man [~thing] ~ 子

남성 man; male [~sex] ~ 性
남성복 men's clothes

남녀 man and woman [~woman] ~ 女
남녀노소 male and female, old and young

미남 good-looking man [beautiful~] 美~

남학생 male student [~student] 學生

43

남창	male prostitute [~prostitute] ~ 娼
남편	husband [~side] ~ 便
유부남	married man [exist wife~] 有婦~
장남	eldest son [elder~] 長~
남동생	younger brother [~sibling] ~ 同生
남매	brother and sister [~sister] ~ 妹
처남	one's wife's brother [wife~] 妻~
무남독녀	only daughter [no~only female] 無~獨女
남존여비	male superiority [~honorable female low] ~ 尊女卑

남 ʷ(南)	**south**
남쪽	southern side [~side] ~K
남부	southern part [~part] ~ 部
남대문	South Gate of Seoul [~big gate] ~ 大門
남미	South America [~America] ~ 美
남극	the South Pole [~pole] ~ 極
남북	south and north [~north] ~北
남한	South Korea [~Korea] ~ 韓
이남	South Korea [from~] 以~
월남*	coming south (from North Korea) [cross over~] 越~
남침*	invasion of South Korea [~invade] ~ 侵
남향	(house) southern exposure [~to face] ~向
남방	aloha shirt [~direction] ~ 方

납(納)	**give; receive**
납부*	paying (tax, bills, etc.) [~pay] ~ 付
납득*	understanding; being convinced [~acquire] ~ 得
용납*	toleration; permission [permit~] 容~

낭(浪)	**wave; wasteful** (/랑)
풍랑	wind and waves [wind~] 風 ~
낭만	romance [~romance] ~ 漫 낭만적 romantic
낭비*	waste [~spend] ~ 費

내(內)	**inside**
내면	the inside [~side] ~ 面
내부	the inside [~part] ~ 部
실내	indoors [room~] 室~
내복	underwear [~clothes] ~ 服
내의	underwear [~clothes] ~ 衣
내장	internal organs [~viscera] ~ 臟
내·과	dept. of internal medicine [~department] ~ 科
국내	domestic [country~] 國 ~
내륙	inland [~land] ~ 陸 내륙지방 inland area
내란	civil war [~chaos] ~ 亂
내무부	Ministry of Domestic Affairs [~affairs section] ~務部
시내	within the city; downtown [city~] 市 ~
교내	intramural; on-campus [school~] 校~

구내   a compound; (on) the campus [structure~] 構~
구내식당 (school) cafeteria

내용   contents [~permit] ~ 容

내막   inside story [~curtain] ~ 幕

내색하다   let one's face show one's thoughts [~color] ~ 色

내성적   introverted [~examine] ~ 省的

이내   within; not more than [with~] 以~
일주일 이내 within a week

안내*   guidance; ushering [desk~] 案~

내 (來)   **come; coming**   (see 래)

냉 (冷)   **cold**

냉수   cold water [~water] ~ 水

냉면   cold noodle [~noodle] ~ 麵

냉차   iced tea [~tea] ~ 茶

냉커피   iced coffee [~coffee] ~ E

냉방   air conditioned room [~room] ~ 房

냉장*   refrigeration [~storage] ~ 藏
냉장고 refrigerator

냉동*   freezing [~freeze] ~ 凍
냉동실 freezer

냉전   cold war [~war] ~ 戰

냉정*   calmness; composure [~quiet] ~ 靜

냉철하다   be cool-headed [~penetrate] ~ 徹

녀 (女)   **female**   (see 여)

년 (年)   **year; age**   (/연)

연도   year [~limit] ~度
1996년도 the year 1996

금년   this year [now~] 今~

내년   next year [coming~] 來~

작년   last year [yesterday~] 昨~
재작년 the year before last

후년   the year after next [after~] 後~

왕년   the years past [go~] 往~

윤년   leap year [leap month~] 閏~

풍년   year of good harvest [abundant~] 豊~

흉년   year of bad harvest [unlucky~] 凶~

연말   end of the year [~end] ~ 末

연봉   yearly stipend; annual salary [~salary] ~ 俸

연금   annuity; pension [~money] ~ 金

연평균   yearly average [~average] ~ 平均

연하.장   New Year's card [~congratulate letter] ~ 賀狀

학년   school year; grade [school~] 學~

(일)주년   (first) anniversary [first revolve~] 一週~
결혼 일주년 first wedding anniversary

연대   years and generations; chronology [~generation] ~代
연대순 chronological order
90년대 nineties

연령   age; years [~age] ~ 齡

연세   age (hon.) [~age] ~ 歲

노년   old age [old~] 老~

중년   middle age [middle~] 中~

소년	young boy [young~] 少~	염불*	Buddhist invocation [~Buddha] ~ 佛

노 (老) old   (/로)

연로하다 be old; be aged [age~] 年~

노년 old age [~age] ~ 年

노인 elderly person [~person] ~ 人

노약자 elderly person; the old and the weak [~weak person] ~ 弱者

경로 respect for elderly people [respect~] 敬~
경로석 seats for the elderly

양로원 nursing home [care~institution] 養~院

노처녀 old maid [~Miss] ~ 處女

노총각 old bachelor [~bachelor] ~ 總角

노화현상 symptoms of aging [~change phenomenon] ~化現象

노안 eyesight of the aged; far-sightedness [~eye] ~ 眼

노망 dotage [~absurd] ~ 妄

노련하다 be experienced and skilled [~trained] ~ 鍊

노숙하다 be mature and experienced [~mature] ~ 熟

노파·심 excessive solicitude [~old woman mind] ~ 婆心

노 (露) reveal   (/로)

폭로* disclosure; divulgence [suddenly~] 暴~

노출* exposure [~come out] ~ 出

노점 street stall [~store] ~ 店

청년 young man [green~] 靑~
청소년 young boys and girls; teen agers

연로하다 be old; be aged [~old] ~ 老

연상 senior in age [~above] 上

연하 junior in age [~below] 下

념 (念) think; thought   (/염)

잡념 distracting thoughts [mixed~] 雜~

여념이 없다 be absorbed (in) [surplus~not exist] 餘 ~ K

묵념* silent prayer [silent~] 默 ~

전념* undivided attention; mental concentration [exclusive~] 專~

집념* concentration of one's attention [grasp~] 執~
집념이 강하다 be tenacious

신념 belief; faith [believe~] 信 ~

관념 concept; idea [view~] 觀~
시간관념이 없다 have no sense of time
강박관념 obsession; persecution complex

이념 ideology [principle~] 理~

염려* worry; concern [~worry] ~ 慮

염두 mind; one's attention [~head] ~ 頭
...을 염두에 두다 keep...in mind

단념* giving up; abandonment [cut off~] 斷 ~

체념* giving up; resignation [resign~] 諦 ~

기념* commemoration [record~] 紀 ~

46

노골.적   outspoken; plain
[~bone] ~ 骨的
노골.적으로 말하다
call a spade a spade

피로연   reception (for making
an announcement)
[expose~banquet] 披~宴

노 (路)   **road**   (see 로)

노 (勞)   **toil**   (see 로)

녹 ʷ(綠) **green; rust**   (/록)

초록색   grass green color
[grass~color] 草~色

녹차   green tea [~tea] ~ 茶

녹말   starch [~end] ~ 末

녹슬다   become rusty ~ K

녹 (錄)   **record**   (see 록)

논 (論)   **discuss**   (/론)

논하다   argue; discuss

의논*   consultation; discussion
[discuss~] 議~

토론*   debate; discussion
[discuss~] 討~

언론   speech; the press
[talk~] 言~

논쟁*   a dispute; argument
[~fight] ~ 爭

논리   logic [~principle] ~ 理
논리적   logical

논문   thesis; dissertation
[~writing] ~ 文

이론   theory [principle~] 理~

평론*   criticism; review
[comment~] 評~

중론   general opinion
[crowd~] 衆~

논란*   negative criticism
[~difficulty] ~ 難

농 (農)   **agricultural**

농촌   agricultural village
[~village] ~ 村

농업   agricultural industry
[~industry] ~ 業

농장   farm; plantation
[~place] ~ 場

농토   farmland [~land] ~ 土

농부   farmer [~artisan] ~ 夫

농민   farmer; peasantry
[~people] ~ 民

농사   farming [~business] ~ 事
농사꾼   farmer
농사짓다   do farming

농산물   agricultural products
[~products] ~ 産物
농수산물   agricultural
and marine products

농작물   crops; farm produce
[~make things] ~ 作物

농약   herbicides and insecticides
[~medicine] ~ 藥

농대   college of agriculture
[~college] ~ 大
(<농·과대학)

농협   agricultural cooperative
association [~cooperative
association] ~ 協
(<농업협동조합)

뇌 ʷ(腦) **brain**

두뇌   brain [head~] 頭~

뇌염   brain inflammation;
encephalitis
[~inflammation] ~ 炎

47

뇌진탕   cerebral concussion [~shake dissipate] ~ 震蕩

세**뇌***   brainwashing [wash~] 洗 ~

능 (能)   able; ability

능하다   be capable

능력   capability [~strength] ~ 力

예**능**   art; artistic ability [art~] 藝 ~

지**능**   intelligence [know~] 知 ~

능률   efficiency [~rate] ~ 率
(비)능률.적   (in)efficient

능숙하다   be skillful; be proficient [~experienced] ~ 熟

만**능**   omnipotent [all~] 萬 ~
황금만능
Money is everything.

가**능**하다   be possible [alright~] 可 ~

본**능**   basic instinct [basic~] 本 ~

무**능**하다   be incompetent [no~] 無 ~

유**능**하다   be competent [exist~] 有 ~

재**능**   talent; skill [talent~] 才 ~
다재다능*   versatile talents

기**능**   function [mechanism~] 機 ~

성**능**   performance; capacity [essential quality~] 性 ~

ㄷ

다 (多)   many; much

다수   large number [~number] ~ 數
다수결   majority vote

다량   large quantity [~amount] ~量

허**다**하다   be numerous; be common [permit~] 許 ~

다소   more or less [~little] ~ 少

다방면   many quarters; various fields [~field] ~ 方面

다양하다   be varied [~pattern] ~ 樣

다행*   good fortune [~fortune] ~ 幸

다정하다   be affectionate [~affection] ~ 情

다사**다**난하다   be eventful [~matters~difficulty] ~ 事 ~ 難

파**다**하다   be widely rumored [sow (seed)~] 播 ~

단 (斷)   cut off; stop

절.**단***   cutting; amputation [cut~] 切 ~

재**단***   garment cutting [make clothes~] 裁 ~

단발*   bobbed hair; a bob [~hair] ~ 髮

단절*   discontinuation; breaking off [~cut] ~ 絶

중**단***   discontinuance [middle~] 中 ~

분**단***   division; partition [divide~] 分 ~
한반도의 분단   division of the Korean Peninsula

단면   a section; a phase [~surface] ~ 面

단편적   fragmentary; piecemeal [~piece] ~ 片的

차**단***   interception; blocking [block~] 遮 ~
자외선차단제
sunscreen products

횡단*	crossing [across~] 橫~ 횡단보도 crosswalk	단어	vocabulary item [~word] ~ 語
단식*	fasting [~eat] ~ 食	간.단하다	be simple; be brief [simple~] 簡 ~
단념*	giving up; abandonment [~think] ~ 念	단순하다	be simple; be simple- minded [~pure] ~ 純
부단하다	be incessant [no~] 不~	단색	monochrome [~color] ~ 色
결.단*	determination [decide~] 決~	단조롭다	be monotonous [~control] ~ 調
판단*	judgment [judge~] 判 ~	단·과대학	college [~department college] ~科大學
속단*	hasty conclusion [speedy~] 速~	단도직입적	straightforward [~knife straight enter] ~刀直入的
단정*	conclusion; decision [~decide] ~ 定	단위	a unit [~position] ~ 位
진단*	diagnosis [medical examination~] 診 ~	식단	menu [food~] 食~
단호하다	be firm; be determined [~exclamation] ~ 乎	명단	roster [name~] 名~
우유부단*	being indecisive [excellent soft no~] 優柔不~	**단 (團)**	**group**
강단	persevering strength; tenacity [metal~] 剛 ~ 강단이 있다 be strong and tenacious	단체	group; organization [~body] ~ 體 단체여행* group tour 단체활.동* group activity
단 (單)	**single; unit**	단결*	unity; solidarity [~tie] ~ 結
단수	singular number [~number] ~ 數	단합*	unity; solidarity [~unite] ~ 合
단식	(tennis) singles [~style] ~式	집단	collective body; group [gather~] 集~ 집단자살* mass suicide
단층	one-story (building) [~story] ~ 層	악단	orchestra; band [music~] 樂~
단독	singleness [~alone] ~ 獨 단독주택 independent house	단지	housing complex [~place] ~ 地 아파트단지 apartment complex 공업단지 industrial complex
단짝	inseparable friend; shadow [~pair] ~K	재단	benefactive foundation [property~] 財 ~
단번에	at one try; all at once [~number] ~ 番K	단속*	regulation; crackdown [~bind] ~ 束
단숨에	in one breath; in a sitting [~breath] ~ K		

단 (短)　short

단거리	short distance [~distance] ~ 距離
단시간	short period of time [~time] ~ 時間
단편	short piece (writing) [~book] ~ 篇
단축*	shortening [~shrink] ~ 縮
단.점	shortcoming [~point] ~ 點 장단.점　merits and demerits
일.장일.**단**	merits and demerits [one superior one~] 一長一~
장**단**	rhythm [long~] 長~

단 (端)　pointed end; beginning

첨**단**	spearhead; vanguard [sharp~] 尖~ 유행의 첨단을 걷다 lead the fashion
극**단**적	extreme [extreme~] 極~的 양극단　both extremes
양**단**간	one way or the other; between two alternatives [both~between] 兩~間
단서	clue (for investigation) [~clue] ~緖
야**단**	commotion; scolding; trouble [provoke ~] 惹~ 야단나다　be in trouble 야단하다　scold 야단맞다　be scolded

단 (段)　step; section

계**단**	stairs [stairs~] 階~
단계	stages (of development) [~stairs] ~ 階
수**단**	means; resource [means~] 手~
문**단**	paragraph [writing~] 文~

단 ᵂ(壇)　altar

제**단**	altar (for sacrifice) [sacrificial rite ~] 祭~
교**단**	teacher's platform [teach~] 敎~
화**단**	flower bed [flower~] 花~

달 (達)　achieve

달.성*	achieving; attaining [~to complete] ~ 成
숙**달***	attaining proficiency; getting a mastery (of) [experienced~] 熟~
발.**달***	development; growth [rise~] 發~
전**달***	delivery; conveyance [transmit~] 傳~
배**달***	delivery [distribute~] 配~
속**달***	express mail [speedy~] 速~
도**달***	arrival; reaching [arrive~] 到~
미**달***	shortage [not yet~] 未~ 정원미달　for want of quorum

담 (談)　converse; saying

회**담***	parley; a talk [meeting~] 會~
진**담***	serious talk [true~] 眞~
잡**담***	idle talk; desultory chat [mixed~] 雜~
음**담**패설*	obscene talk [obscene perverse talk] 淫~悖說
상**담***	consultation; counsel [mutual~] 相~
농**담***	joke [play with~] 弄~
험**담***	slanderous remark [rough~] 險~

ㄷ

장담* assurance; guarantee [robust~] 壯 ~

속담 proverb [vulgar~] 俗 ~

담 (擔) carry; sustain

전담* whole responsibility; complete charge [whole~] 全 ~

분담* division of labor or responsibility [divide~] 分 ~

부담 a burden; a charge [carry~] 負 ~
부담스럽다 be burdensome
부담하다 bear the expense

담당* being in charge [~ought] ~ 當
담당자 person in charge

담임* teacher in charge (of a class) [~be in charge] ~ 任

담보 security; mortgage [~protect] ~ 保

답 ᵂ(答) reply; answer

응답* a reply [respond~] 應 ~

답변* an answer [~eloquence] ~ 辯

대답* an answer [opposite~] 對 ~

정답 correct answer [right~] 正 ~

해답 correct answer; solution [solve~] 解 ~

확답* definite answer [certain~] 確 ~

명답 brilliant answer; repartee [famous~] 名 ~

동문서답* irrelevant reply [east ask west~] 東問西 ~

답장* letter of reply [~letter] ~ 狀

회답* letter of reply [return~] 回 ~

답안 written answers to exam questions [~document] ~ 案
답안지 answer sheet

보답* repay; reward [give back~] 報 ~

답례* a return favor [~courtesy] ~ 禮
...에 대한 답례로 in return for...

당 (當) ought; suitable; correct

당직* being on (night) duty [~direct] ~ 直

당번 person on duty [~number] ~ 番

담당* being in charge [carry~] 擔 ~

당연하다 be natural; be a matter of course [~as such] ~ 然
당연히 of course

해당하다 correspond to; be applicable to [apply to~] 該 ~
해당사항 pertinent data

감당하다 be capable of carrying out; take care of [endure~] 堪 ~

상당하다 be proportionate; be considerable [mutual~] 相 ~

적당하다 be suitable; be appropriate [suitable~] 適 ~

합당하다 be suitable; be appropriate [join~] 合 ~

지당하다 be quite right; be reasonable [extreme~] 至 ~

타당하다 be reasonable; be proper [reasonable~] 妥 ~

당사자 the person concerned [~matter person] ~ 事者

당국 the authorities concerned [~office] ~ 局

51

배당*	apportionment; a share [distribute~] 配~	혈.당	blood sugar [blood~] 血~
할.당*	allotment [divide~] 割~	포도당	glucose [grape~] 葡萄~
일인당	per person [one person~] 一人~	사탕	candy [gravel~] 砂~
일.당	daily allowance [day~] 日~	당뇨.병	diabetes [~urine disease] ~尿病
수당	allowance; compensation [means~] 手~	탕수육	sweet and sour pork [~water meat] ~水肉
충당*	appropriation; meeting (the demand) [full~] 充~		

당 ʷ(黨) **political party**

당시	at that time; in those days [~time] ~時
당일	the day (in question) [~day] ~日
당장	on the spot; immediately [~place] ~場
당부*	request; entreaty [~give] ~付 신신당부하다 ask earnestly
당치않다	be unreasonable [~not] ~K
정당하다	be just; be legitimate [right~] 正~
부당하다	be unjust; be unfair [not ~] 不~
당선*	getting elected; winning an election [~select] ~選
당첨*	prizewinning; drawing a prize [~draw lots] ~籤
당하다	have (something undesirable) done; experience

당 ʷ(糖) **sugar**

설탕	sugar [snow~] 雪~ 백설탕 white sugar 흑설탕 brown sugar
당분	sugar content [~share] ~分
무가당	sugar-free [not add~] 無可~

정당	political party [politics~] 政~
당수	(political) party leader [~head] ~首
야당	opposition party [outside~] 野~
여당	ruling party [grant~] 與~
당파싸움	party dispute [~branch fight] ~派K
탈.당*	secession [escape~] 脫~
악당	scoundrel; rascal [evil~] 惡~

당 (堂) **hall**

강당	auditorium [lecture~] 講~
식당	restaurant [eat~] 食~
성당	Catholic church [holy~] 聖~
천당	heaven [heaven~] 天~

대 (大) **big; great**

최대	the largest; maximum [the most~] 最~
특대	extra large [special~] 特~
대회	large meeting; rally [~meeting] ~會

대형	big size; large model [~model] ~ 型	교대	teachers' college [education~] 教~ (<교육대학)
대량	large quantity [~amount] ~量	여대	women's college [woman~] 女~ (<여자대학)
대부분	for the most part; mostly [~part] ~ 部分	대인	adult (for admission purposes) [~person] ~ 人
대다수	great number; majority [~large number] ~ 多数	대가족	big family [~family] ~ 家族
대만원	full house; crowdedness [~full house] ~ 滿員	대차없다	make no great difference [~difference not exist] ~ 差 K
대규모	large scale [~scale] ~ 規模	중대하다	be important; be serious [weighty~] 重~
대대적	large-scale ~ ~ 的 대대적으로 on a large scale	지대하다	be immense; be great [extreme~] 至~
대문	main gate [~door] ~ 門	막대하다	be enormous; be colossal [extremely~] 莫~
대교	grand bridge [~bridge] ~ 橋	거대하다	be huge; be gigantic [big~] 巨~
대포	gun; cannon [~cannon] ~ 砲	성대하다	be grand; be magnificent [prosper~] 盛~
대장	large intestine [~intestine] ~ 腸	위대하다	be great [great~] 偉~
대머리	bald head [~head] ~ K	무한대	infinite magnitude [no limit~] 無限~
대륙	a continent [~land] ~ 陸	확대*	enlargement [enlarge~] 擴~
대학	college [~school] 學	관대하다	be generous [generous~] 寬~
대졸	college graduate [~graduation] ~ 卒 (<대학졸업)	대장	a general; head; chief [~officer] ~ 將
법대	law school [law dept.~] 法~ (<법과대학)	대장부	manly man; heroic man [~strong man] ~ 丈夫
의대	medical school [medical dept.~] 醫~ (<의·과대학)	대법원	the Supreme Court [~court] ~ 法院
약대	college of pharmacology [pharmacology~] 藥~ (<약학대학)	대중	masses; general public [~crowd] ~ 衆
공대	engineering college [engineering dept.~] 工~ (<공·과대학)	대개	in general [~outline] ~ 槪
농대	college of agriculture [agricultural dept.~] 農~ (<농·과대학)	대강	an outline; roughly [~principle] ~ 綱
사대	college of education [teacher~] 師~ (<사범대학)	대략	an outline; approximately [~abbreviate] ~ 略

대체로	on the whole [~body] ~ 體 K	상대	partner; rival; relativity [mutual~] 相 ~ 상대편 the opposite party 상대하다 keep company (with); contend (with) 상대적으로 relatively
대담하다	be bold; be daring [~liver] ~ 膽		
대범하다	be not overly fussy about trifles; be open-handed [~careless] ~ 泛	대등하다	be equal; be on an equal footing with [~equal] ~ 等
		절.대(로)	absolutely [absolute~-ly] 絶 ~ K

대 (對) oppose; opposite; comparative

반대*	the opposite; objection [opposite~] 反 ~ 반대편 opposite side		

대 (待) wait (for); treat

대면*	facing [~face] ~ 面	대기*	waiting (for a chance) [~opportunity] ~ 機
대책	countermeasure [~plan] ~ 策	고대하다	wait eagerly [bitter~] 苦 ~ 학수고대하다 look forward to
대립*	opposition; confrontation [~stand] ~ 立		
대결*	confrontation; showdown [~decide] ~ 決	기대*	expectation; anticipation [period~] 期 ~
대항*	counteraction; defiance [~resist] ~ 抗	대합실	(railroad station) waiting room [~join room] ~ 合室
대적하다	to match; rival [~enemy] ~ 敵	대피*	taking shelter [~escape] ~ 避
대조*	contrast [~illumine] ~ 照	우대*	preferential treatment [superior~] 優 ~
적대시하다	regard with hostility [enemy~look at] 敵 ~ 視	천대*	contemptuous, cold treatment [lowly~] 賤 ~
대비*	provision (for); preparation (for) [~prepare] ~ 備	대접*	a treat; hospitality [~receive] ~ 接 대접받다 be treated 푸대접* unkind treatment
대처하다	cope with [~manage] ~ 處		
대각선	diagonal line [~angle line] ~ 角線	대우*	treatment; behavior toward [~entertain] ~ 遇 차별대우* discriminatory treatment
대답*	an answer [~answer] ~ 答	학대*	maltreatment [cruel~] 虐 ~
대화*	dialogue; conversation [~talk] ~ 話	초대*	invitation [invite~] 招 ~
대상	objective; target [~representation] ~ 象 ...를 대상으로 하다 make...an object (of)	접대*	reception; welcome [receive~] 接 ~ 손님접대* receiving (serving) guests

대 (代)   **substitute; generation**

대용*   substitution [~use] ~ 用
대용품 a substitute article

대신*   substitution; replacement
[~body] ~ 身
...대신(에)   instead of...

대치*   replacement [~to place] ~ 置

대리*   proxy; an agent
[~manage] ~ 理
대리점 agency;
commercial agent

대표*   representation;
a representative
[~manifest] ~ 表

대·가   price; cost [~price] ~ 價

교대*   taking turns; shift
[exchange~] 交~
교대로 by turns

시대   time; era [time~] 時~

현대   modern times [current~] 現~

세대   generation [generation~] 世~

연대   years and generations;
chronology [year~] 年~

십대   teenager; teen years
[ten~] 十~

대 (帶)   **belt**

혁대   leather belt [leather~] 革~

붕대   bandage [bind~] 繃~

안대   eyepatch [eye~] 眼~

생리대   sanitary napkin
[physiology~] 生理~

열.대   tropics [heat~] 熱~

지대   zone; area [earth~] 地~
녹지대 green belt

일.대   the whole area; the
neighborhood (of)
[one~] 一 ~
서울 일.대에 all over Seoul

휴대*   carrying along
[take with~] 携~
휴대용 portable (use)

대 (臺)   **tower; terrace**

등대   lighthouse [light~] 燈~

기상대   meteorological
observatory [atmospheric
phenomena~] 氣象~

축대   embankment [axis~] 築~

토대   foundation; groundwork
[soil~] 土~

화장대   dressing table; dresser
[makeup~] 化粧~

무대   stage [dance~] 舞~

침대   bed [sleep~] 寢~

청와대   Blue House (Korean
presidential mansion)
[blue tile~] 靑瓦~

대 (貸)   **lend; borrow**

대출*   lending out; loan [~exit] ~出

대여*   lending [~give] ~ 與

대부*   loaning [~give] ~ 付

임대*   lease; hiring out [lease~] 賃~
임대아파트 leased apartment

대절*   chartering (a vehicle)
[~earnest] ~ 切

대 (隊)   **army**

군대   army; troops [military~] 軍~

입대*   enlistment [enter~] 入~

제대* discharge from military service [eliminate~] 除~

부대 (military) unit; troops; large group [section~] 部~

덕 ᵂ(德) **virtue**

도덕 moral [principle~] 道~

배은망덕* ingratitude [a back favor forget~] 背恩忘~

감지덕지 very gratefully [feeling of~of] 感之~之
감지덕지하다
feel very grateful

덕분 indebtedness; thanks to [~a share] ~分
...덕분에 thanks to...
...덕분이다 I owe it to...

덕택 indebtedness; thanks to [~favor] ~澤

변덕 caprice [change~] 變~

도 ᵂ(道) **way; principle; province**

편도 one-way (ticket) [piece~] 片~

도로 road [~road] ~路
고속도로 expressway

철·도 railroad [iron~] 鐵~

인도 sidewalk [person~] 人~

보도 sidewalk [walk~] 步~

차도 driveway; traffic lane [vehicle~] 車~

지하도 underpass [underground~] 地下~

복도 corridor; hallway [double~] 複~

수도 waterworks; waterway [water~] 水~
하수도 sewer system

적도 equator [red~] 赤~

도구 tool; implement [~tool] ~具

도리 propriety; duty; way [~principle] ~理

도덕 morality; morals [~virtue] ~德
공중도덕 public morals

도의 morality [~right conduct] ~義
도의에 어긋나다
be against public morals

효도* filial duty [filial piety~] 孝~

기사도 knighthood; chivalry [knight~] 騎士~

태.권도 taekwondo [kick fist~] 跆拳~

도청 provincial office [~government office] ~廳

도지사 provincial governor [~know matters] ~知事

경기도 Kyonggi Province 京畿~

강원도 Kangwon Province 江原~

충청도 Chungchong Province 忠淸~

경상도 Kyongsang Province 慶尙~

전라도 Cholla Province 全羅~

도 ᵂ(度) **degree; limit**

각도 angle [angle~] 角~

정도 degree; extent [measure~] 程~

도.수 (lense) power; (alcohol) proof [~number] ~數

온도 degree (temp.) [warm~] 溫~
체감온도
perceived temperature

영도 zero degrees centigrade [zero~] 零~

습도	humidity [wet~] 濕~	도표	chart; diagram [~display] ~ 表
속도	speed [speed~] 速~	도장	a seal; stamp [~a seal] ~ 章
척도	yardstick [yardstick~] 尺~	의도*	intention [intention~] 意~
빈도	frequency [frequent~] 頻~	시도*	trying out; attempt [try~] 試~
진도	the rate of progress (of classwork) [advance~] 進~		

도 (島) island

극도로   extremely [extreme~-ly] 極~ K

무인도	uninhabited island [no person~] 無人~

차도   improvement (of illness) [difference~] 差~

반도	peninsula [half~] 半~ 한반도 the Korean Peninsula

절·도   moderation [moderation~] 節~

제주도	Cheju Island 濟州~

한도   a limit [limit~] 限~

연도   year [year~] 年~
1996년도   the year 1996

도 (盜) steal; rob

태도   attitude; manner [attitude~] 態~

강도	armed robbery [forceful~] 强~

제도   system; institution [govern~] 制~
교육제도
educational system

절·도	theft; larceny [steal~] 竊~
도난	robbery; burglary [~difficulty] ~ 難 도난당하다 be burglarized

도 (圖) drawing; map; diagram

도둑	thief 도둑질* theft

축도   reduced-size drawing; miniature copy [shrink~] 縮~

도청*	wiretapping; bug [~listen] ~ 聽

도화지   drawing paper [~picture paper] ~ 畵紙

도 (導) lead

도서	books [~book] ~ 書
지도	map [earth~] 地~
약도	street map [abbreviated~] 略~

주도*	leading; taking the initiative [chief~] 主~ 주도권 leadership; initiative

전도   whole map [whole~] 全~
대한민국전도
complete map of Korea

유도*	leading out; guide [induce~] 誘~ 유도신문* leading question

괘도   wall map; wall chart [hang~] 掛~

인도*	guidance; leading [pull~] 引~

도형   figure; diagram [~form] ~ 形

지도*	guidance [to point~] 指~ 지도교수 (academic) advisor 개인지도* private tutoring

ㄷ

도 (都) metropolis; all

도시 city [~city] ~ 市
수도 capital city [head~] 首~
도회지 urban area [~gather place] ~ 會地
도매* wholesale [~sell] ~ 賣

도 (倒) fall down; invert

졸·도* fainting; passing out [suddenly~] 卒~
타도* overthrowing [hit~] 打~
압도* overwhelming [press~] 壓~
도치* inversion [~to place] ~ 置

독 (獨) alone

단독 singleness [single~] 單~
　　　 단독으로 single-handed
독신 single; unmarried person [~person] ~ 身
　　　 독신주의자 celibate person
고독* solitude [alone~] 孤~
독립* independence [~stand] ~ 立
독백* monologue [~tell] ~ 白
독특하다 be unique [~special] ~ 特
독창* (vocal) solo [~sing] ~ 唱
독주* (instrumental) solo [~play music] ~ 奏
독재* dictatorship [~judge] ~ 裁
독점* monopolization [~seize] ~ 占
독차지* having all to oneself [~taking up] ~ K
독창적 original; creative [~beginning] ~ 創 的
독단적 dogmatic; peremptory [~cut off] ~ 斷 的

독불장군 stubborn fellow; self-assured person [~not a general] ~ 不將軍

독 ʷ(毒) poison

독약 poisonous drug [~medicine] ~ 藥
독사 venomous snake [~snake] ~ 蛇
독극물 toxic chemicals [~violent thing] ~ 劇物
유독하다 be poisonous [exist~] 有~
　　　 유독가스 poisonous gas
중독 poisoning [middle~] 中~
　　　 알콜중독 alcoholism
　　　 식충독 food poisoning
해독제 antidote [loosen~medicine] 解~劑
소독* sterilization [disperse~] 消~
　　　 소독약 disinfectant; antiseptic
독감 flu; bad cold [~feeling] ~ 感
혹독하다 be severe; be harsh [severe ~] 酷~
(지)독하다 be vicious; be severe [extreme~] 至~

독 (讀) read

독서* reading [~book] ~ 書
　　　 독서실 reading room; study room
독자 reader [~person] ~ 者
독해* reading comprehension [~explain] ~ 解
낭독* reading (aloud) [clear~] 朗~
정독* careful reading [fine~] 精~
독후감 impressions of a book [~after feeling] ~ 後感

58

해독* decoding; deciphering [solve~] 解~

구독* subscription (to a newspaper) [buy~] 購~

돌 (突) sudden; collide

돌변* sudden change [~change] ~變
돌연변이 mutation

돌풍 sudden gust of wind [~wind] ~風

돌.진* a rush; a dash [~advance] ~進

충돌* collision [collision~] 衝~

돌파* breaking through; exceeding [~break] ~破
돌파구 a breakthrough

동 (同) same; together

동일하다 be identical [~one] ~一

동감* same feeling; same opinion [~feeling] ~感

동지 like-minded person; kindred spirit [~mind] ~志

동시 same time [~time] ~時
동시통역* simultaneous interpretation

동성 same sex [~sex] ~性

동.점 same score; a tie [~point] ~點

동의* same opinion; agreement [~opinion] ~意

동족 same race; brethren [~tribe] ~族

동포 brethren [~womb] ~胞

동갑 same age [~armor] ~甲

동생 younger sibling [~be born] ~生

동등하다 be equal; be of the same rank [~equal] ~等

동기 graduates of the same year [~period] ~期
대학동기 contemporaries at college

동창(생) fellow student; schoolmate [~window student] ~窓生
동창회 alumni association

동문 fellow student; schoolmate [~gate] ~門
동문회 alumni association

동료 colleague [~companion] ~僚

동거* living together [~dwell] ~居

동침* sleeping together [~sleep] ~寢

동업* running business together [~business] ~業

동조* acting in concert; aligning oneself [~harmonize] ~調

합동* combination; union [join~] 合~
합동결혼식* group wedding

협동* cooperation [harmony~] 協~

공동 cooperation; collaboration; union [cooperate~] 共~
공동생활* community life

일.동 all the persons concerned [one~] 一 ~

동정* sympathy [~feeling] ~情
동정.심 sympathy

동화* assimilation [~change] ~化

동행* going together; company [~go] ~行

동반* accompanying; being accompanied by [~companion] ~伴

동부인*	accompanying one's wife [~wife] ~ 夫人
혼동*	confusion; mixing [confused~] 混~

동 (動) move

작동*	(machine) operation [make~] 作~
자동	automatic (movement) [self~] 自~ 자동차 automobile
수동	manual operation [hand~] 手~
노동*	labor [toil~] 勞~
가동*	operation [operate~] 稼~ 에어콘 가동중 air conditioner in operation
시동	starting (an engine) [begin~] 始~ 시동걸다 start an engine
동작	motion; gesture [~make] ~作
발·동*	putting in motion; putting in action [depart~] 發~ 발·동을 걸다 start an engine
기동력	mobility [machine~power] 機~力
이동*	movement; migration [move~] 移~
출·동*	going out; mobilization [exit~] 出~ 경찰의 출·동 the moving in of the police
동원*	mobilization [~member] ~員 관객을 동원하다 draw an audience
유동적	fluctuating [flow~] 流~的
파동	fluctuation; undulation; crisis [wave~] 波~
충동*	instigation; impulse [rush into~] 衝~ 충동적 impulsive

제동	braking; damping [regulate~] 制~ 제동을 걸다 put on the brakes
동물	animal [~thing] ~物
행동*	behavior; action [act~] 行~
거동	conduct; behavior [lift~] 舉~
활·동*	activity [lively~] 活~ 활·동적 active
수동적	passive [receive~] 受~
선동*	instigation [agitate~] 煽~
주동*	masterminding [chief~] 主~ 주동자 a mastermind
반동*	reaction; counteraction [opposite~] 反~ 반동분자 reactionary elements
소동	agitation; tumult [agitate~] 騷~
폭동	riot; rebellion [cruel~] 暴~ 폭동을 일으키다 raise a riot
동기	motive; incentive [~mechanism] ~機
동향	tendency; trend [~to face] ~向
운동*	sports; exercise; campaign [transport~] 運~ 운동장 playground; athletic field 운동부족 lack of exercise 선거운동* election campaign
동맥	artery [~vein] ~脈
동사	verb [~words] ~詞

동 (童) child(ren)

아동	children [child~] 兒~
쌍동이	twin children [pair~] 雙~K
목동	shepherd boy [herd animals~] 牧~

ㄷ

신동	child prodigy [god~] 神~
동심	child's mind; naiveté [~mind] ~ 心
동요	children's song [~song] ~ 謠
동화	fairy tale; children's story [~story] ~ 話
동시	children's verse [~poetry] ~ 詩
동안	childlike face [~face] ~ 顏

동 ʷ(東) east

동쪽	eastern side [~side] ~ K
동서남북	east, west, south, north [~west south north] ~ 西南北
동아시아	East Asia [~Asia] ~ E
중동	Middle East [middle~] 中~
동양	the Orient [~ocean] ~ 洋

동 (冬) winter

춘하추동	four seasons [spring summer fall~] 春夏秋~
동복	winter clothes [~clothes] ~服
월.동준비*	preparation for winter [cross over~preparation] 越~準備

동 ʷ(銅) copper; bronze

동전	(copper) coin [~money] ~ 錢
동메달	copper medal [~medal] ~ E
동상	bronze statue [~statue] ~ 像

두 (頭) head

| 두통 | headache [~pain] ~ 痛 편두통 migraine |

두뇌	brain [~brain] ~ 腦
염두	mind; one's attention [think~] 念~ …을 염두에 두다 keep...in mind
몰.두하다	be absorbed in [sink~] 沒~
박두하다	be imminent; be near at hand [oppress~] 迫~
두목	ringleader (of a gang) [~item] ~ 目
선두	the forefront; the lead [the first~] 先~
구두로	orally; verbally [mouth~-ly] 口 ~ K
만두	a bun stuffed with seasoned meat and vegetables [steamed bread~] 饅~

득 ʷ(得) gain; acquire

이득	gains; profits [profit~] 利~
소득	income; earnings [whatsoever~] 所~
득점*	a score; scoring (a point) [~point] ~ 點
취득*	attainment (of diploma, certificate, etc.) [obtain~] 取~
습득*	picking up; finding; acquisition [study~] 習~ 습득물 findings 언어습득* language acquisition
획득*	acquiring; winning (medals) [acquire~] 獲~
터득*	learning; grasping [grasp~] 攄~ 요령을 터득하다 get the knack

ㄹ

납득* — understanding; being convinced [receive~] 納~

설.득* — persuasion [explain~] 說~

부득이 — unavoidably [no~already] 不~已

자업자득 — natural consequences of one's (mis)deed; serves one right [self business self~] 自業自~

일거양득 — killing two birds with one stone [one action two~] 一擧兩~

등 (等) rank; equal

일.등* — first rank; top [first~] 一~

등급 — a grade; a rank [~grade] ~級

등.수 — ratings; a grade [~number] ~數
등.수를 매기다 get ratings

고등 — higher; advanced [high~] 高~
고등교육 higher education

월.등하다 — be superior by far [crossover~] 越~

평등* — equality; impartiality [even~] 平~

동등하다 — be equal; be of the same rank [same~] 同~

균등하다 — be equal; be even [equal~] 均~

등분* — division into equal parts [~divide] ~分
이등분* splitting into two

하등 — (nothing) whatever [whatever~] 何~

등한히하다 — neglect; make light of [~leisure] ~閑 K

등 ʷ(燈) light; lamp

신호등 — signal light [signal~] 信號~

가로등 — street light [street road~] 街路~

형광등 — fluorescent lamp [fluorescence~] 螢光~

백열.등 — incandescent lamp [white heat~] 白熱~

전등 — electric lamp [electric~] 電~

외등 — outdoor lamp [outside~] 外~

등.불 — light; lamplight [~fire] ~ K

등대 — lighthouse [~tower] ~臺

등잔 — oil cup for a lamp [~cup] ~盞
등잔밑이 어둡다
The darkest place is under the candlestick.

등 (登) mount; advance

등산* — mountain climbing [~mountain] ~山

등장* — advent; appearance [~place] ~場
등장인물 dramatis personae

등록* — registration [~register] ~錄
등록금 tuition; registration fee

ㄹ

락 (落) fall; omit; scatter (/낙)

낙엽 — fallen leaves [~leaf] ~葉

낙하산 — parachute [~descend umbrella] ~下傘

추**락*** (airplane) fall; crash [fall~] 墜~

폭**락*** (stock/price) heavy fall [cruel~] 暴~

전**락*** downfall; degradation [turn~] 轉~

몰**락*** collapse; ruin [sink~] 沒~

낙오* falling behind [~rank] ~伍

낙제* flunking [~grade] ~第

타**락*** depravity; corruption [fall~] 墮~

탈**락*** being omitted; being eliminated [escape~] 脫~
예선에서 탈락하다 be eliminated from the tournament

낙태* abortion [~pregnant] ~胎

낙서* scribbling; graffiti [~writing] ~書

영**락**없다 be infallible [zero~not exist] 零~K

락 ᵂ(樂) **joy(ful)** (/낙)

희노애**락** joy, anger, sorrow, and pleasure [joy anger sorrow~] 喜怒哀~

오**락** amusement; recreation [amuse~] 娛~
오락실 game room

쾌**락** pleasure; enjoyment [pleasant~] 快~

낙원 paradise [~garden] ~園

낙천적 optimistic [~sky] ~天的
낙천주의자 optimist

락(諾) **answer** (see 낙)

란(亂) **chaos; chaotic; reckless** (/난)

난장판 chaotic scene [~place scene] ~場K

혼**란*** confusion; disorder; chaos [confused~] 混~

난리 uproar; commotion [~separate] ~離
난리나다 be an uproar

난잡하다 be disorderly; be lawless; be indecent [~mixed] ~雜

문**란**하다 be disorderly [disorder~] 紊~
풍기문란* demoralization

심**란**하다 be in mental turmoil [mind~] 心~

소**란*** commotion; noise [agitate~] 騷~

산**란**하다 be dispersed; be scattered about [disperse~] 散~

내**란** civil war [inside~] 內~

반**란** rebellion [opposite~] 反~

난폭하다 be rough; be violent [~cruel] ~暴

음**란**하다 be lewd [obscene~] 淫~
음란비디오 sex video

람(覽) **view; look at**

관**람*** (movie) watching [view~] 觀~

열**람*** (book) perusal; reading [inspect~] 閱~
열람실 reading room

전**람**회 exhibition [spread~meeting] 展~會

박**람**회 exposition; fair [extensive~meeting] 博~會

일**람**표 table; chart [one~display] 一~表

랑 (浪)	**wave; wasteful** (see 낭)	간략하다	be brief; be informal [simple~] 簡 ~
래 (來)	**come; coming** (/내)	대략	an outline; roughly [big~] 大 ~
왕래*	going and coming; mutual visit [go~] 往 ~	약도	outline map [~map] ~ 圖
내빈	guest (formal) [~guest] 賓	약소하다	(gift) be little; be scanty [~little] ~ 少
초래*	bringing about; incurring [invite~] 招 ~	침략*	invasion [invade~] 侵 ~
유래*	origin; originating [cause~] 由 ~	량 ʷ(量)	**amount; to measure (/양)**
원래	originally; by nature [the first~] 元 ~	분량	amount [share~] 分 ~
본래	originally; by nature [origin~] 本 ~	강수량	amount of rainfall [descend water~] 降水 ~
근래	recent times; these days [recent~] 近 ~	수량	quantity; volume [number~] 數 ~
미래	future [not yet~] 未 ~	소량	small quantity [little~] 少 ~
장래	future; prospect [future~] 將 ~	대량	large quantity [big~] 大 ~
내일	tomorrow [~day] ~ 日	주량	one's drinking capacity [liquor~] 酒 ~
내주	next week [~week] ~ 週	계량기	meter; gauge [calculate~utensil] 計 ~器
내년	next year [~year] ~ 年	측량*	measuring; (land) survey [measure~] 測 ~
전래*	transmission; handing down [transmit~] 傳 ~	중량	weight [weight~] 重 ~
이래	from that time on; ever since [from~] 以~ 유사이래 since the dawn of history	열량	calorie [heat~] 熱 ~
		함량	content (proportion) [include~] 含 ~ 알콜함량 alcohol content
략 (略)	**abbreviate(d); strategy (/약)**	용량	dosage [use~] 用 ~
약자	acronym; abbreviation [~character] ~ 字	가량	approximately [temporary~] 假 ~ 20살·가량의 남자 a man about twenty years of age
생략*	omission; abbreviation [abbreviate~] 省 ~	아량	magnanimity [elegant~] 雅 ~
요약*	summary [important~] 要 ~		

재량 discretion; judgment [judge~] 裁~
재량에 맡기다 leave (a matter) to (a person's) discretion

양껏 as much as one can (eat) [~to the full extent of] ~ K

량 (良) good(ness) (see 양)

려 (慮) **worry; think**

염려* worry; concern [think~] 念~

우려* worry; apprehension [anxiety~] 憂~

배려* care; concern; good offices [suitable~] 配~

고려* consideration [consider~] 考~

사려깊다 be thoughtful [consider~deep] 思 ~ K

무려 as many as [not~] 無~
무려 5000명 as many as five thousand people

력 (力) **strength; power** (/역)

체력 physical strength [body~] 體~

정신력 mental strength [mind~] 精神~

기력 energy [energy~] 氣~
무기력하다 feel lethargic; feel spiritless

정력 energy; stamina [essential~] 精~

활력 vitality; vital power [lively~] 活~

전력 all one's energies [all~] 全~
...에 전력을 기울이다 devote all one's energies to...

주력하다 concentrate one's effort [pour~] 注~

기억력 memory power [memory~] 記憶~

시력 eyesight [look at~] 視~

세력 influence; power [power~] 勢~

권력 authority; power [authority~] 權~

유력하다 be influential; be powerful [exist~] 有~
유력한 후보 strong candidate

국력 national power [nation~] 國~

전력 electric power [electricity~] 電~

화력 thermal power [fire~] 火~

입력* power input [enter~] 入~

박력 force; power [oppress~] 迫~
박력있다 be powerful; be of strong appeal

능력 ability [able~] 能~
...할 능력이 있다 be capable of doing...

실력 real ability [real~] 實~
영어실력 English proficiency

역부족 being beyond one's ability [~not sufficient] ~ 不足

효력 effect; validity [effect~] 效~

노력* effort [toil~] 努~

협력* cooperation [union~] 協~

지구력 staying power; tenacity [sustain longtime~] 持久~

순발력 ability to respond quickly and appropriately [moment rise~] 瞬發~

매력 attractiveness [bewitch~] 魅~

탄력 elasticity [a spring~] 彈~

중력   gravity [weight~] 重~

속력   speed [speed~] 速~

기동력   mobility [maneuvering~] 機動~

통솔력   leadership [command~] 統率~

무력   armed force [military~] 武~

폭력   violence [cruel~] 暴~

역도*   weight lifting [~principle] ~ 道

력 (歷)   pass; go by   (/역)

역사   history [~history] ~ 史

이력   personal record [walk~] 履~
이력서   resumé

경력   career record; experience [pass through~] 經~

내력   (family) tradition [coming~] 來~

력 (曆)   calendar

달력   calendar [month~] K~

일력   daily calendar pad [day~] 日 ~

양력   solar calendar [sun~] 陽~

음력   lunar calendar [dark~] 陰~

련 (練 / 鍊)   practice; to train   (/연)

연습*   practice; exercise [~practice] ~ 習

훈련*   training; drill [teach~] 訓 ~
맹훈련*   intense training

교련*   military drill [teach~] 敎~

단련*   training; discipline [to train~] 鍛~
심신을 단련하다   train one's body and mind

시련   trial; ordeal [test~] 試~

노련하다   be experienced and skilled [experienced~] 老~

세련되다   be polished; be refined [wash~become] 洗 ~ K

미련   lingering attachment [not yet~] 未 ~

련 (聯)   association   (see 연)

렬 (烈)   vehement   (/열)

강렬하다   be intense [strong~] 强~

맹렬하다   be rigorous; be vehement [intense~] 猛~

격렬하다   be severe; be intense [intense~] 激~

열렬하다   be fiery; be passionate [hot~] ~ 烈

치열하다   (competition) be intense; be ferocious [intense~] 熾~

렴 (廉)   incorruptible; honest; moderate   (/염)

청렴결백*   integrity; uprightness [clear~innocence] 淸 ~ 潔白

염치   sense of shame [~shameful] ~ 恥
염치없다   be shameless

염·가   low price [~price] ~ 價

저렴하다   be low priced [low~] 低~

렴 (炎)   inflammation   (see 염)

령 (領) **command; receive** (/**영**)

영역 territory; domain
[~boundary] ~ 域

영토 territory [~land] ~ 土

대통령 president of a country
[great govern~] 大統~

영사 consul [~matters] ~ 事
영사관 consulate

점령* occupation; capture
[seize~] 占 ~

횡령* usurpation; embezzlement
[unreasonable~] 橫 ~

요령 knack [~important] 要 ~

영수증 receipt
[~collect evidence] ~ 收證

령 (令) **command; honorable**
(/**영**)

명령* an order; a command
[command~] 命 ~

구령* verbal order [mouth~] 口 ~

지령 an order; a directive
[to point~] 指 ~
지령을 내리다 issue an order

영.장 warrant [~document] ~ 狀
구속영.장 arrest warrant

영감 old man [~oversee] ~ 監

영부인 esteemed wife [~wife] ~夫人
대통령 영부인
president's wife; first lady

령 (靈) **spirits** (/**영**)

영혼 spirit; soul
[~heavenly spirit] ~ 魂

신령 divine spirit [god~] 神 ~

유령 spirit of the dead; ghost
[illusion~] 幽 ~

망령 dotage; second childhood
[foolish~] 妄 ~

례 ʷ (例) **example; usual** (/**예**)

일례 one example [one~] 一 ~

예를 들다 give an example [~lift] ~ K
예를 들면 for example

유례 similar example
[a kind~] 類 ~
유례없는 unprecedented

실례 actual example [real~] 實 ~

전례 a precedent [before~] 前 ~
전례없는 unprecedented

사례 instance; case [matter~] 事 ~

예년 ordinary year [~year] ~ 年
예년에 비해서
compared with other years

예사 common practice; usual
matter [~matter] ~ 事

의례 customarily; usually
[depend on~] 依 ~

예외 exception (to the rule)
[~outside] ~ 外

차례 (sequence) order;
(one's) turn [next~] 次 ~

비례* proportion [compare~] 比 ~
정비례* direct proportion
반비례* inverse proportion

례 ʷ (禮) **etiquette; rites** (/**예**)

예의 courtesy; etiquette
[~rites] ~ 儀
예의바르다 be courteous;
be well-behaved
예의가 없다 have no manners
예의를 지키다
observe decorum

예절 requirements of etiquette;
formality [~moderation] ~ 節

무례하다	be impolite [no~] 無~
실례*	discourtesy; breach of etiquette [lose~] 失~ 실례지만 Excuse me, but ... 실례합니다 Excuse me.
답례*	a return favor [reply~] 答~
사례*	thanks; reward [thank~] 謝~
경례*	salutation [respect~] 敬~ 거수경례* military salute
목례*	a nod (of greeting) [eye~] 目~
예식장	wedding hall [~ceremony place] ~式場
주례*	officiating at a ceremony; officiator [chief~] 主~
세례받다	be baptized [wash~receive] 洗~K
예배*	worship; (church) service [~bow] ~拜

로 (路)	road	(/노)
도로	road [road~] 道~	
대로	big road [big~] 大~	
교차로	crossroads [crossing~] 交叉~	
선로	railroad; track [line~] 線~	
항로	(sea, air) route [navigate~] 航~	
활.주로	runway [gliding~] 滑走~	
노선	(bus) route; line [~line] ~線	
경로	course; channel; route [pass through~] 經~	
통로	passage; aisle [go through~] 通~	
진로	the way ahead; one's path in life [advance~] 進~	
미로	maze [confusing~] 迷~	

로 (勞)	toil	(/노)
노고	labor; pains [~suffering] ~苦	
노동*	labor [~move] ~動 막노동* rough physical labor 중노동* heavy labor 노동자 laborer	
근로자	laborer [work~person] 勤~者	
노조	labor union [~union] ~組 (<노동조합)	
노사	labor and management [~employ] ~使 노사관계 relations between labor and management	
피로*	tiredness; fatigue [tired~] 疲~	
과로*	overexertion; overwork [exceed~] 過~	
위로*	solace; consolation [console~] 慰~	
공로	meritorious deed [merit~] 功~	

로 (老)	old	(see 노)
로 (露)	expose	(see 노)
록 (錄)	record; register	(/녹)
녹음*	(sound) recording [~sound] ~音 녹음기 tape recorder	
녹화*	videorecording [~picture] ~畵 녹화방송 filmed TV broadcast	
기록*	putting on record; a record [record~] 記~ (신)기록을 세우다 set up a (new) record	

68

주소록	address book [address~] 住所~
목록	list; catalogue [item~] 目~
부록	appendix (in a book) [append~] 附~
등록*	registration [advance~] 登~

록 ᵂ(綠) **green; rust** (see 녹)

론 (論) **discuss** (see 논)

롱 (弄) **play with** (/농)

농담*	joke [~converse] ~ 談
재롱	(baby's) cute tricks [talent~] 才~ 재롱부리다 do cute things
농간	machination; trickery [~crafty] ~ 奸 농간부리다 play tricks
희롱*	ridiculing; toying (with) [play games~] 戲~
조롱*	ridicule; derision [ridicule~] 嘲~
우롱*	mockery; making a fool of [stupid~] 愚~

뢰 (雷) **thunder**

피뢰침	lightning rod [avoid~needle] 避~針
우뢰	thunder [rain~] 雨~
지뢰	land mine [earth~] 地~

료 (料) **material; estimate** (/요)

재료	materials; ingredients [material~] 材~

자료	materials; data [funds~] 資~ 연구자료 research materials 통계자료 statistical data
원료	raw materials [origin~] 原~
음료	beverage [drink~] 飮~ 청량음료 soft drinks
조미료	condiments [control taste~] 調味~
요리*	cooking [~manage] ~ 理
연료	fuel [burn~] 燃~
비료	manure [fertile~] 肥~
사료	(livestock) feed [feed animal~] 飼~
요금	fee; fare [~money] ~ 金 요금인상/인하 fee hike/cut 기본요금 basic rate
연체료	overdue fee [delay obstructed~] 延滯~
입장료	entrance fee [entrance~] 入場~
통행료	toll [passing~] 通行~
무료	no charge [no~] 無~ 무료입장* admission free
유료	toll [exist~] 有~ 유료주차장 toll parking lot
위자료	compensation; alimony [console help~] 慰藉~

료 (療) **medical treatment** (/요)

의료	medical service [medical science~] 醫~
치료*	medical treatment [treat~] 治~
요양*	medical care; recuperating [~care] ~ 養
진료*	medical examination and treatment [medical examination~] 診~

요.법 treatment method;
a remedy [~method] ~ 法
식이요.법* dietary treatment

요기* appeasing hunger
[~hunger] ~ 飢

류 (流) stream; flow (/유)

주류 mainstream [main~] 主~

상류 upper stream; upper class
[upper~] 上~

중류 midstream; middle class
[middle~] 中~

하류 downstream; low class
[below~] 下~

전류 electric current
[electricity~] 電~

유선형 streamlined shape
[~line type] ~ 線型

유동적 fluctuating [~move] ~ 動的

교류* interchange [exchange~] 交~

유행* fashion; vogue [~go] ~ 行
유행가 popular song

유창하다 be fluent [~pleasant] ~ 暢

유산* miscarriage; abortion
[~produce] ~ 産

유언비어 groundless, false rumor
[~talk fly words] ~言蜚語

일류 first-rate; top-ranking
[first~] 一 ~

이류 second-rate [second~] 二 ~

삼류 third-rate [third~] 三 ~

류 (類) a kind; a sort (/유)

종류 a kind; a sort [a kind~] 種~

부류 class; category [part~] 部 ~

분류* classification [divide~] 分 ~

인류 humankind [person~] 人 ~

육류 meats [meat~] 肉 ~

의류 clothing; garment
[clothes~] 衣 ~

서류 document [writing~] 書 ~

유형 type; pattern [~type] ~ 型

유례 similar example
[~example] ~ 例

유사하다 be similar [~similar] ~ 似
유사품 an imitation (product)

유달리 conspicuously;
uncommonly
[~differently] ~ K

륙 (陸) land (see 육)

률 (率) rate; ratio (see 율)

**리 (理) reason(ing); principle;
manage (/이)**

일리 some reason; truth
[one~] 一 ~
일리가 있다
contain some truth

이유 cause; reason [~cause] ~ 由

이치 good reason; principle
[~reach] ~ 致
이치에 맞지않다
be contrary to reason

원리 (underlying) principle
[origin~] 原 ~

이해* understanding
[~explain] 解

이론 theory [~discuss] ~ 論

합리적 rational; reasonable
[unite~] 合 ~ 的
합리화* rationalization

추리* reasoning; inference
[infer~] 推 ~

무리하다 be unreasonable; overwork [no~] 無~

이성 reasoning power [~essential quality] ~性
이성적 rational

궁리* deliberation; thinking over [used up~] 窮~

심리 mentality; psychology [mind~] 心~

생리 physiology [life~] 生~

논리 logic [discuss~] 論~

이념 ideology [~thought] ~念

이상 an ideal [~think] ~想
이상적 ideal

진리 truth [true~] 眞~

도리 propriety; duty; way [principle~] 道~
도리에 어긋나다 be against propriety
부모의 도리 parents' duty
도리가 없다 there is no way

의리 sense of duty; loyalty [right conduct~] 義~

비리 wrongdoings (of public officials) [wrong~] 非~

지리 geography [earth~] 地~

섭리 providence [hold~] 攝~
자연의 섭리 the providence of nature

관리* administration; management [govern~] 管~

처리* management; handling; disposal (of a matter) [manage~] 處~

정리* arrangement; putting things in order; settlement [be in order~] 整~

국무총리 prime minister [nation affairs general~] 國務總~

이사 director; trustee [~matters] ~事
이사장 chairman of a board of directors

대리 proxy; an agent [substitute~] 代~

경리 accounting [govern ~] 經~
경리·과 payroll department

수리* repairs; remodelling (house, car, etc.) [repair~] 修~

이발* haircut; hairdressing [~hair] ~髮

요리* cooking [ingredients~] 料~

리 ʷ (利) benefit; gain (see 이)

리 (離) leave; separate (see 이)

립 (立) stand; establish (/입)

입석 standing room [~seat] ~席

설립* establishment [establish~] 設~

국립 national establishment [nation~] 國~

공립 public establishment [public~] 公~

사립 private establishment [private~] 私~

시립 municipal; city-established [city~] 市~

입증* establishment of a fact [~evidence] ~證

조립* assembly; assembling [weave~] 組~

독립* (personal, political) independence [alone~] 獨~

ㅁ

자립* (personal, economical) independence [self~] 自~

고립* isolation [alone~] 孤~

입후보* standing as a candidate [~candidate] ~候補
입후보자 candidate

중립 neutrality [middle~] 中~

입체 a solid; three-dimensional body [~body] ~體

입장 position; situation [~place] ~場
입장이 곤란하다 be in a difficult situation

입각하다 be based on [~leg] ~脚
사실에 입각하다 be based on facts

ㅁ

마 (馬) horse

승마* horseback riding [ride~] 乘~

경마* horse racing [compete~] 競~
경마장 race track

목마 rocking horse [wood~] 木~

마차 carriage [~vehicle] ~車
포장마차 covered wagon bar

출마* running for election [appear~] 出~

하마 hippopotamus [water~] 河~

천고마비 term describing autumn [sky high~fat] 天高~肥

마 ᵂ (魔) demon

마귀 devil [~ghost] ~鬼

악마 devil; Satan [evil~] 惡~

마술 magic [~art] ~術

마 ᵂ (麻) hemp; anesthetic

대마초 hemp leaf cigarette [big~grass] 大~草

마약 narcotics; drug [~drug] ~藥

마 (痲) paralysis

마비 paralysis [~paralysis] ~痺
마비되다 be paralyzed
심장마비 heart attack
소아마비 polio

마취* anesthesia [~intoxicated] ~醉
마취약 an anesthetic

막 (莫) extremely; not

막대하다 be huge; be enormous [~big] ~大

막중하다 be very important [~weighty] ~重
책임이 막중하다 Responsibility is grave.

막심하다 (loss, regret) be tremendous [~intense] ~甚

막론하고 not to speak of [~discuss] ~論K
남녀노소를 막론하고 regardless of sex and age

막상막하 neck and neck [~above~below] ~上~下

무지막지하다 be ignorant and uncouth [not know~know] 無知~知

72

막 ^w(幕)	**curtain; an act**		만반의 준비	thorough preparation [~general preparation] ~般K準備

막 ᵂ(幕) **curtain; an act**

천막	tent; pavilion [sky~] 天~ 천막을 치다 set up a tent
막간	interval between acts or scenes [~between] ~間
내막	inside story [inside~] 內~
흑막	something fishy [black~] 黑~
자막	subtitle [character~] 字~
주막	tavern [liquor~] 酒~

막 (漠) **desert**

사막	a desert [sand~] 沙~
삭막하다	be dreary; be bleak [rope~] 索~
막연하다	be vague [~as such] ~然

만 ᵂ(萬) **ten thousand; all**

만세	hurrah; cheers; long live... [~year] ~歲 만세부르다 cry 'hurrah!'
백만	million [hundred~] 百~ 백만장자 millionaire
천만	ten million; countless number; extremely [thousand~] 千~
만물	all things [~thing] ~物 만물박사 walking dictionary
만사	all affairs [~matters] ~事
만인	everyone [~person] ~人
만방	all nations of the world [~country] ~邦
만병	all kinds of diseases [~disease] ~病
만능	many abilities; omnipotent [~capable] ~能

만반의 준비	thorough preparation [~general preparation] ~般K準備
만년필	fountain pen [~year pen] ~年筆
만수무강*	longevity [~life no end] ~壽無疆
만무하다	cannot be [~no] ~無 그럴리가 만무하다 It cannot be true.
만일	if; in case [~one] ~一 만일 비가오면 if it rains 만일의 경우 in case
만약	if; in case [~if] ~若

만 (滿) **full**

만.점	full marks; perfect score [~point] ~點
만원	full house [~member] ~員 만원버스 jam-packed bus
만족*	satisfaction [~sufficient] ~足 불만족* dissatisfaction
불만	dissatisfaction [not~] 不~
만끽하다	enjoy fully [~eat] ~喫
만장일치*	unanimity [~place agreement] ~場一致
자신만만*	being full of self-confidence [self~~] 自信~~
원만하다	be harmonious; be well-rounded [round~] 圓~
비만	obesity [fat~] 肥~
풍만하다	be plump [abundant~] 豊~
만삭	full term of pregnancy [~month] ~朔

만 (慢) **arrogant; gradually**

거만*	arrogance [arrogant~] 倨~

ㅁ

자만*	self-conceit [self~] 自~	가망	hope; possibility [alright~] 可~ 가망없다 there is no hope
교만하다	be haughty [proud~] 驕~	욕망	desire; ambition [desire~] 欲~
태만*	negligence; dereliction [lazy~] 怠~	갈망*	earnest desire [thirsty~] 渴~
완만하다	(slope) be gentle; be easy [slow~] 緩~	소망*	desire; wish [whatsoever~] 所~
만성	chronic condition [~nature] ~性	지망*	wish; choice (for college or career) [intention~] 志~ 지망대학 college one hopes to enter

말 ᵂ(末) **end**

연말	end of the year [year~] 年~
월말	end of the month [month~] 月~
주말	weekend [week~] 週~
기말	end of semester [term~] 期~ 기말고사 final exam
종말	the end (of the world) [finish~] 終~
말·세	the end of the world; corrupt world [~world] ~世
말기	the last period [~period] ~期
말일	the last day (of period) [~day] ~日 이달 말일 the last day of this month
결말	conclusion; an end [tie~] 結~ 결말이 나다 come to a conclusion 결말을 내다 bring to a conclusion
말·단사원	minor clerk [~tip company employee] ~端社員
분말	powder [powder~] 粉~
녹말	starch [green~] 綠~

망 (望) **hope; observe**

희망*	hope [hope~] 希~

전망*	prospect [unfold~] 展~
야망	ambition [wilderness~] 野~
유망하다	be promising [exist~] 有~
실망*	disappointment [lose~] 失~
절망*	despair; hopelessness [cut~] 絕~
망보다	keep watch (against) [~see] ~ K
망원경	telescope [~far mirror] ~遠鏡
원망*	resentment [grudge~] 怨~
책망*	reproach; blame [reprove~] 責~

망 (亡) **perish; lose**

망하다	perish
사망*	death [die~] 死~
도망*	running away [escape~] 逃~ 도망가다 run away
멸망*	collapse [destroy~] 滅~
흥망	rise and fall [prosper~] 興~
망신*	losing face [~person] ~身

74

망 (忘) forget

망 (忘) forget

건망증 forgetfulness [strong~symptom] 健~症

망각* oblivion [~reject] ~却

망년회* year-end party [~year meeting] ~年會

망 (妄) absurd; foolish

망상 wild fantasy [~thought] ~想

망령 dotage [~spirit] ~靈

노망 dotage [old~] 老~

망 (網) net

철망 wire net [iron~] 鐵~

방충망 insectproof net [defend insect~] 防蟲~

망사 gauze [~thread] ~紗

매 (賣) sell

매매* buying and selling [~buy] ~買

매점 a stand; booth [~store] ~店

매진* selling out [~entirely] ~盡
매진되다 be sold out

판매* sale; selling [sell~] 販~
(자동)판매기 (automatic) vending machine

예매* advance sale [beforehand~] 豫~

도매* wholesale [all~] 都~
도매상 wholesale store

소매* retail sale [small~] 小~
소매상 retail store

매 (每) each; every

매년 every year [~year] ~年

매달 every month [~month] ~ K

매주 every week [~week] ~週

매일 every day [~day] ~日

매번 every time [~number] ~番

매사 every matter [~matter] ~事

매한가지 all the same [~one kind] ~ K

매 (買) buy

매매* buying and selling [sell~] 賣~

예매* advance purchase [beforehand~] 豫~

매수* buying over; bribing [~collect] ~收

매 (魅) attract

매력 attractiveness [~power] ~力
매력적 attractive

매혹 fascination; captivation [~mislead] ~惑
매혹적 captivating

맥 ᵂ(脈) pulse; vein

맥박 pulse [~hit] ~搏

동맥 artery [move~] 動~

정맥 vein [still~] 靜~

맥빠지다 be exhausted [~leak out] ~ K

맥없다 feel tired; feel dejected [~not exist] ~ K

산맥 mountains [mountain~] 山~

문맥 context of a passage [writing~] 文~

맹 (盲) blind

맹인	blind person [~person] ~ 人
맹목적	blind [~purpose] ~ 目的 맹목적 사랑 blind love
색맹	color blind [color~] 色~
문맹	illiteracy; an illiterate [letter~] 文~
맹장	appendix (organ) [~gut] ~ 腸

맹 (猛) wild; intense

맹수	wild animal [~animal] ~ 獸
맹연습*	intensive practice [~practice] ~ 練習
맹훈련*	intense training [~training] ~ 訓練
맹렬하다	be rigorous; be vehement [~vehement] ~ 烈

면 ʷ(面) (sur)face; side; aspect

앞면	front side [front~] K~
뒷면	reverse side [back~] K~
정면	front side; facade [straight~] 正~
측면	the side; side surface [side~] 側~
평면	a plane; a level [even~] 平~
표면	surface [surface~] 表~
겉면	surface side [surface~] K~
전면	the whole surface [whole~] 全~
내면	the inside [inside~] 內~
이면	the other side [back~] 裏~
반면	the other hand [opposite~] 反~ 반면에 on the other hand

단면	a section; a phase [cut~] 斷~
체면	face; honor; dignity [body~] 體~ 체면상 for honor's sake
면목없다	be ashamed [~eye not exist] ~ 目 K
액면	face value [amount of money~] 額~
가면	mask [false~] 假~
방독면	gas mask [prevent poison~] 防毒~
면도*	shaving [~knife] ~ 刀 면도칼 razor 면도날 razor blade
직면하다	face; confront [straight~] 直~
대면*	facing [opposite~] 對~
외면*	turning one's face away; looking away [outside~] 外~
안면	face; acquaintance [face~] 顔~ 안면이 있다 be acquainted with (a person)
구면	old acquaintance [old~] 舊~
초면	meeting for the first time [first~] 初~
면담*	interview; personal communication [~talk] ~ 談
면회*	visiting; meeting [~meeting] ~ 會
면접*	interview; oral test [~touch] ~ 接
화면	screen [picture~] 畵~
면적	square measure [~pile up] ~ 積
방면	direction; field [direction~] 方~ 다방면 many-sidedness

면 (免) exempt

- 면세*   duty-free [~tax] ~ 稅
- 면제*   exemption [~eliminate] ~ 除
- 면역   immunity [~sick] ~ 疫
  면역이 되다 become immune
- 면허   license [~permit] ~ 許
- 파면*   dismissal [cease~] 罷 ~

면 ʷ(麵) noodle

- 냉면   cold noodle [cold~] 冷 ~
  비빔냉면 cold noodle mixed with seasoning
  물냉면 noodle in cold soup
- 쫄면   chewy noodle
- 라면   ramen; instant noodle
  컵라면 noodle-in-a-cup
- 짜장면   noodles with bean sauce

면 ʷ(綿) cotton

- 순면   pure cotton [pure~] 純 ~
- 면양말   cotton socks [~socks] ~洋 襪
- 탈·지면   absorbent cotton
  [take off oil~] 脫 脂~

멸 (滅) destroy

- 전멸*   total destruction; annihilation [whole~] 全~
- 파멸*   ruin; destruction [break~] 破~
- 멸망*   downfall; collapse [~perish] ~ 亡
- 멸·종*   extinction of a species [~seed] ~ 種
- 박멸*   eradication [beat~] 撲~
- 멸균*   pasteurization [~germ] ~ 菌

환멸   disillusionment
[illusion~] 幻~

명 (名) name; famous

- 성명   full name [family name~] 姓 ~
- 별명   nickname [different~] 別~
- 가명   false name; alias
  [false~] 假~
- 본명   original name [origin~] 本~
- 지명*   nomination [to point~] 指 ~
- 명사   noun [~words] ~ 詞
- 명함   namecard [~title] ~ 銜
  명함판 namecard size (picture)
- 명찰   name tag [~document] ~ 札
- 명단   roster [~unit] ~ 單
- 무기명   secret ballot
  [not record~] 無記~
- (한)명   (one) person [one~] K~
- 유명하다   be famous [exist~] 有~
  유명상표 famous brand
- 명예   honor; reputation
  [~honor] ~ 譽
  불명예 dishonor
  명예훼손* defamation
- 악명높다   be notorious
  [bad~high] 惡 ~ K
- 명곡   famous music [~tune] ~曲
- 명언   wise saying [~saying] ~ 言
- 명답   brilliant answer; repartee
  [~answer] ~ 答
- 명절   festive days [~festival] ~ 節

명 (明) bright; clear

- 명암   brightness and darkness
  [~dark] ~ 暗
- 광명   light; hope [brightness~] 光 ~

조**명*** lighting; illumination [illumine~] 照 ~

명확하다 be definite; be clear [~certain] ~ 確

명백하다 be clear; be evident [~clear] ~ 白

명시* clear statement; elucidation [~manifest] ~ 示

선**명**하다 be clear; be distinctive [fresh~] 鮮 ~

판**명**되다 become clear; prove to be [judge~become] 判 ~ K

분**명**하다 be clear; be obvious [divide~] 分 ~

투**명**하다 be transparent [transparent~] 透 ~

설**명*** explanation [explain~] 說 ~

해**명*** elucidation; explanation [explain~] 解 ~

증**명*** verification [testify~] 證 ~

현**명**하다 be wise [wise~] 賢 ~

변**명*** an excuse; justification [eloquence~] 辯 ~

발**명*** invention [depart~] 發 ~

문**명** civilization [writing~] 文 ~

명랑하다 be cheerful [~cheerful] ~ 朗

선견지**명** foresight [precede see of~] 先見之 ~

명 (命) **life; destiny; command**

생**명** life [life~] 生 ~
생명보험 life insurance

인**명** human life [person~] 人 ~
인명피해 loss of human lives

수**명** life span [life~] 壽 ~

치**명**적 fatal [result in~] 致 ~ 的

운**명** fate; destiny [luck~] 運 ~

숙**명** fate [stellar-mansion~] 宿 ~

명령* order; command [~order] ~ 令

사**명** mission [employ~] 使 ~
사명감 sense of mission

임**명*** appointment; nomination [entrust~] 任 ~

혁**명*** revolution [revolt~] 革 ~
혁명을 일으키다
start a revolution

모 (母) **mother**

모친 one's mother (formal) [~parents] ~ 親

계**모** stepmother [adopt~] 繼 ~

장**모** man's mother-in-law [adult~] 丈 ~

현**모**양처 a wise mother and goodwife [wise~good wife] 賢 ~ 良妻

부**모**(님) parents [father~ respected person] 父 ~ K

모성애 maternal love [~nature love] ~ 性愛

모유 mother's milk [~milk] ~ 乳

모국 mother country [~country] ~ 國
모국어 mother tongue

모교 alma mater [~school] ~ 校

모음 vowel [~sound] ~ 音

식**모** kitchen-maid [food~] 食 ~

모 (模) **sample; pattern**

모범 model; example [~sample] ~ 範

모형 model; miniature [~model] ~ 型

모양	shape; form [~pattern] ~ 樣 겉모양 outer appearance	무모하다	be reckless [no~] 無~
모방*	imitation; copying [~imitate] ~ 倣	참모	staff officer; brain truster [participate~] 參~

모 (募) collect

모조품	an imitation; a fake [~make article] ~ 造品
모창*	imitative singing [~sing] ~唱
모호하다	be vague; be equivocal [~paste] ~ 糊 애매모호하다 be vague
규모	scale; scope [scale~] 規~

모집*	recruitment; invitation [~gather] ~ 集
모금*	fund raising [~money] ~ 金
응모*	applying for; entry for (a contest) [reply~] 應~

모 ʷ(毛) wool; hair

순모	pure wool [pure~] 純~
모직	woolen fabric [~weave] ~ 織
모피	fur [~skin] ~ 皮
모발	(head) hair [~hair] ~ 髮
탈모	hair loss [escape~] 脫~

모 (貌) countenance

외모	outer appearance [outside~] 外~
미모	beautiful appearance [beautiful~] 美~
용모	looks; appearance [face~] 容~ 용모단정* decent looking
모습	figure; appearance [~surprise attack] ~ 襲 뒷모습 one's appearance from the back

모 (謀) plot; strategy

음모*	plot; frame-up [dark~] 陰~
모의*	conspiracy [~discuss] ~ 議 역적모의* conspiracy to rebel

목 (目) eye; item

목격*	witnessing [~strike] ~ 擊 목격자 a witness
일목요연*	being clear at a glance [one~clear] 一 ~瞭然
지목*	pointing out; spotting [to point~] 指~
주목*	paying attention [pour in~] 注~
이목	public attention [ear~] 耳~
목례*	a nod (of greeting) [~courtesy] ~ 禮
목적*	purpose; aim [~target] ~ 的
목표*	aim; goal [~mark] ~ 標
항목	item [item~] 項~
품목	a list of articles; item [article~] 品~
조목	articles; items [clause~] 條~
제목	subject; title [subject~] 題~
목차	table of contents [~order] ~ 次
종목	(sports) an event [a kind~] 種~
과목	course (subject) of study [course~] 科~

두목	ringleader (of a gang) [head~] 頭~	몰·살*	massacre; annihilation [~kill] ~ 殺
		몰·수*	confiscation [~collect] ~ 收

목 (木) wood; tree

목재	lumber [~material] ~ 材
목탁	wood block [~bell] 鐸
목발*	a crutch [~foot] ~ K
목수	carpenter [~means] ~ 手
목마	rocking horse [~horse] ~ 馬 회전목마 merry-go-round
묘목	sapling; seedling [seed~] 苗~
식목일	Arbor Day [plant~day] 植 ~ 日
산천초목	mountains, streams, grass, and trees [mountain stream grass ~] 山川草~
목석같다	be insensible [~stone be like] ~ 石 K

목 (牧) raise; herd

목축*	cattle raising [~livestock] ~ 畜
목장	ranch [~place] ~ 場
목동	shepherd boy [~child] ~ 童
목사	pastor; minister [~teacher] ~ 師

몰 (沒) lack; sink

몰·상식하다	lack common sense [~common sense] ~ 常識
몰지각하다	lack discretion [~discretion] ~ 知覺
침몰*	(boat) sinking [sink~] 沈~
몰락*	collapse; ruin [~fall] ~ 落
몰·두하다	be absorbed in [~head] ~ 頭

몽 (夢) dream

길몽	lucky dream [lucky~] 吉~
악몽	nightmare [bad~] 惡~
태몽	dream that one is going to get pregnant [pregnant~] 胎~
해몽*	dream interpreting [solve~] 解~
비몽사몽	neither asleep nor awake [not~resemble~] 非 ~ 似~

묘 (妙) exquisite

묘하다	be exquisite; be strange
기묘하다	be strange; be queer [strange~] 奇~
묘기	exquisite skill [~skill] ~ 技
묘미	exquisiteness; subtle charm [~taste] ~ 味
교묘하다	be clever; be dexterous [clever~] 巧~
미묘하다	be subtle [minute~] 微~
묘안	excellent plan [~plan] ~ 案

묘 ᵂ(墓) a grave

묘지	a grave [~place] ~ 地
성묘*	visiting ancestral graves [examine~] 省~

무 (無) no; not; nothing

무색	colorlessness [~color] ~ 色
무취	odorlessness [~odor] ~ 臭

ㅁ

무난하다 be not difficult; be easily passable [~difficult] ~ 難

무사하다 be safe [~accident] ~ 事
무사히 safely

무례하다 be impolite [~courtesy] ~ 禮

무식하다 be ignorant; be illiterate [~know] ~ 識

무책임하다 be irresponsible [~responsibility] ~ 責任

무의미하다 be meaningless [~meaning] ~ 意味

무한하다 be infinite [~limit] ~ 限

무수하다 be innumerable [~number] ~ 數

무지방 nonfat; skim [~fat] ~ 脂肪

무질·서* disorder [~order] ~ 秩序

무죄 being not guilty [~guilt] ~ 罪

무직 being unemployed [~post] ~ 職

무표정* being expressionless [~facial expression] ~ 表情

무진장* being inexhaustible [~exhaust storage] ~ 盡藏

무료 no charge [~estimate] ~ 料

무소식 no news [~news] ~ 消息
무소식이 희소식
No news is good news.

무허가 no permit; illegal [~permission] ~ 許可
무허가 건물
unauthorized building

무승부 undecided match; tie game [~victory defeat] ~ 勝負

무경험 inexperience [~experience] ~ 經驗
무경험자 inexperienced person

무관심* indifference [~interest] ~ 關心

무성의* insincerity [~sincerity] ~ 誠意

무효 invalidity [~effect] ~ 效

무자비하다 be merciless [~mercy] ~ 慈悲

무정하다 be heartless [~feeling] ~ 情

무심하다 be unwitting [~mind] ~ 心

무감각하다 be insensible; be callous [~sense] ~ 感覺

무신경하다 be insensible; be apathetic [~nerve] ~ 神經

무모하다 be reckless [~plan] ~ 謀

무리하다 be unreasonable; overwork [~reason] ~ 理

무료하다 be bored; be tedious [~happy] ~ 聊

무생물 inanimate object [~living thing] ~ 生物

무시하다 disregard [~look at] ~ 視

무의식 unconsciousness [~consciousness] ~ 意識
무의식중에 unconsciously

무조·건 unconditional(ly) [~condition] ~ 條件

무작정* without any definite plan [~definite plan] ~ 酌定

무안 shame [~face] ~ 顔
무안하다 be embarrassed

만무하다 cannot be [ten thousand~] 萬~
그럴 리가 만무하다
That cannot be so.

무려 as many as [~think] ~ 慮

허무하다 be futile; be vain [empty~] 虛~

인생무상 futility of life [life~constant] 人生~常

81

무 (務) duty; affairs

임무	duty; task [be in charge~] 任~
의무	duty; obligation [right conduct~] 義~ 의무교육 compulsory education
근무*	service; work [work~] 勤~
사무	office work; business matter [business~] 事~
업무	business; work [business~] 業~
급선무	the most urgent business [urgent first~] 急先~
총무	general affairs; manager [general~] 總~
전무	executive director [exclusive~] 專~
상무	managing director [usual~] 常~

무 (武) military

무술	military arts [~art] ~術
무력	armed force [~power] ~力
무기	weapon [~utensil] ~器
무장*	armaments [~decorate] ~裝

무 (舞) dance

무용*	dance [~jump] ~踊 무용단 ballet troupe
안무	choreography [stroke~] 按~
무대	stage [~terrace] ~臺

묵 (默) silent

묵묵하다	be silent 묵묵히 silently
침묵*	silence [sink~] 沈~ 침묵을 지키다 keep silent
묵념*	silent prayer [~think] ~念
묵인*	tacit approval; connivance [~consent] ~認
묵살*	ignoring (a person's remarks by keeping silence) [~kill] ~殺

문 (文) letter; figure; writing

문·자	written character [~character] ~字
문맹	illiteracy; an illiterate [~blind] ~盲
작문*	composition; writing [make~] 作~
산문	prose writing [disperse~] 散~
한문	Chinese writing [China~] 漢~
천자문	the (Chinese) Thousand-Character Text [thousand character~] 千字~
문학	literature [~study] ~學 영문학 English literature
문헌	literature; (documentary) records [~offer] ~獻
본문	main text [origin~] 本~
문단	paragraph [~section] ~段
문장	sentence; a piece of writing [~paragraph] ~章
문·법	grammar [~law] ~法
논문	thesis; dissertation [discuss~] 論~
문서	document [~writing] ~書
문(방)구	stationery [~room tool] ~房具
기행문	travel description [record go~] 紀行~
문맥	context of a passage [~pulse] ~脈

주문* an order; request
[pour~] 注~

문화 culture; civilization
[~change] ~ 化
문화재 cultural assets

문명 civilization [~bright] ~ 明

문 ʷ(門) **door**

앞문 front door [front~] K ~

방문 room door [room~] 房 ~

문턱 doorsill [~chin] ~ K

문·고리 door knob [~knob] ~ K

문패 doorplate [~plate] ~ 牌

창문 window [window~] 窓 ~

대문 gate [big~] 大~
동/서/남대문 East/West/
South Gate of Seoul

교문 school gate [school~] 校~

정문 front gate; main entrance
[right~] 正~

후문 back gate [back~] 後~

뒷문 back gate [back~] K ~

동문 schoolmate [same~] 同~

전문 specialty [exclusive~] 專 ~

말문이 막히다 be struck dumb
[speech~be blocked] K~ K

항문 anus; back passage
[anus~] 肛 ~

가문 family; clan [family~] 家~

문 (問) **ask; inquire**

의문 question; doubt
[doubt~] 疑~
의문문 interrogative sentence

반문* counterquestion
[opposite~] 反~

질문* question [substance~] 質 ~

문제 problem; question
[~subject] ~ 題
사회문제 social problem
문제내다 make up a question

불문하고 regardless of [not~] 不 ~ K
남녀를 불문하고
regardless of sex

신문* cross-examination
[investigate~] 訊 ~
유도신문* leading question

고문* torture [beat~] 拷 ~

검문* a check; inspection
[inspect~] 檢~

문의* inquiry [~discuss] ~ 議

위문* consolatory visit; inquiry
[console~] 慰~

방문* a call; a visit [visit~] 訪 ~

문병* visiting a sick person
[~sickness] ~ 病

병문안* checking on someone's
well-being
[sickness~peaceful] 病~安

학문* (the pursuit of) learning;
studies [learn~] 學~

동문서답* irrelevant reply
[east~west reply] 東~西答

문 (聞) **hear**

금시초문 hearing (something)
for the first time
[now time first~] 今時初~

신문 news [new~] 新~

소문 rumor [thing~] 所~
헛소문 groundless rumor
수소문* inquiring into
rumors; asking around

추문 scandal; ill fame
[ugly~] 醜 ~

물 (物) things; object

사물 things [matter~] 事 ~

물·가 price of things [~price] ~ 價

물·정 condition of things
[~circumstance] ~情
세상물·정 world affairs

물건 article; goods [~thing] ~ 件
물건하다 make
a wholesale purchase

물품 goods; articles [~goods] ~ 品

보물 treasure [precious~] 寶 ~

뇌물 bribe [bribe~] 賂 ~

제물 sacrificial offering
[sacrifice~] 祭 ~

생물 living thing [living~] 生 ~
무생물 inanimate object
미생물 microorganism

인물 person; character; figure
[person~] 人 ~

속물 worldly person
[vulgar~] 俗 ~

실물 real thing/person
[real~] 實 ~

동물 animal [move~] 動 ~

괴물 monster [strange~] 怪 ~

식물 plant; vegetation
[plant~] 植 ~

음식물 foods [food~] 飲食 ~

농작물 agricultural products
[agricultural make~] 農作 ~

해물 marine products
[ocean~] 海 ~

산물 product [produce~] 産 ~

거물 big shot [big~] 巨 ~

건물 building [build~] 建 ~

유물 relic; antiquity
[bequeath~] 遺 ~

화물 freight [cargo~] 貨 ~

선물* gift [tasty food~] 膳 ~

물물교환* bartering
[~~exchange] ~ ~ 交換

금물 prohibited thing
[prohibit~] 禁 ~

폐기물 waste matter
[abolish abandon~] 廢棄 ~

무용지물 useless thing
[no use of~] 無用之 ~

물·색하다 search for; hunt
[~color] ~ 色

물의 public criticism
[~discuss] ~ 議
물의를 빚다/일으키다
bring on public criticism

물체 a physical solid; an object
[~body] ~ 體

물·질 material; matter
[~substance] ~ 質

물리 physics [~principle] ~ 理

미 ʷ (美) beautiful; beauty; America

미모 beautiful appearance
[~appearance] ~ 貌

미인 beautiful woman
[~person] ~ 人

미남 handsome man [~male] ~ 男

미관 beautiful view [~view] ~ 觀
미관상 for the sake of beauty

미용 cosmetology [~face] ~ 容
미용사 beautician; hairdresser
미용실 beauty parlor

미장원 beauty parlor
[~makeup institution] ~ 粧院

미술* fine arts [~art] ~ 術

건강미	healthy beauty [health~] 健康~	미흡하다	be insufficient [~sufficient] ~ 洽
자연미	natural beauty [nature~] 自然~	미달*	shortage [~achieve] ~ 達
육체미	physical beauty; body building [body~] 肉體~	미만	under; less than [~full] ~ 滿 이십세 미만 under twenty years old
각선미	the beauty of shapely legs [leg line~] 脚線~	미지.수	unknown quantity [~know number] ~ 知數
미.적	esthetic ~ 的 미.적 감각 esthetic sense	미심쩍다	be questionable; be dubious [~judge] ~ 審K
미화*	beautification; embellishment [~change] ~ 化	미안하다	be sorry; be regrettable [~peaceful] ~ 安
불미스럽다	be ugly; be scandalous [not~] 不~	미련	lingering attachment [~practice] ~ 練
미사여구	flowery words [~speech beautiful phrase] ~ 辭麗句	**미 (味)**	**taste**
미국	U.S.A. [~country] ~ 國	미각	sense of taste [~sense] ~ 覺
미군	U.S. Armed Forces [~military] ~ 軍	구미	appetite; taste [mouth~] 口 ~ 구미에 맞다 be to one's taste
남미	South America [south~] 南~	조미료	condiments [control~material] 調~料
미화	American money [~goods] ~ 貨	감미롭다	be sweet [sweet~] 甘~
		미원	Miwon; monosodium [~the first] ~ 元
미 (未)	**not yet; no**	취미	hobby; taste [hobby~] 趣~
미래	future [~come] ~ 來	흥미	an interest; an appeal [fun~] 興~
미정이다	be undecided [~decide be] ~ 定K	음미*	appreciation; savoring [recite~] 吟~
미혼	unmarried; single [~marriage] ~ 婚	묘미	exquisiteness; subtle charm [exquisite~] 妙~
미성년	under age [~adult age] ~成年	의미*	meaning; significance [meaning~] 意~
미숙하다	be inexperienced [~experienced] ~ 熟	성미	disposition; temperament [nature~] 性~
미완성*	being unfinished [~completion] ~ 完成		
미개하다	be uncivilized [~open] ~ 開		

ㅁ

미 (微)	**minute; tiny**
현미경	microscope [manifest~mirror] 顯~鏡
미소*	(faint) smile [~laugh] ~笑 미소짓다 wear a smile
미생물	microbe [~living thing] ~生物
미묘하다	be delicate; be subtle [~exquisite] ~妙
희미하다	be dim; be vague [scarce~] 稀~

미 (米)	**rice**
현미	brown rice [black~] 玄~
일반미	traditional variety of rice [general~] 一般~
정부미	state-held rice [government~] 政府~
미색	pale yellow [~color] ~色

미 (迷)	**be confused**
미로	maze [~road] ~路
미신	superstition [~belief] ~信

민 (民)	**people**
국민	a nation; a people [nation~] 國~
민족	race; people [~tribe] ~族 소수민족 a minority
서민	the common people [people~] 庶~
빈민	poor people [poor~] 貧~
농민	farmer; peasantry [agricultural~] 農~
시민	citizen [city~] 市~
주민	resident [reside~] 住~ 원주민 native; aborigine

이민	emigration; immigration; emigrant; immigrant [move~] 移~
민간인	civilian [~between person] ~間人
민방위	civil defense [~defense] ~防衛
민주주의	democracy [~host principle] ~主主義
민속	folk customs [~customs] ~俗 민속무용 folk dance
민요	folk song [~song] ~謠

민 (敏)	**sharp**
민감하다	be sensitive; be susceptible [~feeling] ~感
과민하다	be oversensitive [excessive~] 過~ 과민반응* oversensitive reaction
예민하다	be sensitive [sharp~] 銳~

밀 (密)	**secret; intimate; thorough**
비밀	secret [conceal~] 秘~
은밀하다	be covert; be confidential [hide~] 隱~
밀·수*	smuggling [~transport] ~輸
밀·접하다	(connection) be close [~connect] ~接
밀·도	density [~degree] ~度 인구밀·도 density of population
밀폐*	shutting tightly; sealing up [~to close] ~閉
세밀하다	be minute; be detailed [minute~] 細~
정밀*	minuteness; accuracy [fine~] 精~

치밀하다   be minute; be elaborate
        [minute~] 緻~
        치밀한 계획   elaborate plan

엄밀하다   be strict; be precise
        [strict~] 嚴~
        엄밀히 말해서
        strictly speaking

ㅂ

박 (迫)   **persecute; oppress**

압박*   pressure; oppression
      [press~] 壓~

협박*   a threat [threaten~] 脅~

구박*   cruel treatment [expel~] 驅~

촉박하다   be urgent; be imminent
       [urge~] 促~

박력   force; power [~power] ~力

임박하다   be near at hand; draw near
       [come to~] 臨~

박두하다   be imminent; be near at
       hand [~head] ~頭

박 (泊)   **stay; to anchor**

숙박*   lodging; accommodation
      [lodge~] 宿~
      숙박시설   accommodations

외박*   sleeping away from home
      [outside~] 外~

민박*   lodgings at a private house
      [people~] 民~

(일)박(이)일   (one) night, (two) days
      [one~two day] 一~二日

박 (博)   **extensive**

박람회   exposition
      [~view meeting] ~覽會

박물관   museum
      [~things building] ~物館

박사   Ph. D. [~scholar] ~士

도박*   gambling [steal~] 賭~

박 (拍)   **clap; slap**

박수*   clapping of hands
      [~hands] ~手
      박수치다   clap hands
      기립박수   standing ovation

박자   beat; rhythm [~thing] ~子
      박자맞추다 keep time with

박차   a spur; acceleration
      [~vehicle] ~車
      박차를 가하다   give impetus

반 (反)   **opposite**

반대*   the opposite; opposition
      [~oppose] ~對
      반댓말   opposite words
      정반대   the exact opposite

반면   the other side; the other
      hand [~side] ~面
      반면에   on the other hand

찬반   for and against; pros
      and cons [agree~] 贊~

반응*   reaction; response
      [~respond] ~應

반동   reaction; counteraction
      [~move] ~動
      반동분자
      reactionary elements

반항*   rebellion; defiance
      [~resist] ~抗

반란   rebellion [~chaos] ~亂
      반란을 일으키다
      rise in revolt

ㅂ

반발* resistance; insubordination [~overturn] ~ 撥

반격* a counterattack [~attack] ~ 擊

반공 anti-Communism [~Communism] ~ 共

반정부 antigovernment [~government] ~ 政府

반복* repetition [~return] ~ 復

반성* reflection; self-examination [~reflect] ~ 省

반사* reflection (of light) [~shoot] ~ 射

반영* reflection (of opinion) [~reflect] ~ 映

배반* betrayal [a back~] 背 ~

위반* violation [violate~] 違 ~

반칙* violation of rules; a foul in sports [~rule] ~ 則

적반하장 shifting the blame [thief~bear weapon] 賊 ~ 荷杖

반 ʷ(半) half

절반 a half [cut~] 折 ~

반반 half-and-half; fifty-fifty 반의반 one-fourth; a quarter

반값 half-price [~price] ~ K

반액 half the price [~amount of money] ~ 額

반달 half-moon [~moon] ~ K

전반전 the first half of a game [former~fight] 前 ~ 戰

후반전 the second half of a game [later~fight] 後 ~ 戰

반도 peninsula [~island] ~ 島 한반도 the Korean Peninsula

반소매 short-sleeve [~sleeve] ~ K

반숙* sunny side up or soft-boiled (egg) [~ripe] ~ 熟

반지름 radius [~diameter] ~ K

태반 the most part; majority [greatest~] 太 ~

반올림* rounding off [~raising] ~ K

반말* impolite speech; neutral style of speech [~speech] ~K

반 (盤) tray; slab

쟁반 tray [gong~] 錚 ~

선반 shelf

음반 a (phonograph) record [sound~] 音 ~

나침반 a compass [magnet needle~] 羅針 ~

골반 pelvis [bone~] 骨 ~

기반 foundation [base~] 基 ~

초반 opening phase; early stage [beginning~] 初 ~

반 (伴) companion

수반* accompaniment [follow~] 隨 ~

동반* accompanying; being accompanied by [together~] 同 ~ 부부동반* husband and wife company

반주* (music) accompaniment [~play music] ~ 奏

반 (般) sort; class; all kinds

전반 the whole; all [whole~] 全 ~

일반 general; common [one~] 一 ~ 일반적으로 in general

88

일반 ·사람 the common run of people

만반의 준비 thorough preparation [all~'s preparation] 萬 ~ K 準備

발 (發) depart; shoot; rise

출**발***	departure [exit~] 出 ~ 새출발* fresh start
발차*	departure (of a vehicle) [~vehicle] ~ 車
발·동*	putting in motion; putting in action [~move] ~ 動
발견*	discovery [~see] ~見
발명*	invention [~bright] ~ 明
순**발**력	ability to respond quickly and appropriately [moment~power] 瞬~力
발·사*	firing; blast-off [~shoot] ~射
폭**발***	explosion; detonation [explode~] 爆 ~
발·생*	occurrence [~be born] ~ 生
재**발***	relapse; recurrence [again~] 再 ~
유**발***	induction; triggering [induce~] 誘 ~
증**발***	evaporation [steam~] 蒸 ~
휘**발**유	volatile oil; gasoline [wield~oil] 揮 ~ 油
발·전*	growth; prosperity [~unfold] ~ 展
발·달*	development; growth [~achieve] ~ 達
개**발***	development [open~] 開 ~
발·작*	fit; spasm [~make] ~ 作
발광하다	act crazily [~mad] ~ 光
활**발**하다	be lively; be active [lively~] 活 ~

발표*	announcement; presentation [~manifest] ~ 表
발음*	pronunciation [~sound] ~ 音
발휘*	manifestation; demonstration (of one's ability) [~wield] ~ 揮
발행*	publishing; issuing [~act] ~ 行
발급*	issuing (a passport, license, etc.) [~give] ~ 給
고**발***	(legal) accusation; complaint [accuse~] 告 ~
적**발***	exposing; uncovering [pick~] 摘 ~

발 (髮) hair

모**발**	hair [hair~] 毛 ~
금**발**	blond hair [gold~] 金 ~
백**발**	white/grey hair [white~] 白 ~
장**발**	(men's) long hair [long~] 長 ~
단**발**	(women's) short hair [short~] 斷 ~
가**발**	wig [false~] 假 ~
이**발***	(men's) haircut; hairdressing [manage~] 理 ~
삭**발***	shaving one's head [shave~] 削 ~

발 (拔) extract; pull out

발췌*	extraction; excerpt [~gather] ~ 萃
선**발***	selection; picking out [select~] 選 ~

기**발**하다	(idea) be extraordinary; be striking [mysterious~] 奇~	한**방**	Chinese medicine [China~] 漢~
해**발**	above sea level; elevation [sea~] 海~	처**방***	prescription [manage~] 處~
		방편	expedient [~convenience] ~便 임시**방**편 makeshift
방 (方)	**square; direction; method; just now**	**방**금	just now; a moment ago [~now] ~今
평**방**미터	square meter [even~meter] 平~E	금**방**	just now; a moment ago [now~] 今~
방석	cushion [~seat] ~席		
방위	compass direction [~position] ~位	**방** ʷ(房)	**room**
방향	direction [~to face] ~向	공부.**방**	study room [study~] 工夫~
방면	direction; field [~side] ~面	안.**방**	main room [inside~] K~
사**방**	four sides; all directions [four~] 四~	주**방**	dining room [kitchen~] 廚~
일**방**적	one-sided; unilateral [one~] 一 ~的	골**방**	back room; closet [alley~] K~
팔**방**	all directions; every side [eight~] 八~	난**방**	heated room; heating (a room) [warm~] 煖~
전**방**	the front (line) [front~] 前~	냉**방**	air-conditioned room [cold~] 冷~
후**방**	the rear (base) [back~] 後~	**방**.바닥	floor of a room [~bottom] ~ K
근**방**	neighborhood; vicinity [near~] 近~	**방**문	door of a room [~door] ~門
지**방**	area; locality [place~] 地~ 중부.지**방** central area 지**방**대학 local college	세.**방**	room for rent [rent~] 貰~ 세**방**살이* living in a rented room
행**방**	whereabouts [go~] 行~	**방**.세	rent for a room [~rent] ~ 貰
방언	dialect [~talk] ~言	**방**.값	charge for a room [~price] ~ K
남**방**	aloha shirt [south~] 南~	다**방**	tea room; tea house [tea~] 茶~
방법	method; way [~law] ~法	책**방**	bookstore [book~] 冊~
방식	form; method [~style] ~式	금.**방**	goldsmith's shop; jewelry store [gold~] 金~
방책	measures; policy [~plan] ~策	구듯**방**	(dress) shoe store [shoes~] K~
방침	plan; policy [~needle] ~針	약**방**	pharmacy [medicine~] 藥~

복덕**방** realtor's office [blessing virtue~] 福德 ~

머리**방** hair salon [hair~] K~

노래**방** karaoke room [song~] K~

감.**방** cell; ward [supervise~] 監 ~

유**방** woman's breast [milk~] 乳 ~

방 (防) defend; protect

방위* defense [~guard] ~ 衛
방위(군) defense corps
민방위 civil defense

방어* defense [~resist] ~ 禦

국**방** national defense [nation~] 國~

방수* waterproof [~water] ~ 水

방음* soundproof [~sound] ~ 音

방패 a shield [~board] ~ 牌

방독면 gas mask [~poison face] ~ 毒面

방부제 preservative [~rotten medicine] ~ 腐劑

예**방*** prevention; precaution [beforehand~] 豫 ~

방지* prevention [~stop] ~ 止

방 (放) release

해**방*** release; liberation [release~] 解 ~

석**방*** release; acquittal [release~] 釋 ~

방학* school vacation [~study] ~ 學

방송* broadcasting [~send] ~ 送
방송국 broadcasting station

방사선 radiation; x rays [~shoot ray] ~ 射線

개**방*** opening; lifting the ban [open~] 開 ~

자유분**방**하다 be unrestrained; be wild [freedom run~] 自由奔 ~

방심* inattention; being off one's guard [~mind] ~ 心

방치* leaving (things) neglected [~to place] ~ 置

추**방*** driving out; banishment [pursue~] 追 ~

방탕* dissipation; debauchery [~dissipation] ~ 蕩

배 (配) distribute; suitable

배부* distribution; passing out [~give] ~ 付

분**배*** distribution; giving out [divide~] 分 ~

배당* apportionment; a share [~suitable] ~ 當

배달* delivery [~achieve] ~ 達
우편배달* mail delivery

배치* arrangement; placement [~to place] ~ 置

지**배*** governing; domination [manage~] 支 ~

배려* consideration [~think] ~ 慮

배역* the cast (of a play) [~role] ~ 役

배우자 spouse [~pair person] ~ 偶者

배 (排) push out; reject

배설* excretion [~flux] ~ 泄

배수* drainage [~water] ~ 水

배란* ovulation [~egg] ~ 卵
배란기 ovulating period

배제*   ruling out (a possibility) [~exclude] ~ 除

배척*   rejection; expulsion [~refuse] ~斥

배타적   exclusive (of others) [~others] ~ 他的

배구*   volleyball [~ball] ~ 球

배열*   arranging things in order [~line] ~ 列

배 （背） the back

배낭   backpack [~sack] ~ 囊

배영*   backstroke [~swim] ~ 泳

배경   background scenery [~scenery] ~ 景

배반*   betrayal [~oppose] ~ 反

배신*   betrayal [~believe] ~ 信
배신자   betrayer

위배*   violation; infringement [oppose~] 違~
...에 위배되다
run counter to...

배은망덕*   ingratitude [~favor forget virtue] ~ 恩忘德

배 （輩） fellow member

선배   one's senior (in school) [precede~] 先~

후배   one's junior (in school) [later~] 後~

배출*   producing (scholars) [~produce] ~ 出

배 （杯） cup; glass

축배*   celebratory drink; toast [celebrate~] 祝 ~

건배*   making a toast [dry~] 乾 ~

백 （白） white; clear; tell

흑백   black and white [black~] 黑~

백금   white gold [~gold] ~ 金

백인   Caucasian [~person] ~ 人

백지   white paper; blank paper [~paper] ~ 紙
얼굴이 백지장 같다
look as pale as a sheet

공백   blank; blank space [empty~] 空~

백발   white/grey hair [~hair] ~髮

창백하다   be pale [blue~] 蒼 ~

표백*   bleaching [launder~] 漂~

백조   swan [~bird] ~ 鳥

백반   plain cooked rice [~cooked rice] ~ 飯

백설탕   white sugar [~snow sugar] ~ 雪糖

단백질   protein [egg~substance] 蛋~質

백열등   incandescent lamp [~heat lamp] ~ 熱燈

명백하다   be clear; be evident [clear~] 明~

담백하다   (food) be light; be plain [clear~] 淡~

결백*   innocence [clean~] 潔~

독백*   monologue [alone~] 獨~

자백*   confession (of one's crime) [self~]自~

고백*   confession [tell~] 告~

백치   moron [~imbecile] ~ 痴

백 ᵂ（ 百 ） one hundred

수백   hundreds of [several~] 數 ~
수백명   hundreds of people

백일	the hundreth day of a newborn baby [~day] ~ 日
백점	a hundred points; full marks [~point] ~ 点
백퍼센트	100 percent [~percent] ~ E
백분율	percentage [~divide rate] ~ 分率
백발백중	a hundred percent accurate [~shoot~center] ~ 發 ~ 中
백팔십도	180 degrees [~eighty degree] ~ 八十度 백팔십도 달라지다 undergo a radical change
백만	million [~ten thousand] ~ 萬 백만장자 millionaire
백날	all the time [~day] ~ K
백화점	department store [~goods store] ~ 貨店

번 (番)	number; repeat
번호	number [~number] ~ 號 전화번호 phone number
국번	area code [position~] 局~
번지	street number [~place] ~ 地
번번이	each time ~ ~ K
이번	this time [this~] K~ 이번.주 this week 이번 일요일 this coming Sunday
여러번	several times [several~] K ~
지난번	last time [passed~] K~
전번	the other day; former occasion [former~] 前~
당번	person on duty [ought~] 當~
십팔번	one's forte; one's favorite song [eighteen~] 十八~

번 (繁)	prosper
번영*	prosperity (of a country) [~glory] ~ 榮
번창*	prosperity (in business) [~flourish] ~ 昌
번화하다	(street) be busy; be lively [~splendid] ~ 華 번화가 busy street
빈번하다	be frequent [frequent~] 頻~
번식*	propagation [~birth] ~ 殖

번 (飜)	overturn
번역*	translation [~translate] ~ 譯
번복*	reversing (one's former words) [~overturn] ~ 覆

벌 ʷ(罰)	punish
벌받다	be punished [~receive] ~ K
엄벌*	severe punishment [severe~] 嚴 ~
처벌*	(official) punishment [manage~] 處~
형벌	(legal) punishment; penalty [punishment~] 刑~
벌금	a fine [~money] ~ 金
벌칙	penal regulations [~rule] ~ 則
천벌	heaven's vengeance [heaven~] 天~ 천벌을 받다 be punished by heaven

범 (犯)	offense
범죄	crime [~crime] ~ 罪 경범·죄 misdemeanor
범행*	criminal act [~act] ~ 行
범인	criminal [~person] ~ 人

주**범**	chief criminal [chief~] 主~
공**범**	accomplice [together~] 共~
침**범***	invasion; encroachment [invade~] 侵~

범 (範) **law; pattern**

모**범**	model; example [pattern ~] 模~
시**범**	demonstrating (by examples); model [manifest~] 示~ 시범을 보이다 demonstrate
규**범**	rule; norm [regulation~] 規~
범위	scope [~surround] ~圍
솔.선수**범***	taking the lead; setting an example to others [to lead first hang down ~] 率先垂~

법 ᵂ(法) **law; rule; method**

법률	law [~rule] ~律 법률가 lawyer
법칙	law; rule [~rule] ~則
법규	laws and regulations [~regulation] ~規 교통법규 traffic regulations
상.**법**	business law [trade~] 商~
형.**법**	criminal law [punishment~] 刑~
헌.**법**	constitutional law [constitution~] 憲~
법원	court (of law) [~institution] ~院
법대	law school [~college] ~大 (<법과대학)
법관	a judge; the judiciary [~official] ~官
합**법**적	lawful; legal [join~] 合~的

준.**법**정신	law-abiding spirit [obey~spirit] 遵~精神
문.**법**	grammar [writing~] 文~
방**법**	method; way [method~] 方~
비.**법**	secret method [secret~] 秘~
요.**법**	treatment method; a remedy [medical treatment~] 療~
수.**법**	technique; trick [hand~] 手~

벽 ᵂ(壁) **wall**

장**벽**	wall; barrier [obstruct~] 障~
벽지	wallpaper [~paper] ~紙
벽시계	wall clock [~watch] ~時計
벽난로	fireplace [~stove] ~煖爐
벽걸이	wall tapestry [~hanger] ~ K
벽보	poster [~report] ~報
절**벽**	cliff [cut~] 絶~

변 (變) **change; alter**

변하다	change
변화*	change [~change] ~化
변경*	change; modification [~alter] ~更 날짜를 변경하다 change the date
변동*	change; fluctuation [~move] ~動 물·가변동 fluctuation in prices
돌**변***	sudden change [sudden~] 突~
급**변***	fast change [fast~] 急~
이**변**	unusual change; accident [different~] 異~

변심* change of mind; falling out of love [~mind] ~ 心

변질* change in quality; (food) going bad [~quality] ~ 質

변형* transformation [~form] ~ 形

변장* disguise; masquerade [~costume] ~ 裝

변덕 caprice [~virtue] ~ 德
변덕스럽다 be capricious
변덕쟁이 capricious person

봉변* mishap; bitter experience [meet with~] 逢 ~

천재지변 natural disaster [sky calamity earth~] 天災地~

임시변통* makeshift measure [temporary~through] 臨時~通

변 ᵂ (便) excrement

대변 dung; feces [big~] 大 ~

소변 urine [small~] 小 ~

변소 toilet [~place] ~ 所
공중변소 public washroom

변기 toilet bowl [~utensil] ~ 器
양변기 western toilet bowl

변비 constipation [~secret] ~ 秘

변 (辯) eloquence

웅변* eloquence; oratory [virile~] 雄 ~

열변 vehement speech [heat~] 熱~
열변을 토하다 make a vehement speech

변호* defense; vindication [~guard] ~ 護
변호사 attorney

답변* an answer [reply~] 答~

변명* an excuse; justification [~bright] ~ 明

변 (邊) edge; side

주변 outskirts; vicinity [encircle~] 周 ~

변두리 outskirts (of a town) [~around] ~ K

도로변 roadside [road~] 道路~

강변 riverside [river~] 江 ~

해변 beach [ocean~] 海~

별 (別) special; separate

특별하다 be special; be particular [special~] 特 ~

별나다 be peculiar; be eccentric [~come out] ~ K
유별나다 be distinctive; be peculiar

별다르다 be of a particular kind [~different] ~ K
별다른 일 something in particular

별일 particular thing [~matter] ~K
별일 없으면 if you don't have anything particular to do

별도리없다 there is no alternative [~way not exist] ~ 道理K

별·도 separate way [~way] ~ 途
...과는 별·도로 apart from...

별개 a different one [~piece] ~ 個
별개의 문제 another question

개별 individuation [piece~] 個 ~

구별* differentiation [distinguish~] 區 ~

판별* distinction; discernment [judge~] 判 ~

식별* discernment [recognize~] 識 ~

차별* discrimination
[difference~] 差~
남녀차별* sexual
discrimination

성별 distinction of sex
[sex~] 性~

천차만별 infinite variety
[thousand difference
ten thousand~] 千差萬~

별식 rare dish [~food] ~食

별꼴 obnoxious thing/person;
eyesore [~appearance] ~ K

별종 weirdo [~a kind] ~ 種

별명 alias [~name] ~ 名

이별* parting; separation
[leave~] 離~

별거* living separately;
separation [~dwell] ~ 居

송별* farewell; send-off
[send~] 送~

작별* leave-taking; good-by
[make~] 作 ~
작별인사*
farewell expression

별고없다 be well
[~cause not exist] ~ 故 K

별장 villa; country house
[~villa] ~ 莊

병 ᵂ(病) **disease; sickness**

질병 disease [sickness~] 疾~

병균 (disease) germ [~germ] ~菌

병환 sickness (hon.)
[~suffering] ~患

병나다 fall sick [~come out] ~ K

병들다 fall sick [~enter] ~ K

병이 낫다 recover from illness
[~get better] ~ K

병적 pathological; sick

눈병 eye disease [eye~] K~

심장병 heart disease [heart~] 心臟~

위장병 stomach disease
[stomach~] 胃腸~

당뇨병 diabetes
[sugar urine~] 糖尿~

폐병 lung disease [lung~] 肺~

피부병 skin disease [skin~] 皮膚~

성병 venereal disease [sex~] 性~

중병 serious illness
[weighty~] 重~

꾀병 pretended sickness
[trick~] K~

불치병 incurable disease
[not cure~] 不治~

전염병 contagious/communicable
disease [contagion~] 傳染~

상사병 lovesickness
[mutual think~] 相思~

투병* fighting against a disease
[fight~] 鬪 ~

병원 hospital [~institution] ~院

병실 sickroom [~room] ~室

병자 sick person [~person] ~者

병신 deformed person; a fool
[~body] ~身

문병* visiting a sick person
[inquire~] 問~

병문안* checking on someone's
well-being [~inquire peaceful]
~問安

병 ᵂ(瓶) **bottle; jar**

유리병 glass bottle [glass~] K~

술병 liquor bottle [liquor~] K~

맥주.병	beer bottle; person who cannot swim (slang) [beer~] 麥酒~	확보*	securing; insuring [certain~] 確~
젖병	nursing bottle [milk~] K ~	보수적	conservative [~guard] ~ 守的
병마개	bottle cap [~lid] ~ K	보류*	deferring [~stay] ~ 留
병따개	bottle opener [~opener] ~ K	담보	security; mortgage [sustain~] 擔~
꽃병	flower vase [flower~] K~		
보온.병	a thermos (bottle) [protect heat~] 保温 ~		

보 (報) report; give back

화염.병	Molotov cocktail [fire flame~] 火焰~

보고*	report [~inform] ~ 告 보고서 written report
보도*	report [~way] ~ 道 신문보도* press report

병 (兵) soldier; military

장병	officers and men; military men [military officer~] 將~
특보	special report [special~] 特~
통보*	notification [circulate~] 通~
졸병	common soldier [underling~] 卒~
경보*	alarm; warning [warn~] 警~
호위병	bodyguard [guard~] 護衛~
예보*	forecast [beforehand~] 豫~
헌병	military police [constitution~] 憲~
벽보	wall newspaper; poster [wall~] 壁~

보 (保) protect

일보	daily newspaper [day~] 日 ~ X일보 X daily newspaper
보호*	protection [~guard] ~ 護
전보	telegram [electricity~] 電~ 전보치다 send a telegram
보험	insurance [~rough] ~ 險 의료보험 medical insurance
정보	information; intelligence [circumstances~] 情~ 중앙정보부 C. I. A
보건	preservation of health [~healthy] ~ 健
보존*	preservation [~exist] ~ 存
보답*	repayment; recompense [~reply] ~ 答
보관*	storage; keeping [~manage] ~ 管
보수	remuneration; salary [~repay] ~ 酬
보온	heat insulation [~warm] ~ 温

보 (步) walk; step

보증*	guaranteeing [~evidence] ~ 證 보증금 deposit
보행*	going on foot; walking [~go] ~ 行 보행자 pedestrian
보장*	guaranteeing; security [~obstacle] ~ 障 사회보장 social security
경보*	walking race [compete~] 競~
안보	national security [peaceful~] 安~

산·보*	taking a walk [disperse~] 散~		보배	treasure
보조	pace [~harmonize] ~調 보조를 맞추다 keep step		국보	national treasure [nation~] 國~
보도	sidewalk [~way] ~道 횡단보도 pedestrian crossing		보석	jewelry [~stone] ~石
초보	beginning; novice [first~] 初~		가보	heirloom [family~] 家~

보 (普) usual; ordinary

보통 (being) ordinary; common [~go through] ~通

보급* spread; dissemination [~give] ~及

보편적 universal; general [~everywhere] ~遍的

진보* progress; advancement [advance~] 進~

퇴보* retrogression [retreat~] 退~

보초 sentry [~protect] ~哨

양보* concession [decline~] 讓~

일보직전 being on the brink (of) [one~right before] 一 ~直前

오십보 백보 little difference between the two [fifty~hundred~] 五十~百~

복 (服) clothes; submit

복장 dress; uniform [~costume] ~裝

한복 Korean dress [Korea~] 韓~

양복 (men's) western clothes [western~] 洋~

제복 uniform [govern~] 制~

군복 military uniform [military~] 軍~

교복 school uniform [school~] 校~

사복 civilian clothes [private~] 私~

평상복 everyday clothes [ordinary usual~] 平常~

외출복 street wear [going out~] 外出~

작업복 work clothes [work~] 作業~

기성복 ready-made clothes [already complete~] 既成~

하복 summer clothes [summer~] 夏~

동복 winter clothes [winter~] 冬~

보 (補) supplement; mend

보충* supplementation [~full] ~充 보충수업* supplementary class

보강* supplementary lecture [~lecture] ~講

보조* assistance [~assist] ~助

보상* compensation [~compensation] ~償 보상금 compensation money

(몸)보신* invigorating one's body by taking tonics [body~body] K ~身

보약 tonic [~medicine] ~藥

보수* mending; repair [~repair] ~修

보 (寶) treasure

보물 treasure [~thing] ~物

춘추복	spring/autumn clothes [spring autumn~] 春秋~
아동복	children's clothes [child~] 兒童~
임신복	maternal dress [pregnancy~] 姙娠~
수영복	swimsuit [swim~] 水泳~
내복	underwear [inside~] 內~
굴복*	submission; surrender [bend~] 屈~
복종*	obedience [~follow] ~從
복용*	taking medicine [~use] ~用

복 (復) recover; restore; return

회복*	recovery [return~] 回~
복구*	restoration; repair [~old] ~舊
왕복*	going and returning; roundtrip [go~] 往~
복귀*	a return; making a comeback [~return] ~歸
반복*	repetition [opposite~] 反~
복학*	resumption of school [~study] ~學 복학생 student back from the army
복습*	review (of studies) [~study] ~習
복수*	revenge [~enemy] ~讐

복 ʷ(福) blessing; fortunate

축복*	blessing [congratulate~] 祝~
복스럽다	be (chubby and) prosperous looking
복권	lottery ticket [~ticket] ~券
복점	good-luck freckle [~spot] ~點

행복	happiness [fortunate~] 幸~
유복하다	be rich; be well-off [abundant~] 裕~
복지	welfare [~fortune] ~祉
복덕방	realtor's office [~virtue room] ~ 德房

복 ʷ(伏) to prostrate; dog days

복날	any one of the three dog days [~day] ~ K
복중	middle of dog days [~middle] ~ 中
초복	first period of dog days [first~] 初~
중복	middle period of dog days [middle~] 中~
말복	final period of dog days [end~] 末~
삼복	three dog days; hottest period of summer [three~] 三 ~
복더위	heat wave during the dog days [~heat] ~ K

복 (複) double; complex

복사*	duplication; copy [~copy] ~寫 복사기 copy machine
복수	plural [~number] ~數
복식	(tennis) doubles [~style] ~式
중복*	overlapping; redundancy [layer~] 重~ 중복되다 be overlapped
복잡하다	be complex [~mixed] ~雜
복도	corridor; hallway [~way] ~道

ᄇ

복 (腹) **abdomen**

복통　　stomachache [~ache] ~ 痛

공복　　empty stomach
　　　　[empty~] 空~

할복*　　disembowelment [cut~] 割~
　　　　할복자살* suicide
　　　　by disembowelment

본 ʷ(本) **origin; base; sample**

원본　　original copy [origin~] 原~

사본　　a duplicate [copy~] 寫~

본래　　originally [~come] ~ 來

본능　　basic instinct [~ability] ~ 能

본성　　original nature; real
　　　　character [~nature] ~ 性

본색　　true character [~color] ~ 色
　　　　본색을 드러내다
　　　　reveal one's true character

본전　　original cost [~money] ~ 錢

본심　　real intention [~mind] ~ 心

본의　　real intention
　　　　[~intention] ~ 意
　　　　본의 아니게 unwillingly

본토　　mainland [~land] ~ 土

본론　　main topic [~discuss] ~ 論

본교　　main campus (of a school)
　　　　[~school] ~ 校

본점　　main store [~store] ~ 店

본사　　main company
　　　　[~company] ~ 社

본부　　headquarters [~section] ~ 部

본적　　permanent residence
　　　　[~register] ~ 籍

기본　　basis [foundation~] 基~

근본　　root; foundation [root~] 根~

자본　　capital; funds
　　　　[property~] 資~

교본　　manual; textbook
　　　　[teach~] 敎~

견본　　sample [see~] 見~

표본　　specimen; sample
　　　　[mark~] 標~

제본*　　bookbinding [make~] 製~

본.격적　full-scale; real
　　　　[~ pattern] ~ 格的
　　　　본.격적인 여름 real summer
　　　　본.격적으로 in earnest

각본　　(movie) scenario; script
　　　　[leg~] 脚~

본인　　the person in question
　　　　[~person] ~ 人

봉 (封) **seal(ed); closed**

봉하다　to seal; to close

봉투　　envelope [~wrapper] ~ 套

봉지　　paper bag [~paper] ~ 紙

개봉*　　opening (a letter);
　　　　releasing (a movie)
　　　　[open~] 開~

밀봉*　　tight seal [tight~] 密~

봉 (俸) **salary**

봉급　　salary [~pay] ~ 給

초봉　　starting pay [first~] 初~

연봉　　yearly stipend; annual
　　　　salary [year~] 年~

부 (部) **part; section**

부분　　part; section [~divide] ~ 分
　　　　부분적으로 partly

일부　　a part [one~] 一 ~

100

부품	parts [~article] ~品 자동차부품 automobile parts
부위	a part (of a body) [~position] ~位
환부	affected part [trouble~] 患~
남부	southern part [south~] 南~
중부	middle part [middle~] 中~
북부	northern part [north~] 北~
내부	the inside [inner~] 內~
외부	the outside [outer~] 外~
내무부	Ministry of Domestic Affairs [inside affairs~] 內務~
외무부	Ministry of Foreign Affairs [foreign affairs~] 外務~
학부	undergraduate school [study~] 學~
본부	headquarters [base~] 本~
부류	class; category [~a kind] ~類
전부	all; the entire [all~] 全~
간부	managing staff; executive members [trunk~] 幹~
부장	department manager [~superior] ~長
부하	subordinate; underling [~below] ~下

부 (不)	**no; not**
부정*	injustice [~just] ~正
부단하다	be incessant [~stop] ~斷
부당하다	be unjust; be unfair [~suitable] ~當
부족*	insufficiency [~sufficient] ~足

부실하다	be lacking; be insincere [~reality] ~實
부주의*	inattention; carelessness [~attention] ~注意
부적당하다	be inappropriate [~appropriate] ~適當
부조리*	irregularity [~logic] ~條理 사회 부조리 social irregularities
부도덕*	immorality [~morality] ~道德
부진*	inactivity; slump [~move] ~振
부도	dishonor; nonpayment [~crossover] ~渡 부도나다 be dishonored
부득이*	unavoidably; against one's will [~benefit already] ~得已 부득이한 사정으로 due to unavoidable circumstances
부동산	real estate [~movables] ~動産

부 (婦)	**(married) woman; wife**
부인	married woman [~person] ~人 산부인·과 obstetrics and gynecology
신부	bride [new~] 新~
주부	housewife [chief~] 主~
유부남	married man [exist~man] 有~男
부부	husband and wife [husband~] 夫~
부녀자	women and girls; womenfolk [~woman] ~女子
임산부	pregnant mother [pregnant produce~] 妊産~
파출부	visiting housemaid [branch come out~] 派出~

ㅂ

부 (夫)	husband; man; artisan
부부	husband and wife [~wife] ~ 婦
부인	wife [~person] ~ 人
유부녀	married woman [exist~woman] 有 ~ 女
형부	a female's elder sister's husband [elder brother~] 兄 ~
농부	farmer [agricultural~] 農 ~
광부	mine worker [mining~] 鑛 ~
대장부	manly man [big adult~] 大丈 ~
공부*	study; learning [labor~] 工 ~

부 (附)	paste to; append
부착*	sticking; adhesion [~attach] ~ 着
부속	attachment; affiliation [~belong] ~ 屬 자동차부속품 automobile accessories 부속병원 affiliated hospital
첨부*	appending; accompanying [add~] 添 ~
부록	appendix (in a book) [~record] ~ 錄
부근	neighborhood; vicinity [~near] ~ 近
기부*	donating [entrust~] 寄 ~
조.건부	conditional [condition~] 條件 ~
아부*	flattery [flatter~] 阿 ~

부 (副)	second; extra; support
부업	second job [~job] ~ 業
부수입	second income [~income] ~ 收入

부작용	side effect [~effect] ~ 作用
부회장	vice-president of an association [~president] ~ 會長
부반장	vice-president of a class [~class president] ~ 班長
부심	assistant referee [~judge] ~ 審
부통령	vice-president of a nation [~president] ~ 統領 (<부대통령)

부 (父)	father
부친	one's father (formal) [~parents] ~ 親
부모	parents [~mother] ~ 母 학부모 parents of students
학부형	parents of students [study~elder brother] 學 ~ 兄
부전자전	like father like son [~transmit son transmit] ~ 傳子傳
신부	Catholic priest [god~] 神 ~

부 ʷ(富)	rich
부자	rich person [~person] ~ 者
빈부	poverty and wealth [poor~] 貧 ~ 빈부의 격차 the gulf between rich and poor
부티나다	look rich [~an air come out] ~ K
부유하다	be wealthy [~abundant] ~ 裕
풍부하다	be abundant; be rich [abundant~] 豊 ~

부 (否)	on the contrary; not alright
부정*	denial; negation [~decide] ~ 定

부인*	denial [~approve] ~ 認
거부*	refusal; rejection [refuse~] 拒~ 거부반응 rejection symptoms 거부감 repulsive feeling
가부간	whether yes or no [alright~between] 可~間
안부	well-being [peaceful~] 安~ 안부를 묻다 inquire after (a person) ...에게 안부 전해주세요 Please give my regards to...

부 (付) give; pay

부탁*	entrusting; asking [~entrust] ~ 託
배부*	distribution; passing out [distribute~] 配~
납부*	paying (tax, bills, etc.) [give~] 納~
대부*	loaning [lend~] 貸~
당부*	request; entreaty [ought~] 當~
결부*	linking; involving [tie~] 結~

부 (負) carry (on the back); lose

부담	a burden; a charge [~carry] ~ 擔 부담주다 burden (a person) 부담을 느끼다 feel obligated 부담하다 bear (the expense)
부상*	injury [~injury] ~ 傷 부상당하다 get injured
포부	ambition; wishes [embrace~] 抱~
자부하다	be self-confident [self~] 自~ 자부.심 pride
승부	victory or defeat; outcome [win~] 勝~

부 (簿) account book

장부	account book [accounts~] 帳~
가계부	housekeeping book [housekeeping~] 家計~
출석부	attendance book [attendance~] 出席~
명부	roster [name~] 名~
전화번호부	telephone directory (book) [telephone number~] 電話番號~

부 (賦) pay; give

월부	monthly installment [month~] 月~
할부	installment [divide~] 割~
부과*	levy; imposition [~task] ~ 課 세금을 부과하다 levy a tax

북 ʷ(北) north

남북	south and north [south~] 南~ 동서남북 east, west, south, and north
북부	northern part [~part] ~ 部
북쪽	northern direction [~direction] ~ K
북한	North Korea [~Korea] ~ 韓
이북	North Korea [from~] 以~
북경	Beijing [~capital] ~ 京

분 ʷ(分) a minute; divide; share

(일)분	(one) minute [one~] 一~
부분	a part [part~] 部~
구분*	division; classification [distinguish~] 區~
분류*	classification [~a kind] ~ 類

ㅂ

분리* separation; division [~separate] ~ 離

분할* division; partition [~divide] ~ 割

분단* division; partition [~cut] ~ 斷

분담* division of labor or responsibility [~carry] ~ 擔

분배* distribution; giving out [~suitable] ~ 配

분해* decomposition [~loosen] ~ 解

분석* analysis [~analyze] ~ 析

분간* distinguishing; discerning [~choose] ~ 揀

분점 branch store [~store] ~ 店

분교 branch school [~school] ~ 校

분야 field; area [~field] ~ 野

성분 ingredient; constituent [to complete~] 成~
주성분 main ingredient

분량 quantity [~amount] ~ 量

수분 water; moisture [water~] 水~

염분 salt content [salt~] 鹽~

당분 sugar content [sugar~] 糖~

철분 iron content [iron~] 鐵~

영양분 nutritive elements [nutrition~] 營養~

여분 remainder; excess; leftover [surplus~] 餘~

충분하다 be enough; be sufficient [full~] 充~

분수 discretion; one's place; one's means; fraction [~number] ~ 數
분수가 없다 be indiscreet
농담을 해도 분수가 있지
(You) carry your joke too far.

분수를 알다
know one's place
분수에 맞게 살다
live within one's means

과분하다 be more than one deserves [exceed~] 過~

신분 social standing; identity [person~] 身~

기분 feeling [spirit~] 氣~

분명하다 be clear; be obvious [~clear] ~ 明

연분 preordained tie; fate [affinity~] 緣~

처분* disposal (of one's property) [manage~] 處~

분양* initial sale (apartment) [~cede] ~ 讓

덕분 indebtedness; thanks to [virtue~] 德~
…덕분에 thanks to …

당분간 for the time being [suitable~interval] 當~間

분 ᵂ(粉) powder

분말 powder [~end] ~ 末

분유 powdered milk [~milk] ~ 乳

분필 chalk [~pen] ~ 筆

분식 flour-based meals [~food] ~ 食
분식하다
eat flour-based meals

분 ᵂ(憤) anger

분노* anger [~angry] ~ 怒

분개하다 be enraged [~pitiful] ~ 慨

분통터지다 be greatly vexed [~pain explode] ~ 痛 K

분하다 be indignant; be resentful

ㅂ

불 (不) **no; not**

불행* unhappiness; misfortune [~fortune] ~ 幸

불편* discomfort; inconvenience [~convenient] ~ 便

불안* uneasiness [~peaceful] ~ 安

불쾌하다 be unpleasant; be displeased [~pleasant] ~ 快

불평* complaints [~peaceful] ~ 平

불만 dissatisfaction [~full] ~ 滿

불.신* distrust [~believe] ~ 信

불화 discord; trouble [~harmonize] ~ 和
가정불화 family troubles

불길하다 be ill-omened; be inauspicious [~lucky] ~ 吉

불리하다 be disadvantageous [~benefit] ~ 利

불량하다 be bad; be poor [~good] ~ 良

불결* uncleanliness [~clean] ~ 潔

불참* absence; nonattendance [~attend] ~ 參

불효* undutifulness to parents [~filial piety] ~ 孝

불친절* unkindness [~kindness] ~ 親切

불가능* impossibility [~possibility] ~可能

불규칙* irregularity [~regularity] ~ 規則

불공평하다 be unfair [~fair] ~ 公平

불투명하다 be opaque [~transparent] ~ 透明

불면.증 insomnia [~sleep symptom] ~ 眠症

불찰 lack of attention; mistake [~observe] ~ 察

불구 deformity [~tool] ~ 具
불구자 deformed person

불통 impassability; no communication [~go through] ~ 通

불의 unexpectedness; suddenness [~intention] ~ 意
불의의 사고 unexpected accident

불·시에 unexpectedly; by surprise [~time] ~ 時 K

불과* no more than; merely [~exceed] ~ 過

불구하고 in spite of; regardless of [~restrain] ~ 拘 K
비가 오는데도 불구하고 in spite of the rain

불황 (business) depression; slump [~situation] ~ 況

불경기 (business) depression [~tone of the market] ~ 景氣

불 (拂) **pay**

지불* payment; defrayment [pay~] 支 ~

선불* advance payment [precede~] 先 ~

후불* postpayment [after~] 後 ~

일시불 lump-sum payment [one time~] 一時 ~

환불* refund [return~] 還 ~

가불* salary advance [temporary~] 假 ~

비 (備) **prepare; provided with**

예비* preparation; a reserve [beforehand~] 豫 ~

준비* preparation [standard~] 準 ~

105

대비* preparation (for)
[oppose~] 對~
시험에 대비하다
prepare for an exam

설비* equipment; facilities
[establish~] 設~

장비 equipment [pack~] 裝~
등산장비 hiking equipment

구비하다 have all; be fully equipped
[tool~] 具~

완비* being fully equipped
[complete~] 完~

비치* furnishing; equipping
[~to place] ~ 置

비품 fixtures [~article] ~ 品

겸비* combine (one thing with
another); have both
[combine~] 兼~

경비* defense; guard [warn~] 警~
경비실 security office

수비* defense [guard~] 守~

우비 raincoat [rain~] 雨~

유비무환 Preparing is preventing.
[exist~no worry] 有~無患

비 (費) expense; use

비용 expenses; cost [~use] ~ 用

경비 expenses [govern~] 經~

학비 school expenses
[learning~] 學~

식비 grocery expenses
[food~] 食~

호텔비 hotel expenses [hotel~] E ~

자비 one's own expenses
[self~] 自~

회비 membership fee
[meeting~] 會~

차비 car fare [vehicle~] 車~

낭비* waste [wasteful~] 浪~
시간낭비* waste of time

허비* waste [empty~] 虛~

소비* consumption
[dissolve~] 消~
소비자 consumer

비 (非) no; not; wrong

비상 extraordinariness;
emergency [~usual] ~ 常
비상하다 (brain) be
extraordinary

비정하다 be heartless
[~feeling] ~ 情

비정상 abnormality
[~normality] ~ 正常

비능률.적 inefficient
[~efficient] ~ 能率的

비공식 informality;
being unofficial
[~officialness] ~ 公式

비매품 articles not for sale
[~sell article] ~ 賣品

비싸다 be expensive [~cheap] ~ K

시비* a quarrel [right~] 是~
시비걸다 start a quarrel

사이비 pseudo-; false
[similar by~] 似而~

비난* criticism; blame
[~difficult] ~ 難

비몽사몽 half-dreaming, half-awake
[~dream similar dream]
~夢似夢

비 (秘) secret; conceal

비밀 secret [~secret] ~ 密
일급비밀 top secret

극비 top secret [extreme~] 極~

비결 secret; key [~depart] ~ 訣
성공의 비결 key to success

신비* mystery [divine~] 神~

비서 (private) secretary
[~writing] ~ 書

변비 constipation
[excrement~] 便~

비 (比) compare

비하다 compare
...에 비해 compared with...

비교* comparison [~compare] ~ 較
비교적 relatively
비교가 안되다
be incomparable

비유* metaphor; comparison
[~simile] ~ 喩

비율 ratio [~rate] ~ 率

비례* proportion [~example] ~ 例
정비례* direct proportion
반비례* inverse proportion

비중 specific gravity; relative
importance [~weight] ~ 重
비중이 크다 be important

비 (悲) sad

비참하다 be miserable
[~miserable] ~ 慘

비관* pessimism [~view] ~ 觀
비관적 pessimistic

비극 tragedy [~drama] ~ 劇

비명 cry of distress; a shriek
[~cry] ~ 鳴
비명을 지르다 scream

자비 mercy [benevolent~] 慈~

비 (卑) low

비천하다 be lowly; be low-born
[~lowly] ~ 賤

비열하다 be mean [~inferior] ~ 劣

비겁하다 be cowardly
[~cowardice] ~ 怯

야비하다 be mean; be of bad taste
[wilderness~] 野~

비굴하다 be servile; be obsequious
[~bend] ~ 屈

비 (肥) fat; fertile

비만* obesity [~full] ~ 滿

비계 (hog) fat

비둔하다 be heavily clothed
[~dull] ~ 鈍

비료 manure [~material] ~ 料

비 (飛) to fly

비행기 airplane [~go machine] ~行機

비약* leap of logic; jumping to
a conclusion [~leap] ~ 躍

빈 (貧) poor

빈부 poverty and wealth
[~rich] ~ 富

빈민 poor people [~people] ~ 民
빈민굴 a slum

빈티나다 look poor
[~an air come out] ~K

빈약하다 be scanty; be meager
[~weak] ~ 弱
내용이 빈약하다
lack substance

빈혈 anemia [~blood] ~ 血

빈 (賓) guest

귀빈 important guest; VIP
[honorable~] 貴~

주빈 guest of honor [main~] 主~

내빈	guest (formal) [come~] 來~
빙 (氷)	**ice**
빙수	shaved ice [~water] ~ 水 팥빙수 shaved ice with red bean
빙판	icy road; icy place [~board] ~ 板

入

사 (事)	**matters; business; serve**
사항	items; matters [~item] ~ 項 중요사항 important matters
매사	every matter [every~] 每~
만사	all matters [all~] 萬~ 만사태평 being carefree in all matters
시사	current events [time~] 時~
사례	instance; case [~example] ~ 例
사정	circumstances; reasons consideration [~circumstance] ~ 情 사정하다 solicit (special consideration)
사연	origin and circumstances of a matter; full story [~cause] ~ 緣
사태	situation; the state of things [~situation] ~ 態 비상사태 a state of emergency
사전에	before the fact; in advance [~before] ~ 前 K
사실	fact; truth [~reality] ~ 實

기사	a report (in newspaper/ magazine) [record~] 記~ 신문기사 newspaper article
사.건	event; happening [~thing] ~ 件 사사.건.건 each and every matter
경사	happy event [congratulate~] 慶~
행사	event; function [act~] 行~ 국제행사 international event
불.상사	mishap [not lucky~] 不詳~
사고	accident [~cause] ~ 故 사고가 나다 an accident happens
무사하다	be safe [no~] 無~
사무	office work; business matter [~duty] ~ 務 사무실 office 사무적 businesslike
사업*	enterprise; business [~business] ~ 業
종사*	following a profession [follow~] 從 ~
농사	farming [agricultural~] 農~ 농사짓다 do farming
가사	housework [house~] 家~
식사*	(having) a meal [eat~] 食 ~
공사*	construction work [labor~] 工~
판사	a judge [judge~] 判 ~
검사	public prosecutor [inspect~] 檢~
형사	(police) detective [punishment~] 刑~
인사*	greeting; thanking; personnel management [person~] 人~
선사하다	give a present [good~] 善~

치사하다	be shameful; be mean [shameful~] 恥~	사원	company employee [~member] ~ 員
허사	vain attempt; failure [empty~] 虛~	입사*	becoming a member of a company [enter~] 入~
장사지내다	hold a funeral [funeral~hold] 葬~K	여행사	travel agency [travel~] 旅行~
		장의사	funeral parlor [funeral rite~] 葬儀~
		사회	society [~meeting] ~ 會

사 (士) scholar; gentleman; soldier

박사	Ph. D. [extensive~] 博~
석사	master's (degree) [great~] 碩~
도사	enlightened Buddhist; expert [principle~] 道~
변호사	attorney [vindication~] 辯護~
신사	gentleman [nobility~] 紳~ 신사용 for gentlemen
장사	strong man [robust~] 壯~ 천하장사 strongest man in the world
운전사	driver [driving~] 運轉~
조종사	pilot [operation~] 操縱~
군사	soldier [military~] 軍~
기사	knight [horse riding~] 騎~ 기사도 knighthood; chivalry
육사	military academy [army~] 陸~ (<육군사관학교)
사기	morale; spirit [~spirit] ~ 氣 사기가 떨어지다 become demoralized

사교	social relationships [~exchange] ~ 交 사교적이다 be sociable
사설	an editorial (article) [~speech] ~ 說

사 (師) teacher; master

교사	school teacher [teach~] 敎~
강사	lecturer [lecture~] 講~ 시간강사 part-time lecturer 전임강사 full-time lecturer
사대	college of education [~college] ~ 大 (<사범대학)
의사	medical doctor [medical science~] 醫~
약사	pharmacist [medicine~] 藥~
기사	engineer; technician [skill~] 技~
미용사	beautician; hairdresser [beauty art~] 美容~
곡예사	acrobat [bend art~] 曲藝~
목사	pastor; minister [herd~] 牧~

사 (社) company; society

회사	company [meeting~] 會~
본사	main company [origin~] 本~
지사	branch company [branch~] 支~
사장	president of a company [~superior] ~ 長

사 (沙) sand

백사장	sandy beach [white~place] 白~場
사막	desert [~desert] ~ 漠
황사현상	dust storm [yellow~ phenomenon] 黃~現象

(산)**사**태   landslide
[mountain~landslide] 山~汰
눈사태 avalanche (of snow)

사기   porcelain; earthenware
[~vessel] ~器

사발   porcelain bowl [~bowl] ~鉢

사공   boatman [~artisan] ~工

사과   apple [~fruit] ~果

사 (死)   **die**

사망*   death [~die] ~亡

즉**사***   immediate death
[immediate~] 卽~

사형*   death penalty
[~punishment] ~刑

전**사***   death in battle [war~] 戰~

익**사***   death (from drowning)
[drown~] 溺~

한**사**코   to the death; persistently
[limit~] 限 ~ K

구**사**일.생   narrow escape from
death [nine~one live]
九~一生
구사일.생으로 살아나다
have a narrow escape
from death

필**사**적   desperate
[inevitably~] 必~的

사 (辭)   **speech; resign**

축**사***   congratulatory speech
[congratulate~] 祝~

찬**사**   laudatory remark;
compliment [praise~] 讚~

공치**사***   self-praise; admiration
of one's own merit
[merit achieve~] 功致~

미**사**여구   flowery words
[beautiful~beautiful phrase]
美~麗句

사양*   courteous refusal
[~decline] ~讓

사표   letter of resignation
[~manifest] ~表
사표내다 submit
one's resignation

사퇴*   resignation
[~retreat] ~退

사전   dictionary [~code] ~典

사 ʷ (四)   **four**

사철   four seasons [~season] ~ K

사계절   four seasons
[~season] ~季節

사거리   intersection [~street] ~ K

사방   four directions; all
directions [~direction] ~方

사각형   quadrangle
[~angle shape] ~角形

사촌   cousin [~relation] ~寸

사 (使)   **employ; messenger**

사용*   a use; making use of
[~use] ~用

구**사***   command (of a language)
[drive~] 驅~

사명   mission [~command] ~命

혹**사***   slave-driving; abuse
[severe~] 酷~

설·**사**   granted that; even if
[establish~] 設~

천**사**   angel [God~] 天~

대**사**관   embassy
[great~building] 大~館

ㅅ

사 (査) **inspect; examine**

검사*   inspection; examination
[inspect~] 檢~

조사*   investigation; survey
[control~] 調~
뒷조사* secret investigation

수사*   investigation (by police, prosecutors)
[investigate~] 搜~

고사   examination [examine~] 考~
중간고사 mid-term exam

심사*   judging [judge~] 審~

사돈   relatives by marriage; in-laws [~bow the head] ~頓

사 (史) **history**

역사   history [pass~] 歷~

세계사   world history
[world~] 世界~

사상   in history [~above] ~上
사상 최대 the greatest in history

유사이래   since the dawn of history
[exist~ever since] 有~以來

사극   historical drama
[~drama] ~劇

여사   Mrs.; madame
[female~] 女~

사 (私) **private; personal**

사.적   private; personal ~的
사.적인 일
something personal

사복   private clothes
[~clothes] ~服

사립   private establishment
[~establish] ~立
사립학교 private school

사생활   private life [~life] ~生活

사서함   post-office box
[~writing box] ~書函

사 (思) **think; consider**

사고*   thinking [~think] ~考
사고방식 way of thinking

의사   thought; mind
[intention~] 意~

사상   thought; ideology
[~think] ~想

사려깊다   be thoughtful
[~think deep] ~慮 K

상사.병   lovesickness
[mutual~disease] 相~病

사춘기   adolescence; puberty
[~spring period] ~春期

심사숙고*   thorough consideration
[deep~mature think] 深~熟考

사 (詞) **words**

작사*   lyric making; song writing
[make~] 作~

동사   verb [move~] 動~

명사   noun [name~] 名~

형용사   adjective
[description~] 形容~

부사   adverb [support~] 副~

사 (謝) **thank; apologize**

감사하다   thank; feel grateful
[feeling~] 感~

사례*   thanks; reward
[~etiquette] ~禮

사은   grateful appreciation
[~favor] ~恩
사은품 thank-you gifts

사과*   apology [~to err] ~過

111

ㅅ

사절* refusal; declining [~cut] ~絕
면회사절* No visitors

삭발* shaving one's head [~hair] ~髮

사 (寫) sketch; copy

묘사* description; portrayal [sketch~] 描~

사본 a duplicate [~origin] ~本

복사* duplication; copy [double~] 複~

사진 photograph [~true] ~眞
사진찍다 take pictures
사진·기 camera

사 (似) resemble; similar

흡사하다 resemble closely [similar~] 恰~

유사하다 be similar [a kind~] 類~

사이비 pseudo-; false [~by wrong] ~而非

비몽사몽 neither asleep nor awake [not dream~dream] 非夢~夢

사 (射) shoot

사격* firing; shooting [~attack] ~擊
사격장 shooting range

발·사* firing; blast-off [shoot~] 發~

주사* injection [pour~] 注~
주사맞다 be injected

반사* reflection (of light) [opposite~] 反~

삭 (削) cut; subtract

첨삭* addition and deletion; correction [add~] 添~

삭제* elimination; erasure [~eliminate] ~除

산 ʷ(山) mountain

산맥 mountains [~vein] ~脈

산꼭대기 mountaintop [~top] ~K

산중턱 hillside [~midslope] ~中K

야산 small hill [field~] 野~

등산* mountain climbing [climb~] 登~

산·골 mountain district [~valley] ~K

강산 rivers and mountains; native land [river~] 江~
팔·도강산 (the scenery of) all parts of Korea

화산 volcano [fire~] 火~

광산 a mine [ore~] 鑛~

산장 villa in a mountain [~villa] ~莊

태산 high mountain; tremendous thing [big~] 泰~

산·더미 huge amount [~pile] ~K
할 일이 산·더미같다 have tons of work to do

산·불 forest fire [~fire] ~K

산토끼 wild rabbit [~rabbit] ~K

산나물 wild edible greens [~vegetable] ~K

산소 grave [~place] ~所

산 (算) calculate

계산* calculation [calculate~] 計~

추산* estimate; calculation [infer~] 推~

ㅅ

암산*	mental calculation [dark~] 暗~	재산	property; estate [property~] 財~
주산*	abacus calculation [beads~] 珠~	부동산	real estate [not move~] 不動~
오산*	miscalculation; wrong estimate [mistake~] 誤~	파산*	bankruptcy [break~] 破~
타산적	calculating; mercenary [hit~] 打~的	유산	inheritance [bequeath~] 遺~

산 （散） **disperse**

전산	computation [electricity~] 電~	산란하다	be dispersed; be scattered about [~chaotic] ~亂
산수	arithmetic [~number] ~數		정신이 산란하다 feel dispersed
합산*	adding up [unite~] 合~		
예산*	estimate; budget [beforehand~] 豫~	확산*	spreading; dissemination [enlarge~] 擴~
결산*	settlement of accounts [decide~] 決~	산만하다	be distracted; be scatter-brained [~diffused] ~漫
청산*	clearing off; squaring accounts [clear~] 淸~	해산*	(meeting) breaking up [release~] 解~
환산*	conversion [exchange~] 換~ 달러를 원으로 환산하다 convert dollars into won	산산·조각	broken pieces [~~piece] ~~K 산산·조각이 나다 be broken into pieces
산통깨지다	scheme is ruined [~bamboo tube break] ~ 筒K	이산가족	separated family (between North and South Korea) [separate~family] 離~家族

산 （産） **produce; possession**

생산*	production [be born~] 生~	한산하다	be inactive; be slack (in traffic/trade) [leisure~] 閑~
국산	domestic production [nation~] 國~	음산하다	be gloomy and chilly [dark~] 陰~
산물	product [~thing] ~物 농산물 agricultural products 수산물 marine products	산·보*	taking a walk [~walk] ~步
산업	industry [~business] ~業	산책*	taking a walk [~a plan] ~策
출·산*	baby delivery [come out~] 出~	산문	prose (writing) [~writing] ~文
유산*	miscarriage; abortion [flow~] 流~		

산 ʷ（酸） **acid; sour**

산부인·과	obstetrics and gynecology [~married woman department] ~婦人科	산성	acidity [~nature] ~性
		위산	stomach acid [stomach~] 胃~

113

염산	hydrochloric acid [salt~] 鹽 ~
산소	oxygen [~element] ~ 素

산 (傘) umbrella

우산	umbrella [rain~] 雨 ~
양산	parasol [sun~] 陽 ~
낙하산	parachute [fall down~] 落下 ~

살 (殺) kill

살인*	homicide; murder [~person] ~ 人
살해*	murder; killing [~harm] ~ 害
타살	homicide; murder [others~] 他~
피살되다	get killed [suffer~become] 被 ~ K 피살·자 murder victim
암살*	assassination [secret~] 暗 ~
총살*	execution by shooting [gun~] 銃~
몰·살*	massacre; annihilation [sink~] 沒 ~
학살*	massacre [cruel~] 虐~
자살*	suicide [self~] 自 ~
박살*	clubbing (someone/ something) to death/pieces [beat~] 撲~
살균*	sterilization [~germ] ~ 菌
살벌하다	be bloody; be warlike [~chastise] ~ 伐
살충제	insecticide [~insect medicine] ~ 蟲 劑

묵살*	ignoring (a person's remarks by keeping silent) [silent~] 默 ~

삼 ᵂ(三) three; third

삼각형	triangle [~angle shape] ~角形
삼복	three dog days; hottest period of summer [~dog days] ~ 伏
삼위일체	Trinity [~position one body] ~位一體
삼류	third-rate [~stream] ~ 流
제삼자	third party; outsider [order~person] 第~者
삼관왕	triple gold medalist [~crown king] ~冠王
삼팔선	the thirty-eighth parallel (dividing Korea) [~eight line] ~ 八線
삼수*	preparing for the college entrance exam after two failures [~cultivate] ~ 修
삼촌	uncle (on the father's side) [~relation] ~ 寸

상 (上) above; ascend; supreme

상체	upper part of the body [~body] ~ 體
상반신	upper half of the body [~half body] ~ 半身
상류	(river) upstream; (society) upper class [~flow] ~ 流 상류계급 the upper class
영상	above zero (temp.) [zero~] 零~
옥상	rooftop [building~] 屋 ~
정상	peak; top [summit~] 頂 ~

114

향상* elevation; improvement [to face~] 向~

인상* (price) raising [pull~] 引~

상경* coming up to the capital (Seoul) [~capital] ~京

상행 (train) going up toward Seoul [~go] ~行

상륙* landing; disembarkation [~land] ~陸

상관 superior official [~official] ~官

연상 senior in age [age~] 年~

조상 ancestor [ancestor~] 祖~

막상막하 neck and neck [not~not low] 莫~莫下

상책 best plan [~plan] ~策

최상 the best [the most~] 最~
최상품 highest-quality article

상영* screening; showing [~reflect] ~映
영화상영* movie showing

이상 more than; now that [from~] 以~
두시간 이상
more than two hours
이렇게 된 이상 now that
such things have come to pass

세상 the world [world~] 世~

상 ᵂ(相) **mutual; face; minister**

상담* consultation; counsel [~converse] ~談

상의* consultation; discussion [~discuss] ~議

상대 partner; rival; relativity [~opposite] ~對
상대방 the other person
상대하다 keep company (with); contend (with)

상대가 안되다
be no match for
상대적으로 relatively

상관* connection; meddling; concern [~concern] ~關

상종* keeping company with; associating [~follow] ~從

상당하다 be suitable for; be considerable [~suitable] ~當
상당히 fairly; considerably

상속* succession; inheritance [~continue] ~續

울.상 tearful face [cry~] K~

관상 physiognomy [view~] 觀~
관상을 보다 read one's
character/fortune by the face

인상 physiognomy; looks [person~] 人~

피상적 superficial [skin~] 皮~的

양상 aspect; phase [appearance~] 樣~

진상 real facts of a case; true picture [true~] 眞~

수상 prime minister [head~] 首~

상 (常) **constantly; usual**

항상 always [constant~] 恒~

상비약 reserve medicine [~prepare medicine] ~備藥

일.상 everyday; usually [day~] 日~
일.상생활 everyday life

상습 habitual practice [~practice] ~習
상습범 habitual criminal

상투적 commonplace; hackneyed [~customary] ~套的
상투적인 말
hackneyed words

상식 common sense [~know] ~識

정상 normality [right~] 正~
비정상 abnormality

상무 managing director [~duty] ~務

비상 extraordinariness; emergency [not~] 非~
비상하다 be extraordinary
비상구 emergency exit
비상금 emergency money

이상하다 be strange; be unusual [different~] 異~

수상하다 be suspicious; be fishy [different~] 殊~

괴상하다 be strange; be odd [strange~] 怪~

상스럽다 be vulgar; be indecent

상 (想) think; reflect

감상 thoughts; impressions [feeling~] 感~
감상문 description of one's impressions

상상* imagination [~image] ~像
상상력이 풍부하다 be imaginative

연상* association (of ideas) [association~] 聯~
연상되다 be reminded (of)

회상* reminiscing [return~] 回~

명상* meditation; contemplation [close eyes~] 瞑~

구상* visualization; plan; idea [compose~] 構~

예상* expectation [beforehand~] 豫~

이상 an ideal [principle~] 理~
이상적 ideal

환상 fantasy; illusion [illusion~] 幻~

공상* idle fantasy; daydream [empty~] 空~

망상* wild fantasy [absurd~] 妄~
과대망상 megalomania
피해망상 persecution mania

상 (商) business; trade

상업 commerce [~occupation] ~業
상공업 commerce and industry

상.법 business law [~law] ~法

상인 merchant; shopkeeper [~person] ~人

상가 shopping mall [~street] ~街
지하상가 underground shopping mall

상점 a store [~store] ~店

도매상 wholesale store [wholesale~] 都賣~

상표 trademark; brand [~mark] ~標
유명상표 famous brand

상품 goods; merchandise [~article] ~品

협상* negotiation [harmony~] 協~

상술 business trick [~skill] ~術

상 (傷) injure; wound

상처 injury; scar [~place] ~處
상처입다/받다 get hurt

부상* injury; wound [carry~] 負~
부상자 wounded person

중상 serious injury [heavy~] 重~

화상 a burn [fire~] 火~
화상을 입다 be burned

동상 frostbite [freeze~] 凍~
동상걸리다 get frostbitten

타박상 a bruise; contusion [hit hit~] 打撲~

상하다 (food) go bad

116

ㅅ

손상* damage [damage~] 損~
명예를 손상시키다
disgrace one's reputation

상 ᵂ(賞) **prize; award; appreciate**

상품 prize; trophy [~article] ~ 品

상금 prize money [~money] ~ 金
현상금 bounty; reward

상타다 win a prize [~receive] ~ K

수상* receiving a prize
[receive~] 受~

입상* winning a prize [enter~] 入~

상패 medal [~signboard] ~ 牌

상.장 award certificate
[~document] ~ 狀

최우수상 the highest award
[the very best~] 最優秀~

우등상 prize for excellent
scholarship
[excellent rank~] 優等~

감상* appreciation (of a movie,
music, poetry, etc.)
[mirror~] 鑑~

상 (狀) **form; shape**

상태 condition; state
[~situation] ~ 態

상황 situation; circumstances
[~situation] ~ 況

증상 symptom; condition
of a patient [ailment~] 症~

이상 abnormality; something
wrong [different~] 異~
정신이상 mental disorder

궁상 extreme straits [poor~] 窮~

험상궂다 be rough; be savage-
looking [rough~bad] 險 ~ K

상 ᵂ(床) **table; bench**

밥상 eating table [rice~] K~

책상 desk [book~] 冊~
책상다리* sitting
on crossed legs

걸.상 chair

온상 greenhouse; hotbed
[warm~] 溫 ~

기상* rising from bed
[rise~] 起~

상 (象) **image; representation**

인상 impression [seal~] 印~
인상적 impressive
첫인상 first impression

추상적 abstract [extract~] 抽~ 的

현상 phenomenon [appear~] 現~

대상 the object; target
[opposite~] 對~

상징* symbol [~symptoms] ~ 徵

상 ᵂ(像) **appearance; image; statue**

상상* imagination [think~] 想~

현상* (film) developing
[appear~] 現~

자화상 self-portrait
[self picture~] 自畵~

동상 bronze statue [bronze~] 銅~

상 (償) **compensation**

보상* compensation
[supplement~] 補~

배상* indemnification
[reparation~] 賠~
손해배상* indemnity
for damage done

117

변상* (making up for) damage [distinguish~] 辨~

색 ᵂ(色) **color**

색깔 color ~ K

흰색 white color [white~] K~

하얀색 white color [white~] K~

미색 cream color [rice~] 米~

노란색 yellow color [yellow~] K~

주황색 orange color [red yellow~] 朱黃~

분홍색 pink color [powder red~] 粉紅~

빨간색 red color [red~] K~

갈.색 brown color [brown~] 褐~

파란색 blue color [blue~] K~

청색 blue color [blue~] 靑~

하늘.색 sky blue color [sky~] K~

회색 grey color [ash~] 灰~

검정색 black color [black~] K~

까만색 black color [black~] K~

초록색 grass-green color [grass green~] 草綠~

원색 primary color [origin~] 原~

단색 monochrome [single~] 單~

바탕색 ground color [ground~] K~

무색 colorlessness [no~] 無~

탈.색* discoloration; fading [escape~] 脫~

색칠* coloring; painting [~painting] ~ 漆

색종이 colored paper [~paper] ~ K

색연필 color pencil [~pencil] ~ 鉛筆 (pron=생년필)

색소 pigment [~element] ~ 素 식용색소 food colors

염색* dyeing [dye~] 染~

색안경 tinted glasses; unfairly biased view [~glasses] ~ 眼鏡 색안경을 쓰고 보다 be unfairly biased

색맹 color blindness [~blind] ~ 盲

혈.색 complexion; color [blood~] 血~

안색 countenance [face~] 顔~ 안색이 좋다 /나쁘다 look well/unwell

내색하다 let one's face show one's thoughts [inside~]

본색 true character [original~] 本~ 본색을 드러내다 reveal one's true character

정색하다 put on a serious look [true~] 正~

특색 specific character; characteristic [special~] 特~

색다르다 be of a different cast; be unique [~different] ~ K

가지각색 various kinds [a kind every~] K 各~

생색내다 pose as a benefactor; emphasize the favor done for (a person) [raw~bring out] 生 ~ K

손색없다 stand comparison (with) [humble~not exist] 遜 ~ K

물.색하다 search for; hunt [thing~] 物~

색 (索) **grope; seek**

탐색* investigation; probe [search~] 探~

수색* searching; investigation [investigate~] 搜~

색출* ferreting out (a criminal) [~come out] ~出

생 (生) **be born; life; living; raw; student**

출.생* birth [come out~] 出~

탄생* birth [be born~] 誕~

생일 birthday [~day] ~日
생년월일 year, month, and date of birth

동생 younger sibling [together~] 同~
여동생 younger sister
남동생 younger brother

생산* production [~produce] ~産

천생 by nature [nature~] 天~

생명 life [~life] ~命
생명보험 life insurance

생활* life; living [~live] ~活
생활비 cost of living

인생 (human) life; existence [person~] 人~

생물 living thing [~thing] ~物

생기 animation; vitality [~spirit] ~氣

일.생 one's lifetime [one~] 一~

평생 lifetime [even~] 平~

생전 lifetime [~before] ~前
생전처음 for the first time in one's life

전생 former life [before~] 前~

여생 rest of one's life [remain~] 餘~

재생* regeneration; recycling [again~] 再~

발.생* occurrence [arise~] 發~

생존* existence [~exist] ~存
생존경쟁* struggle (competition) for existence

생방송* live broadcast [~broadcasting] ~放送

구사일.생 narrow escape from death [nine die one~] 九死一~

위생 hygiene; sanitation [guard~] 衛~

생리 physiology [~principle] ~理
생리현상 physiological phenomenon
생리대 sanitary napkin

생화 real flower [~flower] ~花

생수 mineral water [~water] ~水

생맥주 draft beer [~beer] ~麥酒

생머리 natural hair (vs. permed hair) [~hair] ~K

생사람잡다 accuse an innocent person [~person arrest] ~K

생색내다 pose as a benefactor; emphasize the favor done for (a person) [~color bring out] ~色K

생소하다 be unfamiliar [~far apart] ~疎

생생하다 be vivid; be fresh

생선 raw fish [~fresh] ~鮮
생선회 sashimi
생선구이 grilled fish

학생 student [study~] 學~
국민학생 elementary school student
중학생 middle school student
고등학생 high school student
대학생 college student
남학생 male student
여학생 female student
장학생 scholarship student

신입생 new student; freshman [new enter~] 新入~

119

졸업생	graduate; alumni [graduation~] 卒業~
동창생	fellow student; schoolmate [same window~] 同窓~
수험생	student preparing for an entrance exam [receive examine~] 受驗~
재수생	student repreparing for college entrance exam [repreparing for exam~] 再修~
선생님	teacher [precede~ respected person] 先~K

서 (書) **book; writing**

서적	books; publications [~book] ~籍
교·과서	textbook [teach course~] 教科~
참고서	reference book [reference~] 參考~
안내서	guidebook [guide~] 案內~
원서	original (language) edition; original text [origin~] 原~
서점	bookstore [~store] ~店
도서	books [drawing~] 圖~ 도서관 library (building) 도서실 library (room)
서재	a study [~library] ~齋
독서*	reading [read~] 讀~
서예	calligraphy [~art] ~藝
정서*	square handwriting; printed-style writing [correct~] 正~
낙서*	scribbling; graffiti [scatter~] 落~
혈·서	writing in blood [blood~] 血~

유서	suicide note [bequeath~] 遺~
서류	document [~a kind] ~類
증서	certificate [evidence~] 證~
이서*	endorsing (a cheque) [inside~] 裏~
계산서	bill; cheque [calculation~] 計算~
원서	application form [desire~] 願~ 입학원서 application form for admission to a school
신청서	application form [request~] 申請~
추천서	letter of recommendation [recommendation~] 推薦~
보고서	a report [report~] 報告~
이력서	resumé [personal history~] 履歷~
엽서	postcard [leaf~] 葉~ 그림엽서 picture postcard 우편엽서 postcard 관제엽서 (government) postcard
투서*	(sending an) anonymous letter [throw~] 投~
비서	(private) secretary [secret~] 秘~

서 ᵂ (西) **west**

서쪽	western side [~side] ~K
서해안	west coast [~coast] ~海岸
서양	the West [~ocean] ~洋
서구문명	Western civilization [~Europe civilization] ~歐文明
서기	A. D. [~record] ~紀

서 ᵂ **(署)** public office

관공서   government and public offices [official public~] 官公~

경찰서   police station [police~] 警察~

소방서   fire station [dissolve defend~] 消防~

세무서   tax office [tax affair~] 稅務~

서 (序) **(sequence) order**

순서   (sequence) order [order~] 順~

질서   order; system [order~] 秩~
    질서를 지키다   keep order

장유유서   order between the old and the young; the elder first [elder child exist~] 長幼有~

석 (石) **stone**

비석   tombstone [tombstone~] 碑~

투석전   stone-throwing fight [throw~fight] 投~戰

채석장   quarry [dig up~place] 採~場

자석   magnet [magnet~] 磁~

보석   jewelry [treasure~] 寶~

화석   fossil [change~] 化~

석고   plaster [~fat] ~膏

치석   tartar on the teeth [tooth~] 齒~

석탄   coal [~charcoal] ~炭

석유   petroleum [~oil] ~油

정석   formula; established form [decide~] 定~

목석같다   be insensible [tree~be like] 木~K

석 (席) **seat; place**

경로석   seats for the elderly [respect old~] 敬老~

좌석   seat [sit~] 坐~
    좌석버스   bus with guaranteed seating

방석   cushion [square~] 方~

입석   standing room [stand~] 立~

합석*   sitting together [join~] 合~

참석*   attendance; presence [participate~] 參~

출.석*   (school) attendance [appear~] 出~

결.석*   absence (from school) [deficient~] 缺~

즉석   on the spot; improvised; instant [immediate~] 卽~
    즉석구이   things grilled on the spot

석차   class standing [~order] ~次

수석*   the top [head~] 首~

석 (釋) **release; explain**

석방*   release; acquittal [~release] ~放

해석*   interpretation [explain~] 解~

주석   annotation [explanatory notes~] 註~
    주석을 달다   append notes (to a book)

석가모니   Buddha ~迦牟尼

석 (夕) **evening**

석간(신문)   evening paper [~publish newspaper] ~刊新聞

추석   harvest full moon festival on Aug. 15th by lunar calendar [autumn~] 秋~

선 ᵂ(線) **line; cord**	
점선	dotted line [dot~] 點~
직선	straight line [straight~] 直~ 수직선 vertical line
곡선	curved line [bend~] 曲~
사선	slanted line; slash [inclined~] 斜~
대각선	diagonal line [opposite angle~] 對角~
수평선	horizon [water even~] 水平~
유선	wire [exist~] 有~ 유선텔레비전 cable TV
전선	electric wire [electricity~] 電~
무선	wireless [no~] 無~ 무선전화기 cordless phone
혼선되다	(lines) be crossed [confused~become] 混 ~ K
노선	(bus) route [road~] 路~
차선	(traffic) lane [vehicle~] 車~
선로	railroad; track [~road] ~路
경부선	Seoul-Pusan line [capital Pusan~] 京釜~
탈.선*	derailment; aberration [escape~] 脫~
광선	ray of light [light~] 光~
적외선	infrared rays [red outside~] 赤外~
자외선	ultraviolet rays [violet outside~] 紫外~
방사선	radiation; x rays [release shoot~] 放射~
삼팔.선	the thirty-eighth parallel (dividing Korea) [three eight~] 三八~
시선	line of vision; one's gaze [look at~] 視~ 시선을 끌다 attract attention

선 ᵂ(先) **precede; the first**	
우선하다	take precedence (over) [superior~] 優~ 우선.권 priority; right to preferential treatment
선불*	prepayment [~pay] ~拂
선약*	previous engagement [~promise] ~約
선입견	preconception; prejudice [~enter view] ~入見
선배	one's senior (in school) [~fellow member] ~輩
선생님	teacher [~student respected person] ~生 K
선조	forefathers [~ancestor] ~祖
선구자	forerunner [~drive person] ~驅者
선두	the forefront; the lead [~head] ~頭
선견지명	foresight [~see of clear] ~見之明
우선	first of all [from~] 于~
선진국	developed country [~advance country] ~進國
선천적	innate; inherited [~nature] ~天的

선 (選) **select; elect**	
선정*	selection [~decide] ~定
선발*	selection; picking out [~pull out] ~拔
엄선*	careful selection [strict~] 嚴~
예선	preliminary selection/ match [beforehand~] 豫~
입선*	being selected for a competition [enter~] 入~
선수	player [~hand] ~手

선호하다	prefer (over) [~like] ~ 好		선 (宣)	**proclaim; spread**
선택*	choice; option [~select] ~ 擇 선택과목 optional subject		선포*	proclamation [~notify] ~ 布
선거*	election [~lift] ~ 擧		선언*	pronouncement; declaration [~talk] ~ 言
선출*	electing [~come out] ~ 出 선출되다 be elected		선고*	pronouncement; a sentence [~tell] ~ 告
당선*	getting elected; winning an election [suitable~] 當~		선서*	oath; pledge [~oath] ~ 誓
			선교*	missionary work [~religion] ~ 敎
선 (船)	**ship; boat**		선전*	propaganda; advertisement [~propagate] ~ 傳
선박	ship [~ship] ~ 舶			
어선	fishing boat [fishing~] 漁~		선 (鮮)	**fresh**
화물.선	freight vessel; cargo boat [freight~] 貨物~		생선	fresh fish [raw~] 生~
유람선	sightseeing boat [sightseeing tour~] 遊覽~		신선하다	be fresh [new~] 新~
여객선	passenger boat [passenger~] 旅客~		선명하다	be clear; be distinctive [~clear] ~ 明
선장	(ship's) captain [~superior] ~ 長		**설 w(說)**	**theory; explain; talk**
선원	crew; mariner [~member] ~ 員		학설	theory [study~] 學~
			가설	hypothesis [temporary~] 假~
선 w(善)	**the good; virtue**		설명*	explanation [~clear] ~ 明
선하다	be good-natured		해설*	explanation; commentary [explain~] 解~
선량하다	be good-natured [~good] ~ 良		설득*	persuasion [~acquire] ~ 得
선악	good and evil [~evil] ~ 惡		설교*	sermon; preaching [~religion] ~ 敎
선의	good intention [~intention] ~ 意		연설*	public speech [perform~] 演~
최선	one's best [the most~] 最~ 최선의 노력 the utmost efforts		발.설*	divulging; announcement [put forth~] 發~
개선*	improvement; betterment [amend~] 改~		사설	an editorial (article) [society~] 社~
			소설	a novel [small~] 小~
선사하다	give a present [~matter] ~ 事		전설	legend [transmit~] 傳~

음담패설* obscene talk
[obscene conversation perverse~] 淫談悖~

횡설수설* random talk; nonsense
[unreasonable~establish~] 橫~竪~

설 (設) establish

설립* establishment [~stand] ~ 立

창설* establishment; founding
[beginning~] 創~

신설* new establishment;
founding [new~] 新~

설.정* establishment; setting up
[~decide] ~ 定

설치* establishment; installation
[~to place] ~ 置

시설 facilities [grant~] 施~

설계* plan; design [~plan] ~ 計

설사 granted that; even if
[~employ] ~ 使
설·사 그렇다 하더라도
granting that it is so

설 (雪) snow

설경 snowscape [~scenery] ~ 景

폭설 heavy snowfall [cruel~] 暴~

제설작업* snow removal
[remove~] 除~

설.상가상 to make matters worse
[~above add frost] ~上加霜

설탕 sugar [~sugar] ~糖

성 w(性) sex; nature (quality)

성교육* sex education
[~education] ~ 教育

성기 sexual organ [~utensil] ~ 器

성욕 sexual desire [~desire] ~ 慾

성교* sexual intercourse
[~intercourse] ~ 交

성.병 venereal disease
[~disease] ~ 病

남성 man; male [male~] 男~

여성 woman; female
[female~] 女 ~

동성 same sex [same~] 同~
동성연애자 homosexual

이성 opposite sex [different~] 異~

성별 distinction of sex
[~separate] ~ 別

중성 sexlessness; neuter gender
[middle~] 中~

산성 acidity [acid~] 酸~

알칼리.성 alkalinity [alkali~] E ~

식물.성 vegetable property
[plant~] 植物~

동물.성 animal property
[animal~] 動物~
동물·성 단백질
animal protein

양성 positivity [positive~] 陽~

음성 negativity [negative~] 陰~

급성 acute form of a disease
[urgent~] 急~

만성 chronicity [gradual~] 慢~

우성 genetic dominance
[superior~] 優~

본성 original nature; real
character [origin~] 本~

성질 nature; disposition
[~disposition] ~ 質

성미 disposition; temperament
[~taste] ~ 味
성미가 급하다
be short-tempered

ㅅ

천성　nature; innate disposition [nature~] 天~

근성　fundamental nature [root~] 根~

성.격　character; personality [~category] ~格

개성　individuality [individual~] 個~

특성　distinctive quality; characteristic [special~] 特~

속성　essential character [class~] 屬~

이성　reasoning power [principle~] 理~
이성적 rational

실.성하다　become insane [lose~] 失~

중요.성　importance [important~] 重要~

신빙.성　reliability [believe evidence~] 信憑~

식성　likes and dislikes in food; taste [eat~] 食~

성급하다　be hasty [~urgent] ~急

참을.성　patience [to endure~] K~

융통.성　adaptability; flexibility [accommodation~] 融通~

일관.성　consistency; coherence [consistent~] 一貫~

주체.성　subjecthood; self-reliance [chief body~] 主體~

감수.성　sensitivity; susceptibility [feel receive~] 感受~

성능　capacity; efficiency; performance [~ability] ~能
고성능 high fidelity

성 (成)　to complete; make

완성*　completion; finishing [complete~] 完~

달.성*　achieving; attaining [achieve~] 達~
목적을 달.성하다
achieve one's goal

성취*　accomplishing; realization [~complete] ~就
소원성취하다
realize one's wish

성공*　success [~merit] ~功

성.과　result; outcome [~fruit] ~果

형성*　formation [shape~] 形~

구성*　composition; organization [compose~] 構~

성분　ingredient; constituent [~share] ~分

작성*　drawing up (papers); writing out (a contract) [make~] 作~

조성*　creation (of an atmosphere); preparation (of a housing site) [make~] 造~

성인　adult [~person] ~人

성숙하다　be mature [~ripe] ~熟

성장*　growth [~long/elder] ~長

성적　a score; a grade [~result] ~績

찬성*　approval; agreement [agree~] 贊~

성화*　vexation; irritation [~anger] ~火

자수성가*　making one's own fortune [self hand~home] 自手~家

성 (誠)　sincere; sincerity

성의　sincerity [~intention] ~意
성의껏 sincerely; wholeheartedly
성의있다 be sincere

성실하다   be sincere; be faithful
[~genuine] ~ 實

정성   true heart; devotion
[fine~] 精 ~
정성껏 with utmost devotion

효성   filial devotion
[filial piety~] 孝 ~

열.성   earnestness; enthusiasm
[hot~] 熱 ~

성금   donation (of money)
[~money] ~ 金

성 (聲)   voice

음성   voice [sound~] 音 ~

언성   tone of voice [talk~] 言 ~
언성을 높이다
raise one's voice

환성   a shout of joy
[cheerful~] 歡 ~

성악   vocal music [~music] ~ 樂
성악가 vocalist

성우   radio actor/actress;
dubbing artist [~actor] ~ 優

이구동성   (with) one voice; (in)
chorus [different mouth
same~] 異口同 ~

성 (盛)   prosper

왕성하다   be prosperous; be
flourishing [prosper~] 旺 ~
식욕이 왕성하다 have a
strong appetite

풍성하다   (harvest) be abundant
[abundant~] 豊 ~

성황   boom; success
[~situation] ~ 況
성황을 이루다 be a great
success; be well attended

성대하다   be grand; be magnificent
[~big] ~ 大
성대한 파티 splendid banquet

전성기   golden period; one's best
days [all~period] 全 ~期

극성   (personality) being
extreme [extreme~] 極 ~
극성스럽다 be impatient;
be overeager

성 (星)   star; planet

화성   Mars [fire~] 火 ~

토성   Saturn [soil~] 土 ~

혜성   comet; sudden prominence
[comet~] 彗 ~

직성풀리다   be satisfied;
be appeased
[direct~solved] 直 ~ K

성 (聖)   holy; saint

성경   the Holy Bible
[~scripture] ~ 經

성당   Catholic church [~hall] ~ 堂

성인   saint [~person] ~ 人

성탄절   Christmas Day
[~birth festival] ~ 誕節

세 (世)   world; generation

세계   the world [~boundary] ~ 界
세계적 worldwide
세계사 world history

세상   the world [~above] ~ 上
이세상 this world
저세상 the next world
세상없어도 under
any circumstances
세상에 on earth;
(what) in the world

속세   this world; mundane life
[vulgar~] 俗 ~

126

ㅅ

출·세*	success (in life); rising in the world [come out~] 出~	세 (税)	**tax**
처세*	conduct of life [manage~] 處~	세금	tax [~money] ~金
신세	one's circumstances; one's lot [person~] 身~	세무서	tax office [~affair office] ~務署
세대	generation [~generation] ~代 세대차이 generation gap	자동차·세	auto tax [automobile~] 自動車~
이세	second generation [second~] 二~	소득세	income tax [income~] 所得~
후세	future generation [later~] 後~	부가가치·세	value-added tax [add value~]附加價値~
세기	century [~century] ~紀	탈·세*	evasion of taxes [escape~] 脱~

세 (勢) **power; conditions**

세력	influence; power [~strength] ~力
허세	false show of power; a bluff [empty~] 虛~
우세하다	be predominant [superior~] 優~
강세	stress (on a syllable) [strong~] 強~
증세	symptoms [symptom~] 症~
정세	state of affairs [circumstances~] 情~ 국내정세 domestic situation
추세	tendency; trend [hasten~] 趨~
시세	current market price [time~] 時~
자세	posture [nice figure~] 姿~
태세	posture; preparedness [attitude~] 態~ 태세를 갖추다 get fully prepared

면세*	duty-free [exempt~] 免~ 면세점 duty-free shop 면세품 duty-free goods
세관	customhouse [~customhouse] ~關

세 (洗) **wash**

세수*	washing hands and face [~hand] ~手
세탁*	washing clothes [~wash clothes] ~濯 세탁기 washer 세탁소 laundromat; dry cleaning shop
세차*	car washing [~vehicle] ~車 세차장 car wash place
세제	detergent [~medicine] ~劑
세면기	wash bowl [~face utensil] ~面器
세련되다	be polished; be refined [~to train become] ~ 鍊 K
세뇌*	brainwashing [~brain] 腦
세례받다	be baptized [~rite receive] ~ 禮 K

세 ʷ (貰) **rent**

세놓다	rent (to); hire out [~put] ~ K

127

월·세	monthly rent [month~] 月~	주유소	gas station [pour oil~] 注油~
집세	rent for a house [house~] K~	휴게소	rest stop [rest rest~] 休憩~
방·세	rent for a room [room~] 房~	매표소	ticket office [sell ticket~] 賣票~
세·방	room for rent [~room] ~房	형무소	prison [punishment affairs~] 刑務~
전세	rental contract involving prepayment [transmit~] 傳~	파출·소	police substation [branch come out~] 派出~
전세내다	reserve (a vehicle/place) [exclusive~take out] 專~ K 전세버스 chartered bus	발·전소	power plant [shoot electricity~] 發電~
		연구소	research institute [research~] 研究~
세 (歲)	**year; age**	주소	one's address [reside~] 住~ 현주소 current address
세월	time (and tide) [~month] ~月 세월이 빠르다 Time flies.	숙소	temporary abode [lodge~] 宿~
세배*	bow performed on New Year's Day [~bow] ~拜	변소	toilet [excrement~] 便~
만세	hurrah; cheers; long live... [ten thousand~] 萬~	산소	a grave [mountain~] 山~
연세	age (hon.) [year~] 年~	소중하다	be important; be valuable [~weighty] ~重
세 (細)	**minute; delicate**	소지*	possession [~possess] ~持 소지품 one's belongings
세밀하다	be minute; be detailed [~intimate] ~密	소속*	belonging [~belong] ~屬
자세하다	be detailed [tiny~] 仔~	소감	one's impression; opinion [~feeling] ~感
상세하다	be detailed [detail~] 詳~	소행	one's actions; behavior [~act] ~行
세균	germ; microbe [~germ] ~菌	소원*	one's wish [~desire] ~願
세포	cell [~placenta] ~胞	소망*	desire; wish [~hope] ~望
세심하다	be careful; be prudent [~mind] ~心	소득	income; earnings [~gain] ~得
소 (所)	**place; thing; whatsoever**	소유*	possession [~exist] ~有
장소	place [place~] 場~	소용	use; usefulness [~use] ~用
세탁소	laundromat; dry cleaning shop [washing clothes~] 洗濯~	소위	so-called [~speak of] ~謂

ㅅ

소 (素)   **element; simple; ordinary**

요소   essential element [essential~] 要~

소질   makings; talents [~quality] ~ 質
소질이 있다 have the makings (of)

소재   material; subject matter [~material] ~ 材

산소   oxygen [acid~] 酸~

염소   chlorine [salt~] 鹽~

탄소   carbon [coal~] 炭~
이산화탄소 carbon dioxide

질소   nitrogen [obstructed~] 窒~

효소   enzyme [ferment~] 酵~

활력소   tonic; vitamin [vitality~] 活力~

색소   pigment [color~] 色~

소박하다   be simple; be artless [~honest] ~ 朴

검소하다   be frugal [frugal~] 儉~

평소   ordinary times [ordinary~] 平~

소 (消)   **dissolve; disperse; negative**

소독*   disinfection; sterilization [~poison] ~ 毒

해소*   clearing up; solving [release~] 解~
스트레스를 해소하다 get rid of stress

소화기   fire extinguisher [~fire utensil] ~ 火器

소방서   fire station [~defend office] ~ 防署

소방차   fire engine [~defend vehicle] ~ 防車

취소*   cancellation [take~] 取~

소화*   digestion [~change] ~ 化
소화제 digestive aid

소비*   consumption [~spend] ~ 費
소비자 consumer

소모*   consumption; waste [~diminish] ~ 耗

소식   news; information [~news] ~ 息

소풍   picnic; excursion [~wind] ~ 風

소극적   negative; passive [~pole] ~ 極的

소 (小)   **small**

소형   small size; compact model [~model] ~ 型
소형차 small vehicles

소규모   small scale [~scale] ~ 規模

최소   the smallest; minimum [the most~] 最~

협소하다   be small and narrow [narrow~] 狹~

축소*   reduction [shrink~] 縮~

소수   decimal (fraction) [~number] ~ 數

소심하다   be timid [~mind] ~ 心

소포   parcel; package [~wrap] ~ 包

소매*   retail sale [~sell] ~ 賣

소변   urine [~excrement] ~ 便

소설   a novel [~talk] ~ 說

소 (少)   **little; young**

소량   small quantity [~amount] ~ 量

소수   small number; minority [~number] ~ 數

다소   more or less [much~] 多~

129

약소하다	(gift) be little; be scanty [abbreviated~] 略~
감소*	decrease [decrease~] 減~
사소하다	be trivial [little~] 些~
소녀	young girl [~female] ~女
소년	young boy [~age] ~年
연소자	minors; underage people [age~person] 年~者
남녀노소	male and female, old and young [male female old~] 男女老~

소 (疏) loose; far apart

소홀하다	be indifferent; be negligent [~disregard] ~忽 소홀히하다 neglect
소탈하다	be unceremonious; be informal [~escape] ~脫
소통*	mutual understanding [~communicate] ~通 의사소통* communication
소외감	sense of alienation [~outside feeling] ~外感 소외당하다 be alienated
생소하다	be unfamiliar [raw~] 生~

소 (訴) accuse; tell

고소*	(legal) accusation; (filing) a complaint [accuse~] 告~
항소*	an appeal to a higher court [resist~] 抗~
소송*	lawsuit [~suit] ~訟
호소*	an appeal; a petition [call~] 呼~

속 (速) speed(y)

속력	speed [~power] ~力
속도	speed [~degree] ~度 속도위반* speed violation 가속도 degree of acceleration
초속	speed per second [second~] 秒~
시속	speed per hour [hour~] 時~
과속*	excessive speed [excessive~] 過~
감속*	reducing speed [decrease~] 減~
속달	express mail [~delivery] ~達
속기*	shorthand; quick writing [~record] ~記
속단*	hasty conclusion [~cut off] ~斷
신속하다	be prompt [rapid~] 迅~
속히	quickly; promptly [~-ly] ~K

속 (俗) vulgar; customs

저속하다	be vulgar; be base [low~] 低~
속되다	be secular; be earthly [~be] ~K
속세	this world; mundane life [~world] ~世
속물	worldly person [~thing] ~物
속어	slang [~words] ~語
속담	proverb [~saying] ~談
통속적	popular; non-technical [circulate~] 通~ 통속소설 popular novel
풍속	customs; manners [customs~] 風~
민속	folk customs [people~] 民~ 민속촌 folk village
야속하다	be unsympathetic; be unkind [wilderness~] 野~

속 (續) sequel; continue

속편	a sequel [~print] ~ 編
연속*	series; succession [connect~] 連~ 연속해서 consecutively 연속극 soap opera
계속*	continuation [continue~] 繼~
지속*	continuation; maintenance [sustain~] 持~
접속*	connection [connect~] 接~ 접속사 conjunctive word 접속곡 medley (songs)
수속*	procedure [means~] 手~

속 (屬) belong to; class

속하다	belong to
소속*	belonging [thing~] 所~ 소속감 sense of belonging
부속	attachment; affiliation [append~] 附~
금속	metal [metal~] 金~
속성	essential character [~nature] ~性

속 (束) bind; arrest

속박*	restraint; shackles [~tie] ~縛
구속*	restraint; arrest [restrain~] 拘~
단속*	regulation; crackdown [surround~] 團~
약속*	promise; appointment [promise~] 約~
속수무책	helplessness; resourcelessness [~hand no plan] ~手無策

손 (損) lose; damage

손실	loss [~lose] ~失
손해	loss; damage [~harm] ~害 손해보다 suffer a loss
손상*	damage [~injure] ~傷 손상되다 get damaged
파손*	damage; breakage [break~] 破~
결.손가정	dysfunctional family [defect~family] 缺~家庭

손 ʷ(孫) grandchildren; descendant

손자	grandson [~son] ~子
손녀	granddaughter [~female] ~女
자손	offspring [children~] 子~
후손	descendants [after~] 後~

솔 (率) to lead

인솔*	guiding (a group) [pull~] 引~ 인솔·자 leader; guide
통솔*	command; leadership [govern~] 統~ 통솔력 leadership
솔.선수범*	taking the lead; setting an example to others [~ first hang down pattern] ~先垂範
솔.직하다	be frank [~straight] ~直
경솔하다	be thoughtless; be frivolous [light~] 輕~

송 (送) send

우송*	sending by mail [mail~] 郵~
수송*	transportation; conveyance [transport~] 輸~

송금* remittance [~money] ~ 金

환송* farewell; send-off
[cheerful~] 歡 ~
환송회* farewell party

송별* farewell; send-off
[~separate] ~別
송별회* farewell party

전송* seeing off
[farewell entertainment~] 餞 ~

방송* broadcasting [release~] 放 ~

송구* handball [~ball] ~ 球

송 (悚) **fear; regret**

황송하다 be awestruck; be
grateful [emperor~] 皇~

죄송하다 be sorry (for) (hon.)
[guilt~] 罪~
죄송하지만 I am sorry, but...

송구스럽다 feel much obliged;
feel ashamed [~fear] ~ 懼

수 (水) **water**

수분 water; moisture [~share] ~分

냉수 cold water [cold~] 冷~

온수 warm/hot water
[warm~] 溫~

식수 potable water [food~] 食~

음료수 potable water; beverage
[beverage~] 飮料~

폐수 waste water
[abolished~] 廢~

지하수 underground water
[underground~] 地下~

생수 mineral water [living~] 生~

약수 mineral water
[medicine~] 藥~
약숫물 mineral water
약수터 mineral spring resort

수압 water pressure [~press] ~壓

수질 quality of water
[~quality] ~ 質

정수기 water purifier
[clean~machine] 淨~機

방수* waterproof [defend~] 防~

강수량 amount of rainfall
[descend~amount] 降~量

수도 waterworks; waterway
[~way] ~ 道
하수도 sewage system
수돗물 tap water

호수 lake [lake~] 湖~

홍수 flood [vast~] 洪~
홍수나다 be flooded

수해 flood damage [~harm] ~ 害
수해를 입다
suffer flood damage

배수* drainage [push out~] 排~

탈.수* dehydration [take off~] 脫~

수세식 flushing (toilet)
[~wash style] ~ 洗式

식염수 saline salution
[food salt~] 食鹽~

빙수 shaved ice [ice~] 氷~

육수 beef broth [meat~] 肉~

향수 perfume [fragrant~] 香~

분수 a jet; fountain [spout~] 噴~

수평선 horizon [~even line] ~ 平線

수영* swimming [~swim] ~ 泳

수상스키 water skiing
[~above ski] ~ 上E

잠수* submerging [submerge~] 潛~

수산물 marine products
[~produce thing] ~ 産物

수력발전 water-power generation
[~power shoot electricity]
~ 力發電

수채화	watercolor painting [~color picture] ~ 彩畵
수박	watermelon [~gourd] ~ K
수정	crystal [~crystal] ~ 晶
수준	standard; level [~measure] ~ 準
수은	mercury [~silver] ~ 銀 수은주 mercurial column

수 ᵂ (數) number; several; fate

단수	singular number [single~] 單~
복수	plural number [double~] 複~
홀·수	odd number [single~] K~
짝수	even number [pair~] K~
다수	large number [many~] 多~ 대다수 majority
소수	small number; minority [little~] 少~ 극소수 small minority
정수	whole number [right~] 正~
수·자	numeral; figure [~letter] ~ 字
소수	decimal (fraction) [small~] 小~ 소수.점 decimal point
분수	discretion; one's place; one's means; fraction [divide~] 分~ 삼분의 일 one third 가분수 improper fraction
수학	mathematics [~study] 數~
무수하다	be innumerable [no~] 無~
수량	quantity [~amount] ~ 量
수치	numerical value [~value] ~ 值
지·수	numerical index [to point~] 指~

불쾌지.수	discomfort index
물가지.수	price index
햇수	number of years [year~] K~
호.수	the number (of a house) [number~] 號~
회.수	the number of times; frequency [times~] 回~
점.수	marks (grade); score [point~] 點~
등.수	ratings; a grade [rank~] 等~
부지기.수	being numberless [not know that~] 不知其~
치.수	size; measurements [inch~] K~
과반.수	majority [exceed half~] 過半~
수차	several times; time and again [~sequence] ~次
수천	thousands of [~thousand] ~千
수백	hundreds of [~hundred] ~百
재수	one's luck; fortune [property~] 財~
운수	fortune; luck [luck~] 運~
술.수	artifice; trick [artifice~] 術~

수 (手) hand; means

수족	hands and feet; limbs [~foot] ~ 足
악수*	handshaking [grasp~] 握~
세수*	washing hands and face [wash~] 洗~
수건	(hand) towel [~towel] ~ 巾 손.수건 handkerchief
수공	manual work [~work] ~ 工
입수*	coming to hand; obtaining [enter~] 入~

수갑	handcuffs [~case] ~ 匣
수류탄	hand grenade [~pomegranate bullet] ~ 榴彈
수동	manual operation [~move] ~ 動
수술*	surgical operation [~skill] ~ 術
수.법	technique; trick [~rule] ~ 法
수속	procedure [~sequel] ~ 續 수속을 밟다 follow a procedure
수표	cheque [~ticket] ~ 票
수첩	pocket notebook [~document] ~ 帖
수기	memoirs [~record] ~ 記
자수성가*	making one's own fortune [self~make home] 自 ~ 成家
실.수*	mistake [lose~] 失 ~
착수*	launching; embarking on [reach~] 着 ~
조수	an assistant; helper [assist~] 助 ~
투수	(baseball) pitcher [throw~] 投 ~
포수	(baseball) catcher [catch~] 捕 ~
선수	player [select~] 選 ~ 농구선수 basketball player
포수	hunter [gun~] 砲 ~
적수	a rival; a match [enemy~] 敵 ~
수단	means; resource [~step] ~ 段 별수단을 다쓰다 try every possible means 수단이 좋다 be resourceful
가수	singer [song~] 歌 ~
목수	carpenter [wood~] 木 ~
수당	allowance; compensation [~suitable] ~ 當

수 (修)	**cultivate; repair**
수양*	cultivation of the mind; mental training [~raise] ~ 養 정신수양* spiritual culture
연수*	research training; study and training [research~] 研 ~
수학여행*	school excursion (pursuit of knowledge) (pron.=수항녀행) [~learn travel] ~ 學旅行
수료*	completion (of a course) [~complete] ~ 了
재수*	repreparing for college entrance exam [again~] 再 ~
삼수*	preparing for college entrance exam after two failures [third~] 三 ~
수식*	rhetorical flourish [~decorate] ~ 飾
수녀	nun [~woman] ~ 女
보수*	mending; repair [mend~] 補 ~ 보수공사* repair work
수리*	repairs; remodelling (house, car, etc.) [~manage] ~ 理 내부수리중 Closed for alterations
수선*	repairs; mending (clothes, watch, shoes, etc.) [~mend] ~ 繕
수정*	amendment; correction [~correct] ~ 正
수라장	pandemonium [~spread out place] ~ 羅場
수 (收)	**harvest; collect; bind**
추수*	autumn harvest [autumn~] 秋 ~

수확*	harvest; crop [~harvest] ~ 穫	수난*	sufferings; ordeal [~difficulty] ~ 難
징수*	levy; collection (of taxes) [collect~] 徵~	수정*	fertilization [~sperm] ~ 精 인공수정* artificial insemination
매수*	buying over; bribing [buy~] 買~	수동적	passive [~move] ~ 動的
회수*	withdrawal; retrieval [return~] 回~	수강*	taking a course [~lecture] ~ 講
몰.수*	confiscation [sink~] 沒~	수업*	a class [~job] ~ 業

수흡*
수난*
수정*

수확* harvest; crop [~harvest] ~ 穫

징수* levy; collection (of taxes) [collect~] 徵~

매수* buying over; bribing [buy~] 買~

회수* withdrawal; retrieval [return~] 回~

몰.수* confiscation [sink~] 沒~

흡수* absorption [inhale~] 吸~

수입 income [~enter] ~ 入
월수입 monthly income
부수입 side income

수지맞다 (business) be profitable; (person) make profit [~pay agree] ~ 支 K

수습하다 have (the situation) under control; settle [~pick up] ~ 拾

수용* accommodation [~permit] ~ 容
수용인원 the number of persons to be admitted

철.수* withdrawal (of troops) [remove~] 撤~

수축* shrinkage [~shrink] ~ 縮

수 (受) receive

수화기 telephone receiver [~talk machine] ~ 話機

수상* receiving a prize [~prize] ~ 賞
수상자 prize winner

수락* acceptance [~consent] ~ 諾

접수* receipt of an application [receive~] 接~
접수번호 receipt number

감수하다 be ready to suffer; willingly submit [sweet~] 甘 ~

수난* sufferings; ordeal [~difficulty] ~ 難

수정* fertilization [~sperm] ~ 精
인공수정* artificial insemination

수동적 passive [~move] ~ 動的

수강* taking a course [~lecture] ~ 講

수업* a class [~job] ~ 業

수 (首) head

당수 (political) party leader [political party~] 黨 ~

수상 prime minister [~minister] ~ 相

수석* the top [~seat] ~ 席
수석졸업* graduating at the top (of the list)

수도 capital city [~metropolis] ~ 都
수도.권 metropolitan area

수긍* assent; a nod [~affirm] ~ 肯
수긍이 가다 be convinced

교수형 punishment by hanging [hang~punishment] 絞 ~ 刑

자수* self-surrender [self~] 自 ~

수 (守) guard; observe

수위 security guard; custodian [~guard] ~ 衛

수비* defense [~prepare] ~ 備

고수하다 hold fast to [firm~] 固 ~

보수적 conservative [protect~] 保~的

엄수* strict observance [strict~] 嚴 ~

준수* observance (of the law) [conform~] 遵~

135

ㅅ

수 (輸) transport

수송* transportation; conveyance [~send] ~ 送

수입* import [~enter] ~ 入

수출* export [~exit] ~ 出

밀.수* smuggling [secret~] 密~

수혈* blood transfusion [~blood] ~ 血

수 (秀) excellent

우수하다 be excellent [superior~] 優~

준수하다 be superior and refined [excellent~] 俊~

수재 brilliant person [~talent] ~ 才

수 (需) require; essential

수요 a demand [~demand] ~ 要

혼수 articles essential to a marriage [marriage~] 婚~

필.수품 necessities [surely~article] 必~品

숙 (熟) ripe; experienced

반숙* sunnyside-up or soft-boiled (egg) [half~] 半~

성숙하다 be mature [to complete~] 成~

노숙하다 be mature and experienced [old~] 老~

조숙하다 be precocious [early~] 早~

미숙하다 be inexperienced [not yet~] 未~

능숙하다 be skillful; be proficient [ability~] 能~

숙달* attaining proficiency; getting a mastery (of) [~achieve] ~達

친숙하다 be familiar; be well acquainted [friendly~] 親~

익숙하다 be accustomed to [ripe~] K~

숙어 idiomatic phrase [~words] ~ 語

숙 (宿) lodge

숙박* lodging; accommodation [~stay] ~ 泊
숙박료 lodging charges

합숙* lodging together [join~] 合~
합숙훈련* camp training

하숙* boarding; lodging [below~] 下~
하숙집 boarding house

숙식* room and board [~food] ~食

숙소 (temporary) abode [~place] ~ 所

여인숙 second-class inn [travel person~] 旅人~

숙제* homework [~subject] ~ 題

숙직* night duty [~direct] ~ 直

순 (順) (sequence) order; gentle

순서 (sequence) order [~order] ~ 序

순위 order; rank [~position] ~ 位

키순 order in terms of height [height~] K~

나이순 order in terms of age [age~] K~

가나다순 (Korean) alphabetical order K~

어순 word order [words~] 語~

선착순 first come, first served [first arrive~] 先着~

식순 program for a ceremony [ceremony~] 式~

136

순하다	be gentle; be mild	하순	the last ten days of a month [below~] 下 ~
순순히	tamely; without resistance [~~ -ly] ~~ K	육순	being sixty years old [sixth~] 六~
순종하다	follow obediently [~follow] ~ 從	칠.순	being seventy years old [seventh~] 七~
온순하다	be gentle; be docile [warm~] 溫 ~		
유순하다	be docile; be meek [soft~] 柔~	술 (術)	skill; art(iface)
순조롭다	be favorable; be smooth-going [~control] ~調	기술	skill; technique [skill~] 技 ~
		화술	conversational skill [talk~] 話~
순 (純)	pure	예술	art [art~] 藝 ~
순수하다	be pure; be genuine [~pure] ~ 粹	학술	arts and sciences [study~] 學~
불.순하다	be impure [not~] 不~	미술	fine arts [beauty~] 美~
순결*	purity; chastity [~clean] ~潔	호신술	the art of self-defense [protect body~] 護身~
순거짓말	pure fabrication [~lie] ~K	침술	the art of acupuncture [acupuncture needle~] 鍼~
순금	pure gold [~gold] ~ 金	의술	medical arts; medical practice [medical science~] 醫~
순면	pure cotton [~cotton] ~ 綿		
순모	pure wool [~wool] ~ 毛	수술*	surgical operation [hand~] 手 ~
순정	pure heart [~feeling] ~ 情		성형수술* plastic surgery 정형수술* orthopedic operation
청순하다	be pure and innocent [clean~] 清 ~		
순진하다	be innocent; be naive [~genuine] ~ 眞	술.수	artifice; trick [~number] ~ 數 술.수를 쓰다 resort to tricks
단순하다	be simple; be simple-minded [simple~] 單 ~	상술	business trick [business~] 商~
순전히	completely; utterly [~complete -ly] ~全 K	요술	magic; witchcraft [bewitching~] 妖~ 요술부리다 use magic
		마술	magic [demon~] 魔~ 마술부리다 use magic
순 (旬)	ten days/years	최면술	hypnotism [hypnotism~] 催眠~
초순	the first ten days of a month [beginning~] 初 ~		
중순	the middle ten days of a month [middle~] 中~		

심술   ill-natured temperament
[mind~] 心~

習 (習)   **study; practice**

학습*   studying; drilling
[study~] 學~

자습*   self-study [self~] 自~

예습*   preview (of studies)
[beforehand~] 豫~

복습*   review (of studies)
[return~] 復~

습득*   learning; acquisition
[~acquire] ~ 得

연습*   practice; exercise
[practice~] 鍊~

강습*   (short) training course
[lecture~] 講~
강습을 받다
take a short course

실습*   practical training [real~] 實~

습관*   habit [~habit] ~ 慣
습관적 habitual

습성   habit; second nature
[~nature] ~ 性

관습   custom; convention
[habit~] 慣~

풍습   customs; manners
[customs~] 風~

상습   habitual practice
[usual~] 常~

習 (濕)   **wet; damp(ness)**

습하다   be damp; be moist

습기   moisture; dampness
[~energy] ~ 氣
습기가 많다 be damp

습도   humidity [~degree] ~ 度
습도가 높다 be humid

가습기   humidifier
[add~machine] 加~機

습진   eczema; moist tetter
[~pustule] ~ 疹

習 (襲)   **surprise attack**

기습*   surprise attack
[mysterious~] 奇~

습격*   an attack; a raid
[~attack] ~ 擊

공습*   air raid [air~] 空~
공습경보 air raid alarm

모습   figure; appearance
[countenance~] 模~

勝 (勝)   **win**

승자   winner [~person] ~ 者

승리*   victory [~gain] ~ 利

우승*   victory; championship
[superior~] 優~
준우승* victory
in the semi-finals

연승*   victories in a row
[connected~] 連~

필승   certain victory
[certainly~] 必~

승부   victory or defeat; outcome
[~lose] ~ 負
무승부 undecided match

승패   victory or defeat;
outcome [~lose] ~ 敗

결승(전)   championship game
[decide~fight] 決~戰

판정승*   a win on a decision
[judge decide~] 判定~

乘 (乘)   **ride**

승마*   horseback-riding
[~horse] ~ 馬

합승* riding together; sharing a vehicle [join~] 合~

탑승* boarding (a plane; a ship) [board~] 搭~

승차* getting in a vehicle [~vehicle] ~車
승차.권 passenger ticket

승객 passenger [~guest] ~客

승용차 passenger car [~use vehicle] ~用車

(삼)인승 for (three) passengers [three person~] 三人~

승무원 (member of) the crew [~duty member] ~務員
비행기 승무원 flight attendant

시 (時) **time**

시일 time; days [~day] ~日
시일이 걸리다 take time (many days)

시간 hour; time [~interval] ~間
시간표 time table
시간이 걸리다 take time

동시 same time [same~] 同~
동시에 at the same time
동시상영* a double feature

평상시 ordinary times; normally [ordinary usual~] 平常~

시사 current events [~matter] ~事
시사영어 current English
시사문제 current issues

시국 situation; the times [~circumstances] ~局

시차 jet lag [~difference] ~差

잠시 a short while [moment~] 暫~

임시 temporary [temporary~] 臨~
임시로 temporarily

일시적 transient; passing [one~] 一 ~的

시세 current market price [~conditions] ~勢

즉시 immediately [immediate~] 即~

시속 speed per hour [~speed] ~速

우천시 in case of rain [rain sky~] 雨天~

불·시에 unexpectedly; by surprise [no~] 不~ K

한시도 even for a moment [one~even] K~ K

당시 at that time; in those days [suitable~] 當~

수시로 at any time; from time to time [follow~] 隨~ K

시한폭탄 time bomb [~limit bomb] ~限爆彈

시계 watch; clock [~calculate] ~計
손목시계 wrist watch
탁상시계 table-top clock
벽시계 wall clock

시급하다 be urgent [~urgent] ~急

비상시 emergency [emergency~] 非常~

시기 opportunity; the right time [~opportunity] ~機

시대 time; era [~generation] ~代
원자력시대 the atomic age
시대에 뒤떨어지다 be out-of-date

시절 time; period [~season] ~節
학생시절 school days

시 ᵂ (市) **city; market**

도시 city [metropolis~] 都~

시청 city hall [~government office] ~廳

시내 within the city; downtown [~inside] ~內

139

시외	outskirts of a city; suburbs [~outside] ~ 外
시민	citizen [~people] ~民
시립	municipal; city-established [~establish] ~ 立
특별시	special city (Seoul) [special~] 特別~
직할시	special city under the direct control of the central government [direct control~] 直轄~
시장	mayor [~superior] ~ 長
시장	market place [~place] ~ 場
시중	the open market [~middle] ~ 中
시판*	marketing; sale at a market [~sell] ~ 販
시·가	market price [~price] ~ 價
개시*	first sale (of the day) [open~] 開~

시 (視) look at

시청*	seeing and hearing (TV) [~hear] ~ 聽 시청자 TV audience 시청각 audiovisual
시력	eyesight [~power] ~力
근시	nearsightedness [near~] 近~
원시	farsightedness [far~] 遠~
시선	line of vision; one's gaze [~line] ~ 線 시선을 끌다 attract gaze
주시하다	stare at; observe closely [pour~] 注~
시찰*	inspection; observation [~observe] ~ 察
중(요)시하다	take a serious view of; make much of [important~] 重要~

경시하다	make little of [light~] 輕~
천시*	looking down on; slight [lowly~] 賤~
무시*	disregarding [not~] 無~
멸·시*	contempt; disdain [despise~] 蔑~ 멸·시당하다 be held in contempt

시 (示) manifest; show

표시*	indication; expression; a sign [manifest~] 表~
명시*	clear statement; elucidation [clear~] 明~
암시*	allusion; a hint [secret~] 暗~
게시*	a notice; bulletin [raise~] 揭~ 게시판 bulletin board
전시*	exhibition; display [unfold~] 展 ~
지시*	instruction; direction [to point~] 指~
제시*	presentation (of ideas, etc.) [suggest~] 提~
과시*	ostentation; showing off [brag~] 誇~
시범*	demonstrating (by examples); model [~pattern] ~ 範 시범을 보이다 demonstrate
시위*	demonstration (rally) [~dignity] ~威 반정부 시위* antigovernment demonstration

시 (媤) husband's home

시댁	one's husband's family/house (hon.) [~house (hon.)] ~ 宅

ㅅ

시집   one's husband's family/house [~house] ~ K
시집가다   marry (a man)
시집살이*   living with one's husband's parents

시부모   one's husband's parents [~parents] ~ 父母

시아버지   one's husband's father [~father] ~ K

시어머니   one's husband's mother [~mother] ~ K

시누이   one's husband's sister [~male's sister] ~ K

시동생   one's husband's younger brother [~younger sibling] ~ 同生

시 (試) test; try

시험*   exam; test [~examine] ~ 驗
시험삼아   as an experiment
시험공부*   preparation for an examination

고시   exam [examine~] 考~
검정고시   equivalency exam

응시*   applying for an exam; taking an exam [respond~] 應~

입시   entrance exam [school admission~] 入~ (<입학시험)

시도*   trying out; attempt [~diagram] ~ 圖

시련   trial; ordeal [~to train] ~ 鍊

시합*   a match; game [~join] ~ 合

시행착오   trial and error [~act error] ~ 行錯誤

시 (始) begin

시초   beginning; inception [~beginning] ~ 初

시작*   beginning [~make] ~ 作

시동   starting (an engine) [~move] ~ 動
시동을 걸다   start an engine

창시*   originating; founding [beginning~] 創~
창시자   originator; founder

원시적   primitive [origin~] 原~的

시종일관   consistently; from start to finish [~finish consistent] ~ 終一貫

시 (施) grant

시행*   putting in force; enforcing [~act] ~ 行

실시*   putting in practice; enforcing [real~] 實~

시설   facilities [~establish] ~ 設

시 ʷ (詩) poetry

시인   poet [~person] ~ 人

시집   collection of poems [~gather] ~ 集

동시   children's verse [children~] 童~

식 (食) food; eat

음식   food [drink~] 飮~
음식점   restaurant

양식   foodstuffs [food~] 糧~

식량   provisions; foodstuffs [~food] ~ 糧

식품   foodstuffs; groceries [~goods] ~ 品
불량식품   substandard, unsanitary food
식료품   foodstuffs; groceries

주식   staple food [chief~] 主~

ㅅ

한식   Korean food [Korea~] 韓~

양식   western food [western~] 洋~

후식   dessert [after~] 後~

별식   rare dish [special~] 別~

정식   (restaurant's) regular meal [decide~] 定~

혼식*   meal of mixed rice [mix~] 混~

분식   flour-based meals [powder~] 粉~

식빵   (plain) bread; table bread [~bread] ~ K

침식   sleep and food; room and board [sleep~] 寢~

숙식*   room and board [lodge~] 宿~

식중독   food poisoning [~poisoning] ~ 中毒

식사*   (having) a meal [~matter] ~ 事

식후   after meals [~after] ~ 後

외식*   eating out [outside~] 外~

회식*   dining together (in a group with coworkers) [gather~] 會~

포식*   eating one's fill; satiation [full stomach~] 飽~

과식*   overeating [excessive~] 過~

간식*   eating between meals; snack [between~] 間~

식비   grocery expenses [~expense] ~ 費

식권   meal ticket [~ticket] ~ 券

식당   restaurant [~hall] ~ 堂

식단   menu [~unit] ~.單

식탁   dining table [~table] ~ 卓

대식가   big eater [big~person] 大~家

식욕   appetite [~desire] ~ 慾

식성   likes and dislikes in food; taste [~nature] ~ 性
식성이 까다롭다
be particular about food

육식*   meat diet [meat~] 肉~

채식*   vegetarian diet [vegetable~] 菜~

이유식*   weaning diet [leave milk~] 離乳~

편식*   unbalanced diet [lean toward~] 偏~

식이요.법*   dietary treatment [~bait treatment method] ~餌療法

단식*   fasting [cut off~] 斷~
단식투쟁*   hunger strike

식인종   cannibal tribe [~person a kind] ~ 人種

식기   tableware [~utensil] ~ 器

식칼   kitchen knife [~knife] ~ K

식모   kitchen-maid [~mother] ~ 母

식수   potable water [~water] ~ 水
식염수   saline salution

식초   (table) vinegar [~vinegar] ~ 醋

식용유   cooking oil [~use oil] ~ 用油

식혜   fermented rice punch [~sweet-sour wine] ~ 醯

식구   family members [~mouth] ~ 口

식 ᵂ(式) **style; ceremony; formula**

신식   new style; new mode [new~] 新~

구식   old style [old~] 舊~

재래식	conventional style [conventional~] 在來~	주식	stocks [stock~] 株~ 주식회사 company
양식	mode; style [pattern~] 樣~		
형식	formality [form~] 形~	식 (識)	**know; recognize**
격식	rule; formality [rule~] 格~ 격식을 차리다 stick to formality	지식	knowledge [know~] 知~
		유식하다	be learned; be educated [exist~] 有~
공식	formula; official ceremony [official~] 公~	무식하다	be ignorant; be illiterate [not~] 無~
정식	regular form; (legal) formalities [right~] 正~ 정식으로 formally; in due form	상식	common sense [usual~] 常~
		인식*	cognition; understanding [consent~] 認~
방식	form; method [method~] 方~	의식*	consciousness; awareness [intention~] 意~ 무의식 unconsciousness 무의식중에 involuntarily 잠재의식 subconsciousness
단식	(tennis) singles [single~] 單~		
복식	(tennis) doubles [double~] 複~		
수세식	flushing (toilet) [water wash~] 水洗~	식별*	discernment [~separate] ~別
장례식*	funeral rites [funeral~] 葬禮~	식 (植)	**plant**
결혼식*	wedding ceremony [wedding~] 結婚~	식물	plant; vegetation [~thing] ~物
졸업식*	graduation ceremony [graduation~] 卒業~	식목일	Arbor Day [~tree day] ~木日
기념식*	commemorative ceremony [commemoration~] 紀念~	이식*	transplantation [move~] 移~ 심장이식* heart transplant
개막식*	opening ceremony (for a sporting event) [open curtain~] 開幕~	식민지	colony; settlement [~people place] ~民地
폐막식*	closing ceremony (for a sporting event) [close curtain~] 閉幕~	식 (飾)	**decorate**
		장식*	ornament; decoration [decorate~] 裝~
착복식*	celebration for wearing new clothes [wear clothes~] 着服~	가식	hypocrisy; dissimulation [false~] 假~
식장	ceremonial hall [~place] ~場	수식*	rhetorical flourish [cultivate~] 修~
식순	program of a ceremony [~order] ~順		

신 (新)	**new; fresh**
최신	the newest [the most~] 最~
신식	new style; new mode [~style] ~ 式 최신식 newest style
신형	new model [~model] ~ 型 최신형 latest model
신설*	new establishment; founding [~establish] ~ 設
신곡	new song [~song] ~ 曲
신기록	new record [~record] ~ 記錄
신제품	new product [~product] ~ 製品
신생아	newborn baby [~born child] ~ 生兒
신인	new face (entertainer) [~person] ~ 人
신참	newcomer [~participate] ~ 參
신입생	new student; freshman [~enter student] ~ 入生
신정	New Year's Day (by solar calendar) [~January] ~ 正
신문	newspaper [~hear] ~ 聞
신혼	new marriage [~marriage] ~ 婚
신랑	bridegroom [~husband] ~ 郎
신부	bride [~married woman] ~ 婦
혁신*	a reform; innovation [revolt~] 革~
신선하다	be fresh [~fresh] ~鮮
참신하다	be original; be novel [behead~] 斬~

신 (身)	**body; person**
전신	whole body [whole~] 全~

신체	body; physique [~body] ~體 신체검사 physical checkup 신체장애자 physically handicapped person
상반신	upper half of the body [above half~] 上半~
하반신	lower half of the body [below half~] 下半~
신장	stature; height [~long] ~ 長
장신구	personal ornaments; personal outfittings [decorate~tool] 裝~具
(몸)보신*	invigorating one's body by taking tonics [body supplement~] K 補~
출.신	a graduate; affiliation; origin [come out~] 出~
팔.등신	well-proportioned figure [eight equal~] 八等~
피신*	secret escape [escape~] 避~
문신	tattoo [writing~] 文~
신분	social standing; identity [~share] ~ 分 신분증명서 ID card
신원	one's identity [~principal] ~元
신세	one's circumstances; one's lot [~world] ~ 世 신세타령하다 bewail one's lot
대신*	substitution; replacement [substitute~] 代~ ...대신(에) instead of...
처신*	behavior; conduct [manage~] 處~
망신*	losing face [lose~] 亡~
헌신*	self-sacrifice; devotion [offer~] 獻~

신 (信)	**believe**
신념	belief; faith [~thought] ~ 念
확신*	firm belief; conviction [certain~] 確~
신앙	belief; religion [~respect] ~ 仰
신자	believer [~person] ~ 者 불교신자 Buddhist 기독교신자 Christian
신도	believer [~disciple] ~ 徒
신용*	trust; credit [~use] ~ 用 신용있다 be trustworthy 신용을 잃다 lose one's credit 신용카드 credit card
신뢰*	trust [~trust] ~ 賴
불.신*	distrust [not~] 不~
자신*	self-confidence [self~] 自~ 자신있다 have confidence 자신감 confident feeling
과신*	overconfidence [excessive~] 過~
신조	creed; principle [~clause] ~ 條 생활신조 principles of life
신빙.성	reliability [~evidence nature] ~ 憑性 신빙.성이 있다 be reliable
위신	prestige; dignity [dignity~] 威~
배신*	betrayal [the back~] 背~
통신*	correspondence; communication [communicate~] 通~
신호*	a signal [~number] ~ 號
미신	superstition [confused~] 迷~

신 ᵂ(神)	**god; spirit**
여신	goddess [female~] 女~
귀신	ghost; demon [ghost~] 鬼~

신령	divine spirit [~spirits] ~ 靈 산신령 mountain god
신부	Catholic priest [~father] ~ 父
신학	theology [~study] ~ 學
신화	myth [~story] ~ 話
신비*	mystery [~secret] ~秘
신기하다	be marvelous; be miraculous [~mysterious] ~奇
신통하다	be marvelous; be extraordinary [~communicate] ~ 通
신동	child prodigy [~child] ~童
정신	mind; spirit [spirit~] 精~ 정신적 mental; psychological
신경	nerve [~pass through] ~ 經 신경쓰다 mind; worry 신경질 nervous temperament 신경통 neuralgia

실 (實)	**fruit; real(ity); genuine**
결.실*	bearing fruit; fruition [result~] 結~ 결.실을 맺다 bear fruits
현실	reality [current~] 現~
실.제	reality; actuality [~about] ~ 際 실.제로 in reality; actually
실물	real thing/person [~thing] ~ 物
실력	real ability [~ability] ~ 力 실력껏 to the full extent of one's ability
실.지	practicality; actuality [~place] ~ 地 실.지로 in practice; practically 실.지경험* practical experience
실기	practical skill [~skill] ~ 技

실.습* practical training [~practice] ~ 習

실용 practical use; utility [~use] ~ 用
실용.성 practicality
실용적 practical

실례 actual example [~example] ~例

실감* actual feeling [~feeling] ~ 感

실.정 actual circumstances [~circumstances] ~ 情

실.적 actual results [~result] ~ 積

실화 true story [~story] ~ 話

실.속 substance; real content [~inside] ~ K
실.속있다 be substantial

충실하다 be substantial; be solid (in contents) [full~] 充~

확실하다 be certain; be sure [certain~] 確~

사실 fact; truth [matter~] 事~
기정사실 established fact

실은 in fact ~ K

실토* true confession; telling the truth [~vomit] ~ 吐

이실직고* reporting the truth [with~straight tell] 以~直告

진실* truth; sincerity [true~] 眞 ~

충실하다 be faithful; be loyal [loyal~] 忠~

성실하다 be sincere; be faithful [sincere~] 誠 ~

실.시* enforcing; putting in practice [~grant] ~施

실천* putting into practice [~tread upon] ~ 踐

실행* carrying out; practice [~act] ~ 行

실현* realization; actualization [~appear] ~ 現
실현되다 come true

실험* experimentation [~examine] ~ 驗

실없다 be untrustworthy; be silly [~not exist] ~K

구실 excuse; pretext [mouth~] 口 ~

착실하다 be steady and honest; be trustworthy [attach~] 着 ~

절.실하다 be immediate; be urgent [earnest~] 切~
절실히 keenly; urgently

유명무실* being titular; being nominal [exist name no~] 有名無~

실 (室) room

교실 classroom [teaching~] 教~

강의실 lecture room [lecture~] 講義~

연구실 research room [research~] 研究~

도서실 library (room) [books~] 圖書~

독서실 reading room [reading~] 讀書~

침실 bedroom [sleep~] 寢~

거실 living room [dwell~] 居 ~

화장실 bathroom [makeup~] 化粧~

욕실 bathing room [bathe~] 浴~

실내 indoors [~inside] ~ 內
실내장식* interior decoration

실외 outdoors [~outside] ~ 外

탈의실 locker room; changing room [take off clothes~] 脫衣~

응접실	reception room [respond receive~] 應接~	실.수*	mistake [~hand] ~ 手
휴게실	a lounge [rest rest~] 休憩~	실례*	discourtesy; breach of etiquette [~etiquette] ~ 禮 실례지만 Excuse me, but...
대합실	(railway station) waiting room [wait join~] 待合~	실책	faulty policy; blunder [~plan] ~ 策
지하실	basement [underground~] 地下~	실패*	failure [~lose] ~ 敗
응급실	emergency room [emergency~] 應急~	실.종*	disappearance; missing [~footprint] ~ 踪
입원실	(sick) ward [hospitalization~] 入院~		
특실	special room [special~] 特~	심 (心)	mind; heart
양호실	school clinic [care care~] 養護~	심리	mentality; psychology [~principle] ~理 심리적 psychological
회의실	conference room [conference~] 會議~	심.적	mental; psychological ~ 的
과장실	(department) chairperson's office [chairperson~] 課長~	동심	child's mind; naiveté [children~] 童 ~
사무실	office [business~] 事務~	안심*	peace of mind; relief [peaceful~] 安~
미용실	beauty parlor [cosmetology~] 美容~	결.심*	making up one's mind; resolution [decide~] 決~
온실	green house [warm~] 溫~	심란하다	be in mental turmoil [~chaotic] ~ 亂
실 (失)	lose; lack of	명심*	bearing in mind [engrave~] 銘~
분실*	losing (things) [confused~] 紛~ 분실물 lost article	변심*	change of mind; falling out of love [change~] 變~
손실	loss [lose~] 損~	이심전심	mental telepathy [with~transmit~] 以~傳~
상실*	loss; forfeiture [lose~] 喪~ 기억상실증 amnesia	본심	real intention [origin~] 本~
실.직*	losing one's job [~post] ~ 職	흑심	evil intention [dark~] 黑~
실업자	unemployed person [~job person] ~ 業者	욕심	greed [greed~] 慾~
실망*	disappointment [~hope] ~ 望	야심	ambition; sinister design [wilderness~] 野~
실연하다	be lovelorn; be broken hearted [~love] ~ 戀	앙심	grudge; spite [grudge~] 怏~ 앙심을 품.다 bear a grudge
실.성하다	become insane [~nature] ~性	인내.심	patience [patience~] 忍耐~

ㅅ

경쟁.심	competitive spirit [competition~] 競爭~
방심*	inattention; being off one's guard [release~] 放~
조심*	carefulness; precaution [hold~] 操~
세심하다	be careful; be prudent [minute~] 細~
유심히	attentively; carefully [exist~-ly] 有~K
관심	concern; interest [concern~] 關~ 관심이 있다 be interested 무관심* indifference
양심	conscience [good~] 良~
수치.심	shame [shame~] 羞恥~
호기.심	curiosity; inquisitiveness [like mysterious~] 好奇~
자부.심	pride; self-conceit [self-confident~] 自負~
근심*	anxiety; worry
의심*	doubt; suspicion [doubt~] 疑~
심술	ill-natured temperament [~artifice] ~術 심술부리다 act cross 심술쟁이/꾸러기 ill-natured person
심·보	nature; temper ~K 심·보가 고약하다 be ill-natured
무심하다	be unwitting [no~] 無~ 무심코 inadvertently
열.심이다	be earnest; be enthusiastic [hot~be] 熱~K
합심하다	be united; be of one accord [unite~] 合~
일.심동체	being one in flesh and spirit [one~same body] 一~同體

소심하다	be timid [small~] 小~
한심하다	be deplorable [cold~] 寒~
작심삼일	resolution good for only three days; short-lived resolution [make~three days] 作~三日
심장	heart; nerve [~viscera] ~臟 심장마비 heart attack 강심장 nerve; guts
진심	true heart; sincerity [true~] 眞~ 진심으로 with true heart
인심	human heart [person~] 人~ 인심좋다 be good-hearted; be generous
인심	benevolent heart [benevolent~] 仁~ 인심쓰다 act generously; display one's liberality
일편단심	devoted heart; fidelity [one piece red~] 一片丹~
심정	one's feelings [~feeling] ~情
환심	good graces; favor [cheerful~] 歡~ 환심을 사다 curry (a person's) good graces
노파.심	excessive solicitude [old woman~] 老婆~
애국심	patriotism [love country~] 愛國~
핵심	core; point [nucleus~] 核~
중심	the center; the middle [middle~] 中~
점심	lunch [dot~] 點~
심 (深)	**deep**
심야	late night [~night] ~夜
심각하다	be serious [~engrave] ~刻

ㅇ

의미심장하다 be profound
in meaning; be
deeply significant
[meaning~long] 意味~長

심 (審) **judge; examine**

심사* judging; screening
[~inspect] ~ 查
심사위원 screening committee

심판* refereeing; a referee
[~judge] ~ 判
심판보다 act as referee

주심 chief referee [main~] 主~

부심 assistant referee
[second~] 副~

미심쩍다 be questionable;
be dubious [no~] 未~ K

십 ʷ(十) **ten**

십대 teenager; teen years
[~generation] ~ 代

십중팔구 nine out of ten; most
likely [~among eight nine]
~中八九

(열)십자 a cross [ten~letter] K~ 字
십자가 crucifix

ㅆ

쌍 (雙) **a pair**

(한)쌍 (a) couple; (a) pair
[one~] K~

쌍꺼풀 double eyelid [~skin] ~ K

쌍둥이 twin children
[~children] ~ 童 K

아 (兒) **child**

아동 children [~children] ~ 童

우량아 physically superior child
[superior good~] 優良~

문제아 problem child
[problem~] 問題~

기형아 deformed child
[deformity~] 畸形~

정박아 mentally retarded child
[essence poor~] 精薄~

아녀자 women and children
[~woman] ~ 女子

고아 orphan [alone~] 孤~

신생아 newborn baby
[new born~] 新生~

유아 infant; baby [infantile~] 幼~
유아용품 baby supplies

태아 embryo; fetus [womb~] 胎~

소아과 pediatrics
[small~department] 小~科

산아제한* population control
[produce~limit] 産~制限

아 (阿) **flatter**

아첨* flattery [~flatter] ~ 諂

아부* flattery [~paste] ~ 附

아교 glue [~glue] ~ 膠

아편 opium [~piece] ~ 片

아 (雅) **elegant**

우아하다 be graceful and elegant
[excellent~] 優~

149

ㅇ

| 아담하다 | be elegant; be dainty [~clear] ~ 淡 |
| 아량 | magnanimity [~amount] ~量 |

악 ᵂ(惡) evil; bad

악하다	be bad; be wicked
선악	good and evil [good~] 善~
악의	malice; bad will [~intention] ~意
악담*	curse; speaking evil [~talk] ~談
악연	unfortunate affinity; evil connection [~affinity] ~緣
악당	scoundrel; rascal [~group] ~黨
악마	evil spirit; devil [~demon] ~魔
악처	bad wife [~wife] ~妻
악질	evil nature; vicious person [~quality] ~質
악종	bad character [~seed] ~種
죄악	crime; sin [crime~] 罪 ~
흉악하다	(crime) be heinous; (looks) be unseemly [cruel~] 凶~
악명높다	be notorious [~name high] ~名K
악랄하다	be vicious; be nasty; be knavish [~peppery] ~辣
우악스럽다	be rough; be crude [stupid~] 愚 ~
최악	the worst [the most~] 最~ 최악의 경우에는 if worst comes to worst
악몽	nightmare [~dream] ~夢
악용*	abuse; improper use [~use] ~用

악순환	vicious cycle [~cycle] ~循環
악화*	worsening; aggravation [~change] ~化
악취	bad smell [~smell] 臭
험악하다	(looks, weather) be threatening; be rough [rough~] 險 ~

악 (樂) music

음악	music [sound~] 音 ~
성악	vocal music [voice~] 聲~
관현악	orchestral music [pipe string~] 管絃~
풍악	traditional Korean music [custom~] 風~
악보	sheet music [~musical note] ~譜
악기	musical instrument [~utensil] ~器
악단	orchestra; band [~group] ~團

악 (握) grasp

파악*	grasping; understanding [hold~] 把 ~
장악*	holding (power) [palm~] 掌 ~
악수*	handshaking [~hand] ~ 手

안 (安) peaceful; safe

안심*	peace of mind; relief [~mind] ~心
편안하다	be peaceful; be comfortable [convenient~] 便~
위안*	consolation; comfort [console~] 慰~

ㅇ

안녕* well-being; good health [~peaceful] ~寧

안락* ease; comfort [~joyful] ~樂
안락사 mercy killing
안락의자 armchair

안정* a rest; repose [~serene] ~靜

불안* uneasiness [not~] 不~

미안하다 be sorry; be regrettable [not~] 未~

안부 well-being; news [~not alright] ~否
...에게 안부 전해 주세요
Please give my regards to...

안정 stability [~decide] ~定
안정되다 be stablized

안도* relief [~embankment] ~堵
안도의 한숨을 쉬다
heave a sigh of relief

안보 national security [~protect] ~保

안전* safety [~whole] ~全
안전벨트 safety belt

안타 a hit (in baseball) [~hit] ~打

안 (眼) eye

육안 naked eye [flesh~] 肉~

혈안이 되다 be frantic about
(e.g., money)
[blood~become] 血 ~ K

안중에 없다 be out of one's thoughts
[~middle not exist] ~中 K

검안* eye examination
[examine~] 檢~

안·과 ophthalmology
[~department] ~科

안약 eye medicine
[~medicine] ~藥

안대 eyepatch [~belt] ~帶

노안 eyesight of the aged;
farsightedness [old~] 老~

안경 glasses [~mirror] ~鏡

안 ᵂ(案) plan; document; desk

방안 plan; scheme [method~] 方~

묘안 excellent plan
[exquisite~] 妙~

고안* devising; contrivance
[think~] 考~

제안* proposal; suggestion
[suggest~] 提~

감안하다 take into account
[consider~] 勘~

답안 written answers to exam
questions [reply~] 答~

안내* guidance; ushering
[~inside] ~內
안내소 information booth
안내방송* information
broadcasting

안 (顔) face

동안 childlike face [child~] 童~

안색 complexion; face color
[~color] ~色
안색이 나쁘다 look unwell

안면 acquaintance [~face] ~面
안면이 있다 be acquainted
with (a person)

무안 shame [no~] 無~
무안하다 be embarrassed
무안을 주다 embarrass
(a person)

암 (暗) dark; secret

암흑 darkness [~black] ~黑

명암 brightness and darkness
[bright~] 明~

151

ㅇ

암담하다	be gloomy; be hopeless [~gloomy] ~ 澹
암시장	black market [~market] ~ 市場
암표	illegal ticket [~ticket] ~ 票 암표상 ticket scalper
암기*	memorization [~record] ~ 記
암산*	mental calculation [~calculate] ~ 算
암시*	hint; suggestion [~manifest] ~ 示
암호	password [~name] ~ 號
암살*	assassination [~kill] ~ 殺

암 ʷ(癌) cancer

피부암	skin cancer [skin~] 皮膚~
위암	stomach cancer [stomach~] 胃 ~
간암	liver cancer [liver~] 肝 ~
유방암	breast cancer [breast~] 乳房~
암세포	cancer cell [~cell] ~ 細胞
암환자	cancer patient [~patient] ~ 患者
항암제	anticancer medicine [defy~medicine] 抗 ~ 劑
발암물.질	carcinogen [rise~material] 發 ~ 物質

암 (岩) rock

암석	rock [~stone] ~ 石
암벽등반*	rock climbing [~wall climbing] ~ 壁登攀
용암	lava [smelt~] 熔~

압 (壓) press(ure); repress

압력	pressure; stress [~strength] ~ 力
혈압	blood pressure [blood~] 血~ 고/저혈압 high/low blood pressure
수압	water pressure [water~] 水 ~
기압	air pressure [air~] 氣~ 고/저기압 high/low atmospheric pressure
전압	voltage [electricity~] 電~
지압	finger-pressure (therapy) [finger~] 指~
압축*	compression [~shrink] ~ 縮
압박*	oppression; persecution [~oppress] ~ 迫
억압*	oppression (of freedom) [suppress~] 抑~
강압적	coercive; oppressive [force~] 強 ~ 的
탄압*	oppression; suppression [a spring~] 彈 ~
진압*	quelling (a riot) [suppress~] 鎭 ~
압도*	overwhelming [~fall down] ~ 倒 압도적 승리 overwhelming victory

압 (押) push; press

압정	tack; pushpin [~nail] ~ 釘
압핀	tack; pushpin [~pin] ~ E
압수*	confiscation [~collect] ~收

애 (愛) love

| 애정 | affection [~feeling] ~ 情 |

ㅇ

애착	attachment [~attach] ~ 着 애착을 가지다/느끼다 be attached to	애걸*	begging; imploring [~beg] ~ 乞
모성애	motherly love [mother nature~] 母性~	애원*	entreaty; supplication [~desire] ~ 願
연애*	(romantic) love; going steady [love~] 戀~	**액 (額)**	**amount (of money)**
애칭	term of endearment [~call] ~ 稱	금액	amount of money [money~] 金~
편애*	being partial to; favoritism [lean toward~] 偏~	액수	amount of money [~number] ~ 數
애교	winsomeness [~charming] ~ 嬌	총액	total amount of money [all~] 總~
우애	brotherliness; fraternity [friend~] 友~	거액	huge amount of money [big~] 巨~
애인	girl/boyfriend; one's love [~person] ~ 人	액면	face value [~face] ~ 面 액면 그대로 at face value
애처가	devoted husband [~wife specialist] ~ 妻家	잔액	balance (in an account) [remainder~] 殘~
애국*	love of one's country [~country] ~ 國	반액	half the price [half~] 半~
총애하다	favor [favor~] 寵~	**액 (液)**	**liquid**
애지중지하다	treasure; love and prize [~it important it] ~之重之	액체	liquid [~body] ~ 體
애주가	alcohol lover [~liquor specialist] ~ 酒家	혈액	blood [blood~] 血~ 혈액순환 blood circulation
애완동물	pet animal [~play with animal] ~ 玩動物 애완견 pet dog	정액	semen [essential~] 精~
애용*	regular use [~use] ~ 用	**야 (野)**	**wilderness; outside; field**
애 (哀)	**sorrow**	야생동물	wild animal [~live animal] ~ 生動物
애도*	deep sympathy; condolences [~grieve] ~ 悼 애도의 뜻을 표하다 express one's condolences	야성적	wild; rough [~nature] ~ 性的 야성미 wild beauty
		야만적	barbarous [~barbarian] ~ 蠻的 야만인 barbarian
애석하다	be regrettable; be lamentable [~reluctance] ~ 惜	야외	open air; outdoor [~outside] ~ 外
		야유회	picnic; outing [~outing meeting] ~ 遊會

야영*	camping [~camp] ~ 營		약물중독	medicinal poisoning [~thing poisoning] ~ 物中毒
야산	small hill [~mountain] ~ 山		약초	medicinal plant [~grass] ~ 草
광야	wide plain [wide~] 廣 ~		구급약	first-aid medicine [save urgent~] 救急 ~
야채	vegetable [~vegetable] ~ 菜			
야망	ambition [~hope] ~ 望		상비약	reserve medicine [constantly prepare~] 常備 ~ 가정상비약 household medicine
야심	ambition; sinister design [~mind] ~ 心			
야비하다	be mean; be of bad taste [~low] ~ 卑		특효약	wonder drug [special efficacy~] 特效 ~
야박하다	be ungenerous; be unfeeling [~stingy] ~ 薄		만병통치약	cure-all [all diseases thorough cure~] 萬病通治 ~
야속하다	be unsympathetic; be unkind [~vulgar] ~ 俗		보약	tonic [supplement~] 補 ~
야구*	baseball [~ball] ~ 球		독약	poisonous drug [poison~] 毒 ~
야당	opposition party [~party] ~ 黨		마약	narcotics; drug [hemp~] 麻
			치약	toothpaste [tooth~] 齒 ~
야 (夜)	**night**		약수	mineral water [~water] ~ 水
야간	nighttime [~interval] ~ 間 야간학교 night school		물약	liquid medicine [water~] K~
심야	late night [deep~] 深~ 심야방송* late-night program		알약	tablet (medicine) [tablet~] K~
야경	night view [~scenery] ~ 景		가루약	powdered medicine [powder~] K~
야광	shining in the dark [~shine] ~ 光 야광시계 luminous watch		고약	sticking plaster [ointment~] 膏 ~
야근*	night duty [~work] ~ 勤		약솜	surgical cotton [~cotton (ball)] ~ K
			약국	pharmacy [~office] ~ 局
약 w(藥)	**medicine**		약방	pharmacy [~room] ~ 房
약품	drugs; medical supplies [~article] ~ 品		약대	college of pharmacology [~college] ~ 大 (<약학대학)
한약	Chinese medicine [China~] 漢 ~		약사	pharmacist [~master] ~ 師
양약	western medicine [western~] 洋 ~		약값	price of medicine [~price] ~ K
			약효	effect of a medicine [~effect] ~ 效

154

좀약   mothballs [moth~] K~

농약   herbicides and insecticides [agricultural~] 農~

모기약   mosquito killer [mosquito~] K~

파리약   fly poison [a fly~] K~

구두약   shoe polish [dress shoe~] K~

염색약   (hair) dye [dyeing~] 染色~

화약   gunpowder [fire~] 火~

약과   a type of Korean cake; nothing (compared to) [~fruit] ~果

약 (約)   promise; be sparing; approximate

약속*   promise; appointment [~bind] ~束

공약*   public promise [public~] 公~ 선거공약*   election pledges

서약*   an oath; a vow [take an oath~] 誓~

기약*   pledge; promise [period~] 期~

계약*   contract [agreement~] 契 ~ 계약서   contract document

해약*   cancellation of a contract [release~] 解~

예약*   reservation [beforehand~] 豫~

선약*   previous engagement [precede~] 先~

조약   treaty; pact [clause~] 條~

약혼*   (marriage) engagement [~marriage] ~婚

절약*   economizing; saving [moderation~] 節~ 시간절약*   economy of time

요약*   summing up [important~] 要~

제약*   restriction; condition [suppress~] 制~ 시간제약*   time restriction

약 (弱)   weak

약하다   be weak

나약하다   be feeble; be weak-minded [timid~] 懦~

허약하다   be weak; be frail [empty~] 虛~

연약하다   be tender and weak [tender~] 軟~

쇠약하다   be weak; be enfeebled [decline~] 衰~ 신경쇠약   nervous breakdown

약골   weakling [~bone] ~骨

약자   the weak; underdog [~person] ~者

약점   weak point; drawback [~point] ~点

빈약하다   be scanty; be meager [poor~] 貧~ 내용이 빈약하다 be poor in substance 몸이 빈약하다 be weak and skinny

약육강식   law of the jungle [~meat strong eat] ~肉強食

약 (躍)   jump

비약*   leap of logic; jumping to a conclusion [fly~] 飛~

일약   at a single jump [one~] 一 ~ 일약 스타가 되었다 became a star overnight

활약*   (great) activity [lively~] 活~

약 (略)   abbreviation   (see 략)

양 (洋) **ocean; western**

태평**양**   the Pacific Ocean [greatest peaceful~] 太平~

대서**양**   the Atlantic Ocean [big west~] 大西~

인도**양**   the Indian Ocean 印度~

동**양**   Orient [east~] 東~

서**양**   West [west~] 西~

양복   man's western-style suit [~clothes] ~ 服

양말   socks [~socks] ~ 襪
양말을 신.다   put on socks

양식   western food [~food] ~ 食

양약   western medicine [~medicine] ~ 藥

양주   western liquor [~liquor] ~ 酒

양변기   western-style toilet bowl [~toilet bowl] ~ 便器

양.담배   American cigarette [~cigarette] ~ K

양상추   American lettuce [~lettuce] ~ K

양배추   American cabbage [~cabbage] ~ K

양파   onion [~green onion] ~ K

양초   candle [~candle] ~ K

양동이   metal waterpail; bucket [~water jar] ~ K

양철   tinned sheet iron [~iron] ~ 鐵

양탄자   carpet [~rug] ~ K

양 (養) **bring up; care; nourish**

양육*   bringing up; fostering [~raise] ~ 育
양육권   custody

양부모   foster parents [~parents] ~ 父母

입**양***   adopting (a child) [enter~] 入 ~

양자   adopted son [~son] ~ 子

양녀   adopted daughter [~female] ~ 女

부**양***   supporting (family) [assist~] 扶~
부양가족   dependent family

휴**양***   a rest; recuperation [rest~] 休 ~

요**양***   medical care; recuperating [medical treatment~] 療 ~

양호실   school clinic [~care room] ~ 護室

양치(질)*   brushing one's teeth [~tooth doing] ~ 齒 K

영**양**   nutrition [manage~] 營 ~
영양가   nutritive value
(영)양분   nutritive elements
영양제   nutritional supplement
영양실조   malnutrition

교**양**   culture; refinement [teach~] 敎 ~
교양있다   be cultured

양 (兩) **both**

양면   both sides; both aspects [~side] ~ 面

양쪽   both sides [~direction] ~ K

양손   both hands [~hand] ~ K
양손잡이   ambidextrous person

양팔   both arms [~arm] ~ K

양친   both parents (formal) [~parents] ~ 親

양극단   both extremes [~extremes] ~ 極端

양다리걸치다   try to have it both ways; play double [~leg put in] ~K

ㅇ

양자택일* selecting one alternative; choosing between the two [~person select one] ~者擇一

양단간 one way or the other; between two alternatives [~ends between] ~端間

양반 two upper classes of old Korea; aristocratic and noble class [~divisions] ~班

양 (陽) sun(light)

태양 sun [greatest~] 太~
태양열 solar energy

양력 solar calendar [~calendar] ~曆

양지 sunny spot [~place] ~地
양지바르다 be sunny
양지쪽 sunny side

양달 sunny place [~place] ~K

양산 parasol [~umbrella] ~傘

양성 positivity [~nature] ~性
양성반응 positive reaction

양 (良) good(ness)   (/량)

양질 good quality [~quality] ~質

불량하다 be bad; be poor [not~] 不~
불량식품 poor quality food
불량품 poor quality goods

선량하다 be good-natured [good~] 善~

양심 conscience [~mind] ~心

양호하다 be good; be satisfactory [~good] ~好

양순하다 be gentle; be docile [~gentle] ~順

양 (讓) cede; decline

양보* concession [~step] ~步

사양* kind refusal [resign~] 辭~
고맙지만 사양하겠습니다
Thank you, but no thank you.

분양* initial sale (apartment) [divide~] 分~

양 (樣) pattern

모양 form; appearance [pattern~] 模~

양식 mode; style [~style] ~式

양상 aspect; phase [~appearance] ~相

다양하다 be varied [many~] 多~

양 ʷ(量) amount   (see 량)

어 (語) words; language

단어 vocabulary item [single~] 單~

어휘 vocabulary [~collection] ~彙

숙어 idiomatic phrase [ripe~] 熟~

속어 slang [vulgar~] 俗~

구어 colloquial expression [mouth~] 口~

표어 slogan; motto [signboard~] 標~

어감 a feel for words; nuance [~feeling] ~感

유행어 phrase in vogue [vogue~] 流行~

용어 term(inology) [use~] 用~
전문용어
technical terminology

주어 subject (of a sentence) [main~] 主~

목적어 direct object (of a sentence) [object~] 目的~

ㅇ

어원	etymology [~origin] ~ 源	어 (漁)	**fishing**
어순	word order [~order] ~ 順	어부	fisherman [~man] ~ 夫
언어	language [words~] 言~ (언)어학 linguistics	어촌	fishing village [~village] ~村
국어	national language; native language [nation~] 國~ 모국어 native language 한국어 Korean (language) 외국어 foreign language	어업	fishery; fishing industry [~industry] ~ 業
		어선	fishing boat [~boat] ~ 船 원양어선 deep-sea fishing boat
외래어	loanword [foreign come~] 外來~	억 (抑)	**suppress**
영어	English (language) [English~] 英~	억누르다	oppress; suppress [~press]
불어	French (language) [France~] 佛~	억압*	oppression (of freedom) [~repress] ~ 壓
독(일)어	German (language) [Germany~] 獨逸~	억제*	restraint; suppression [~suppress] ~ 制 감정을 억제하다 suppress one's feelings
일(본)어	Japanese (language) [Japan~] 日本~	억울하다	feel unfairly treated [~depressed] ~ 鬱
중국어	Chinese (language) [China~] 中國~	억양	intonation [~raise] ~ 揚
어색하다	be awkward [~block] ~ 塞	언 (言)	**words; talk**
어 (魚)	**fish**	언론	speech; the press [~discuss] ~ 論 언론의 자유 freedom of speech
뱀장어	eel [snake long~] K 長~ 장어구이 broiled eel	언어	language [~words] ~ 語
인어	mermaid [person~] 人~	격언	proverb; maxim [rule~] 格~
어두육미	fish heads and animal tails [~head meat tail] ~ 頭肉尾	명언	wise saying [famous~] 名~
잉어	carp	선언*	pronouncement; declaration [proclaim~] 宣~
붕어	Prussian carp 금붕어 goldfish	발언.권	the right to speak [shoot~rights] 發 ~ 權
고등어	mackerel	과언	saying too much; exaggeration [excessive~] 過~ ...라고해도 과언이 아니다 It is not too much to say that...
오징어	squid		
어항	fish bowl [~jar] ~ 缸		

158

ㅇ

언급*	mention; referring [~extend] ~ 及
일구이언*	being double-tongued [one mouth two~] 一口二~
언성	tone of voice [~voice] ~ 聲 언성을 높이다 raise one's voice
조언*	counsel; advice [assist~] 助~
예언*	prophecy; foretelling [beforehand~] 豫~
증언*	testimony [testify~] 證~
언쟁*	verbal dispute [~fight] ~ 爭
유언*	a will [bequeath~] 遺~

엄 (嚴) strict; severe

엄하다	be strict; be stern
엄밀하다	be strict; be precise [~thorough] ~ 密
엄격하다	be strict; be stern [~rule] ~ 格
엄중하다	(punishment) be strict; be severe [~weighty] ~ 重
엄벌*	severe punishment [~punishment] ~ 罰
엄금*	strict prohibition [~prohibit] ~ 禁
엄수*	strict observance [~observe] ~ 守 시간엄수* punctuality
엄선*	careful selection [~select] ~ 選
엄숙하다	be grave; be solemn [~solemn] ~ 肅
위엄	dignity [dignity~] 威~
근엄하다	be dignified and serious [careful~] 謹 ~
엄포	threat; menace 엄포를 놓다 threaten

업 ᵂ(業) job; business; industry

직업	job; occupation [post~] 職~
부업	second job [second~] 副~
취업*	taking up a job; employment [take~] 就~
업무	business; work [~duty] ~ 務
사업*	business; enterprise [business~] 事~ 자선사업* charitable work
기업	enterprise; company [plan~] 企~ 대기업 large corporation 중소기업 smaller enterprise
작업*	working; operations [do~] 作~ 작업복 work clothes
영업*	(entertainment) business; service (industry) [manage~] 營~ 영업시간 business hours
개업*	opening of a business [open~] 開~ 신장개업* remodeled and newly opened
휴업*	suspension of business [rest~] 休~
동업하다	run business together [together~] 同 ~
분업*	division of work; specialization [divide~] 分~
파업*	a strike; walkout [cease~] 罷 ~
업적	achievements; results [~result] ~ 績
농업	agricultural industry [agricultural~] 農~
공업	(manufacturing) industry [industry~] 工~
상업	commerce [trade~] 商~

어업	fishing industry [fishing~] 漁~
종업원	worker; employee [follow~member] 從~員
실업자	unemployed person [lose~person] 失~者
졸업*	graduation [finish~] 卒~
수업*	a class [give/receive~] 授/受~ 수업료 tuition
자업자득	natural consequences of one's own deed; serves one right [self~self gain] 自~自得

여 (女)	**female; woman** (/녀)
여자	female; woman [~thing] ~子
남녀	man and woman [male~] 男~
숙녀	lady [chaste~] 淑~ 숙녀용 for ladies' use
여성	woman; female [~sex] ~性 여성용 for women's use
여사	Mrs.; madame [~history] ~史 김여사 Mrs. Kim
유부녀	married woman [exist husband~] 有夫~
여편네	married woman; one's wife (vulgar) [~side] ~便 K
처녀	Miss; virgin [manage~] 處~
소녀	young girl [young~] 少~
여동생	younger sister [~younger sibling] ~同生
장녀	first daughter [elder~] 長~
손녀	granddaughter [grandchildren~] 孫~
효녀	dutiful daughter [filial~] 孝~

양녀	adopted daughter [bring up~] 養~
무남독녀	only daughter [no male only~] 無男獨~
여왕	queen [~king] ~王
여신	goddess [~god] ~神
여공	female factory worker [~laborer] ~工
창녀	female prostitute [prostitute~] 娼~
여군	female soldier [~military] ~軍
여학생	female student [~student] ~學生
해녀	woman diver (for seaweed, pearls, etc.) [ocean~] 海~
수녀	nun [cultivate~] 修~
여.권	women's rights [~rights] ~權 여.권신장* extension of women's rights
여고	girls' high school [~high school] ~高 (<여자고등학교)
여대	women's college [~college] ~大 (<여자대학) 여대생 woman college student

여 (餘)	**surplus**
여분	remainder; excess; leftover [~share] ~分
여가	spare time; leisure [~leisure] ~暇 ...ㄹ/할 여가가 없다 have no (leisure) time to do...
여벌	a spare; an extra [~set] ~ K
여유	extra (time, money, space, etc.); composure [~plenty] ~裕

...할 시간 / 마음의 여유가 없다 have no time/room in one's mind to spare to do...

여지 room; margin [~place] ~ 地
의심할 여지가 없다
There is no room for doubt.

여생 rest of one's life [~life] ~ 生

여념 distraction [~thought] ~ 念
...에 여념이 없다
be absorbed in...

여 (與) give

수여* awarding; conferring [give~] 授~

대여* lending [lend~] 貸~

기여* contribution; services [entrust~] 寄~

여.건 given condition; circumstances [~things] ~ 件

관여* being concerned (in); involvement [concern~] 關~

참여* participation [participate~] 參~

여당 ruling party [~party] ~ 黨

여 (旅) travel(er)

여행* travel [~go] ~ 行
여행·가방 suitcase
여행사 travel agency

여인숙 second-class inn [~person lodge] ~ 人宿

여관 hotel; inn [~building] ~ 館

여.권 passport [~document] ~ 券

역 ʷ(逆) disobey; contrary

거역* disobedience; objection [resist~] 拒~

반역* treason [rebel~] 叛~
반역자 traitor

역겹다 feel disgusted [~be more than one can manage] ~ K

역효·과 counterresult; contrary effect [~effect] ~ 效果

역전* reversal of a situation (in a game) [~turn] ~ 轉

역경 adverse circumstances [~circumstances] ~ 境

구역질 nausea [vomit~doing] 嘔 ~ K
구역질나다 have nausea

역 ʷ(役) role; serve

역할 role; part [~divide] ~ 割

배역 the cast (of a play) [suitable~] 配~

중역 director (of a company) [weighty~] 重~

고역 hard work; drudgery [suffering~] 苦~

징역 penal servitude; imprisonment [punish~] 懲~
징역살이* prison life

역 (譯) translate

번역* translation [overturn~] 飜~

직역* literal translation [direct~] 直~

의역* meaning translation [meaning~] 意~

통역* interpreting [communicate~] 通~
동시통역* simultaneous interpretation

역 w (驛) **station**

전철역   subway station [subway~] 電鐵~

종착역   terminal station [finish arrive~] 終着~

서울역   Seoul station [Seoul~] K~

역전   plaza in front of a train station [~front] ~ 前

역 (域) **boundary**

지역   region; area [place~] 地~

구역   district; zone [district~] 區~

영역   territory; domain [govern~] 領~

역 (歷) **past**   (see 력)

연 (演) **perform**

연기*   performance; acting [~skill] ~ 技

공연*   public performance [public~] 公~

연주*   performance on a musical instrument [~play music] ~奏

조연   supporting performance [assist~] 助~

연예인   performer; entertainer [~art person] ~ 藝人

출연*   appearance on stage [come out~] 出~

주연*   playing the leading part; starring [main~] 主~

연극*   play; drama [~drama] ~ 劇

연출*   production; staging [~produce] ~ 出

연설*   public speech [~speech] ~ 說

강연*   lecture; speech [lecture~] 講~

연 (連) **connect(ed)**   (/련)

연결*   connection; linking [~tie] ~ 結

연속*   series; succession [~continue] ~ 續

연쇄   chain; series [~a chain] ~ 鎖
연쇄살인사.건   serial murders
연쇄반응   chain reaction

연달아   continuously; one after another ~K

연거푸   consecutively; in a row ~ K

연휴   consecutive holidays; long weekend [~rest] ~ 休

연승*   victories in a row [~win] ~ 勝
(이)연승   winning (two) games in a row

연패*   victories in a row [~chief] ~ 覇

연패*   consecutive defeats [~lose] ~ 敗

연재*   publication in serial form [~to load] ~ 載
연재만화   serial cartoon strips
연재소설   serial novel

연락*   contact; communication [~connection] ~ 絡

연 (聯) **relation; association** (/련)

연상*   association (of ideas) [~think] ~ 想

연관*   connection; correlation [~concern] ~ 關

관련*   connection; correlation [concern~] 關~

연방   federation [~relation] ~ 邦
연방정부   federal government

ㅇ

연합* union; alliance [~join] ~ 合
국제연합 U.N.

연맹 league; union
[~swear an oath] ~ 盟

연립주택 tenement house;
row houses
[~stand house] ~ 立住宅

연 (然) as such

자연 nature [self~] 自~
자연적 natural
자연스럽다 be natural
자연식품 natural food
자연환경 natural environment
자연보호* nature preservation

천연* being natural [nature~] 天~
천연자원 natural resources

우연* chance; accident
[accidental~] 偶~
우연히 by chance; by accident

필연적 inevitable [surely~] 必~的

당연하다 be natural; be a matter of
course [ought~] 當~

막연하다 be vague [desert~] 漠~

태연하다 be calm; be undisturbed
[big~] 泰~

초연하다 be aloof; be transcendental
[jump over~] 超~

연 (緣) affinity

악연 unfortunate affinity;
evil connection [evil~] 惡~

인연 predestined tie; affinity
[cause~] 因~

연분 preordained tie; fate
[~share] ~ 分
천생연분 marriage ties
preordained by Providence

자매결연 sisterhood relationship
[sister tie~] 姉妹結~

자매결연을 맺다
set up sister relationship

혈연 blood relation [blood~] 血~

연줄 pull; connections [~line] ~ K

연 (延) extend; delay

연장* extension; lengthening
[~long] ~ 長

연기* postponement; deferment
[~period] ~ 期

지연* delay [late~] 遲~
지연되다 be delayed

연착* delayed arrival [~arrive] ~ 着

연체료 overdue fee
[~obstructed estimate] ~ 滯料

연 (軟) soft

유연하다 be soft; be pliable
[soft~] 柔~

연하다 (color, coffee, etc.) be
mild; (meat, etc.) be tender

연보라 light purple [~purple] ~ K

연약하다 be tender; be weak
[~weak] ~ 弱

연고 ointment [~ointment] ~ 膏

연 (煙) smoke

연기 smoke [~air] ~ 氣
담배연기 cigarette smoke
연기나다 smoke rises
아니땐 굴둑에 연기나랴
There is no smoke
without fire.

흡연* smoking [inhale~] 吸~

금연* prohibition against
smoking [forbid~] 禁~

연통 stovepipe [~tube] ~ 筒

163

연 (戀)　**love**

연애＊　(romantic) love;
going steady [~love] ~ 愛
연애편지　love letter
연애결혼＊　marriage of love
동성연애＊　homosexual love

연인　romantic partner; lover
[~person] ~ 人

실연하다　be lovelorn; be broken-
hearted [lose~] 失~

연연해하다　have a lingering
affection ~~ K

연 (研)　**research**

연구＊　research [~research] ~ 究

연수＊　research training; study
and training [~cultivate] ~ 修
해외연수＊　overseas training
연수원　training institute

연 (年)　**year**　(see **년**)

연 (練 / 鍊)　**practice; to train**
(see **련**)

열 w(熱)　**heat; hot**　(/렬)

열기　heat; heated atmosphere
[~energy] ~ 氣

가열＊　heating [add~] 加~

열.대　tropics [~belt] ~ 帶
열.대지방　tropical region

태양열　solar energy [sun~] 太陽~

열량　calorie [~amount] ~ 量

열창＊　passionate singing
[~sing] ~ 唱

열.전　heated battle; close game
[~fighting] ~ 戰

열렬하다　be fiery; be passionate
[~vehement] ~ 烈
열렬히　ardently; passionately

열.정　ardor; passion [~feeling] ~ 情

정열　passion; enthusiasm
[feeling~] 情 ~
정열.적　passionate

열나다　become feverish; get
angry [~come out] ~ K
열나게　feverishly; ardently

열띤　heated; enthusiastic ~ K

열받다　feel angry and heated
(slang) [~receive] ~ K

열.중하다　be absorbed (in)
[~middle] ~ 中

열.성　earnestness; enthusiasm
[~sincerity] ~ 誠

열.심이다　be earnest; be enthusiastic
[~mind be] ~ 心 K
열.심히　enthusiastically

열의　zeal; enthusiasm
[~wish] ~ 意

열광＊　wild enthusiasm
[~madness] ~ 狂

열변　vehement speech
[~eloquence] ~ 辯

이열치열　Like cures like.
[with~govern~] 以~治~

열 w(列)　**line; row**　(/렬)

일렬　one line/row [one~] 一 ~
일렬로 서다　stand in a line

정렬하다　line up [be in order~] 整 ~

배열＊　arranging things in order
[push out~] 排 ~

행렬　parade; line [go~] 行 ~
가장행렬＊　masquerade parade

열거＊　enumeration [~lift] ~ 擧

열차　train [~vehicle] ~ 車

진열* exhibition; display
[display~] 陳~
진열.장 show window

열 (烈) **violent** (see 렬)

염 (炎) **inflammation** (/렴)

염.증 inflammation
[~symptom] ~ 症

위염 gastritis [stomach~] 胃~

간염 hepatitis [liver~] 肝~

폐렴 pneumonia [lung~] 肺~

뇌염 brain inflammation
[brain~] 腦~

관절염 arthritis [a joint~] 關節~

기관지염 bronchitis
[bronchus~] 氣管支~

맹장염 appendicitis
[appendix~] 盲腸~

염 (鹽) **salt**

염분 salt content [~share] ~ 分

염전 salt pond [~field] ~ 田

식염수 saline solution
[food~water] 食~水

염산 hydrochloric acid
[~acid] ~ 酸

염소 chlorine [~element] ~ 素
염소표백* chlorine bleach

염 (染) **dye; infect**

염색* dyeing [~color] ~ 色

감염 infection [feeling~] 感~
감염되다 get infected

전염 contagion; infection
[transmit~] 傳~

전염.병 contagious/
communicable disease
전염되다 be infected;
be contagious

오염 pollution [dirty~] 汚~
대기오염 air pollution
환경오염
environmental pollution

염 (念) **think; thought** (see 념)

염 (廉) **incorruptible** (see 렴)

엽 (葉) **leaf**

낙엽 fallen leaves [fall~] 落~

엽차 green tea [~tea] ~ 茶

엽서 postcard [~writing] ~ 書

태엽 spring (in a watch)
[pregnant~] 胎~

영 (營) **manage; camp**

경영* management [govern~] 經~

직영* direct management
[direct~] 直~

영업* (entertainment) business;
service (industry)
[~business] ~ 業
영업용 for business use

운영* operation; running
(a business) [transport~] 運~

영양 nutrition [~nourish] ~ 養

야영* camping [outside~] 野~

탈영* desertion [escape~] 脫~

영 (榮) **glory**

영광 glory; honor [~shine] ~ 光
영광스럽다 be glorious;
feel honored

ㅇ

영예	honor; glory [~praise] ~譽	**영** w(零)	**zero**
허영	vanity; vainglory [empty~] 虛~	**영도**	zero degrees centigrade [~degree] ~度
번영*	prosperity (of a country) [prosper~] 繁~	**영상**	above zero (temp.) [~above] ~上
영전*	promotional transfer [~transfer] ~轉	**영하**	below zero (temp.) [~below] ~下
		영락없다	be infallible [~fall not exist] ~落 K 영락없이 without fail

영 (英)   **England; hero**

영국	England [~country] ~國
영문학	English literature [~literature] ~文
영어	English (language) [~language] ~語
영한사전	English-Korean dictionary [~Korea dictionary] ~韓辭典
영웅	hero [~virile] ~雄

영 (映)   **reflect; cinema**

반영*	reflection (of an opinion) [opposite~] 反~
영화	movie [~picture] ~畵 영화관 movie theater
상영*	screening; showing [ascend~] 上~ 동시상영* double feature

영 (永)   **permanent**

영구하다	be permanent; be eternal [~eternity] ~久 영구적 lasting; permanent 영구불변* no change forever
영원하다	be eternal [~far] ~遠
영주*	permanent residence [~reside] ~住
영영	for good; forever

영 (影)   **shadow**

촬영*	photographing; filming [take pictures~] 撮~ 영화촬영* filming
영향	influence [~echo] ~響 영향을 주다 / 끼치다 have an influence (on)

영 (領)   **command; receive** (see 령)

영 (泳)   **swim**

수영*	swimming [water~] 水~ 수영복 swimsuit 수영장 swimming pool
자유영*	free stroke [freedom~] 自由~
평영*	breast stroke [even~] 平~
배영*	back stroke [the back~] 背~

영 (令)   **command; honorable** (see 령)

영 (靈)   **spirits** (see 령)

ㅇ

예 (豫) **beforehand**

예감* premonition; hunch
[~feeling] ~ 感

예상* expectation [~think] ~ 想
예상외 unexpectedness

예언* prophecy; foretelling
[~talk] ~ 言

예보* forecast [~report] ~ 報
일기예보* weather forecast

예견하다 foresee [~see] ~ 見

예습* preview of studies
[~study] ~ 習

예측* pre-estimate [~measure] ~測

예산* estimate; budget
[~calculate] ~ 算

예정* a schedule; a plan
[~decide] ~ 定
예정일 scheduled date

예약* reservation [~promise] ~ 約

예고* advance notice [~tell] ~ 告

예매* advance sale/purchase
[~sell/buy] ~ 賣/買

예방* prevention; precaution
[~defend] ~ 防
예방주사 immunization

예비* preparation; a reserve
[~prepare] ~ 備
예비고사 preliminary exam
예비군 reserve army

예선 preliminary selection/
match [~select] ~ 選

예행연습* rehearsal
[~act practice] ~ 行演習

예 (藝) **art**

예술 art [~art] ~ 術
예술적 artistic

예능 art; artistic ability
[~ability] ~ 能
예능·과목 art subject

서예 calligraphy [writing~] 書~

공예 industrial arts
[industry~] 工~
수공예 handicraft

원예 gardening [garden~] 園~

예 ᵂ (例) **example; usual** (see 례)

예 ᵂ (禮) **etiquette; rites** (see 례)

오 (誤) **mistake**

오류 mistake; error [~error] ~ 謬
오류를 범하다
make a mistake

착오* mistake; error
[mistaken~] 錯~
시대착오 anachronism

오산 miscalculation; wrong
estimate [~calculate] ~ 算

오진* misdiagnosis
[~medical examination] ~ 診

오해* misunderstanding
[~explain] ~ 解

오차 error (in mathematics)
[~difference] ~ 差

오·자 wrong character; typo
[~character] ~ 字

오 (午) **afternoon**

정오 noon [right~] 正~

오전 A. M. [~before] ~ 前

오후 P. M. [~after] ~ 後

ㅇ

옥 ᵂ(獄) prison

감옥	prison [supervise~] 監~
지옥	hell [earth~] 地~ 생지옥 living hell

온 (溫) warm; temperature

온천	hot spring [~a spring] ~ 泉
온수	warm/hot water [~water] ~ 水
온돌	Korean under-floor heating system [~chimney] ~ 突
온상	hotbed; greenhouse [~table] ~ 床
온실	greenhouse [~room] ~ 室
기온	temperature [air~] 氣~
고온	high temperature [high~] 高~
저온	low temperature [low~] 低~
온도	degree (temp.) [~degree] ~ 度 온도계 thermometer
삼한사온	cycle of three cold and four warm days [three cold four~] 三寒四~
체온	body temperature [body~] 體~
보온	heat insulation [protect~] 保~ 보온.병 thermos (bottle) 보온밥통 thermos rice container
온화하다	be mild; be gentle [~harmony] ~ 和
온순하다	be gentle; be docile [~gentle] ~ 順

완 (完) complete

완성*	completion; finishing [~to complete] ~ 成
완료*	completion [~complete] ~ 了 준비완료* completion of preparation 현재완료 present perfect tense
완비*	being fully equipped [~prepare] ~ 備
완공*	completion (of construction) [~labor] ~ 工
완수*	fulfillment [~complete] ~ 遂 책임을 완수하다 fulfill one's responsibilities
완치*	complete cure [~cure] ~ 治
완쾌*	complete recovery [~refreshing] ~ 快
완전*	perfection; completeness [~complete] ~ 全 완전히 completely
완벽*	perfection [~perfect jade] ~ 璧 완벽주의자 perfectionist

완 (緩) slow

완행	(vehicle) going slow [~go] ~ 行 완행열차 slow train
완만하다	(slope) be gentle; be easy [~gradual] ~ 慢
완화*	mitigation; ease [~harmony] ~ 和

왕 ᵂ(王) king

여왕	queen [female~] 女~
왕비	queen [~wife] ~ 妃
왕자	royal prince [~son] ~ 子

왕관	(royal) crown [~crown] ~ 冠	교외	suburbs [suburb~] 郊~
삼관왕	triple gold-medalist [three crown~] 三冠~	해외	overseas [sea~] 海~
왕개미	giant ant [~ant] ~ K	외국	foreign country [~country] ~ 國 외국인 foreigner 외국어 foreign language

왕 (往) **go**

왕래*	going and coming; mutual visit [~come] ~ 來 그친구와 별로 왕래가 없다 That friend and I seldom see each other.
왕복*	going and returning; roundtrip [~return] ~ 復
왕진*	(doctor's) visit (to a patient) [~medical examination] ~ 診
왕년	the years past [~year] ~ 年

외 (外) **outside; foreign; mother's side**

외모	outer appearance [~countenance] ~ 貌
외부	outside; external [~part] ~ 部
외등	outdoor lamp [~lamp] ~ 燈
실외	outdoors [room~] 室~
외출*	going out [~go out] ~ 出
외식*	eating out [~eat] ~ 食
외박*	sleeping away from home [~stay] ~ 泊
외투	overcoat [~wrapper] ~ 套
외·과	dept. of external medicine [~department] ~ 科
시외	outskirts of a city; suburbs [city~] 市~ 시외전화* out-of-town, long-distance call

외무부	Ministry of Foreign Affairs [~affairs section] ~ 務部
외교*	diplomacy [~exchange] ~ 交 외교관 diplomat
외제	foreign-made [~make] ~ 製 외제차 imported car
외화	foreign money [~goods] ~貨
외환은행	foreign exchange bank [~exchange bank] ~ 換銀行
외래어	loanword [~come word] ~ 來語
외삼촌	maternal uncle [~uncle] ~ 三寸
외갓집	mother's family/home [~house house] ~ 家 K
예외	exception (to the rule) [usual~] 例~
이외	except for; other than [with~] 以~ 일요일 이외에는 except on Sundays
제외*	exclusion [eliminate~] 除~ ...을 제외하고 except for...
소외	alienation [far apart~] 疎~ 소외되다 be alienated
의외	unexpectedness [wish~] 意~
예상외	unexpectedness [expectation~] 豫想~
외면*	turning one's face away; looking away [~face] ~ 面
문외한	outsider; layperson [door~person] 門~漢

ㅇ

요 (要) essential; demand

필**요***	necessity [surely~] 必~ 불필요하다 be unnecessary
요하다	require; need
중**요**하다	be important [weighty~] 重~
주**요**하다	be main; be principal [main~] 主~
요·점	main point; gist [~point] ~點
요지	essential point; gist [~purport] ~旨
요는	the point is... ~ K
요인	primary factor; main cause [~cause] ~因
요소	essential element [~element] ~素
요긴하다	be essentially important [~important] ~緊
긴**요**하다	be important; be essential [important~] 緊~
요약*	summing up [~approximate] ~約
요컨대	in short ~ K
강**요***	forcible demand [force~] 强~
수**요**	a demand [require~] 需~
요구*	a request; a demand [~request] ~求
요청*	important request [~request] ~請
요령	knack [~command] ~領

요 (妖) bewitching

요술	magic; witchcraft [~skill] ~術
요정	fairy; elf [~spirit] ~精

요염하다	be bewitching; be voluptuous [~enticing] ~艶
요사스럽다	be wicked; be cunning [~devilish] ~邪

요 (謠) song

가**요**	song [song~] 歌~
동**요**	children's song [child~] 童~
민**요**	folk song [people~] 民~

요 (療) medical treatment (see 료)

요 (料) material; estimate (see 료)

욕 (慾) greed; desire

욕심	greed [~mind] ~心 욕심쟁이/꾸러기 greedy person
욕망	desire; ambition [~hope] ~望
욕구*	desire; wants [~seek] ~求 욕구불만 frustrated desire
의욕	volition; ambition [wish~] 意~
성욕	sexual desire [sex~] 性~
식욕	appetite [eat~] 食~
탐욕스럽다	be avaricious [covet~] 貪~
금욕*	self-restraint; stoicism [forbid~] 禁~

욕 w(辱) insult; disgrace

모욕*	an insult [insult~] 侮~ 모욕적 insulting
욕먹다	be reviled; be spoken ill of [~eat] ~ K

170

ㅇ

욕보다	be put to shame; have a hard time [~see] ~ K	신사용	for gentlemen [gentleman~] 紳士~
치욕	shame; disgrace [shameful~] 恥~	일회용	for one-time use; disposable [one time~] 一回~
굴욕	humiliation [bend~] 屈~ 굴욕적 humiliating	여행용	for travel [travel~] 旅行~
욕하다	abuse; revile	악용*	abuse; improper use [evil~] 惡~

욕 (浴) bath(e)

목욕*	bathing [bathe~] 沐~ 목욕탕 bathhouse; bathing room	이용*	utilization; taking advantage of [benefit~] 利~
욕조	bathtub [~trough] ~ 槽	활용*	utilization; making the most of [lively~] 活~
욕실	(family) bathroom [~room] ~ 室	채용*	employment; appointment [select~] 採~
일광욕*	sunbathing [sunlight~] 日光~	응용*	practical application; adaptation [suitable~] 應~
해수욕장	beach for swimming [sea water~place] 海水~場	적용*	application (of a rule) [suitable~] 適~
		휴대용	portable [carrying along~] 携帶~

용 (用) use

소용	use; usefulness [whatsoever~] 所~ 소용있다/없다 be useful/useless	자가용	one's own car [self house~] 自家~
		용구	tool; instrument [~tool] ~ 具
유용하다	be useful [exist~] 有~	용량	dosage [~amount] ~ 量
사용*	a use; making use of [employ~] 使~ (사)용.법 way of using; directions for use	용품	necessities; supplies [~article] ~ 品
		비용	expense; cost [expense~] 費~
용도	a use; service [~road] ~ 途 다용도 multipurpose	용.돈	pocket money; spending money [~money] ~ K
실용적	practical [real~] 實~的	용.건	important matter; matter of business [~thing] ~ 件
전용*	exclusive use [exclusive~] 專~ 직원전용 for exclusive use of the staff	과용*	spending too much money [exceed~] 過~
		인용*	quotation [pull~] 引~
숙녀용	for ladies [lady~] 淑女~	용어	term(inology) [~words] ~ 語
		신용*	trust; credit [believe~] 信~

171

착용*   putting on; wearing (formal) [wear~] 着 ~

복용*   taking medicine [submit~] 服 ~

용 (容)   face; permit

용모   looks; appearance [~countenance] ~ 貌

미용   beauty; cosmetology [beautiful~] 美 ~

내용   contents [inside~] 內 ~

허용*   permission; allowance [permit~] 許 ~

관용   forgiving with generosity; toleration [generous~] 寬 ~
관용을 베풀다   forgive with generosity

용서*   pardon; forgiveness [~pardon] ~ 恕
용서를 빌다   beg one's pardon

포용하다   embrace; accept with magnanimity [wrap~] 包 ~
포용력   magnanimous capacity

용납*   toleration; permission [~give] ~ 納

용기   receptacle; container [~utensil] ~ 器

용 (勇)   brave

용기   courage [~spirit] ~ 氣
용기있다   be courageous

용감하다   be brave [~dare] ~ 敢

만용   foolhardiness [barbarian~] 蠻 ~

우 (優)   excellent; superior; actor

우수하다   be excellent [~excellent] ~ 秀

우열   superiority and/or inferiority; relative standing [~inferior] ~ 劣
우열을 가리다   distinguish between superior and inferior

우등상   prize for excellent scholarship [~rank prize] ~ 等賞

우월하다   be superior [~leap over] ~ 越
우월감   sense of superiority

우량아   physically superior child [~good child] ~ 良兒

우선하다   take precedence (over) [~precede] ~ 先

우세하다   be predominant [~power] ~ 勢

우성   genetic dominance [~essential quality] ~ 性

우승*   victory; championship [~win] ~ 勝

우대*   preferential treatment [~treat] ~ 待

우아하다   be graceful and elegant [~elegant] ~ 雅

우유부단하다   be indecisive [~soft not cut off] ~ 柔不斷

배우   actor; actress [actor~] 俳 ~

성우   radio actor/actress; dubbing artist [voice~] 聲 ~

우 (雨)   rain

호우   heavy rainfall [violent~] 豪 ~
집중호우   concentrated heavy rain
호우주의보   heavy rain warning

폭우   heavy rain; torrential rain [cruel~] 暴 ~

우천시   in case of rain [~sky time] ~ 天時

172

ㅇ

우비 raincoat [~prepare] ~ 備

우산 umbrella [~umbrella] ~ 傘

우박 hail; hailstone [~hail] ~ 雹

우뢰 thunder [~thunder] 雷
우뢰와 같은 박수
thunderous applause

우 (郵) **mail**

우편 mail [~mail] ~ 便
우편함 letter box
우편번호 zip code
등·기우편 registered mail
항공우편 air mail

우송* sending by mail [~send] ~送

우체통 mailbox [~post tube] ~遞筒

우표 (postage) stamp
[~ticket] ~ 票

우체국 post office
[~post office] ~ 遞局

우 (友) **friend**

우정 friendship [~feeling] ~ 情

죽마고우 bosom buddy
[bamboo horse past~] 竹馬故~

우방 friendly nation
[~nation] ~ 邦

우애 brotherliness; fraternity
[~love] ~ 愛

전우 war buddy [war~] 戰~

우 ᵂ(右) **right**

우측 right side [~side] ~ 側
우측통행* Keep to the right.

우회전* right turn
[~turning] ~ 回轉

좌우 left and right [left~] 左~

우왕좌왕* moving about
in confusion
[~go left go] ~ 往左往

우 (憂) **anxiety**

우려* worry; apprehension
[~worry] ~ 慮

우울하다 feel depressed; feel
gloomy [~depressed] ~ 鬱

우수 melancholy
[~melancholy] ~ 愁

우 (愚) **stupid**

우둔하다 be stupid; be thick-
headed [~dull] ~ 鈍

우롱* mockery; ridicule
[~ridicule] ~ 弄

우악스럽다 be rough; be crude
[~evil] ~惡

운 ᵂ(運) **luck; transport**

운좋다 be lucky [~good] ~ K

운나쁘다 be unlucky [~bad] ~ K

운수 fortune; luck [~fate] ~ 數

행운 good luck [fortunate~] 幸~

운명 fate; destiny [~destiny] ~ 命

운반* conveyance; transport
[~transport] ~ 搬

운전* driving [~turn] ~ 轉
운전사 driver
운전면허 driver's license

운임 freight rates [~wage] ~ 賃

운동* sports; exercise; campaign
[~move] ~ 動

운영* operation; running
(a business) [~manage] ~ 營

운항*   navigation; passage [~navigate] ~ 航

운행*   (vehicle) running; operation [~go] ~ 行

운하   canal [~stream] ~ 河

울 (鬱)   depressed; grow thick

우울하다   feel depressed; feel gloomy [anxiety~] 憂~
우울.증 hypochondria

침울하다   be dismal; be gloomy [sink~] 沈~

울.적하다   feel empty and lonesome [~desolate] ~ 寂

억울하다   feel unfairly treated [suppress~] 抑~

울화   pent-up anger [~fire] ~ 火

울창하다   (forest) be thick [~green] ~ 蒼

웅 (雄)   virile

영웅   hero [hero~] 英~

웅장하다   (building) be grand; be magnificent [~valiant] ~ 壯

웅변*   eloquence; oratory [~eloquence] ~ 辯

원 (原)   origin; plateau

원주민   native; aborigine [~resident] ~ 住民

원시적   primitive [~begin] ~ 始的

원.가   cost price [~price] ~ 價

원본   original copy [~origin] ~ 本

원서   original (language) edition; original text [~writing] ~ 書

원형   original form [~form] ~ 形

원료   raw materials [~material] ~ 料

원자   atom [~thing] ~ 子
원자력 nuclear power
원자폭탄 atomic bomb

원.점   starting point; original place [~point] ~ 点
원.점으로 돌아가다
go back to the starting point

원상복구*   restoring to the original state [~shape restoration] ~ 狀復舊

원인   cause; factor [~cause] ~ 因

원리   (underlying) principle [~principle] ~ 理

원칙   fundamental rule; general rule [~rule] ~ 則

원판   negative (film) [~printing board] ~ 版

원색   primary color [~color] ~ 色

원고   manuscript [~manuscript] ~ 稿

원고   plaintiff [~accuse] ~ 告

초원   grassy plain; prairie [grass~] 草~

원 (員)   member

회원   member (of an association) [meeting~] 會~
회원.권 membership card

전원   all the members [all~] 全~

국회의원   member of Congress [Congress discuss~] 國會議~

직원   staff; personnel [office~] 職~

공무원   public service personnel [public affairs~] 公務~

ㅇ

사원	company employee [company~] 社~ 신입사원 incoming employee
종업원	worker; employee [follow job~] 從業~
공원	factory worker [industry~] 工~
점원	store clerk [store~] 店~
외판원	(traveling) salesperson [outside sell~] 外販~
은행원	bank teller [bank~] 銀行~
간호원	nurse [nursing~] 看護~
승무원	(member of) the crew [ride duty~] 乘務~
선원	the crew; mariner [ship~] 船~
임원	an executive [be in charge~] 任~
정원	the fixed (seating) capacity [fix~] 定~ 정원초과* exceeding capacity
만원	no vacancy; full house [full~] 滿~
인원	the number of persons [person~] 人~
동원*	mobilization [move~] 動~ 관객을 동원하다 draw an audience

원 (園) garden

정원	garden [yard~] 庭~
원예	gardening [~art] ~藝
화원	flower shop [flower~] 花~
과수원	orchard [fruit tree~] 果樹~
공원	park [public~] 公~
전원	countryside [field~] 田~ 전원생활* rural life
낙원	paradise [pleasant~] 樂~

유아원	nursery (school) [infant~] 幼兒~
유치원	kindergarten [babyhood~] 幼稚~

원 (院) court; institution

법원	court (of law) [law~] 法~ 대법원 Supreme Court
병원	hospital [disease~] 病~
의원	clinic [medical~] 醫~
입원*	hospitalization [enter~] 入~
퇴원*	discharge from a hospital [leave~] 退~
양로원	nursing home [care old~] 養老~
학원	educational institution [learning~] 學~ 외국어학원 foreign language institute
원장	director of an institute [~superior] ~長
미장원	beauty parlor [beautiful decorate~] 美裝~

원 (元) the first; principal

원조	originator; founder [~ancestor] ~祖
원래	originally; by nature [~come] ~來
원체	originally; by nature [~body] ~體
차원	dimension [place~] 次~ 삼차원 three-dimensional
원금	principal sum [~money] ~金
신원	one's identity [person~] 身~
미원	Miwon; monosodium [taste~] 味~

175

o

원 (援)	help
원조*	assistance; aid [~assist] ~助 경제원조* economic aid
구원*	relief; rescue [rescue~] 救~
지원*	support [support~] 支~
후원*	support; backing [back~] 後~ 후원자 supporter; sponsor
응원*	moral support; cheering [respond~] 應~ 응원가 rooter's song 응원단 cheering group

원 ʷ(圓)	round; circle
원탁	round table [~table] ~卓
원형	round shape [~shape] ~形 원형극장 amphitheater
원통	cylinder [~tube] ~筒
원만하다	be harmonious; be well-rounded [~full] ~滿
원활하다	be smooth; be harmonious [~slippery] ~滑

원 ʷ(願)	desire; request
원하다	desire; want
소원*	one's wish [whatsoever~] 所~
기원*	prayer [pray~] 祈~
자원하다	volunteer [self~] 自~ 자원봉사* volunteer service
지원*	application; volunteering [intention~] 志~
원서	application form [~writing] ~書

원 (怨)	grudge
원망*	resentment [~hope] ~望

원한	grudge; spite [~grudge] ~恨 원한을 사다 earn a grudge 원한을 품다 bear a grudge
원수	enemy [~enemy] ~讐 원수갚다 revenge; get even

원 (遠)	far
원시	farsightedness [~see] ~視
망원경	binoculars [observe~mirror] 望~鏡
원양어업	deep-sea fishing industry [~ocean fishing industry] ~洋漁業
영원하다	be eternal [permanent~] 永~

월 (月)	month; moon
(일)개월	(one) month [one individual~] 一個~
유월	June [sixth~] 六~
시월	October [tenth~] 十~
월말	end of a month [~end] ~末
월급	monthly salary [~pay] ~給
월수입	monthly income [~income] ~收入
월·세	monthly rent [~rent] ~貰
월간	monthly publication [~publish] ~刊
월부	monthly installment [~pay] ~賦 월부로 by monthly installment
월요일	Monday [~day of the week] ~曜日
세월	time (and tide) [year~] 歲~

월 (越)	cross over
추월*	passing (another car) [follow~] 追~ 추월금지 No passing

ㅇ

초월하다 transcend; go beyond
[excel~] 超~
상상을 초월하다
be unimaginable

월.등하다 be superior by far
[~equal] ~ 等

우월하다 be superior [superior~] 優~

월남* coming south (from
North Korea) [~south] ~ 南

월.동준비* preparation for winter
[~winter preparation] ~冬準備

위 (位) position

지위 position; status [place~] 地~
사회적 지위 social status

직위 position; status [post~] 職~

위치* location [~to place] ~ 置

순위 order; ranking
[sequence~] 順~

방위 compass direction
[direction~] 方~

단위 a unit [single~] 單~

부위 a part (of a body)
[part~] 部~

품위 grace; dignity [grade~] 品~

위 ʷ (胃) stomach

위산 stomach acid [~acid] ~ 酸
위산과다 excessive
stomach acid

위궤양 stomach ulcer [~ulcer] ~潰瘍

위장 stomach and intestines
[~intestine] ~ 腸
위장.병 gastroenteric disorder

위암 stomach cancer
[~cancer] ~ 癌

비위 spleen and stomach;
taste [spleen~] 脾 ~

비위가 좋다
have a strong stomach
비위에 맞다 suit one's tastes
비위맞추다 curry favor with
비위상하다 feel nauseated

위염 gastritis [~inflammation] ~ 炎

위 (危) dangerous

위험* danger [~rough] ~ 險
위험물 dangerous article

위태롭다 be dangerous; be critical
[~dangerous] ~ 殆

위기 critical moment; crisis
[~opportunity] ~ 機

위급하다 be critical; be an
emergency [~urgent] ~ 急

위독하다 (illness) be in critical
condition [~true] ~ 篤

위 (慰) console

자위* self-consolation;
masturbation [self~] 自~

위로* solace; consolation
[~toil] ~ 勞

위안* consolation; comfort
[~peaceful] ~ 安
...에서 위안을 얻다
find one's comfort in...

위문* consolatory visit; inquiry
[~inquire] ~ 問
위문편지 letter of consolation
위문품 care package

위자료 compensation; alimony
[~help estimate] ~ 藉料

위 (威) dignity; stern

위엄 dignity [~solemn] ~ 嚴

위신 prestige; dignity
[~believe] ~ 信
위신문제 a matter of prestige

권위	authority; prestige [authority~] 權~
시위*	demonstration (rally) [manifest~] 示~
위협*	intimidation [~threaten] ~ 脅

위 (衛) guard

방위*	defense [defend~] 防~ 민방위 civil defense
수위	security guard [guard~] 守~
위생	hygiene; sanitation [~life] ~生 위생적 hygienic; sanitary
위성	satellite [~planet] ~星 위성도시 satellite city 인공위성 man-made satellite

위 (僞) false

허위	falsehood [unreal~] 虛~
위조*	forgery; fabrication [~make] ~造 위조지폐 counterfeit bank note
위선	hypocrisy [~goodness] ~善 위선자 hypocrite
위장*	camouflage; disguise [~costume] ~裝

위 (圍) circumference

주위	environs; vicinity [encircle~] 周~
포위*	encirclement; beleaguerment [wrap~] 包~
분위기	atmosphere; ambience [fog~atmosphere] 雰~氣
범위	scope [pattern~] 範~ 광범위* wide scope

유 (有) exist

유용하다	be useful [~use] ~用
유리하다	be advantageous [~benefit] ~利
유익하다	be beneficial; be instructive [~profit] ~益
유효하다	be valid; be effective [~effect] ~效
유독하다	be poisonous [~poison] ~毒
유해하다	be noxious [~harm] ~害
유력하다	be influential; be powerful [~power] ~力
유명하다	be famous [~name] ~名
유별나다	be distinctive; be peculiar [~special come out] ~別 K
유식하다	be learned; be educated [~know] ~識
유망하다	be promising [~hope] ~望
특유하다	be peculiar [special~] 特~
고유하다	be peculiar; be native (to) [firm~] 固~
유선	wire [~line] ~線 유선방송 cable broadcasting
유료	toll [~estimate] ~料 유료도로 toll highway
소유*	possession [whatever~] 所~ 소유.권 ownership
유심히	attentively; carefully [~mind -ly] ~心 K

유 (遺) bequeath

유언*	a will [~words] ~言
유산	inheritance [~possession] ~産
유물	relic; antiquity [~thing] ~物
유품	relic; article left by the deceased [~article] ~品

○

유적	vestige; relic [~trace] ~ 跡
유전*	hereditary transmission [~transmit] ~ 傳
유가족	bereaved family [~family] ~ 家族
유서	suicide note [~writing] ~ 書
유감	regrettable feeling [~remorse] ~ 憾 유감이다 (I) regret (that)

유 (油) oil

석유	petroleum [stone~] 石~
경유	light oil; gasoline [light~] 輕~
휘발유	volatile oil; gasoline [volatilization~] 揮發~
주유소	gas station [pour~place] 注~所
윤활유	lubricating oil [luster slippery~] 潤滑~
식용유	cooking oil [food use~] 食用~
유화	oil painting [~picture] ~ 畵
유부	fried bean curd [~rotten] ~腐 유부국수 noodle with fried bean curd

유 (乳) milk

우유	cow's milk [cow~] 牛~
분유	powdered milk [powder~] 粉~
모유	mother's milk [mother~] 母~
유지방	milk fat [~fat] ~ 脂肪
유제품	dairy product [~product] ~ 製品
이유식*	weaning diet [leave~food] 離~食
유방	woman's breast [~room] ~房

유 (誘) induce

권유*	inducement; exhortation [encourage~] 勸~
유혹*	temptation; seduction [~mislead] ~ 惑
유인*	allurement; inducement [~pull] ~ 引
유도*	leading out; guide [~lead] ~ 導
유발*	induction; triggering [~rise] ~ 發
유괴*	kidnapping [~entice] ~ 拐

유 (遊) outing

유람선	sightseeing boat [~view boat] ~ 覽船
유원지	amusement park [~garden place] ~ 園地
유흥	amusement; pleasure-seeking [~fun] ~ 興
선거유세*	electioneering tour [election~persuade] 選擧 ~ 說

유 (由) cause; from

이유	cause; reason [reason~] 理~
유래*	origin; originating [~come] ~ 來
경유*	passing through; via [pass through~] 經~
자유	freedom; liberty [self~] 自~

유 (幼) infantile

유치하다	be childish; be immature [~child] ~ 稚 유치원 kindergarten
유아원	nursery (school) [~child garden] ~兒園

179

ㅇ

유 (類)　**a kind; a sort**　(see 류)

유 (流)　**stream**　(see 류)

육 (肉)　**meat; flesh**

육류　meats [~a kind] ~ 類
육식*　meat diet [~eat] ~ 食
육수　beef broth [~water] ~ 水
육포　beef jerky [~sliced meat] ~ 脯
육개장　hot shredded beef soup
정육점　butcher shop [fine~store] 精 ~ 店
탕수육　sweet and sour pork [sugar water~] 糖水 ~
어두육미　fish heads and animal tails [fish head~tail] 魚頭 ~ 尾
육체　flesh; body [~body] ~ 體
　　　육체파 glamor
근육　muscle [muscle~] 筋 ~
육안　naked eye [~eye] ~ 眼

육 (陸)　**land**　(ﾉ륙)

육지　land (vs. ocean) [~place] ~ 地
내륙지방　inland area [inside~area] 內 ~ 地方
대륙　a continent [big~] 大 ~
착륙*　landing; touchdown [reach~] 着 ~
이륙*　take off [leave~] 離 ~
상륙*　landing; disembarkation [ascend~] 上 ~
육상경기　track and field events [~above event] ~ 上競技
육교　overpass [~bridge] ~ 橋

육군　army [~military] ~ 軍
육사　military academy [~officers' school] ~ 士 (<육군사관학교)

육 (育)　**raise; bring up**

양육*　bringing up [raise~] 養 ~
　　　양육비 cost of raising a child
사육*　breeding; raising (cattle, etc.) [feed animals~] 飼 ~
교육*　education [teach~] 敎 ~
체육　physical education [body~] 體 ~

윤 (潤)　**luster**

윤·기　luster; shine [~energy] ~ 氣
윤나다　be lustrous; be shiny [~come out] ~ K
윤활유　lubricating oil [~slippery oil] ~ 滑油

율 (率)　**rate; ratio**　(ﾉ률)

이율　interest rate [benefit~] 利 ~
환율　exchange rate [exchange~] 換 ~ (pron.=환뉼)
비율　ratio [compare~] 比 ~
백분율　percentage [hundred divide~] 百分 ~ (pron.=백분뉼)
확률　probability [certain~] 確 ~
능률　efficiency [able~] 能 ~
효율.적　efficient [effect~] 效 ~ 的
경쟁률　amount of competition [competition~] 競爭 ~

180

융 (融) melt; blend

융합*   fusion; harmony
[~unite] ~ 合

융통.성   adaptability; flexibility
[~circulate nature] ~ 通性

금융   finance; monetary market
[money~] 金 ~

융자*   financing; loaning funds
[~funds] ~ 資
학자금 융자   loan
for school expenses

은 ^w(銀) silver; money

은메달   silver medal [~medal] ~ E

은전   silver coin [~money] ~ 錢

은수저   silver spoon and
chopsticks
[~spoon and chopsticks] ~ K

은쟁반   silver tray [~tray] ~ 錚盤

은박지   silver foil
[~thin paper] ~ 箔紙

은하수   Milky Way; galaxy
[~stream water] ~ 河水

수은   mercury [water~] 水 ~

은행   bank [~act] ~ 行
은행원 bank teller
외환은행 foreign
exchange bank

은 (恩) a favor; indebtedness

은총   a favor; grace [~favor] ~ 寵
신의 은총 God's grace

은혜   a favor; indebtedness;
obligation [~a favor] ~ 惠
은혜를 알다/모르다
be grateful/ungrateful
은혜를 갚다
repay one's obligations

사은   grateful appreciation
[thank~] 謝~
사은품 thank-you gifts

은인   person to whom one
is beholden [~person] ~人
생명의 은인
savior of one's life

은 (隱) hide

은밀하다   be covert; be confidential
[~secret] ~ 密

은퇴*   retirement from a post;
withdrawal from
public life [~retreat] ~ 退

은은하다   (sound) be dim;
be distant

음 ^w(音) sound

음성   voice [~voice] ~ 聲

음절   syllable [~joint] ~ 節

모음   vowel [mother~] 母~

자음   consonant [son~] 子~

소음   noise [annoy~] 騷~
소음방지* noise pollution

잡음   noise; jarring and grating
[mixed~] 雜~

방음*   soundproof [defend~] 防~
방음장치* soundproof facility

음악   music [~music] ~ 樂

음정   musical interval; tone
[~measure] ~ 程

저음   bass; low voice [low~] 低~

고음   high tone [high~] 高~

음치   tone deafness; lack
of musical ability
[~imbecile] ~ 癡

녹음*   (sound) recording
[to record~] 錄 ~

음반   a (phonograph) record
[~tray] ~ 盤

음질   sound quality (of a stereo)
[~quality] ~ 質

음 (陰)   **dark; negative**

음산하다   be gloomy and chilly
[~disperse] ~ 散

음침하다   be somber [~sink] ~ 沈

음성   negativity [~nature] ~ 性

음모   plot; frame-up [~plot] ~ 謀

음흉하다   be wicked and treacherous
[~evil] ~ 凶

음력   lunar calendar
[~calendar] ~ 曆

음 (飮)   **drink**

과음*   overdrinking
[excessive~] 過 ~

음주운전*   drunken driving
[~liquor driving] ~ 酒運轉

음료   beverage [~material] ~ 料
음료수   beverage;
potable water

음식   food [~eat] ~ 食

음 (應)   **respond; suitable**

응하다   respond to; comply with

응답*   a reply [~answer] ~ 答
(자동)응답기 (automatic)
answering machine

반응*   reaction; response
[opposite~] 反 ~

호응*   response (to a request);
acting in concert [call~] 呼 ~

응낙*   consent [~consent] ~ 諾

적응*   adaptation; adjustment
[suitable~] 適 ~

응용*   practical application;
adaptation [~use] ~ 用

임기응변*   adaptation to
circumstances; an
expedient [temporary
opportunity~change] 臨機 ~ 變

응급   emergency [~urgent] ~ 急
응급치료* first-aid treatment

응모*   applying for; entering
(a contest) [~gather] ~ 募

응원*   moral support; cheering
[~help] ~ 援

의 (意)   **wish; intention; meaning**

의욕   volition; ambition
[~desire] ~ 慾

의지   will; volition [~intention] ~志
의지가 강하다
have a strong will

열의   zeal; enthusiasm
[hot~] 熱 ~

성의   sincerity [sincere~] 誠 ~

의도*   intention [~diagram] ~ 圖

의향   intention; inclination;
willingness [~to face] ~ 向

저의   real intention; ulterior
motive [bottom~] 底 ~

선의   good intention [good~] 善 ~
선의의 경쟁
competition in good faith

호의   goodwill; friendliness
[good~] 好 ~

고의   willfulness; intentionality
[cause~] 故 ~
고의로 intentionally

악의   bad intention [evil~] 惡~

임의로   at one's option
[be in charge~] 任 ~ K

의견   opinion; view
[~opinion] ~ 見

의사   thought; mind
[~think] ~ 思
의사를 밝히다
speak one's mind; make
known one's intentions
의사소통*
mutual communication

개의하다   care about; mind
[mediate~] 介 ~

의식*   consciousness; awareness
[~recognize] ~ 識

경의   respect; homage
[respect~] 敬~

합의*   mutual agreement
[unite~] 合 ~
합의이혼*
uncontested divorce

조의   mourning; condolences
[condole~] 弔~
조의를 표하다
express one's condolences

의의   meaning; significance
[~meaning] ~ 義

의미   meaning; significance
[~taste] ~ 味
의미 있는/없는
meaningful/meaningless
어떤 의미에서는 in a sense
의미심장하다
be profound in meaning

의역*   meaning translation
[~translate] ~ 譯

주의*   attention; caution
[pour~] 注~
주의깊다 be attentive
주의를 주다 give warnings

유의하다   keep in mind; be mindful
(of) [detention~] 留 ~

불의   unexpectedness;
suddenness [no~] 不~
불의의 사고
unexpected accident

의외   unexpectedness
[~outside] ~ 外
의외로 unexpectedly

의 (議) discuss

의논*   consultation; discussion
[~discuss] ~ 論

협의*   consultation; discussion
[harmony~] 協 ~

토의*   debate; discussion
[discuss~] 討 ~

회의*   conference; meeting
[meeting~] 會 ~

문의*   inquiry [ask~] 問~

모의*   conspiracy [plot~] 謀~

이의   different opinion
[different~] 異 ~

건의*   proposal; suggestion
[establish~] 建~

항의*   protestation; remonstrance
[resist~] 抗 ~

의 (疑) doubt

의심*   doubt; suspicion
[~mind] ~ 心
의심스럽다 be doubtful
의심이 많다 be incredulous
의심을 받다/사다
incur suspicion

의혹   suspicion [~mislead] ~ 惑
의혹을 품다 harbor suspicion

혐의   suspicion; charge
[hate~] 嫌~
살인혐의 charge of murder

의문   question; doubt [~ask] ~ 問

o

의아하다	be dubious; be doubtful [~suspicion] ~ 訝	의원	clinic [~institution] ~ 院 한의원 Chinese herb clinic
회의	skepticism [inmost desire~] 懷~ 회의적 skeptical		
		의 (依)	**depend on**
의처.증	obsessive suspicion of one's wife's chastity [~wife symptom] ~ 妻症	의존하다	depend on; rely on [~exist] ~ 存
		의지하다	lean on; turn to [~support] ~ 支
의 (義)	**right conduct; loyal; meaning**	의뢰*	request; commission; relying on [~trust] ~ 賴
도의	morality [principle~] 道~ 도의적 책임 moral responsibility	의례	customarily; usually [~usual] ~ 例
의리	sense of duty; loyalty [~principle] ~ 理	의하다	be based on (소문)에 의하면 according to (rumors)
정의	justice; righteousness [right~] 正~	**의 (衣)**	**clothes**
의무	duty; obligation [~duty] ~ 務	의식주	clothes; food and shelter [~food dwell] ~ 食住
주의	principle; -ism [chief~] 主~ 민주주의 democracy 공산주의 communism 개인주의 individualism	의류	clothing; garments [~a sort] ~ 類
		의상	dress; costume [~dress] ~ 裳
		내의	underwear [inside~] 內~
정의*	definition [decide~] 定~ 정의를 내리다 give a definition	금의환향*	returning home in glory [silk~return hometown] 錦~還鄉
강의*	a lecture [lecture~] 講~		
		이 (利)	**benefit; gain (/리)**
의 (醫)	**medical science**	이롭다	be profitable; be beneficial
의학	medical science [~study] ~學	이익	gains; profits; advantage [~profit] ~ 益
의대	medical school [~college] ~大 (<의·과대학)	이득	gains; profits [~gain] ~ 得
의사	medical doctor [~master] ~師 전문의(사) specialist (doctor) 돌팔이 의사 quack (doctor)	폭리	excessive profits [cruel~] 暴~ 폭리를 취하다 profiteer
의료보험	medical insurance [~treatment insurance] ~療保險	이자	interest (on money) [~thing] ~ 子
의술	medical arts; medical practice [~skill] ~ 術	이율	interest rate [~rate] ~ 率

이.점 advantage [~point] ~ 點

유리하다 be advantageous [exist~] 有~

불리하다 be disadvantageous [no~] 不~

이용* utilization; taking advantage of [~use] ~ 用

이기적 selfish; egoistic [~self] ~ 己的
이기주의 egoism
이기주의자 egoist

편리* convenience [convenient~] 便~

승리* victory [win~] 勝~

이 (以) from; with

이후 from now on; thereafter [~after] ~ 後

이래 from that time on; ever since [~come] ~ 來

이전 prior to; before [~before] ~ 前

이상 more than; now that [~above] ~ 上

이하 not exceeding; under [~below] ~ 下

이내 within; not more than [~inside] ~ 內

이외 except for; other than [~outside] ~ 外

이남 South Korea [~south] ~ 南

이북 North Korea [~north] ~ 北

이 (異) different

차이 difference [differ~] 差~

이상하다 be strange; be unusual [~usual] ~ 常

이국적 exotic [~country] ~ 國的

특이하다 be unique [special~] 特 ~

이의 different opinion [~discuss] ~ 議

이변 unusual change; accident [~change] ~ 變

이상 abnormality; something wrong [~shape] ~ 狀
이상있다/없다
There is something/ nothing wrong.

이성 opposite sex [~sex] ~ 性

이 (離) leave; separate (/리)

이별* parting; separation [~separate] ~ 別

이륙* take off [~land] ~ 陸

이탈* secession; breakaway [~escape] ~ 脫

분리* separation; division [divide~] 分~

이혼* divorce [~marriage] ~ 婚

격리* isolating (a patient) [isolate~] 隔~

거리 distance [distance~] 距~

난리 uproar; commotion [chaos~] 亂~

이 ʷ (二) two; second

이중 double; twofold [~layers] ~ 重
이중인격 double personality

이등분* splitting into two [~equal divide] ~ 等分

이차 the second [~sequence] ~ 次

이류 second-rate [~stream] ~ 流

ㅇ

이세	second generation [~generation] ~ 世	노인	elderly person [old~] 老~
		행인	passer-by [go~] 行~
이 (移)	**move**	미인	beautiful woman [beautiful~] 美~
이동*	movement; migration [~move] ~ 動 이동도서관 bookmobile	부인	married woman [married woman~] 婦~
이사*	(house) moving [~change residence] ~ 徙 이사가다/오다 move out/in 이삿짐 house-moving baggage	부인	wife [husband~] 夫~
		거인	gigantic person [big~] 巨~
		군인	soldier [military~] 軍~
이전*	(business, office) moving [~transfer] ~ 轉	민간인	civilian [civilian~] 民間~
이민*	emigration; immigration emigrant; immigrant [~people] ~ 民 이민가다 emigrate 이민오다 immigrate	연예인	performer; entertainer [perform art~] 演藝~
		신인	new face (entertainer) [new~] 新~
		시인	poet [poetry~] 詩~
이 (理)	**reasoning; principle manage** (see 리)	지성인	an intellectual [intelligence~] 知性~
		맹인	blind person [blind~] 盲~
익 (益)	**profit**	외국인	foreigner [foreign country~] 外國~
이익	gains; profits; advantage [gain~] 利~	백인	Caucasian [white~] 白~
유익하다	be beneficial; be instructive [exist~] 有~	흑인	black person [black~] 黑~
		상인	merchant; shopkeeper [trade~] 商~
		범인	criminal [offence~] 犯~
인 (人)	**person**	죄인	criminal; sinner [crime~] 罪~
개인	an individual [individual~] 個~	인질	hostage [~substance] ~ 質 인질로 잡히다 be held hostage
타인	unrelated person; stranger [others~] 他~	증인	witness; testifier [testify~] 證~ 보증인 guarantor; sponsor
인물	person; character; figure [~object] ~ 物 등장인물 dramatis personae 위험인물 dangerous character	고인	the deceased [the past~] 故~
		하인	servant [below~] 下~
인간	human being [~between] ~間 인간성 human nature	교인	believer; Christian [religion~] 敎~

ㅇ

애인	boy/girlfriend; one's love [love~] 愛~	인심	human heart [~heart] ~ 心
연인	romantic partner; lover [love~] 戀~	인공	human work; artificiality [~labor] ~ 工
은인	person to whom one is beholden [favor~] 恩~		인공수정* artificial insemination 인공호흡* artificial respiration
주인	proprietor; owner [host~] 主~	인사	greeting; thanking; personnel management [~matters] ~ 事
본인	the person in question [origin~] 本~ 장본인 ringleader		인사성 courteousness 인사이동* personnel changes
장인	wife's father [an elder~] 丈~	인격	character; personality [~frame] ~ 格
성인	saint [holy~] 聖~	인형	doll [~shape] ~ 形
성인	adult [to complete~] 成~	인어	mermaid [~fish] ~ 魚
초인	superhuman [excel~] 超~	인삼	ginseng [~ginseng] ~ 蔘
인파	surging crowd; waves of people [~wave] ~ 波	인도	sidewalk [~way] ~ 道
인류	humankind [~a kind] ~ 類 인류학 anthropology	**인 (引)**	**pull**
인종	(human) race [~a kind] ~種 인종차별* racial discrimination	유인*	allurement; inducement [induce~] 誘~
인구	population [~mouth] ~ 口 인구밀도 population density	인도*	guidance; leading [~lead] ~ 導
인·기	popularity [~spirit] ~ 氣	인솔*	guiding (a group) [~to lead] ~ 率
인체	human body [~body] ~ 體	인상*	(price) raising [~above] ~ 上
인상	physiognomy; facial looks [~face] ~ 相	인하*	(price) lowering [~below] ~ 下
인원	the number of persons [~member] ~ 員	견인지역	tow-away zone [drag~zone] 牽~地域
인재	talented person [~material] ~ 材	인용*	quotation [~use] ~ 用
인명	human life [~life] ~ 命 인명피해 loss of human lives	색인	index [seek~] 索~
인생	(human) life; existence [~life] ~ 生 인생관 view of life	**인 (印)**	**seal; stamp**
		검인	seal of approval [inspect~] 檢~
인정	humaneness; compassion [~feeling] ~ 情	날인*	affixing a seal [press~] 捺~

인쇄*	printing [~print] ~ 刷
인지	paper stamp [~paper] ~ 紙 수입인지 revenue stamp
인주	red stamping ink [~red] ~ 朱
인상	impression [~image] ~ 象
낙인	a brand; stigma [to brand~] 烙 ~ 낙인찍히다 be branded

인 (認) consent

승인*	approval [consent~] 承 ~
묵인*	tacit approval; connivance [silent~] 默 ~
확인*	confirmation [certain~] 確~ 재확인* reconfirmation
부인*	denial [on the contrary~] 否~
인정*	acknowledgment; recognition [~decide] ~ 定 인정받다 receive recognition
인식*	cognition; understanding [~recognize] ~ 識

인 (因) cause

원인	cause; factor [origin~] 原~
요인	primary factor; main cause [essential~] 要~
인하다	be caused by
인연	predestined tie; affinity [~affinity] ~ 緣

일 ᵂ(一) one; first

일렬	one line/row [~line] ~ 列
일례	one example [~example] ~ 例
일.종	a kind (of) [~a kind] ~ 種
일방적	one-sided; unilateral [~direction] ~ 方的

일방통행*	one-way traffic [~direction traffic] ~ 方通行
일일이	one by one; in detail ~ ~ K
일.단	once; first [~morning] ~ 旦 일.단 약속을 했으면 지켜야 한다 Once one has made a promise, one should keep it. 일.단 먹고나서 생각하자 Let's eat first and think about it later.
일약	at a single jump [~jump] ~ 躍
유일하다	be single; be unique [only~] 唯~
일.시적	transient; passing [~time] ~ 時的
일.시불	lump-sum payment [~time pay] ~ 時拂
일.제히	all at one time; with one accord [~uniform] ~ 齊K
일.동	all the persons concerned [~together] ~ 同 가족일.동 all the family
일.대	the whole area; the neighborhood (of) [~belt] ~ 帶
일부	a part [~section] ~ 部
일행	company, troupe [~go] ~ 行
일.주*	making the rounds (of) [~encircle] ~ 周
일.생	one's lifetime [~life] ~ 生
일인당	per person [~person suitable] ~ 人當
일치*	agreement; consensus [~reach] ~ 致 만장일치 unanimity
통일*	unification; uniformity [govern~] 統~ 남북통일* unification of North and South (Korea) 평화통일* peaceful unification

동**일**하다	be identical [same~] 同~
균**일**하다	be uniform; be even [equal~] 均~
일.정하다	be fixed; be regular [~fix] ~定
일관.성	consistency; coherence [~pierce nature] ~貫性
일.절	entirely (not) [~cut] ~切 술은 일.절 금해야한다 (You) must not drink at all.
일체	all; any and every thing [~all] ~切
일리	some reason; truth [~reason] ~理
일반	general; common [~general] ~般
만**일**	if; in case [ten thousand~] 萬~
일.석이조	killing two birds with one stone [~stone two birds] ~石二鳥
일편단심	devoted heart; fidelity [~piece red heart] ~片丹心
일.등*	first rank; top [~rank] ~等
일류	top-ranking [~stream] ~流
제**일**	the first; number one [order~] 第~
일차	the first [~sequence] ~次
일품	(article of) top quality [~article] ~品

일 (日) day; sun

요**일**	day of the week [brightness~] 曜~ 월/화/수/목/ 금/토/일(요일) Mon-/Tues-/ Wednes-/Thurs-/ Fri-/Satur/Sun-(day)
생**일**	birthday [be born~] 生~

일력	daily calendar pad [~calendar] ~曆
일.상	everyday; usually [~usual] ~常
(**일**)주**일**	(one) week [one week~] 一週~
기념**일**	anniversary [commemoration~] 紀念~ 결혼기념일 wedding anniversary
평**일**	weekdays [ordinary~] 平~
휴**일**	holiday [rest~] 休~ 공휴일 official holiday
공**일**	holiday; Sunday [empty~] 空~
국경**일**	national holiday [nation congratulate~] 國慶~
식목**일**	Arbor Day [plant tree~] 植木~
시**일**	time; days [time~] 時~
예정**일**	scheduled date [schedule~] 豫定~
당**일**	the day (in question) [suitable~] 當~ 당일치기* a day's trip; one day's cramming for an exam
종**일**	all day [finish~] 終~ 하루종일 all day
일보	daily newspaper [~report] ~報 X일보 X daily paper
일용품	daily necessities [~use article] ~用品
일과	daily task; schedule [~task] ~課
일기	diary [~record] ~記
일.정	day's schedule; itinerary [~route] ~程
일.당	daily allowance [~suitable] ~當

ㅇ

일.진   day's luck [~dragon] ~辰

작심삼일   resolution good for only three days; short-lived resolution [make mind three~] 作心三~

일광욕*   sunbathing [~shine bathe] ~光浴

임 (任)   be in charge; entrust

주임   person in charge; a head [main~] 主~

담임*   teacher in charge (of a class) [carry~] 擔~

임원   an executive [~member] ~員

임기   one's term of service [~period] ~期

임무   duty; task [~duty] ~務

전임*   exclusive duty; a full-time (position) [exclusive~] 專~
전임강사   full-time lecturer

책임   responsibility [responsible~] 責~
책임지다   take responsibility
무책임하다   be irresponsible
책임감   sense of responsibility
책임자   person in charge

취임*   assumption of office; inauguration [take~] 就~

임명*   appointment; nomination [~command] ~命

후임   successor (to a post) [after~] 後~

임의로   at one's option [~wish] ~意.K

임 (臨)   come to; temporary

임하다   stand in the presence of; face (a danger)

임박하다   be near at hand; draw near [~oppress] ~迫

임종   one's last moment of life [~finish] ~終

임시   temporary [~time] ~時
임시로   temporarily
임시변통*   makeshift measure

임기응변*   adaptation to circumstances; an expedient [~opportunity respond change] ~機應變

임 (姙/妊)   pregnant

임신*   pregnancy [~pregnant] ~娠

피임*   contraception [avoid~] 避~
피임약   contraceptive

임산부   pregnant mother [~produce woman] ~産婦

임 (賃)   wages; lease

임금   wage [~money] ~金
임금인상*   wage increase

운임   freight rates [transport~] 運~

임대*   lease; hiring out [~lend] ~貸
임대아파트   leased apartment

입 (入)   enter

입구   entrance [~opening] ~口

입장*   entrance; admission [~place] ~場
입장권   admission ticket
입장료   entrance fee
무료입장*   free admission

입국*   entry into a country [~country] ~國

출입*   exit and entrance [exit~] 出~
미성년자 출입금지
No minors

입학*	admission into a school [~study] ~ 學
입시	entrance exam [~exam] ~ 試 (<입학시험)
편입*	transfer (to another school) [weave~] 編~
입원*	hospitalization [~institution] ~ 院
입사*	becoming a member of a company [~company] ~ 社
입대*	enlistment [~army] ~ 隊
가입*	joining (an association) [apply~] 加~
개입*	intervention [mediate~] 介~
주입*	pouring in; instillment [pour~] 注~
삽입*	insertion [insert~] 揷~
투입*	putting in; investing [throw~] 投~
침입*	invasion; trespass [invade~] 侵~
수입*	import [transport~] 輸~
기입*	writing in; filling in (a form) [record~] 記~
입력*	power input [~power] ~ 力
입상*	winning a prize [~prize] ~ 賞
입선*	being selected in a competition [~select] ~ 選
입수*	coming to hand; obtaining [~hand] ~ 手 정보를 입수하다 obtain information
입양*	adopting (a child) [~bring up] ~ 養
입 (立)	establish (see 립)

ㅈ

자 (自)	self; from
자기	self [~self] ~ 己 자기중심적 self-centered 자기생각만 하다 think of oneself only
자신	one's self [~person] ~ 身 자기자신 one's own self
자체	oneself; itself [~body] ~ 體 그 생각 자체 the thought itself
자립*	independence; self-support [~stand] ~ 立
자신*	self-confidence [~believe] ~ 信
자만*	self-admiration; self-conceit [~arrogant] ~ 慢
자존.심	self-respect; pride [~respect mind] ~ 尊心
자습*	self-study [~study] ~ 習
자위*	self-consolation; masturbation [~console] ~ 慰
자제*	self-restraint; self-control [~regulate] ~ 制 자제력 power of self-control
자취*	self-boarding; cooking food for oneself [~cook] ~ 炊
자칭*	self-styled; self-appointed [~call] ~ 稱
자수*	self-surrender [~head] ~ 首
자율.적	self-regulating; autonomous [~rule] ~ 律的
자화상	self-portrait [~picture appearance] ~ 畵像
자축*	self-celebration [~celebrate] ~ 祝

자화자찬* self-praise;
self-admiration
[~picture~praise] ~ 畵 ~ 讚

자초하다 bring upon oneself; incur
(blame) [~invite] ~ 招

자포자기* self-abandonment;
despair [~cruel~abandon]
~ 暴 ~ 棄

자살* suicide [~kill] ~ 殺

자부하다 be self-confident
[~carry] ~ 負
자부.심 pride; self-conceit

자원하다 volunteer [~request] ~ 願

자청하다 volunteer [~request] ~ 請

자발.적 voluntary; spontaneous
[~rise] ~ 發的
자발.적으로 voluntarily

자퇴* voluntary withdrawing
(from school) [~leave] ~ 退

자진하다 do (something) of one's
own accord [~advance] ~ 進
자진해서
of one's own accord

자비 (at) one's own expense
[~expenditure] ~ 費

자가용 one's own car
[~family use] ~ 家用

자필 one's own handwriting
[~writing] ~ 筆
자필 이력서 resumé written
in one's own handwriting

자서전 autobiography
[~narrate transmit] ~ 敍 傳

각자 each one; individually
[each~] 各 ~

자택 private residence;
one's house (hon.)
[~residence] ~ 宅

자동 automatic movement
[~move] ~ 動

자동문 automatic door
자동차 automobile

자전거 bicycle [~revolve cart] ~ 轉車

자명종 alarm clock
[~chirp bell] ~ 鳴鐘

자백* confession (of
one's crime) [~tell] ~ 白

자유 freedom; liberty
[~cause] ~ 由

자연 nature [~as such] ~ 然

자고로 from ancient times;
traditionally
[~past -ly] ~ 故K

자 (者) **person**

부자 rich person [rich~] 富 ~

승자 winner [win~] 勝 ~

패자 loser [lose~] 敗 ~

강자 the strong [strong~] 强 ~

약자 the weak [weak~] 弱 ~

학자 scholar [study~] 學 ~
과학자 scientist

독자 reader [read~] 讀 ~

저자 author [write~] 著 ~

기자 journalist; reporter
[record~] 記 ~

타자 (baseball) hitter [hit~] 打 ~

신자 believer [believe~] 信 ~

병자 sick person [sickness~] 病 ~

환자 a patient [suffering~] 患 ~

불구자 deformed person
[deformity~] 不具 ~

장애자 handicapped person
[obstacle~] 障碍 ~

노약자 elderly person; the old and
the weak [old weak~] 老弱 ~

ㅈ

연소자	minors; underage people [age young~] 年少~	자 (子)	**son; children; thing**
살인자	murderer [murder~] 殺人~	자녀	sons and daughters; children [~female] ~女
피살·자	murder victim [being killed~] 被殺~	손자	grandson [grandchildren~] 孫~
피해자	victim; injured party [damage~] 被害~	효자	dutiful son [filial piety~] 孝~
기술·자	technician [technique~] 技術~	양자*	adopted son [bring up~] 養~
노동자	laborer [labor~] 勞動~	부전자전	like father like son [father transmit~transmit] 父傳~傳
근로자	laborer [labor~] 勤勞~	자식	one's children; a fellow (vulgar) [~son] ~息 처자식 one's wife and children 개자식 son of a bitch
실업자	unemployed person [lose job~] 失業~		
교육자	teacher; educator [education~] 敎育~		
선구자	forerunner [the lead~] 先驅~	자손	descendants [~grandson] ~孫
후계자	successor [after continue~] 後繼~	왕자	royal prince [king~] 王~
애국자	patriot [love of one's country~] 愛國~	남자	male; man [male~] 男~
		공자	Confucius [Confucius~] 孔~
책임자	responsible person; person in charge; [responsibility~] 責任~	제자	disciple; pupil [junior~] 弟~
		여자	female; woman [female~] 女~
적임자	person fit for the post [suitable in charge~] 適任~	자궁	womb [~mansion] ~宮
		자음	consonant [~sound] ~音
위선자	hypocrite [false good~] 僞善~	모자	hat; cap [hat~] 帽~
배우자	spouse [suitable pair~] 配偶~	과자	cookie; confectionery [sweets~] 菓~
당사자	the person concerned [suitable matter~] 當事~	전자	electron [electricity~] 電~
제삼자	a third party; outsider [order third~] 第三~	원자	atom [origin~] 原~
백만장자	millionaire [million superior~] 百萬長~	눈·동자	pupil (of the eye) [eye pupil~] K 瞳~
임자	owner; person to whom someone/a thing belongs	종자	seed [seed~] 種~
		주전자	kettle; tea kettle [liquor simmer~] ~煎子
전자	the former [before~] 前~	판자	wooden board; plank [plank~] 板~ 판잣집 a shack
후자	the latter [later~] 後~		

의자	chair [chair~] 椅~ 긴의자 bench 흔들의자 rocking chair
탁자	table [table~] 卓~
상자	box [basket~] 箱 ~
이자	interest (on money) [gain~] 利~
골·자	the pith and marrow; the essentials [bone~] 骨~
박자	beat; rhythm [clap~] 拍~
액자	(picture) frame [forehead~] 額 ~
족자	wall hangings [collect~] 簇~
국자	soup ladle; dipper [soup~] K~

자 (字) (written) character; letter

글·자	letter; character [writing~] K~
수·자	numeral; figure [number~] 數~ 아라비아 수·자 Arabic numerals
문·자	letter; character [literary~] 文~ 대문·자 capital letter 소문·자 small letter
철·자	spelling [spell~] 綴~
한·자	Chinese character [China~] 漢~
정·자	print letters; correct characters [correct~] 正~ 정·자로 기재하시오 Please print clearly.
약자	acronym; abbreviation [abbreviated~] 略~
오·자	wrong character; typo [mistake~] 誤~

적자	red letters; deficit [red~] 赤~
흑자	figures in black ink [black~] 黑~
타자	typing [hit~] 打~ 타자치다 type 타자기 typewriter
활·자	printing type; font [lively~] 活~
자막	subtitle [~curtain] ~ 幕
(열)십자	a cross [ten ten~] K 十~ 적십자 Red Cross
팔·자	destiny; fate [eight~] 八~

자 (資) funds; property

자금	funds [~money] ~ 金
자본	capital; funds [~source] ~ 本 자본주의 capitalism
투자*	investment [throw~] 投~
융자*	financing; loaning funds [blend~] 融~
자원	natural resources [~source] ~ 源
자료	materials; data [~material] ~ 料 연구자료 research materials 통계자료 statistical data
자격	qualification [~frame] ~ 格 자격상실* disqualification

자 (慈) benevolent

인자하다	be benevolent [benevolent~] 仁 ~
자비	mercy [~sorrowful] ~ 悲 자비를 베풀다 show mercy
자선	charity [~goodness] ~ 善 자선사업* charitable work

작 (作)　**make; do**

작품　a work; production
[~article] ~ 品
문학작품　literary work

제작*　(film) production
[manufacture~] 製~

합작*　joint work [join~] 合~

걸.작　masterpiece; buffoon
[outstanding~] 傑~

명작　masterpiece; fine work
[famous~] 名~

조작*　concoction; fabrication
[make~] 造~

작사*　song writing
[~words] ~ 詞

작곡*　musical composition
[~tune] ~ 曲
작곡가　composer

작문*　composition; writing
[~writing] ~ 文
영작문　English composition

작가　writer [~specialist] ~ 家

작정*　decision; intention
[~decide] ~ 定
...할 작정이다
be decided to do...
...하기로 작정하다
decide to do...

작성*　drawing up (the papers);
writing out (a contract)
[~to complete] ~ 成

작동*　(machine) operation
[~move] ~ 動

조작*　(machine) operation;
handling [hold~] 操~

작업*　work; operations
[~job] ~ 業
작업복　work clothes

타작*　threshing [hit~] 打~

동작　motion; gesture [move~] 動~

작별*　leave-taking; parting
[~separate] ~ 別

작용*　action; function; effect
[~use] ~ 用

작전　strategy; tactics
[~fighting] ~ 戰
작전을 짜다　elaborate
a plan of action

발.작*　fit; spasm [arise~] 發~
발.작을 일으키다　have a fit

잔 (殘)　**remainder; cruel**

잔금　balance; rest of the money
[~money] ~ 金

잔액　balance (in an account)
[~amount of money] ~ 額

잔고　balance (in an account)
[~high] ~ 高

잔인하다　be cruel [~endure] ~ 忍

잔 (盞)　**a glass; cup**

술.잔　wine glass [liquor~] K~

찻잔　tea cup [tea~] 茶~

커피.잔　coffee cup [coffee~] E~

유리잔　a glass [glass~] K~

등잔　oil cup for a lamp
[lamp~] 燈~

잠 (潛)　**submerge**

잠수*　submerging [~water] ~ 水
잠수함　submarine
잠수교　submerging bridge

잠재*　latency; dormancy
[~exist] ~ 在
잠재력　potential ability
잠재의식　subconsciousness

잠적*　concealing oneself;
disappearing [~trace] ~ 跡

잠잠하다	be quiet; be calm	난잡하다	be disorderly; be lawless; be indecent [chaotic~] 亂 ~
		조잡*	crudeness [coarse~] 粗 ~
잡 (雜)	**mixed**	추잡*	filthiness; indecency [ugly~] 醜 ~
잡곡	miscellaneous cereals [~grain] ~ 穀 잡곡밥 rice mixed with miscellaneous cereals	착잡하다	feel entangled; feel mixed up [confused~] 錯 ~
잡채	dish of mixed vegetables, long rice, and beef [~vegetable] ~ 菜	장 (場)	**ground; place**
잡탕	hodgepodge [~soup] ~ 湯	장소	place; location [~place] ~ 所
잡종	hybrid; crossbred [~a kind] ~ 種	광장	open ground; plaza [broad~] 廣 ~ 역전광장 station square
잡초	weed [~grass] ~ 草	주차장	parking lot [parking~] 駐車 ~
잡놈	bastard; son of a bitch [~fellow (vulgar)] ~ K	야구장	ball park [baseball~] 野球 ~
잡념	distracting thoughts [~thought] ~ 念	운동장	playground; stadium [sports~] 運動~
잡담*	idle talk; desultory chat [~converse] ~ 談	골프장	golf course [golf~] E ~
잡음	noise; jarring and grating [~sound] ~ 音	사격장	shooting range [shooting~] 射擊~
잡다하다	be miscellaneous; be sundry [~many] ~ 多	스케이트장	skating rink [skate~] E ~
		스키장	skiing ground [ski~] E~
잡비	sundry expenses [~expenditure] ~ 費	볼링장	bowling alley [bowling~] E~
잡상인	miscellaneous traders; peddlers [~trader] ~ 商人	수영장	swimming pool [swimming~] 水泳~
잡동사니	miscellaneous articles; sundries	백사장	sandy beach [white sand~] 白沙~
잡지	magazine [~record] ~ 誌	경마장	race track [horserace~] 競馬~
혼잡*	congestion; disorder [mix~] 混~	개장*	opening (a place) [open~] 開~
복잡*	complexity [double~] 複~	도장	drill hall; gymnasium [principle~] 道~ 태.권도장 taekwondo drill hall
번잡*	complicatedness; crowding [troublesome~] 煩~	(시)장	market [market~] 市~ 장보러 가다 go shopping
		극장	theater [drama~] 劇~

식장	ceremonial hall [ceremony~] 式~ 예식장 wedding hall	연장*	extension; lengthening [extend~] 延~
정거장	(bus, train) station [stopping of vehicle~] 停車~	신장	stature; height [body~] 身~
정류장	(bus) stop [stoppage~] 停留~	성장*	growth [to complete~] 成~
비행장	airfield; airport [flying~] 飛行~	기장	length of a dress/suit
직장	one's place of work; one's job [post~] 職~	장수*	long life; longevity [~longevity] ~ 壽
공장	factory [industry~] 工~	장거리	long distance [~distance] ~ 距離 장거리 전화* long-distance call
목장	ranch [herd animals~] 牧~	장발	(men's) long hair [~hair] ~ 髮
농장	farm; plantation [agricultural~] 農~		
양계장	poultry (chicken) farm [raise chicken~] 養鷄~	장편	long piece (novel) [~book] ~ 篇
입장	position; situation [stand~] 立~	장남	eldest son [~male] ~ 男
당장	on the spot; immediately [suitable~] 當~	장녀	eldest daughter [~female] ~ 女
현장	the spot (of the action) [current~] 現~	장유유서	order between the old and the young; the elder first [~child exist order] ~ 幼有序
입장*	entrance; admission [enter~] 入~	가장	head of a family [family~] 家~
등장*	advent; appearance [mount~] 登~ 등장인물 dramatis personae	장관	cabinet minister [~official] ~ 官
퇴장*	leaving (the hall); exit; walkout [leave~] 退~	시장	mayor [city~] 市~
		과장	(department) chairperson [department~] 科~
장면	scene [~surface]~ 面	과장	(company) head of a section [section~] 課~
수라장	pandemonium [repair spread out~] 修羅~	회장	(committee) chairperson; (society) president [meeting~] 會~
유치장	police cell; detention house [detention to place~] 留置~	사장	(company) president [company~] 社~
		부장	department manager [department~] 部~
장 (長)	**long; elder; superior**	원장	director of an institute [institution~] 院~
장기	long term [~term] ~ 期 장기계획 long-term plan		

교**장** school principal [school~] 校~

학**장** college dean [learning~] 學~

총**장** president of a university [general~] 總~

반**장** section leader; class president [section~] 班~

선**장** (ship's) captain [ship~] 船~

주방**장** headcook; chef [kitchen~] 廚房~

장·기 special skill; talent [~skill] ~ 技

장.점 merit; good point [~point] ~ .点
장단(점) merit and demerit; strength and weakness

일.**장**일.단 merits and demerits [one~one short] 一~一短

장화 high rubber boots [~shoes] ~ 靴

장작 firewood [~chopper] ~ 斫

장 (裝) **decorate; costume; pack**

장식* ornament; decoration [~decorate] ~ 飾
장식품 ornaments; decorations
실내장식* interior decoration

분**장*** makeup; getup [makeup~] 扮~

장신구 personal ornaments; personal outfittings [~body tool] ~ 身具

복**장** dress; uniform [clothes~] 服~

정**장*** formal dress; full dress [right~] 正~

가**장*** disguise; camouflage [false~] 假~
가장행렬* fancy procession

변**장*** disguise; masquerade [change~] 變~

위**장*** camouflage; disguise [false~] 僞~

포**장*** wrapping [wrap~] 包~

포**장*** paving; pavement [pave~] 鋪~

장비 equipment; fitting [~prepare] ~ 備
등산장비 hiking equipment

장치* equipment; installation; apparatus [~to place] ~ 置
냉방장치* air-conditioning apparatus

무**장*** armaments [military~] 武~

장 (壯) **valiant; strong**

장사 strong man [~man] ~ 士

장정 strong, young man; sturdy youth [~person] ~ 丁

건**장**하다 be robust [healthy~] 健~

웅**장**하다 (building) be grand; be magnificent [virile~] 雄~

장관 magnificent view; grand spectacle [~view] ~ 觀

굉**장**하다 be magnificent; be tremendous [great~] 宏~

장하다 be splendid; be praiseworthy

장담* assurance; guarantee [~talk] ~ 談

장판 floor cover [~printing board] ~ 版

장 (狀) **letter; document**

답**장** letter of reply [reply~] 答~

198

초대.장 invitation card [invitation~] 招待~

연하.장 New Year's card [year congratulate~] 年賀~

청첩.장 wedding invitation card [invitation letter~] 請牒~

안내.장 (commercial) letter of advice [guidance~] 案內~

상.장 award certificate [award~] 賞~

졸업장 diploma (of graduation) [graduation~] 卒業~

영.장 warrant [command~] 令~
구속영.장 arrest warrant

장 (將) **military officer; chess; future**

장교 (military) officer [~field officer] ~校

장병 officers and men; military men [~soldier] ~兵

대장 a general; head; chief [great~] 大~

장군 commander-in-chief; a general [~military] ~軍

주장 captain (of a team) [main~] 主~

장기 chess game [~chess piece] ~棋

장래 future; prospect [~come] ~來

장차 in the future; some day [~next] ~次

장 (醬) **soy sauce**

간장 soy sauce [salty taste~] K~

된장 soybean paste [thick~] K~

고추장 thick soy paste mixed with red peppers [red pepper~] K~

초장 soy sauce mixed with vinegar and pine-nut meal [vinegar~] 醋~

게장 soy sauce in which crabs are preserved [crab~] K~

막장 soybean paste mixed with assorted ingredients [rough~] K~

장조림* beef boiled in soy sauce [~hard-boiled food] ~ K

장 (腸) **intestine**

대장 large intestines [big~] 大~
대장균 colitis germs

간장 liver and intestines; heart [liver~] 肝~

위장 stomach and intestine [stomach~] 胃~

맹장 appendix (organ) [blind~] 盲~
맹장염 appendicitis
맹장수술* appendectomy

관장* rectal injection; enema [irrigate~] 灌~

환장하다 go crazy; be out of one's mind [exchange~] 換~

장티푸스 typhoid fever [~typhus] ~E

장 (欌) **cabinet**

신.장 shoe cabinet [shoes~] K~

찬.장 pantry chest; cupboard [special dish~] 饌~

새장 birdcage [bird~] K~

책장 bookcase [book~] 冊~

옷장 wardrobe cabinet; closet [clothes~] K~

진열.**장**   (store) display window [display~] 陳列~

장 (張)   **stretch; extend; sheet (of paper, stamps, etc.)**

확**장***   extension; enlargement [enlarge~] 擴~

출.**장**   business trip [exit~] 出~

주**장***   a claim [main~] 主~

긴**장***   tension [tense~] 緊~

장본인   ringleader [~the person in question] ~ 本人

겉**장**   front page; (book) cover [surface~] K~

장 (障)   **obstacle; obstruct**

장애   obstacle [~obstruct] ~ 碍
장애가 되다 be an obstacle (to)
장애물 obstacle; hurdle
장애자 disabled person

장벽   wall; barrier [~wall] ~ 壁
언어장벽 language barrier

천**장**   ceiling [sky~] 天~

고**장**   breakdown; out of order [cause~] 故~
고장나다 break down; become out of order

지**장**   hindrance; difficulty [support~] 支~
지장을 주다
cause inconvenience
...하는데 지장없다
have no difficulty in doing...

보**장***   guaranteeing; security [protect~] 保~

장 (葬)   **funeral**

장사지내다 hold a funeral
[~matter hold] ~ 事 K

장례식*   funeral [~ceremony] ~ 禮式

화**장***   cremation [fire~] 火~

매**장***   burial; social ostracism [bury~] 埋~

장의사   funeral parlor [~rite company] ~ 儀社

장 (帳)   **accounts; curtain**

장부   account book [~account book] ~ 簿

통**장**   bankbook; passbook [circulate~] 通~
저금통장 savings passbook

연습**장**   workbook [practice~] 練習~

모기**장**   mosquito net [mosquito~] K~

포**장**마차   covered-wagon bar [cotton~carriage] 布~馬車

장 (臟)   **viscera**

내**장**   internal organs [inside~] 內~

심**장**   heart [heart~] 心~

간(**장**)   liver [liver~] 肝~

신**장**   kidney [kidney~] 腎~

장 (章)   **a seal; badge; paragraph**

도**장**   a seal; a stamp [drawing~] 圖~
도장찍다 affix one's seal

지**장**   thumbprint [finger~] 指~

완**장**   armband [arm~] 腕~

문**장**   a piece of writing; sentence [literary~] 文~

장 (粧)   **makeup**

화**장***   makeup [change~] 化~
화장품 cosmetics

화장지　toilet paper; kleenex
화장실　toilet; bathroom

단장*　dressing; refurbishing
[red~] 丹~

치장*　embellishment
[govern~] 治~

장 (藏)　**storage**

냉**장**고　refrigerator
[cold~storehouse] 冷~庫

저**장***　storing; preservation
[save~] 貯~

무진**장**　being inexhaustible
[not exhaust~] 無盡~

장 (獎)　**encourge**

장려*　encouragement; promotion
[~encourage] ~勵
저축을 장려하다
encourage saving

권**장***　encouragement;
exhortation [encourage~] 勸~

재 (再)　**again; re-**

재고*　reconsideration
[~consider] ~考

재발*　relapse; recurrence
[~arise] ~發

재혼*　remarriage [~marriage] ~婚

재기*　rising again; recovery
[~rise] ~起

재생*　regeneration; recycling
[~life] ~生

재검사*　reexamination
[~examination] ~檢查

재시험　makeup exam
[~exam] ~試驗

재수*　repreparing for
college entrance exam
[~cultivate] ~修
재수생 student repreparing
for college entrance exam

재평·가*　revaluation
[~evaluation] ~評價

재확인*　reconfirmation
[~confirmation] ~確認

재회*　meeting again; reunion
[~meeting] ~會

재결합*　reunion [~union] ~結合

재발급*　reissuance [~issuing] ~發給

재방송*　rebroadcasting
[~broadcasting] ~放送

재작년　the year before last
[~last year] ~昨年

재탕*　second brew; rehashing
[~hot water] ~湯

재 (財)　**property; wealth**

재산　property; estate
[~possession] ~産

재물　property; treasures
[~thing] ~物

재벌　conglomerate; tycoon
[~clique] ~閥

재정　public finance; fiscal
matters [~govern] ~政

재무부　Ministry of Finance
[~affair section] ~務部

재단　benefactive foundation
[~group] ~團
재단법인　juridical foundation

문화**재**　cultural assets
[culture~] 文化~

재수　luck; fortune [~fate] ~數

횡**재***　unexpected fortune;
windfall [unexpected~] 橫~

ㅈ

재 (在)	**exist; be present**	재치	wit [~bring about] ~致
존재*	existence; being [exist~] 存~ 신의 존재 existence of God	재 (裁)	**cut out (clothes); judge**
부재중	absent; out [not~middle] 不~中	재단*	(garment) cutting [~cut] ~斷
재학*	being in school [~study] ~學 재학생 (school) student	재봉*	sewing; needlework [~sew] ~縫 재봉틀 sewing machine
재직*	holding office; being in office [~office] ~職	재판*	judgment; trial [~judge] ~判
재미교포	Korean resident in the U. S. [~U. S. Korean living abroad] ~美僑胞	재량	discretion; judgment [~to measure] ~量 재량껏하다 use one's discretion
재일교포	Korean resident in Japan [~Japan Korean living abroad] ~日僑胞	제재*	sanction; punishment [suppress~] 制~
현재	presently; present time [now~] 現~	결·재*	sanction; approval [decide~] 決~
재고	stock; stockpile [~storehouse] ~庫 재고정리세일* clearance sale	총재	president of a political party [general~] 總~
		독재*	dictatorship [alone~] 獨~
재래식	conventional style [~coming style] ~來式	재 (材)	**material; stuff**
재 (才)	**talent; skill**	재료	material; ingredient [~material] ~料
재능	gift; talent; ability [~ability] ~能 타고난 재능 one's natural gifts	소재	material; subject matter [element~] 素~
		교재	teaching material; text [teach~] 敎~
재간	ability; talent [~main] ~幹 말·재간 gift of gab	취재*	selection of material; news gathering [obtain~] 取~
재주	talent; gift; ability; skill 손·재주 dexterity 재주군 talented person 재주껏 to the best of one's ability	인재	talented person [person~] 人~
		목재	wood; lumber [wood~] 木~
재롱	baby's cute tricks [~play with] ~弄	재 (災)	**calamity**
천재	genius [divine~] 天~	재난	calamity; disaster [~difficulty] ~難
수재	brilliant person [excellent~] 秀~	재해	calamity; disaster [~harm] ~害

ㅈ

천재지변　natural disaster
　　　　　[sky~earth incident] 天~地變

화재　　　fire disaster [fire~] 火~

수재　　　flood disaster [water~] 水~
　　　　　수재민 flood victim

쟁 (爭) fight; dispute

투쟁*　　a fight; a struggle
　　　　　[fight~] 鬪~

전쟁*　　war [war~] 戰~

경쟁*　　competition [compete~] 競~
　　　　　생존경쟁*
　　　　　struggle for existence

쟁탈전　a scramble (for
　　　　　the championship)
　　　　　[~deprive fighting] ~ 奪戰

언쟁*　　verbal dispute [words~] 言~

논쟁*　　a dispute; argument
　　　　　[discuss~] 論~

저 (低) low

최저　　　the lowest; the minimum
　　　　　[the most~] 最~
　　　　　최저기온　the lowest
　　　　　temperature

저온　　　low temperature
　　　　　[~warm] ~ 溫

저기압　low air pressure; bad
　　　　　mood [~air pressure] ~ 氣壓

저혈압　low blood pressure
　　　　　[~blood pressure] ~ 血壓

저음　　　bass; low voice
　　　　　[~sound] ~ 音

저렴하다　be low priced
　　　　　[~moderate] ~ 廉

저질　　　low quality [~quality] ~ 質

저하*　　a decline (in quality, value,
　　　　　etc.); a drop [~descend] ~ 下

저속하다　be vulgar; be base
　　　　　[~vulgar] ~ 俗

저조하다　(market) be dull;
　　　　　(achievements) be poor
　　　　　[~control] ~ 調

저 (著) write; manifest

공저　　　joint work; coauthorship
　　　　　[together~] 共~

저자　　　author [~person] ~ 者

저서　　　one's writings;
　　　　　publications [~writing] ~ 書

저작권　copyright
　　　　　[~make rights] ~ 作權

저명하다　be eminent [~name] ~ 名

현저하다　be notable; be remarkable
　　　　　[conspicuous~] 顯~

저 (貯) save

저금*　　saving money; deposit
　　　　　[~money] ~ 金
　　　　　저금통　savings box;
　　　　　(piggy) bank
　　　　　저금통장　bankbook

저축*　　saving [~store up] ~ 蓄

저장*　　storing; preservation
　　　　　[~to store] ~ 藏

저 (底) bottom

저의　　　real intention; ulterior
　　　　　motive [~intention] ~ 意

저력　　　potential ability
　　　　　[~strength] ~ 力

철·저하다　be thorough [penetrate~] 徹~
　　　　　철·저히　thoroughly

적 (的) target; -ic(al); -ive

목적*　　purpose; aim [eye~] 目~

203

적중하다	hit the mark; guess right [~middle] ~ 中 예상이 적중하다 One's prediction turns out true.
역사적	historic(al) [history~] 歷史~
일시적	transient; passing [one time~] 一時~
주관적	subjective [subjectivity~] 主觀~
객관적	objective [objectivity~] 客觀~
구체적	concrete [concreteness~] 具體~
추상적	abstract [abstraction~] 抽象~
적극적	positive; active [the positive~] 積極~
소극적	negative; passive [negative pole~] 消極~
극단적	extreme [extremity~] 極端~
필사적	desperate [certain death~] 必死~
양.적	quantitative [quantity~] 量~
질.적	qualitative [quality~] 質~
보수적	conservative [conservativeness~] 保守~
개방적	open hearted; liberal [opening~] 開放~
부분적	partial; partly [part~] 部分~
물.질적	material [material~] 物質~
정신적	mental [mind~] 精神~
논리적	logical [logic~] 論理~
감정적	emotional [emotion~] 感情~
극적	dramatic [drama~] 劇~
세계적	worldwide; international [world~] 世界~
일반적	general [general~] 一般~
공.적	public; official [public~] 公~

사.적	private; personal [private~] 私~

적 (適) suitable

적기	right time [~period] ~ 期
적당하다	be appropriate; be suitable [~suitable] ~ 當 적당히 reasonably; as one thinks fit
쾌적하다	(weather) be agreeable; be comfortable [refreshing~] 快~
적응*	adaptation; adjustment [~respond] ~ 應
적격이다	have proper qualification; be fit (for) [~frame be] ~ 格 K
적임자	person fit for the post [~in charge person] ~ 任者
적성	aptitude [~quality] ~ 性 적성검사* aptitude test
적절하다	be pertinent; be adequate [~cut] ~ 切
적합하다	be suitable; be fit (for) [~unite] ~ 合
적용*	application (of a rule) [~use] ~ 用
적자생존	survival of the fittest [~person survival] ~ 者生存

적 (敵) enemy; oppose

적군	enemy forces [~military] ~軍
강적	formidable rival [strong~] 强~
적수	a rival; a match [~hand] ~ 手
대적하다	to match; rival [oppose~] 對~
적의	hostility; animosity [~intention] ~ 意

ㅈ

적대시하다 regard with hostility
[~oppose look at] ~ 對視

적 (赤) red; naked

적십자 Red Cross [~Cross] ~ 十字

적군 enemy force [~military] ~ 軍

적자 red letters; deficit
[~letter] ~ 字

적외선 infrared rays
[~outside line] ~ 外線

적도 equator [~way] ~ 道

적나라하다 (truth, fact) be naked
[~naked naked] ~ 裸裸

적 (迹 / 跡) trace

흔적 a trace; a mark [scar~] 痕迹
흔적을 남기다 leave traces

종적 trace; whereabouts
[heel~] 踪迹
종적을 감추다 disappear;
cover one's tracks

유적 vestige; relic
[bequeath~] 遺跡

추적* chasing; tracking
[follow~] 追跡

잠적* concealing oneself;
vanishing [submerge~] 潛跡

적 (積) pile up; positive

적금 installment savings
[~money] ~ 金

축적* accumulation [store up~] 蓄~

체적 (cubic) volume [body~] 體~

면적 square measure; area
[surface~] 面~

적극적 positive; active
[~pole] ~ 極的
적극적으로 actively

적 (籍) a record

서적 books [book~] 書~

호적 family register
[family~] 戶~
호적등본 a copy
of one's family register

제적 removal from a (school)
register [remove~] 除~
제적당하다 be expelled
from school

국적 nationality [nation~] 國~

부적 amulet [amulet~] 符~

적 (寂) quiet; desolate

한적하다 be quiet and secluded
[leisure~] 閑~

적막하다 be lonely; be desolate
[~lonely] ~ 寞

울.적하다 feel empty and lonesome
[depressed~] 鬱~

적적하다 be lonely

적 (績) merit; result

실.적 actual results [real~] 實~
실.적을 올리다
give actual results

업적 achievements; results
[business~] 業~

성적 a score; a grade
[to complete~] 成~

전 ʷ(前) before; front

오전 A. M. [afternoon~] 午~

기원전 B.C. [epoch~] 紀元~

전후 before and after;
in front of and behind;
approximately [~after] ~ 後

전날	the previous day [~day] ~ K
전야	previous night; eve [~night] ~ 夜 전야제 eve of a festival
전생	former life [~life] ~ 生
전례	precedent; previous example [~example] ~ 例 전례없는 unprecedented
전직	previous post [~post] ~ 職
전편	first volume; part I [~book] ~ 篇
전남편	ex-husband [~husband] ~ 男便
식전	before meals; early morning [eat~] 食~
직전	right before [direct~] 直~ 일보직전 being on the brink (of)
사전에	before the fact; in advance [matter~] 事 ~ K 사전지식 prior knowledge
이전	prior to; before [from~] 以~ 다섯시 이전에 before five o'clock
요전	not long ago; the other day [near at hand~] K~
전번	the other day; former occasion [~number] ~ 番
종전	previous time; former occasion [follow~] 從~ 종전과 같이 as in the past
전자	the former [~person] ~ 者
전제*	premise; assumption [~suggest] ~ 提 전제조건 precondition; prerequisite
예전	former days
역전	plaza in front of a train station [station~] 驛~

전진*	moving forward; advance [~advance] ~ 進
전주	(music) prelude [~play music] ~ 奏
전반전	first half of a game [~half fighting] ~ 半戰
전방	the front line [~direction] ~ 方

전 (電)	electricity
전기	electricity [~energy] ~ 氣 전기료 electricity bill
전선	electric wire [~cord] ~ 線
전등	electric lamp [~lamp] ~ 燈
전구	light bulb [~ball] ~ 球 꼬마전구 miniature bulb
전류	electric current [~flow] ~ 流
전파	electric wave [~wave] ~ 波
전력	electric power [~power] ~ 力
전압	voltage [~pressure] ~ 壓
발.전소	power plant [shoot~place] 發~所 수력발.전소 waterpower plant
정전	power failure; blackout [stop~] 停~
감전	(receiving an) electric shock [feel~] 感~ 감전되다 receive an electric shock
절.전*	power saving [moderation~] 節~
건전지	dry cell; battery [dry~pond] 乾~池
충전*	(battery) charge; electrification [full~] 充~ 재충전* recharging
전철	electric railway; subway [~iron] ~ 鐵

전동(열)차 electric railcar
[~move train] ~ 動列車

전자 electron [~thing] ~ 子
전자계산기
electronic calculator
전자오락실
electronic game room

전축 record player; stereo
[~store up] ~ 蓄

전화* telephone; phone call
[~talk] ~ 話

전보 telegram [~report] ~ 報
전보치다 send a telegram

축전 congratulatory telegram
[congratulate~] 祝 ~

전산 computation [~calculate] ~ 算

전 (戰) **war; fighting**

전쟁* war [~fight] ~ 爭
한국전쟁 the Korean War

세계대전 World War
[world great~] 世界大 ~
일차세계대전 World War I

전사* death in battle [~die] ~ 死

전우 war buddy [~friend] ~ 友

휴전* armistice [rest~] 休 ~

참전* participation in a war
[participate~] 參 ~

선전포고* declaration of war
[proclaim~notify inform]
宣 ~ 布告

신경전 psychological warfare;
war of nerves
[nerve~] 神經 ~

냉전 cold war [cold~] 冷 ~

격전* hot fight; fierce battle
[intense~] 激 ~

열전* hot battle; close game
[hot~] 熱 ~

전투* combat; battle [~fight] ~ 鬪

전경 combat police [~police] ~ 警
(<전투경찰)

투석전 stone-throwing fight
[throw stone~] 投石 ~

고전* hard fight; tough going
[bitter~] 苦 ~

산전수전 fighting all sorts
of hardships
[mountain~water~] 山 ~ 水 ~
산전수전을 겪다
go through many hardships

전략 strategy; tactics
[~strategy] ~ 略

도전* challenge; defiance
[provoke~] 挑 ~

출.전* participating in an athletic
contest [go forth~] 出 ~

전반전 first half of a game
[front half~] 前半 ~

후반전 second half of a game
[after half~] 後半 ~

전 (全) **whole; all; complete**

전반 the whole; all [~general] ~ 般
전반적으로 overall; generally

전체 the whole [~body] ~ 體
학생전체 the whole
student body

전.적으로 fully; completely ~ 的K
전.적으로 찬성하다
fully agree (to)

전교 the whole school
[~school] ~ 校

전국 the whole country
[~country] ~ 國

전세계 the whole world
[~world] ~ 世界

전신 whole body [~body] ~ 身

전도	whole map [~map] ~ 圖 대한민국전도 complete map of Korea
전담*	whole responsibility; complete charge [~carry] ~ 擔
전혀	(not) at all; totally ~ K 전혀 모르다 not know at all 전혀 다르다 be totally different
전부	all; the entire [~part] ~ 部
전원	all the members [~member] ~ 員
전력	all one's energies [~strength] ~ 力
전속력	full speed [~speed] ~ 速力
완전*	perfection; completeness [perfect~] 完~
순전히	purely; completely [pure~-ly] 純 ~ K
전멸*	total destruction; annihilation [~ruin] ~ 滅
안전*	safety [peaceful~] 安~ 안전벨트 safety belt
온전하다	be sound; be unimpaired [calm~] 穩~
전 (傳)	**transmit; propagate; hand down**
전하다	convey; transmit
전염*	contagion; infection [~dye] ~ 染
전달*	delivery; conveyance [~achieve] ~ 達
선전*	propaganda; advertisement [spread~] 宣~
전파*	propagation; spreading [~sow seed] ~ 播
유전*	hereditary transmission [bequeath~] 遺~

전통	tradition [~rule] ~ 統 전통적 traditional
전래*	transmission; handing down [~come] ~ 來
위인전	great people's biography [great person~] 偉人~
전기	biography; life story [~record] ~ 記
자서전	autobiography [self narrate~] 自敍~
전설	legend [~talk] ~ 說 전설적 legendary
전세	rental contract involving prepayment [~rent] ~ 貰
이심전심	telepathy [with mind~mind] 以心~心
전 (轉)	**transfer; turn**
전근*	transfer to another office [~work] ~ 勤
영전*	promotional transfer [glory~] 榮~
전학*	change of schools [~learning] ~ 學
이전*	(business, office) moving [move~] 移~
호전*	favorable turn [good~] 好~
전환*	conversion; diversion [~exchange] ~ 換 기분전환을 위해 for a change
역전*	reversal of a situation (in a game) [contrary~] 逆~
전화위복*	misfortune turning into a blessing [~calamity make blessing] ~ 禍爲福
전락*	downfall; degradation [~fall] ~ 落
회전*	turning; rotation [return~] 回~

좌회전*	left turn
우회전*	right turn
운전*	driving [transport~] 運~
자전거	bicycle [self~cart] 自~車

전 (展) spread out

전람회	exhibition (show) [~view meeting] ~覽會
전시*	exhibition; display [~manifest] ~示 전시회 exhibition (show)
국전	the National Art Exhibition [national~] 國~ (<국립전시회)
전개*	unfolding; development (of a story) [~open] ~開
발.전*	growth; prosperity [arise~] 發~
진전*	development; progress [advance~] 進~
전망*	view; prospect [~hope] ~望

전 (專) exclusive

전념*	undivided attention; mental concentration [~think] ~念
전용*	exclusive use [~use] ~用 한글전용* exclusive use of hangul
전임*	exclusive duty; a full-time (position) [~be in charge] ~任
전세내다	reserve (a vehicle/place) [~rent take out] ~貰K
전문	specialty [~door] ~門 전문가 specialist; expert 전문대학 junior college
전공*	major study; specialization [~attack] ~攻
전무	executive director [~duty] ~務

전 (錢) money; coin

금전	money [money~] 金~
환전*	money exchange [exchange~] 換~
동전	copper coin [copper~] 銅~
은전	silver coin [silver~] 銀~
땡전	penny 땡전 한푼 없다 be penniless

전 (典) code; mortgage

사전	dictionary [speech~] 辭~ 백과사전 encyclopedia 영한사전 English-Korean dictionary 한영사전 Korean-English dictionary
전형적	typical [~form] ~型的
전당포	pawn shop [~suitable shop] ~當鋪

절 (節) joint; season; festival; moderation

관절	joint (bones) [locked~] 關~ 관절염 arthritis
구절	phrase [phrase~] 句~
음절	syllable [sound~] 音~
계절	season [season~] 季~
시절	time; period [time~] 時~ 학생시절 school days
명절	festive days [famous~] 名~
성탄절	Christmas [saint born~] 聖誕~
제헌절	Constitution Day [decide constitution~] 制憲~
광복절	Independence Day [briightness restore~] 光復~
개천절	Foundation Day [open sky~] 開天~

절·도 moderation [~degree] ~ 度
절·도를 지키다
exercise moderation

절약* economizing; saving
[~be sparing] ~ 約

절·전* power saving
[~electricity] ~ 電

절감* curtailment (of expenses)
[~decrease] ~ 減

절·제* control; moderation;
abstinence [~suppress] ~ 制

조절* regulation; adjustment
[control~] 調 ~

절차 procedure [~sequence] ~ 次
절차를 밟다
follow a procedure

절 (絶) discontinue; cut; absolute

단절* discontinuation;
breaking off [cut off~] 斷 ~

두절 stoppage; interruption
[barricade ~] 杜 ~
교통이 두절되다
Traffic is held up (paralyzed).

절교* breaking off friendship
[~exchange] ~ 交

임신중절* abortion [pregnancy
middle~] 妊娠中~

절망* despair; hopelessness
[~hope] ~ 望
절망적이다 be hopeless

기절* fainting [spirit~] 氣~

거절* refusal [refuse~] 拒~

사절* refusal; declining
[apologize~] 謝~

절·정 peak; climax [~summit] ~ 頂

절벽 cliff [~wall] ~ 壁

절호 the very best (chance)
[~good] ~ 好

절호의 기회
the best opportunity

절찬* extolment [~praise] ~ 讚

절·대(로) absolutely
[~comparative -ly] ~ 對 K
절·대반대*
positive opposition

절 (切) cut; earnest; urge

절·단* cutting; amputation
[~cut off] ~ 斷

절개* incision; section
[~open] ~ 開
제왕절개* Caesarean

품절 out of stock [article~] 品~

적절하다 be pertinent; be adequate
[suitable~] 適~

절·실하다 be immediate; be urgent
[~real] ~ 實
절·실하게 느끼다 feel keenly

간절하다 be earnest; be eager
[earnest~] 懇~
간절히 바라다
earnestly hope

친절* kindness [friendly~] 親~

절친하다 be on the best terms (with)
[~friendly] ~ 親

대절* chartering (a vehicle)
[borrow~] 貸~

일·절 entirely (not) [one~] 一~
일·절 관계없다
have nothing to do (with)

절 (折) break off

절반 a half [~half] ~ 半

굴·절* refraction [bend~] 屈~

좌절 discouragement; ruin
[setback~] 挫~
좌절하다 get discouraged
계획이 좌절되다
A plan is ruined.

절충*	compromising [~reach agreement] ~ 衷
곡절	hows and whys; twists and turns [bend~] 曲~

점 (點/点) dot; point; spot

점찍다	make a dot [~place] ~K
점선	dotted line; perforated line [~line] ~ 線
소수.점	decimal point [decimal~] 小數~
구두.점	punctuation mark [phrase start~] 句讀~
기.점	starting point [begin~] 起~
원.점	starting point; original place [origin~] 原~
점수	marks (grade); score [~number] ~ 數
득점*	a score; scoring (a point) [gain~] 得~ 최고득점* marking the highest score
총.점	total score [all~] 總~
만.점	full marks; perfect score [full~] 滿~
백점	a hundred points; full marks [hundred~] 百~
빵.점	zero; no point [bread~] K~
동.점	same score; a tie [same~] 同~
채.점*	marking; grading [select~] 採~
학점	(college) credit [study~] 學~
감.점*	demerit mark [subtract~] 減~
장.점	merit; good point [superior~] 長~

단점	demerit; bad point [short~] 短~
결.점	shortcoming; defect [defect~] 缺~
강.점	one's strength; strong point [strong~] 強~
약점	weak point [weak~] 弱~
이.점	advantage [benefit~] 利~
관.점	viewpoint [view~] 觀~
허.점	blind spot; loophole [empty~] 虛~
요.점	main point; gist [important~] 要~
중.점	emphasis; importance [important~] 重~
초.점	focus [focus~] 焦~ 초.점을 맞추다 adjust the focus (of a lens)
종.점	terminal (point); last stop [end~] 終~
점검*	checking one by one; close inspection [~inspect] ~ 檢
점심	lunch [~mind] ~ 心
복점	lucky freckle [blessing~] 福 ~

점 (店) a store

상점	a store [trade~] 商~
서점	bookstore [book~] 書~
화점	shoestore [shoes~] 靴~
철물점	hardware store [ironware~] 鐵物~
백화점	department store [hundred goods~] 百貨~
면세점	duty-free shop [duty-free~] 免稅~

음식점	restaurant [food~] 飮食~	접 (接)	**contact; connect; receive**
제과점	bakery [confectionery~] 製菓~	접촉*	a contact; a touch [~touch] ~觸
매점	a stand; booth [sell~] 賣~	접착*	adhesion; gluing [~contact] ~着 접착제 an adhesive
양복점	tailor shop (for men) [a suit~] 洋服~	밀.접하다	(connection) be close [intimate~] 密~ 밀.접한 관계 close connection
주점	tavern [liquor~] 酒~	접속*	connection [~continue] ~續
노점	street stall [expose~] 露~ 노점상인 street vendor	접하다	border (on); adjoin
정육점	butcher shop [lean meat~] 精肉~	접붙이다	to graft [~attach] ~K
포목점	linen shop; drapery shop [linen and cotton~] 布木~	접근*	approaching [~near] ~近
연쇄점	chain store [chain~] 連鎖~	직접	direct(ly); in person [direct~] 直~ 직접적으로 directly
본점	main store/office [origin~] 本~	간접	indirect [space between~] 間~ 간접적으로 indirectly
지점	branch store/office [branch~] 支~	접수*	receipt of an application [~receive] ~受
분점	branch store [divide~] 分~	접대*	reception; welcome [~treat] ~待
대리점	agency; commercial agent [agency~] 代理~	응접실	reception room [respond~room] 應~室
개점*	opening of a store [open~] 開~	대접*	a treat; hospitality [treat~] 待~ 푸대접* unkind treatment
점원	store clerk; sales person [~member] ~員	접종	innoculation; vaccination [~seed] ~種 예방접종* preventive innoculation
점 (占)	**prognosticate; seize**		
점장이	fortuneteller [~professional doer] ~K	정 (定)	**decide; fix; settle**
점보다	consult a fortuneteller [~see] ~K	정하다	decide; settle
점치다	tell fortunes [~tell] ~K	결.정*	decision [decide~] 決~
점령*	occupation; capture [~command] ~領	작정*	decision; intention [make~] 作~ ...할 작정이다 be decided to do...
독점*	monopolization [alone~] 獨~		

212

ᄌ

확정*	definite decision [certain~] 確~
미정이다	be undecided [not yet~be] 未~K
판정*	decision; judgment [judge~] 判~ 판정승* a win on a decision
단정*	conclusion; decision [cut off~] 斷~ 단정을 내리다 draw a conclusion
예정*	a schedule; a plan [beforehand~] 豫~
규정*	rules; regulations [regulation~] 規~
협정	agreement; pact [harmony~] 協~
긍정*	affirmation [affirm~] 肯~ 긍정적 positive
부정*	denial; negation [on the contrary~] 否~ 부정적 negative
특정*	specification; designated [special~] 特~
책정*	(budget) appropriation; fixing (prices) [plan~] 策~
측정*	measuring [measure~] 測~
감정*	appraisal [examine~] 鑑~
인정*	acknowledgment; recognition [consent~] 認~
정평	public acknowledgment [~evaluate] ~評 정평이 있다 be generally acknowledged
가정*	assumption; hypothesis [temporary~] 假~
추정*	presumption; estimation [infer~] 推~
잠정적	provisional; tentative [moment~] 暫~的

정·가	fixed price [~price] ~價
고정*	fixing; fixation [firm~] 固~ 고정관념 fixed idea 고정시키다 to fix
일·정하다	be fixed; be regular [one~] 一~
정원	fixed (seating) capacity [~member] ~員
한정*	limitation; restriction [limit~] 限~
지정*	designation; specification [to point~] 指~ 지정석 designated seat
선정*	selection [select~] 選~
설·정*	establishment; setting up [establish~] 設~
정의*	definition [~meaning] ~義
정석	formula; established form [~stone] ~石
정식	(restaurant's) regular meal [~food] ~食
안정	stability [peaceful~] 安~
정기적	periodic; regular [~period] ~期的
정착*	settling down [~arrive] ~着

정 (正) right; straight; January

정의	justice; righteousness [~right conduct] ~義
정당하다	be just; be legitimate [~suitable] ~當 정당화* justification 정정당당하다 be fair and square
공정*	fairness [official~] 公~
부정*	injustice [not~] 不~
정직*	honesty [~straight] ~直
정말	truth; true remark [~talk] ~K

213

정확하다 be accurate; be precise [~certain] ~ 確

정·자 printed letters; correct characters [~character] ~ 字

정서* square handwriting; printed-style writing [~writing] ~ 書

정정* correction; revision [correct~] 訂 ~

개정* amendment; revision [amend~] 改 ~

수정* amendment; correction [repair~] 修 ~

교정* proofreading [revise~] 校 ~

정식 regular form; (legal) formalities [~style] ~ 式

정체 real form; true character [~body] ~ 體
정체불명의 unidentified; (a person) of dubious background

정상 normality [~usual] ~ 常
정상적 normal

정규 regular; formal [~regulation] ~ 規

정장* formal dress; full dress [~costume] ~ 裝

정색하다 put on a serious look [~color] ~ 色

단정하다 be decent; be neat [upright~] 端~

정삼각형 equilateral [~triangle] ~ 三角形

정사각형 square [~quadrangle] ~ 四角形

정·수 whole number [~number] ~ 數

정찰 price tag [~document] ~ 札
정찰제 price tag system; fixed price system

정면 front side; facade [~side] ~ 面

정문 front gate; main entrance [~door] ~ 門

정비례* direct proportion [~proportion] ~ 比例

정반대 exact opposite [~the opposite] ~ 反對

정각 exact time [~engrave] ~ 刻

정오 noon [~afternoon] ~ 午

정초 beginning of January [~beginning] ~ 初

신정 New Year's Day by solar calendar [new~] 新~

구정 New Year's Day by lunar calendar [old~] 舊~

정 ʷ(情) feeling; circumstances

감정 emotion [feeling~] 感~
감정적 emotional

표정 (facial) expression [manifest~] 表~

감정 displeasure; grudge [remorse~] 憾
감정을 사다 arouse displeasure
감정이 있다 bear a grudge

심정 one's feelings [heart~] 心~
울고 싶은 심정이다 feel like crying

진정 genuine feeling; true heart [true~] 眞~

순정 pure heart [pure~] 純~

애정 affection; love [love~] 愛~

동정* sympathy [same~] 同~

우정 friendship [friend~] 友~

인정 humaneness; compassion [person~] 人~

214

	인정이 많다 be compassionate
무**정**하다	be heartless [no~] 無~
비**정**하다	be heartless [no~] 非~
정열	passion; enthusiasm [~heat] ~ 熱
열**정**	ardor; passion [heat~] 熱~
치**정**	foolish passion [foolish~] 癡~ 치정살인* sex murder
정서	(aesthetic) sentiments; atmosphere [~clue] ~ 緒
정들다	become attached [~come in] ~K
정답다	be affectionate; be friendly [~ -ly] ~ K
정나미	attachment; fondness ~ K 정(나미) 떨어지다 be disaffected
진**정***	a petition; an appeal [display~] 陳~ 진정서 written petition
사**정**	circumstances; reasons; consideration [matter~] 事~ 개인사정 personal reasons 사정하다 solicit (special consideration) 사정을 봐주다 make allowances (for) 사정없이 mercilessly
실**정**	actual circumstances [real~] 實~
물**정**	condition of things [things~] 物~ 세상물정 world affairs
정보	information; intelligence [~report] ~ 報 중앙정보부 CIA
정세	state of affairs [~conditions] ~ 勢 국제정세 international situation

정 (停)	**stop**
정지*	stopping; suspension [~stop] ~ 止 정지신호* stop signal
정학	suspension from school [~learning] ~ 學
정차*	stopping of a vehicle [~vehicle] ~ 車
정거*	stopping of a vehicle [~cart] ~ 車 급정거* sudden stop (of a vehicle) 정거장 railroad station
정류장	(bus) stop [~stay place] ~ 留場
정체*	stagnation; (traffic) congestion [~obstructed] ~ 滯
정전	power outage [~electricity] ~ 電
정년퇴직*	retirement at the official age [~age] ~ 年
정 (政)	**politics; govern**
정치*	politics; government [~govern] ~ 治 정치가 politician
정권	political power [~power] ~ 權
정당	political party [~party] ~ 黨
정책	policy [~plan] ~ 策
정부	the government [~prefecture] ~ 府
행**정**	administration [act~] 行~
재**정**	public finance; fiscal matters [property~] 財~
정략결혼*	marriage of convenience [~strategy marriage] ~ 略 結婚

정 (精) essential; fine; spirit

정력 energy; stamina [~strength] ~ 力

정액 semen [~liquid] ~ 液

정성 true heart; devotion [~sincerity] ~ 誠

정교하다 be elaborate; be exquisite [~clever] ~ 巧

정독* careful reading [~read] ~ 讀

정밀* minuteness; accuracy [~thorough] ~ 密
정밀검사* close examination

정신 mind; spirit [~spirit] ~ 神
정신차리다 collect one's mind; pull oneself together
정신나가다 grow absent-minded; become foolish
정신없다 be distracted; be absent-minded
제정신이 아니다 be out of one's mind
정신연령 mental age
정신·병 mental disease
정신·병원 mental institution

요정 fairy; elf [bewitching~] 妖~

정 (程) route; measure

과정 process; course [pass~] 過~

일.정 day's schedule; itinerary [day~] 日~

과정 course of study; curriculum [task~] 課~

이정표 milestone [village~signboard] 里~標

정도 degree; extent [~degree] ~ 度

음정 musical interval; tone [sound~] 音~

정 (整) be in order; regulate

정돈* putting in order; proper arrangement [~order] ~ 頓

정리* putting in order; proper arrangement; settlement [~manage] ~ 理
뒷정리* arrangements for the end; clearing up

질.서정연하다 be arranged in good order; be systematic [order~as such] 秩序 ~ 然

정렬하다 line up [~line] ~ 列

조정* regulation; adjustment [control~] 調~

정비* maintenance; full equipment [~prepare] ~ 備
자동차 정비공장 auto repair shop

정 (靜) quiet; still

정숙* silence; Quiet please. [~quiet] ~ 肅

정맥 vein [~vein] ~脈

정물화 still-life painting [~thing picture] ~ 物畵

냉정* calmness; composure [cold~] 冷~

진정* pacification; calming down [suppress~] 鎭~
진정제 sedative

정 (庭) yard

정원 garden [~garden] ~ 園

교정 school campus [school~] 校~

가정 home; family [house~] 家~

친정 married woman's parents' home [parents~] 親~

제 (制) **suppress; govern; decide**

억제* restraint; suppression
[suppress~] 抑~

절제* control; moderation;
abstinence [moderation~] 節~

통제* control; regulation
[govern~] 統~

강제* compulsion; coercion
[force~] 强~

제한* limitation; restriction
[~limit] ~ 限
제한속도 speed limit
산아제한* birth control

규제* regulation; restriction
[regulation~] 規~

제약* restriction [~be sparing] ~ 約

제재* sanction; punishment
[~judge] ~ 裁
제재를 가하다 take sanctions

제동 braking; damping
[~move] ~ 動
제동을 걸다
put on the brakes

제도 system; institution
[~degree] ~ 度
교육제도 educational system

사년제대학 four-year college
[4 year~college] 四年~大學

제복 uniform [~clothes] ~ 服

제 (劑) **medicine**

조제* medicine compounding
[harmonize~] 調~

소화제 digestive aid
[digestion~] 消化~

진통제 pain killer
[suppress pain~] 鎭痛~

수면제 sleeping medicine
[sleeping~] 睡眠~

항생제 antibiotic [resist life~] 抗生~

진정제 sedative
[pacification~] 鎭靜~

방부제 preservative
[defend rotten~] 防腐~

살충제 insecticide
[kill insect~] 殺蟲~

자외선차단제 sunblock products
[ultraviolet rays block~]
紫外線遮斷~

영양제 nutritional supplement;
vitamin [nutrition~] 營養~

세제 detergent [wash~] 洗~

방향제 air freshener
[fragrant fragrant~] 芳香~

제 (除) **eliminate**

삭제* elimination; erasure
[cut~] 削~

제거* removal; elimination
[~go] ~ 去

제하다 exclude; subtract

제외* exclusion [~outside] ~ 外

공제* deduction [deduct~] 控~

면제* exemption [exempt~] 免~

배제* ruling out (a possibility)
[push out~] 排~

해제* cancellation; removal
(of a ban) [release~] 解~

제설작업* snow-removing work
[~snow work] ~ 雪作業

소제* cleaning [sweep~] 掃~

제적* expulsion from school
register [~a record] ~ 籍

제대* discharge from military
service [~army] ~ 隊

제 (製) **make; manufacture**

제조* making; manufacture [~make] ~ 造

제품 manufactured goods; product [~article] ~ 品
수제품 hand made product

제약 manufacture of medicine; pharmacy [~medicine] ~ 藥
제약회사 pharmaceutical company

제본* bookbinding [~sample] ~ 本

제작* (film) production [~make] ~ 作

제과점 bakery [~cookie store] ~菓店

미제 made in U.S.A. [U.S.~] 美~

일·제 made in Japan [Japan~] 日 ~

외제 foreign-made [foreign~] 外~

제 (題) **subject**

화제 topic of a conversation [talk~] 話~
화제를 돌리다
change the subject

주제 theme; subject [main~] 主~

제목 subject; title [~item] ~ 目

문제 problem; question [ask~] 問~

과제 assignment; question [task~] 課~

숙제* homework [lodge~] 宿~

출·제* making questions for an exam [produce~] 出 ~

제 (祭) **sacrificial rite**

제물 things offered in sacrifice [~things] ~ 物

제단 altar (for sacrifice) [~altar] ~ 壇

제사 memorial service for ancestors [~sacrifice] ~ 祀
제사지내다 hold a memorial service

축제* festival [celebrate~] 祝~

추모제 memorial rite for a deceased person [cherishing the memory of a deceased person~] 追慕~

제 (提) **lift up; suggest**

제시* presentation (of ideas, etc.) [~manifest] ~ 示

제출* submitting; handing in [~put forth] ~ 出

제공* an offer [~offer] ~ 供

제기* instituting (a lawsuit); bringing up (a problem) [~rise] ~ 起

제안* proposal; suggestion [~plan] ~ 案

전제* premise; assumption [before~] 前 ~

제 (弟) **junior (in age)**

형제 brothers/sisters [elder brother~] 兄 ~

처제 one's wife's younger sister [wife~] 妻 ~

제자 disciple; pupil [~thing] ~ 子

조 (調) **control; harmonize**

조절* regulation; adjustment [~moderation] ~ 節

조정* regulation; adjustment [~regulate] ~ 整

조사* investigation; survey [~inspect] ~ 査

강조* emphasizing [strong~] 强 ~

조화* harmony [~harmony] ~ 和

협조* cooperation [union~] 協 ~

동조* acting in concert (with); aligning oneself [together~] 同 ~

곡조 a tune; melody [tune~] 曲~

보조 pace [step~] 步~
보조를 맞추다
keep step (with)

순조롭다 be favorable; be smooth-going [gentle~] 順~

단조롭다 be monotonous [single~] 單~

조제* medicine compounding [~medicine] ~ 劑

조미료 condiments [~taste ingredient] ~ 味料

격조높다 be refined; be high-toned [category~high] 格 ~ K

장난·조 joking manner [play~] K ~
장난·조로 in a joking manner

시비·조 defiant attitude [quarrel~] 是非~

조 (造) **make**

제조* making; manufacture [manufacture~] 製~

구조 structure [structure~] 構~

조성* creation (of an atmosphere); preparation (of a housing site) [~to complete] ~ 成

창조* creation [beginning~] 創 ~
천지창조* the Creation

조물·주 Creator; Maker of the universe [~things lord] ~物主

조화 the creative energy of the universe; the mysterious [~change] ~ 化

개조* remodeling; reconstruct [amend~] 改~

모조품 an imitation; a fake [sample~article] 模 ~品

조화 artificial flower [~flower] ~ 花

위조* forgery; fabrication [false~] 僞 ~
위조지폐 spurious bank note

날·조* fabrication; concoction [fabricate~] 捏~

조작* concoction; fabrication [~make] ~ 作

조예가 깊다 be deeply versed (in) [~reach deep] ~ 詣 K

조 (助) **assist**

원조* assistance; aid [help~] 援 ~

보조* assistance; support [supplement~] 補~

조수 assistant; helper [~hand] ~手

조교 teaching assistant [~teach] ~ 敎

조교수 assistant professor [~professor] ~ 敎授

찬조* support; patronage [help~] 贊 ~
찬조출연*
appearance as a guest

조연 supporting performance [~perform] ~ 演

조언* counsel; advice [~words] ~ 言

구조* rescuing; saving (a life) [rescue~] 救 ~

219

부조* contribution (for a
wedding/funeral)
[assist~] 扶~

조 (早) early

조기 early stage/period
[~period] ~ 期
조기교육* early education

조숙하다 be precocious [~mature] ~ 熟

조퇴* getting off work/school
earlier than usual
[~leave] ~ 退

조만간 sooner or later
[~late between] ~ 晚間

조조할인* early morning discount
(for a movie)
[~morning discount] ~ 朝割引

조 (條) clause

조항 articles and clauses; items
[~item] ~ 項
제일조 일항 Article I Clause 1

조약 treaty; pact [~promise] ~ 約

조목 articles; items [~item] ~目

조·건 condition; stipulation
[~thing] ~ 件
조·건부(로) conditional(ly)
무조·건 unconditionally

신조 creed; principle
[believe~] 信~

조 (朝) morning

조회 morning meeting;
morning session in school
[~meeting] ~ 會

조간(신문) morning paper [~publish
newspaper] ~ 刊 新聞

조선 morning calm; Korea
[~fresh] ~ 鮮

조변석개 changeability; fickleness
[~change evening alter]
~變夕改

조 (組) weave

조직* organization [~weave] ~ 織

조합 union; association
[~together] ~ 合

노조 labor union [labor~] 勞~
(< 노동조합)

조립* assembly; assembling
[~stand] ~ 立

조 (祖) ancestor

선조 ancestor [precede~] 先~

조상 ancestor [~above] ~ 上

조국 one's fatherland
[~country] ~ 國

원조 originator; founder
[the first~] 元~

조 (操) grasp; hold

조종* manipulation; operation
[~control] ~ 縱
조종사 pilot

조작* (machine) operation;
handling [~make] ~ 作

체조* gymnastics [body~] 體~
미용체조* calisthenics

지조 principle; constancy;
integrity [intention~] 志~

조심* carefulness; precaution
[~mind] ~ 心

족 (族) tribe; family

민족 race; people [people~] 民~

동족	same race; brethren [same~] 同~	생존경쟁*	struggle for survival
종족	race; species [seed~] 種~	적자생존	survival of the fittest
가족	family [family~] 家~ 유가족 bereaved family 이산가족 family separated by border between North and South Korea	존재*	existence [~exist] ~ 在 신의 존재 existence of God
왕족	royal family [king~] 王~	보존*	preservation [protect~] 保~
귀족	nobles [honorable~] 貴~	의존하다	depend on; rely on [depend on~] 依~
족보	genealogical record [~genealogy] ~ 譜		

족 (足) foot; sufficient

족발	pig's feet [~foot] ~ K
수족	hands and feet; limbs [hand~] 手~
만족	satisfaction [full~] 滿~ 만족하다 be satisfied
흡족하다	be sufficient; be satisfactory [sufficient~] 洽~
충족하다	be sufficient [full~] 充~ 충족시키다 satisfy (a need)
풍족하다	have plenty; be well off [abundant~] 豊~

존 (尊) honor

존경*	respect; looking up to [~respect] ~ 敬
존중*	respect; valuing [~weighty] ~ 重
존댓말	honorific speech [~treat language] ~ 待 K
존칭	honorific title [~call] ~ 稱

존 (存) exist

생존*	existence; survival [life~] 生~

졸 (卒) finish; underling; suddenly

졸업*	graduation [~business] ~ 業 졸업생 graduate; alumni 졸업반 students of a graduating class 졸업식* graduation ceremony
고졸	high-school graduate [high school~] 高~ (<고등학교 졸업)
대졸	college graduate [college~] 大~ (<대학졸업)
졸병	common soldier [~soldier] ~ 兵
졸·도*	fainting; passing out [~fall down] ~ 倒

종 (種) seed; a kind

종자	seed [~thing] ~ 子
종류	a kind; a sort [~a kind] ~ 類
일·종	one kind [one~] 一~
각종	all kinds [all~] 各~
품종	species; breed [article~] 品~
종족	race; species [~tribe] ~ 族 종족보존* preservation of the species
인종	(human) race [person~] 人~ 식인종 cannibal race
멸·종*	extinction of a species [destroy~] 滅~

순종   pure bred [pure~] 純~

잡종   hybrid; crossbred [mixed~] 雜~

별종   weirdo [different~] 別~

특종   (news) scoop [special~] 特~

종목   (sports) event [~item] ~ 目

종종   often

종 (終) end; finish

최종   the last; the end [the most~] 最~
최종결.정*   final decision

종일   all day [~day] ~ 日

종지부   full stop [~stop credential] ~ 止 符
종지부를 찍다   put an end to

종.점   (bus) terminal; last stop [~point] ~ 点

종착역   terminal station [~arrive station] ~ 着 驛

종말   the end (of the world) [~end] ~ 末

임종*   one's last moment of life [come to~] 臨~

종강*   finishing instruction for the semester [~lecture] ~ 講

자초지종   from the beginning to the end; the whole story [from beginning reach~] 自初至~
자초지종을 이야기하다 give full particulars (of)

종 (從) follow

추종*   following [follow~] 追~
타의 추종을 불허하다 have no superior (in)

순종하다   follow obediently [gentle~] 順~

복종*   obedience [submit~] 服~

종사*   following a profession [~business] ~ 事

상종*   keeping company with associating [mutual~] 相~

종전   previous time; former occasion [~before] ~ 前

종 (鐘) bell

은종   silver bell [silver~] 銀~

초인종   call bell; door bell [call person~] 招人~

종.소리   sound of a bell [~sound] ~K

자명종   alarm clock [self chirp~] 自鳴~

종 (宗) sect

종파   sect; denomination [~branch] ~ 派

종교   religion [~religion] ~ 敎

좌 (左) left

좌우   left and right [~right] ~ 右
좌우간   at any rate; anyway

좌측   left side [~side] ~ 側
좌측통행*   Keep to the left

좌회전*   left turn [~turning] ~ 廻 轉

우왕좌왕*   moving about in confusion [right go~go] 右往~往

죄 (罪) crime; sin; guilt

죄악   crime; sin [~evil] ~ 惡

범죄   crime [offense~] 犯~

ㅈ

| | | | |

살인**죄** crime of murder [murder~] 殺人~

죄짓다 commit a crime [~commit] ~K

죄인 criminal; sinner [~person] ~ 人

무**죄** being not guilty [no~] 無~

속**죄*** atonement for one's sin; redemption [redeem~] 贖~

죄책감 guilty conscience [~reprove feeling] ~ 責感

죄받다 suffer punishment [~receive] ~ K

죄송합니다 be sorry; be regrettable (hon.) [~regret] ~悚

주 (主) **main; host**

주.된 main; primary ~ K

주로 mainly [~ -ly] ~ K

주요하다 be main; be principal [~essential] ~ 要

주성분 main ingredient [~ingredient] ~ 成分

주심 chief referee [~judge] ~ 審

주연* playing the leading part; starring [~perform] ~ 演

주도* taking the initiative leading [~lead] ~ 導

주동* masterminding [~move] ~ 動 주동자 ring leader

주범 chief criminal [~offence] ~犯

주장 captain (of a team) [~officer] ~ 將

주임 person in charge; a head [~be in charge] ~ 任

주관* manage; take charge (of) [~govern] ~ 管

주축 main axis [~axis] ~ 軸

주류 mainstream [~stream] ~ 流

호주 head of a family [family~] 戶 ~

주부 housewife [~woman] ~ 婦

주인 proprietor; owner [~person] ~ 人 주인공 protagonist; main character

주.권 sovereign power [~rights] ~ 權

공주 princess [official~] 公~

구세주 the savior (of the world) [rescue world~] 救世~

주체.성 subjecthood; self-reliance [~body nature] ~ 體性

주의 principle; -ism [~meaning] ~ 義

주빈 guest of honor [~guest] ~ 賓

주례* officiating at a wedding ceremony; officiator [~rite] ~ 禮

주최* sponsorship [~urge] ~ 催 ...주최로 under the sponsorship of...

주식 staple food [~food] ~ 食

주관 subjectivity [~view] ~ 觀 주관적 subjective

주제 theme; subject [~subject] ~題

주어 subject (of a sentence) [~word] ~ 語

주장* a claim [~stretch] ~ 張

주착없다 be senseless; be wishy-washy [~attach not exist] ~ 着 K

주객이 바뀌다 the cart is put before the horse; the tables are turned [~guest switched] ~ 客 K

주 (酒)　liquor

양주	western liquor [western~] 洋~
포도주	wine [grape~] 葡萄~
과실.주	fruit wine [fruit~] 果實~
인삼주	ginseng drink [ginseng~] 人蔘~
소주	soju; distilled liquor [burn~] 燒~
청주	clear-strained rice wine [clear~] 淸~
감주	sweet drink (made from rice) [sweet~] 甘~
주점	tavern [~store] ~ 店 학사주점 college students' tavern
금주*	abstinence from alcohol [prohibit~] 禁~
애주가	alcohol lover [love~specialist] 愛~家
안주*	side dish for drinking [pacify~] 按~
주량	one's drinking capacity [~amount] ~ 量
주정*	drunken frenzy; drunken rowdiness [~intoxicated] ~ 酊 주정뱅이　drunken brawler
음주운전*	drunken driving [drink~driving] 飮~運轉
주전자	kettle; teakettle [~simmer thing] ~ 煎子

주 (週)　week; revolve

(일)주일	(one) week [one~day] 一~日
지난주	last week [past~] K~
이번.주	this week [this time~] K 番~
다음.주	next week [next~] K~

금주	this week [now~] 今~
내주	next week [coming~] 來~
매주	every week [every~] 每~
격주	every other week [isolated~] 隔~
주말	weekend [~end] ~ 末
주간지	weekly magazine [~publish record] ~ 刊誌
주기	period; cycle [~period] ~ 期
(일)주년	(first) anniversary [first~year] 一~年

주 (住)　reside

주민	resident [~people] ~ 民 주민등록증　certificate of residence; resident card
거주*	dwelling; residence [dwell~] 居~ 거주지　place of residence
영주*	permanent residence [permanent~] 永~ 영주.권　green card
주택	house; housing [~residence] ~ 宅
주소	one's address [~place] ~ 所 현주소　current address
의식주	clothing, food, and shelter [clothes food~] 衣食~

주 (注)　pour

주입*	pouring in; instillment [~enter] ~入 주입식 교육　cram method of education
주사*	injection [~shoot] ~ 射
주력하다	concentrate one's effort [~strength] ~ 力
주의*	attention; caution [~intention] ~ 意

주목* (paying) attention [~eye] ~ 目

주시하다 stare at; observe closely [~look at] ~ 視

주문* an order; request [~writing] ~ 文

주 (奏) play music

연주* performance on a musical instrument [perform~] 演 ~ 연주회 (instrumental) recital

독주* (instrumental) solo [alone~] 獨 ~

합주* playing in concert [join~] 合 ~

이중주 (instrumental) duet [two layer~] 二重 ~

전주 (music) prelude [before~] 前 ~

반주* (music) accompaniment [companion~] 伴 ~

주 (周) encircle

일.주* making the rounds (of) [one~] 一 ~ 세계일.주* round-the-world trip

주변 outskirts; vicinity [~edge] ~ 邊

주위 environs; vicinity [~circumference] ~ 圍

주발 brass rice-bowl [~bowl] ~鉢

주선* good offices [~revolve] ~ 旋

주 (走) run

도주* running away [flee~] 逃 ~

경주* (foot) race; running match [compete~] 競 ~

주행거리 mileage [~go distance] ~ 行距離

활.주로 runway [slippery~road] 滑 ~ 路

분주하다 be busy [busy~] 奔 ~

주 (珠) beads

진주 pearl [pure~] 眞 ~

주판 abacus; counting board [~board] ~ 板

주산* abacus calculation [~calculate] ~ 算

주 (駐) stay temporarily

주한미군 U.S. armed forces stationed in Korea [~Korea U.S. forces] ~ 韓美軍

주차* parking a car [~vehicle] ~ 車 주차장 parking lot

주둔* (military) stationing [~camp] ~ 屯

주 (朱) reddish

주홍 bright orange color; scarlet [~red] ~ 紅

주황색 orange color [~yellow color] ~ 黃色

인주 red stamping ink [seal~] 印~

죽 (粥) porridge

팥죽 red-bean porridge [red-bean~] K~

죽쑤다 cook porridge; goof up (slang) [~cook porridge]

준 (準)	**semi; measure**
준결.승	semifinal [~a final] ~ 決勝
표준	standard; norm [signboard~] 標~ 표준말 standard language
기준	a standard; criterion [foundation~] 基~
수준	standard; level [water~] 水~
준비*	preparation [~prepare] ~ 備
중 (中)	**middle; among**
중심	the center; the middle [~heart] ~ 心
중앙	the center; the middle [~center] ~ 央 중앙청 capitol building 중앙난방 central heating
중부	mid part [~part] ~ 部 중부.지방 central area
중간	the middle; midway [~interval] ~ 間 중간고사 midterm
(산)중턱	midslope of a mountain [mountain~hump] 山 ~ K
중류	midstream; middle class [~stream] ~ 流
중복	middle period of dog days [~dog days] ~ 伏
중순	middle ten days of a month [~ten days] ~ 旬
중년	middle age [~age] ~ 年
중소기업	medium and small enterprise [~small enterprise] ~ 小企業
공중	midair [air~] 空~
중도	halfway [~road] ~ 途 중도에서 포기하다 give up halfway
도중	on the way; halfway [road~] 途~ 학교가는 도중에 on one's way to school 식사도중에 in the middle of a meal
오전중	in the A. M. [A. M.~] 午前~
밤.중	during the night [night~] K~ 한밤.중 middle of the night
중단*	discontinuance [~stop] ~ 斷
중지*	discontinuance; stoppage [~stop] ~ 止
중퇴*	dropping out of school [~leave] ~ 退
중학교	junior high school [~school] ~ 學校
중급	intermediate level [~grade] ~ 級
중성	neuter gender; sexlessness [~sex] ~ 性
중화*	neutralization [~harmony] ~ 和
중립	neutrality [~stand] ~ 立 중립을 지키다 maintain neutrality
중용	golden mean; moderation [~middle] ~ 庸
통화중	The line is busy. [phone conversation~] 通話~
공사중	under construction [construction~] 工事~
중국	China [~country] ~國
중동	Middle East [~east] ~ 東
지중해	Mediterranean [earth~sea] 地~海
외출중	not here at the moment; out [going out~] 外出~
적중하다	hit the mark; guess right [target~] 的~

ㅈ

와중	in a whirlpool; in a vortex [whirlpool~] 渦~
안중에 없다	be out of one's thoughts [eye~not exist] 眼~K
열.중하다	be absorbed in [heat~] 熱~
시중	the open market [market~] 市~
오리무중	utter bewilderment; being in the dark [five *ri* fog~] 五里霧~ (1 *ri* = 0.4 km)
집중*	(mental) concentration; convergence [collect~] 集~
중고	the second-hand (article) [~old] ~古
중계*	relay; rebroadcasting [~continue] ~繼
중독	poisoning; addiction [~poison] ~毒 중독되다 be poisoned; be addicted
중풍	palsy; paralysis [~wind] ~風
중 (重)	**weight(y); layer**
중공업	heavy industry [~industry] ~工業
중노동*	heavy labor [~labor] ~勞動
중량	weight [~amount] ~量
체중	body weight [body~] 體~
중력	gravity [~strength] ~力
과중하다	(burden) be too heavy [excede~] 過~
치중하다	attach weight to; lay stress on [put~] 置~
중상	serious injury [~injury] ~傷 중경상 serious and slight injuries
중병	serious illness [~disease] ~病
중태	serious condition (due to an illness/injury) [~form] ~態
중.점	emphasis; importance [~point] ~点 중.점적으로 first in priority ...에 중.점을 두다 put emphasis on...
중(요)하다	be important [~essential] ~要 중요성 importance 중(요)시하다 take a serious view of; make much of
중대하다	be important; be serious [~great] ~大
비중	relative importance [compare~] 比~ 비중이 크다 be important
막중하다	be very important [extremely~] 莫~ 책임이 막중하다 Responsibility is grave.
소중하다	be important; be valuable [actually~] 所~
중역	director (of a company) [~role] ~役
존중*	respect; valuing [honor~] 尊~
귀중하다	be valuable; be precious [valuable~] 貴~
신중하다	be cautious; be prudent [prudent~] 慎~
정중하다	be courteous; be respectful [polite~] 鄭~
엄중하다	(punishment) be strict; be severe [strict~] 嚴~
이중	double; dual [two~] 二~ 이중인.격 dual personality
중복*	overlapping; redundancy [~double] ~複

227

중 (衆) **crowd**	
공중	public [public~] 公~ 공중전화 public phone
대중	masses; general public [big~] 大~ 대중음악 popular music
청중	audience; hearers [hear~] 聽~
관중	(sports) onlookers; audience [view~] 觀~
중론	general opinion [~discuss] ~ 論

즉 (卽) **immediate**	
즉사*	immediate death [~death] ~ 死
즉효	immediate effect [~effect] ~ 效
즉시	immediately [~time] ~ 時
즉각	immediately [~engrave] ~ 刻
즉흥적	impromptu; improvised [~fun] ~ 興的
즉석	on the spot; improvised; instant [~place] ~ 席

증 ᵂ(證) **testify; evidence**	
증인	witness; testifier [~person] ~ 人
증언*	testimony [~talk] ~ 言
증거	evidence; proof [~depend on] ~ 據
확증*	conclusive evidence [certain~] 確 ~
증서	document; certificate [~writing] ~ 書 졸업증서 diploma
증명*	verification; proving [~clear] ~ 明

보증*	a guarantee; guaranteeing [protect~] 保~ 보증인 guarantor; sponsor
입증*	establishment of a fact [establish~] 立~
영수증	receipt [receive collect~] 領收~
신분.증	identification card [identity~] 身分~
학생.증	student ID [student~] 學生~
면허.증	license [license~] 免許~ 운전면허(증) driver's license
자격증	certificate of qualification [qualification~] 資格~ 교사자격증 teaching certificate
주민등록증	certificate of residence; resident card [resident register~] 住民登錄~
증.권	stock; bond [~document] ~ 券 증.권시장 stock market

증 (症) **ailment; symptom**	
증세	symptoms [~conditions] ~ 勢
증상	symptoms [~shape] ~ 狀
염증	inflammation [inflammation~] 炎~
통증	ache; pain [pain~] 痛~
축농.증	asthma; emphysema [store up pus~] 蓄膿~
갈증	thirst [thirsty~] 渴~
불면.증	insomnia [no sleep~] 不眠~
현기.증	dizziness; vertigo [dizzy spirit~] 眩氣~
건망.증	forgetfulness [strong forget~] 健忘~
기억상실.증	amnesia [memory loss~] 記憶喪失~

후유.증	aftereffect (of a disease or injury); aftermath [after bequeath~] 後遺~
식곤.증	after-meal fatigue [eat tired~] 食困~
싫.증나다	get tired of [dislike~come out] K~ K (pron.=실쯩나다)
궁금.증	curiosity [anxiety~] K~
의처.증	obsessive suspicion of one's wife's chastity [doubt wife~] 疑妻~

증 (蒸) steam

수증기	steam; vapor [water~air] 水~氣
한증*	steam bath; sauna [sweat~] 汗~
증발*	evaporation [~arise] ~發

증 (贈) give a present

증정*	presenting (a gift) [~to present] ~呈
기증*	donation; contribution [entrust~] 寄~

지 (地) earth; place

지구	earth; globe [~sphere] ~球
천지	heaven and earth; being full of [heaven~] 天~ 세상천지에 in the world 천지차이 big difference 자동차 천지다 be crowded with cars
지옥	hell [~prison] ~獄
지진	earthquake [~shake] ~震
육지	land (vs. ocean) [land~] 陸~
토지	land [land~] 土~

평지	flat land [even~] 平~
황무지	wasteland [desolate wasteland~] 荒蕪~
지뢰	land mine [~thunder] ~雷
지하	underground [~below] ~下 지하수 underground water 지하실 basement 지하도 underpass 지하철 subway 지하상가 underground shopping mall 지하주차장 underground parking lot
지도	map [~map] ~圖
지리	geography [~principle] ~理
지역	region; zone [~boundary] ~域
지방	area; locality [~direction] ~方
지대	zone; area [~belt] ~帶 비무장지대 demilitarized zone
각지	all places [all~] 各~
객지	place away from home [guest~] 客~
양지	sunny spot [sunlight~] 陽~
현지	the very spot [now~] 現~ 현지생방송* on-the-spot live broadcast
묘지	a grave [grave~] 墓~ 국립묘지 national cemetery
거주지	place of residence [residence~] 居住~
관광지	tourist resort [tour~] 觀光~
유원지	amusement park [outing garden~] 遊園~
목적지	destination [goal~] 目的~
행선지	destination [go precede~] 行先~
식민지	colony; settlement [plant people~] 植民~

단지	housing complex [group~] 團~		휴지	waste paper; toilet paper [rest~] 休~ 휴지통 waste basket
대지	a site; building lot [building area~] 垈~		쪽지	a slip of paper [piece~] K~
번지	street number [number~] 番~		표지	(book) cover [surface~] 表~
여지	room; margin [surplus~] 餘~ 변명의 여지가 없다 There is not the slightest excuse.		신문지	newsprint [newspaper~] 新聞~
처지	situation; position [position~] 處~		편지	letter [mail~] 便~ 연애편지 love letter 편지지 letter paper
지위	position; status [~position] ~位		답안지	answer sheet [written-answer~] 答案~
지경	(bad) situation; condition [~circumstances] ~境		창호지	paper for sliding doors [window door~] 窓戶~
궁지	sad plight; hot seat [poor~] 窮~		인지	paper stamp [seal~] 印~
실·지	practicality; actuality [real~] 實~		딱지	a stamp; (traffic) ticket; pasteboard dump K~ 우표딱지 postage stamp
졸·지에	all of a sudden [sudden~] 猝~ K		지폐	paper money [~money] ~幣
			지갑	purse; wallet [~case] ~匣
			은박지	silver foil [silver thin~] 銀箔~

지 (紙) paper

도화지	drawing paper [drawing picture~] 圖畵~
화선지	Chinese drawing paper [picture wide~] 畵宣~
팔·절·지	octavo size paper [eight cut~] 八切~
십육절·지	8" x 11" paper [sixteen cut~] 十六切~
벽지	wallpaper [wall~] 壁~
포장지	wrapping paper [wrapping~] 包裝~
봉지	paper bag [sealed~] 封~ 비닐봉지 plastic bag
화장지	kleenex; toilet paper [makeup~] 化粧~

지 (指) to point; finger

지목*	pointing out; spotting [~item] ~目
지적*	pointing out (mistakes) [~pick] ~摘
지도*	guidance [~lead] ~導 지도력 leadership 지도자 leader; guide
지시*	instruction; direction [~manifest] ~示
지령	an order; a directive [~command] ~令
지휘*	conducting (orchestra); commanding [~wield] ~揮 지휘자 commander; conductor
지명*	nomination [~name] ~名

지정*	designation; specification [~decide] ~ 定
지탄*	censure; blame [~bullet] ~ 彈
지.수	numerical index [~number] ~ 數 불쾌지.수 discomfort index
지문	fingerprint [~lines] ~ 紋
지압	finger pressure (therapy) [~press] ~ 壓
지장	thumbprint [~a seal] ~ 章
반지	ring [spot~] 斑~ 금반지 gold ring

지 (支) **branch; support; pay; manage**

지사	branch company [~company] ~ 社
지점	branch store/office [~store] ~ 店
지원*	support [~help] ~ 援
지지*	support; upholding [~sustain] ~ 持
지탱하다	prop up; maintain [~prop up] ~ 撑
의지하다	lean on; turn to [depend on~] 依~
지장	hindrance; difficulty [~obstruct] ~ 障
지불*	payment; defrayment [~pay] ~ 拂
지급*	payment; supply [~give] ~給
지출*	expenditure; outlay [~exit] ~ 出
수지 맞다	(business) be profitable; (person) make profit [collect~agree] 收 ~ K
지배*	governing; domination [~distribute] ~ 配 지배인 manager

지 (知) **know**

지능	intelligence [~ability] ~ 能 지능지.수 I Q
지식	knowledge [~know] ~ 識
지성인	an intellectual [~nature person] ~ 性人
미지	unknown [not~] 未~ 미지의세계 the unknown world
철부지	mere child (who lacks common sense) [discretion not~] K 不~
무지 막지*	being ignorant and uncouth [not~not~] 無~莫~
통지*	notice; notification [circulate~] 通 ~
탐지*	detection [search~] 探~

지 (持) **sustain; possess**

지속*	continuance; maintenance [~continue] ~ 續
유지*	maintenance; preservation [tie~] 維~
지지*	support; upholding [support~] 支~
지구력	staying power; tenacity [~long-time strength] ~ 久力
소지*	possession [thing~] 所~ 소지품 one's belongings
지참*	bringing; bearing [~participate] ~ 參 지참금 dowry
차지*	occupying; taking possession of

지 (止) **stop**

정지*	stopping; suspension [stop~] 停~

ㅈ

중지*	discontinuance; stoppage [middle~] 中~
금지*	prohibition [prohibit~] 禁~
방지*	prevention [defend~] 防~
폐지*	abolition [abolish~] 廢~
저지*	hindrance; interception [hinder~] 沮~
지혈*	stanching [~blood] ~血

지 (志) mind; intention

동지	like-minded person; kindred spirit [same~] 同~
지원*	application; volunteering [~desire] ~願
지망*	wish; choice (for college or career) [~hope] ~望
의지	will; intention [intention~] 意~
투지	fighting spirit [fight~] 鬪~
지조	principle; constancy; integrity [~hold] ~操 지조가 있다 be constant; be principled

지 (至) extreme

지극하다	be extreme; be utmost [~extreme] ~極
지급	utmost urgency (telegram) [~urgent] ~急
지대하다	be immense; be great [~great] ~大
지독하다	be vicious; be severe [~poison] ~毒
지당하다	be quite right; be reasonable [~suitable] ~當
지천이다	be abundant; be everywhere [~lowly] ~賤

지 (誌) record

잡지	magazine [mixed~] 雜~
주간지	weekly magazine [week publish~] 週刊~
월간지	monthly magazine [month publish~] 月刊~

지 (遲) late

지각*	being late [~engrave] ~刻
지연*	delay [~delay] ~延
지체*	delay; deferment [~obstructed] ~滯 지체없이 promptly; without delay

직 (直) straight; direct

직선	straight line [~line] ~線 수직선 perpendicular line
직각	right angle [~angle] ~角
직사각형	rectangle [~quadrangle] ~四角形
직진*	going straight [~advance] ~進
직면하다	face; confront [~face] ~面
직전	right before [~before] ~前
직후	immediately after [~after] ~後
직접	direct(ly); in person [~contact] ~接
직사광선	direct ray of (sun)light [~shoot ray of light] ~射光線
직계	direct line (family) [~lineage] ~系
직역*	literal translation [~translate] ~譯
직영*	direct management [~manage] ~營

232

직행*	going nonstop; nonstop (vehicle) [~go] ~ 行	무직	being unemployed [no~] 無~
직통*	through-traffic; direct communication [~go through] ~ 通	퇴직*	retirement [retreat~] 退~
		휴직*	temporary rest from office [rest~] 休~
직감	immediate perception; intuition [~feeling] ~ 感	직원	staff; personnel [~member] ~ 員
정직*	honesty [right~] 正~	직공	factory worker [~laborer] ~工
솔.직하다	be frank [to lead~] 率~		
직성풀리다	be satisfied; be appeased [~star solved] ~星K	**직** (織)	**weave**
		모직	woolen fabric [wool~] 毛~
숙직*	night duty [lodge~] 宿~	면직	cotton fabric [cotton~] 綿~
당직*	being on (night) duty [ought~] 當~	조직*	organization [weave~] 組~

직 (職)	**post; office**	**진** (進)	**advance**
현직	present post; incumbent [current~] 現~	진행*	progress [~go] ~ 行 진행중 in progress
직장	one's place of work; one's job [~place] ~ 場	진도	the rate of progress (of classwork) [~degree] ~ 度
전직	previous post [before~] 前~	진보*	progress; advancement [~step] ~ 步
재직*	holding office; being in office [be present~] 在~	진전*	development; progress [~spread out] ~ 展
취직*	getting a job [take~] 就~	진척*	progress; advance [~progress] ~ 陟
천직	divine calling; mission in life [divine~] 天~	진급*	promotion (in rank) [~grade] ~ 級
직업	job; occupation [~job] ~ 業	진출*	advance; launching into [~come out] ~ 出
관직	government job [official~] 官~	전진*	moving forward; advance [front~] 前~
공직	official position [official~] 公~	추진*	propulsion; carrying forward [push~] 推~
직위	position; status [~position] ~ 位	진화*	evolution [~change] ~ 化
교직	teaching profession [teach~] 敎~	행진*	march; parade [go~] 行~
실.직*	losing one's job [lose~] 失~	직진*	going straight [straight~] 直~

돌·**진***   a rush; a dash [abrupt~] 突~

진로   the way ahead; one's path in life [~road] ~路

진퇴양난   being in a dilemma; being driven to the wall [~retreat both difficult] ~退兩難

진학*   continuing one's schooling at the next level [~learning] ~學

자**진**하다   do (something) of one's own accord [self~] 自~

촉**진***   facilitation; acceleration [urge~] 促~

진 (眞)   **true; genuine**

진리   truth [~principle] ~理

진실*   truth; sincerity [~reality] ~實

진상   real facts of a case; true picture [~appearance] ~相

진짜   genuine article; real stuff [~thing] ~K

진·가   true value [~value] ~價

진심   true heart; sincerity [~heart] ~心

진정*   genuine feeling; true heart [~feeling] ~情

순**진**하다   be innocent; be naive [pure~] 純~

천**진**난만*   innocence; naiveté [nature~bright romance] 天~爛漫

진담   serious talk [~talk] ~談

진지하다   be sincere; be serious [~earnest] ~摯

사**진**   photograph [copy~] 寫~

진공   vacuum [~empty] ~空
진공청소기 vacuum cleaner

진주   pearl [~beads] ~珠

진 (診)   **medical examination**

진찰*   medical examination [~observe] ~察

검**진***   medical checkup [inspect~] 檢~

진료*   medical examination and treatment [~medical treatment] ~療

진단*   diagnosis [~stop] ~斷

오**진***   misdiagnosis [mistake~] 誤~

왕**진***   (doctor's) visit to a patient [go~] 往~

청**진**기   stethoscope [listen~utensil] 聽~器

진 (盡)   **entirely; exhaust**

매**진***   selling out [sell~] 賣~

무**진**장   being inexhaustible [not~storage] 無~藏

탕**진***   dissipating (one's fortune) [dissipation~] 蕩~

극**진**하다   be very kind; be utterly devoted [extreme~] 極~

기**진**맥**진***   complete exhaustion [energy~pulse~] 氣~脈~

진 (鎭)   **suppress**

진압*   quelling (a riot) [~repress] ~壓

진화*   putting out a fire [~fire] ~火

진정*   pacification; calming down [~still] ~靜
진정제 sedative

진통제   pain killer [~pain medicine] ~痛劑

질 (質) **quality; substance; disposition**

품질 quality [article~] 品~

수질 quality of water [water~] 水~

변질* change in quality; (food) going bad [change~] 變~

토질 soil quality [soil~] 土~

음질 sound quality (of a stereo) [sound~] 音~

저질 low quality [low~] 低~

악질 evil nature; viciousness [evil~] 惡~

질.적 qualitative ~ 的

질문* question [~ask] ~ 問

물.질 material; matter [things~] 物~
물.질주의 materialism

인질 hostage [person~] 人~

단백질 protein [egg white~] 蛋白~

체질 physical constitution [body~] 體~

기질 temperament; nature [spirit~] 氣~

성질 nature; disposition [nature~] 性~
성질내다/부리다 show anger

소질 talents; makings [element~] 素~

신경질 nervous temperament; nervousness [nerve~] 神經~
신경질내다/부리다 show nervousness; be irritable

질 (疾) **ailment**

질병 disease [~disease] ~ 病

질환 disease; ailment [~suffering] ~ 患

치질 hemorrhoids [hemorrhoids~] 痔~

간질 epilepsy [epilepsy~] 癎~

감질나다 feel insatiable/tantalized [childhood ailment~come out] 疳 ~ K

질 (窒) **obstructed**

질.식 suffocation [~breath] ~ 息
질.식하다 be suffocated

질.색* abhorrence [~block] ~ 塞

질소 nitrogen [~element] ~ 素

집 (集) **gather**

집합* gathering; a set [~join] ~ 合

집결* gathering [~tie] ~ 結

모집* recruitment; invitation [collect~] 募~

집단 collective body; group [~group] ~ 團

수집* collecting (stamps, coins, etc.) [collect~] 蒐 ~
우표수집* stamp collection

채집* collecting (insects, plants, etc.) [dig up~] 採~
곤충채집* insect collecting

시집 collection of poems [poetry~] 詩~

소집* summoning; convocation [call~] 召~

집중* (mental) concentration; convergence [~middle] ~ 中

집 (執) **grasp**

집게 tongs
쪽집게 tweezers

집착*	being (excessively) attached (to) [~attach] ~ 着	차비	car fare [~expenditure] ~ 費
집념*	concentration of one's attention [~thought] ~ 念	차멀미*	car sickness [~motion sickness] ~ K
고집	stubbornness [firm~] 固~ 고집하다 stick to; insist upon	차고	garage [~storehouse] ~ 庫
집요하다	be persistent; be pertinacious [~twist] ~ 拗	찻길	roadway; driveway [~road] ~ K
		차도	driveway; traffic lane [~way] ~ 道

집 (輯) edit

특집	special edition [special~] 特~	차선	(traffic) lane [~line] ~ 線
편집*	editing; compilation [weave~] 編~	차표	railroad/bus ticket [~ticket] ~ 票
		승차*	getting in a vehicle [ride~] 乘~

징 (徵) symptoms; collect

징조	sign; omen [~omen] ~ 兆	하차*	getting out of a vehicle [descend~] 下~
특징	distinguishing feature; characteristic [special~] 特~	주차*	parking a car [stay~] 駐~ 주차장 parking lot
상징*	symbol [representation~] 象~	정차*	stopping a vehicle [stop~] 停~ 주정차* stopping and parking a vehicle
징수*	levy; collection (of taxes) [~collect] ~ 收		
		발차*	departure of a vehicle [depart~] 發~
		폐차*	auto junking [abolish~] 廢~ 폐차장 auto junkyard

ㅊ

		세차*	car washing [wash~] 洗~
		쓰레기차	garbage truck [garbage~] K~
		똥차	night-soil wagon; ramshackle car [feces~] K~

차 ʷ (車) vehicle; car

차량	vehicle [~vehicle] ~ 輛	소방차	fire engine [dissolve defend~] 消防~
자동차	automobile [self move~] 自動~ 불자동차 fire engine	마차	carriage [horse~] 馬~
		기차	train [steam~] 汽~
		열차	train [line~] 列~
중고차	used car [second-hand~] 中古~	화물차	freight train/truck [freight~] 貨物~
승용차	passenger car [ride use~] 乘用~	첫차	first bus/train [first~] K~
		막차	last bus/train [last~] K~

풍차   windmill [wind~] 風~

박차   a spurt; acceleration
[slap~] 拍~
박차를 가하다 give impetus

차 (差)   **differ(ence)**

차이   difference [~different] ~ 異
천지차이   big difference
수준차이   level gap

격차   difference; gap
[isolated~] 隔~

대차없다   make no great difference
[big~not exist] 大 ~ K

차도   improvement (of illness)
[~degree] ~ 度

세대차   generation gap
[generation~] 世代~

나이차   age gap [age~] K~

시차   jet lag [time~] 時~

차별*   discrimination
[~separate] ~ 別
인종차별*
racial discrimination
차별대우*
discriminatory treatment

오차   error (in mathematics)
[mistake~] 誤~

천차만별   infinite variety
[thousand~ten thousand
separate] 千~萬別

차 (次)   **next; sequence; place**

일차   the first [first~] 一~

이차   the second [second~] 二~

차례   (sequence) order;
(one's) turn [~example] ~ 例
차례차례   in due order;
one by one

차차   bit by bit; gradually

점차   gradually [gradually~] 漸~

수차   several times; time
and again [number~] 數~

누차   many times; repeatedly
[frequently~] 屢~

장차   in the future; some day
[future~] 將~

차원   dimension [~principal] ~ 元
차원이 다르다
be on a different level

절차   procedure [a joint~] 節~

차 ᵂ (茶)   **tea**

녹차   green tea [green~] 綠~

엽차   green tea [leaf~] 葉 ~

인삼차   ginseng tea [ginseng~] 人蔘~

보리차   barley tea [barley~] K~

홍차   black tea [red~] 紅 ~

냉차   iced tea [cold~] 冷~

찻잔   tea cup [~cup] ~ 盞

찻숟갈   tea spoon [~spoon] ~K

찻집   tea house [~house] ~K

찻값   charge for tea/coffee ~ K

착 (着)   **attach; arrive; wear**

부착*   sticking; adhesion
[paste~] 附 ~

접착*   adhesion; gluing
[connect~] 接~
접착제 an adhesive

집착*   being (excessively)
attached (to) [grasp~] 執~

애착*   attachment [love~] 愛~

도착*   arrival [reach~] 到~

연착*   delayed arrival [delay~] 延 ~

선**착**순 first come, first served [first~order] 先~順

착수* launching; embarking on [~hand] ~手

착륙* landing; touch down [~land] ~陸

착용* putting on; wearing (formal) [~use] ~用

착복식* celebration for wearing new clothes [~clothes ceremony] ~服式

정**착*** settling down [settle~] 定~

착착 steadily; in orderly fashion 착착 진행되다 progress steadily

침**착**하다 be composed; be self-possessed [sink~] 沈~

착실하다 be steady and honest; be trustworthy [~reality] ~實

주**착**없다 be senseless; be wishy-washy [main~not exist] 主~K

착석하다 take a chair; sit down (formal) [~seat] ~席

착공* starting (construction) work [~labor] ~工

착 (錯) **mistaken; confused**

착오* mistake; error [~mistake] ~誤 시행착오 trial and error

착각* (optical) illusion; hallucination [~perceive] ~覺

착잡하다 feel entangled; feel mixed up [~mixed] ~雜

찬 (讚) **praise**

칭**찬*** praise [praise~] 稱~

찬양* praise; admiration [~extol] ~揚

찬사 laudatory remark; compliment [~speech] ~辭

과**찬*** excessive praise [excede~] 過~

자화자**찬*** self-praise; self-admiration [self picture self~] 自畵自~

절**찬*** extolment [absolute~] 絶~

찬송가 hymn; psalm [~praise song] ~頌歌

찬 (贊) **agree; help**

찬성* approval; agreement [~to complete] ~成

찬반 for and against; pros and cons [~opposite] ~反

찬조* support; patronage [~assist] ~助 찬조출연* appearance as a guest

찬 w(饌) **(food) dishes**

반**찬** dishes served to go with rice [rice~] 飯~

진수성**찬** various sumptuous dishes [rare food prosperous~] 珍羞盛~

찬.장 pantry chest; cupboard [~cabinet] ~欌

찰 (察) **observe**

관**찰*** observation [see~] 觀~

시**찰*** inspection; observation [look at~] 視~

불**찰** inattention; mistake [not~] 不~

진찰* medical examination [medical examination~] 診~

순찰* patrol [patrol~] 巡~

경찰 the police [warn~] 警~

찰 (札) document

정찰 price tag; fixed price [right~] 正~

현찰 cash; bank notes [current~] 現~

명찰 nameplate [name~] 名~

참 (參) participate; consult

참가* participation [~apply] ~加
참가자 participant

참여* participation [~give] ~與

참전* participation in a war [~war] ~戰

참석* attendance; presence [~seat] ~席

불참* absence; nonattendance [not~] 不~

참견* meddling; minding other's business [~observe] 見

참정·권 suffrage [~govern rights] ~政權

신참 newcomer [new~] 新~

고참 senior; old-timer [old~] 古~

지참* bringing; bearing [possess~] 持~

참고* reference; consultation [~examine] ~考
참고서 reference book

참조* reference; consultation [~illumine] ~照

참작* taking into consideration; making allowances for [~deliberate] ~酌

참모 staff officer; brain truster [~plot] ~謀

참 (慘) miserable

비참하다 be miserable [sad~] 悲~

참혹하다 be pitiable; be miserable [~severe] ~酷

처참하다 be lurid; be ghastly [gruesome~] 慘~

참패* disastrous defeat [~defeat] ~敗

창 (創) beginning

창조* creation [~make] ~造
천지창조* the Creation

독창적 original; creative [alone~] 獨~的

창시* originating; founding [~begin] ~始

창립* establishment; founding [~establish] ~立

창설* establishment; founding [~establish] ~設

창간* first publication [~publish] ~刊

거창하다 be on a large scale [big~] 巨~

창 ʷ(窓) window

창문 window [~door] ~門

유리창 glass window [glass~] K~

창틀 window frame [~frame] ~K

창·가 by the window [~edge] ~K

창호지   paper for sliding doors
[~door paper] ~ 戶紙

들창코   upturned nose
[lift~nose] K~ K

창 ʷ(唱) **sing(ing)**

독창*   (vocal) solo [alone~] 獨~

합창*   singing together;
chorus [unite~] 合~

이중창*   vocal duet
[two layers~] 二重~

모창*   imitative singing
[pattern~] 模~

열창*   passionate singing
[heat~] 熱~

채 (採) **select; dig up**

채택*   selection; adoption
[~select] ~擇

채용*   employment; appointment
[~use] ~用

채.점*   marking; grading
[~point] ~點

채집*   collecting (insects,
plants, etc.) [~gather] ~集

채석장   quarry [~stone place] ~ 石場

채 (菜) **vegetable**

채소   vegetable [~vegetable] ~蔬

야채   vegetable [field~] 野~

생채   raw vegetable [raw~] 生~

잡채   a dish of mixed vegetables,
long rice and beef
[mixed~] 雜~

채식*   vegetarian diet [~eat] ~食
채식주의자 vegetarian

책 ʷ(冊) **book**

헌책   used book [used~] K~
헌책방 used-book store

소설책   a novel [novel~] 小說~

만화책   cartoon; comic book
[cartoon~] 漫畫~

공책   notebook [empty~] 空~

별책부록   separate-volume
supplement [separate~
appendix] 別~附錄

책방   bookstore [~room] ~ 房

책장   bookcase [~cabinet] ~ 欌

책값   price of books [~price] ~K

책가방   book sack [~bag] ~K

책벌레   bookworm [~worm] ~K

책꽂이   bookstand [~insertion] ~K

책상   desk [~table] ~ 床
책상다리* sitting
on crossed legs

책 (策) **a plan**

상책   best plan [supreme~] 上~

해결책   means of settling (a
problem) [settlement~] 解決~

정책   policy [politics~] 政~

실책   faulty policy; blunder
[lose~] 失~

방책   measures; policy
[method~] 方~

대책   countermeasure
[opposite~] 對~
대책을 세우다 work out
a countermeasure

책정*   (budget) appropriation;
fixing (prices) [~fix] ~ 定

240

ᄎ

속수무**책** helplessness; resourcefulness [bind hand no~] 束手無~

산**책*** taking a walk [disperse~] 散~

책 (責) **reprove; responsible**

가**책*** pang; scolding [scold~] 呵~
양심의 가책을 받다
be conscience-stricken

책망* reproach; blame [~observe] ~望

책임 responsibility [~be in charge] ~任

처 ʷ (妻) **wife**

악**처** bad wife [bad~] 惡~

후**처** second wife [after~] 後~

처자식 one's wife and children [~children] ~子息

현모양**처** a wise mother and good wife [wise mother good~] 賢母良~

처남 one's wife's brother [~male] ~男

처제 one's wife's younger sister [~junior] ~弟·

상**처*** loss (death) of one's wife [lose (by death)~] 喪~

처갓집 one's wife's family/house [~house house] ~家K

애**처**가 devoted husband [love~specialist] 愛~家

공**처**가 henpecked husband [fearful~specialist] 恐~家

처 (處) **place; manage**

거**처*** one's place of residence [dwell~] 居~

근**처** neighborhood; vicinity [near~] 近~

처지 situation; position [~place] ~地

난**처**하다 be in a difficult situation [difficult~] 難~

처하다 get faced with
위기에 처하다 face a crisis

출**처** (information) origin; source [come out~] 出~

상**처** injury; scar [injure~] 傷~

처리* management; handling; disposal (of a matter) [~manage] ~理
뒤처리* settlement (of an affair)

처치* disposal; getting rid of [~take action] ~置
처치곤란* being hard to deal with

처분* disposal (of one's property) [~share] ~分

대**처**하다 cope with [oppose~] 對~

처신* behavior; conduct [~body] ~身

처방* prescription [~method] ~方

처벌* (legal) punishment [~punish] ~罰

처세* conduct of life [~world] ~世

처녀 Miss; virgin [~female] ~女

천 (天) **sky; heaven; God; nature**

청**천**하늘 blue sky [blue~sky] 靑~K
청천하늘에 날벼락
thunderbolt out of the blue; sudden and unexpected blow

천하 the universe; the world [~below] ~下
천하에 in the world

241

	천하장사 strongest man in the world 천하일품 the best (quality) on earth
천막	tent; pavilion [~curtain] ~ 幕
천장	ceiling [~obstruct] ~ 障
낙천적	optimistic [pleasant~] 樂 ~ 的
천국	heaven; paradise [~country] ~ 國 지상천국 earthly paradise
천당	heaven [~hall] ~ 堂
천지	heaven and earth; being full of [~earth] ~ 地
천벌	heaven's vengeance [~punish] ~ 罰
천사	angel [~messenger] ~ 使
천주교	Catholicism [~lord religion] ~ 主教
천직	divine calling; mission in life [~post] ~ 職
천성	nature; innate disposition [~nature] ~ 性
천생	by nature [~be born] ~ 生 그는 천생 학자다 He is a scholar by nature. 천생연분 relationship made in heaven
천연*	(being) natural [~as such] ~ 然 천연기념물 natural monument 천연자원 natural resources 천연스럽다 be natural; be unaffected
천부적	natural; endowed [~give] ~ 賦的 천부적 재능 natural talent
선천적	innate; inherited [precede~] 先 ~ 的
후천적	acquired; postnatal [after~] 後 ~ 的
천재	genius [~talent] ~ 才

천진난만*	innocence; naiveté [~genuine bright romance] ~ 眞爛漫
천방지축	headlong [~direction earth axis] ~ 方地軸
천고마비	term describing autumn [~high horse fat] ~ 高馬肥

천 (賤) lowly

귀천	the noble and the lowly [honorable~] 貴~
(비)천하다	be lowly; be lowborn [low~] 卑~
천대*	contemptuous, cold treatment [~treat] ~ 待
천시*	looking down on; slight [~look at] ~ 視
지천이다	be abundant; be everywhere [extreme~] 至~

천 ʷ(千) thousand

수천	thousands of [several~] 數 ~
천만	ten million; countless number; extremely [~ten thousand] ~ 萬 천만에요 not at all; You are welcome. 천만다행이다 be extremely fortunate
천리	thousand li; long distance [~li (= 0.4 km)] ~ 里 천릿길도 한걸음부터 A journey of a thousand miles starts with a single step.
천자문	the (Chinese) Thousand-Character Text [~characters writing] ~ 字文
천층만층	countless varieties; innumerable ranks [~layers ten thousand layers] ~ 層萬層

ㅊ

철 ᵂ(鐵) iron

강철	iron; steel [steel~] 鋼~
양철	tinned sheet iron [western~] 洋~
철모	steel helmet [~hat] ~ 帽
철근	iron reinforcing rod [~muscle] ~ 筋
철봉	iron bar (for exercise) [~stick] ~ 棒
철칙	iron rule [~rule] ~ 則
철분	iron content [~share] ~ 分
철.사	wire [~thread] ~ 絲
철(조)망	wire net; (barbed) wire entanglement [~branch net] ~ 條網
용수철	(coiled steel) spring [dragon beard~] 龍鬚~
철물점	hardware store [~things store] ~ 物店
지남철	magnet [to point south~] 指南~
철.도	railroad [~way] ~ 道
전철	electric railway; subway [electricity~] 電~
철.길	railroad track [~road] ~K
지하철	subway [underground~] 地下~
철판	iron plate; brazen-facedness [~board] ~ 板 얼굴에 철판을 깔다 be brazen-faced
철면피	brazen-facedness; shamelessness [~face skin] ~ 面皮
철통같다	(defense) be impregnable; be rigorously guarded [~tub be like] ~ 桶K

철 (撤) remove

철거*	removal (of a building) [~go away] ~ 去
철.수*	withdrawal (of the troops) [~bind] ~ 收
철폐*	abolition (of a law); lifting (a ban) [~abolish] ~ 廢

철 (徹) penetrate

투철하다	(spirit) be penetrating; be thorough [transparent~] 透~
철.저하다	be thorough [~bottom] ~ 底
철.두철미하다	be thorough [~head~tail] ~ 頭 ~ 尾
냉철하다	be cool-headed [cold~] 冷~

첨 (添) add

첨가*	adding; addition [~add] ~ 加
첨삭*	addition and deletion; correction [~subtract] ~ 削
첨부*	appending; accompanying [~add] ~ 附 첨부서류 accompanying documents

청 (廳) government office

관청	government office [official~] 官~
청사	government building [~building] ~ 舍
중앙청	the capitol building [center~] 中央~
시청	city hall [city~] 市~
도청	provincial office [province~] 道~ 도청소재지 provincial seat

243

군청   county office [county~] 郡 ~

구청   district office [district~] 區 ~

교육청   education building [education~] 敎育 ~

철·도청   office of (Korean National) Railroad [railroad~] 鐵道 ~

청 ʷ(請) request; invite

요청*   important request [essential~] 要 ~

간청*   entreaty [earnest~] 懇 ~

신청*   application; request [petition~] 申 ~

청구*   a demand; a claim [~request] ~ 求
청구서 written claim; bill

초청*   invitation; a call [invite~] 招 ~

청첩*   wedding invitation (card) [~letter] ~ 牒

청혼*   proposal of marriage [~marriage] ~ 婚

자청*   volunteering [self~] 自 ~

청 (聽) listen

경청*   listening attentively [lean~] 傾 ~

방청*   hearing; attending [beside~] 傍 ~
방청객 audience
방청.권 admission ticket for attending (a TV show)

청취*   (radio) listening [~take] ~ 取
청취자 (radio) listener

시청*   seeing and hearing (TV) [look at~] 視 ~

도청*   wiretapping; bug [steal~] 盜 ~

청문회   (public) hearing [~hear meeting] ~ 聞會

청중   audience; hearers [~crowd] ~ 衆

청강*   auditing (a course) [~lecture] ~ 講

청 (靑) blue; green

청색   blue color [~color] ~ 色
청록색 bluish green color

청바지   blue jeans [~pants] ~ K

청와대   Blue House (Korean presidential mansion) [~tile tower] ~ 瓦臺

청천하늘   blue sky [~sky sky] ~天K

청년   young man [~age] ~ 年

청소년   young boys and girls; teenagers [~young age] ~少年

청춘   springtime of life; youth [~spring] ~ 春
이팔청춘 sweet sixteen; flower of youth

청 (淸) clean; clear

청결*   cleanliness [~clean] ~ 潔

청소*   cleaning (a house) [~sweep] ~ 掃
청소기 (vacuum) cleaner
대청소* general cleaning

청산*   clearing off; squaring accounts [~calculate] ~ 算

청순하다   be pure and innocent [~pure] ~ 純

청주   clear strained rice wine [~liquor] ~ 酒

청량음료   cooling beverage; soft drink [~cool beverage] ~ 凉飮料

체 (體) body; frame

신체	body; physique [body~] 身~
체격	physique [~frame] ~格
체구	body; frame [~human body] ~軀
체형	body shape; body type [~shape] ~形
형체	form; shape [form~] 形~
인체	human body [person~] 人~
육체	flesh; body [flesh~] 肉~ 육체노동* physical labor
상체	upper part of the body [upper~] 上~
하체	lower part of the body [below~] 下~
나체	naked body [naked~] 裸~
시체	dead body; corpse [corpse~] 屍~
체중	body weight [~weight] ~重
체온	body temperature [~warm] ~溫
체감온도	perceived temperature [~feeling temperature] ~感溫度
체력	physical strength [~strength] ~力
체질	physical constitution [~disposition] ~質
고체	a solid [firm~] 固~
입체	a solid; three-dimensional body [stand~] 立~
액체	liquid [liquid~] 液~
정체	real form; true character [right~] 正~ 정체를 밝히다 disclose one's identity
체육	physical education [~bring up] ~育

체조*	gymnastics [~grasp] ~操 미용체조* calisthenics
일·심동체	being one in flesh and spirit [one mind same~] 一心同~
삼위일체	Trinity [three position one~] 三位一~
체면	face; honor; dignity [~face] ~面
체통	dignity; respectability [~govern] ~統 체통이 없다 be disrespectable
자체	oneself; itself [self~] 自~
체험*	personal experience [~examine] ~驗
체계	system; organization [~connection] ~系
해체*	dismantling; dissolution [release~] 解~
전체	the whole [whole~] 全~ 전체적으로 on the whole
체적	(cubic) volume [~pile up] ~積
원체	originally; by nature [the first~] 元~
구체적	concrete [implement~] 具~的
주체·성	subjecthood; self-reliance [chief~nature] 主~性

체 (滯) obstructed

체하다	have indigestion
정체*	stagnation; (traffic) congestion [stop~] 停~
침체*	stagnation; dullness [sink~] 沈~
지체*	delay [late~] 遲~
체류*	stay; sojourn [~stay] ~留

ㅊ

초 (初)　first; beginning

최초	the very first [the most~] 最~
초판	first edition [~printing] ~ 版
초반	opening phase; early stage [~slab] ~ 盤
초기	early period/stage [~period] ~ 期
초순	the first ten days of a month [~ten days] ~ 旬
초복	first period of dog days [~dog days] ~ 伏
학기초	beginning of the semester [semester~] 學期~
정초	beginning of January [January~] 正~
초봄	early spring [~spring] ~K
초여름	early summer [~summer] ~K
초가을	early fall [~fall] ~K
초겨울	early winter [~winter] ~K
초저녁	early evening [~evening] ~K
초하루	the first of the month [~one day] ~K
초면	meeting for the first time [~face] ~ 面
시초	beginning; inception [begin~] 始~
초보	beginning; novice [~step] ~ 步 초보자 beginner 초보운전 driving by a novice
초급	elementary level [~grade] ~ 級
초등교육	elementary education [~rank education] ~ 等教育
초봉	starting pay [~salary] ~ 俸
애초	the very first time

초 (超)　excel; jump over

초과*	exceeding; excess [~exceed] ~ 過
초월*	transcendence; going beyond [~cross over] ~ 越
초인	superhuman [~person] ~ 人
초현대적	ultramodern [~modern-times] ~ 現代的
초만원	overcrowding [~full-house] ~ 滿員
초연하다	be aloof; be transcendental [~as such] ~ 然

초 (招)　invite; call

초대*	invitation [~treat] ~ 待 초대.장 invitation card 초대.권 invitation ticket
초청*	invitation; a call [~invite] ~ 請
초빙*	inviting (a lecturer) [~invite] ~ 聘
초래*	bringing about; incurring [~come] ~ 來
자초하다	bring upon oneself; incur (blame) [self~] 自~
초인종	call bell; door bell [~person bell] ~ 人鐘

초 (草)　grass

초원	grassy plain; prairie [~plateau] ~ 原
잡초	weed [mixed~] 雜~
해초	seaweed [sea~] 海~
화초	flowering plants [flower~] 花~
초식동물	herbivorous animal [~eat animal] ~ 食動物

초가집	thatched house [~house house] ~ 家 K		촉진*	facilitation; acceleration [~advance] ~ 進
대마초	hemp leaf cigarette [hemp~] 大麻~		판촉*	sales promotion [sell~] 販 ~
감초	licorice root [sweet~] 甘~ 약방에 감초 indispensable person/thing			

초 ᵂ(醋) vinegar

식초	(table) vinegar [food~] 食~
초간장	soy sauce mixed with vinegar [~soy sauce] ~ K 醬
초밥	Japanese-style vinegared rice delicacies [~rice] ~K
초치다	flavor with vinegar; make a mess of (slang) [~put in] ~ K

초 (焦) focus; burn

초·점	focus [~point] ~ 点
초조하다	be fretful; be anxious [~uneasy] ~ 燥

초 ᵂ(秒) a second (of time)

초침	second hand [~needle] ~ 針
초속	speed per second [~speed] ~ 速
초시계	stopwatch [~watch] ~ 時計

촉 (促) urge

재촉*	pressing; urging
촉박하다	be urgent; be imminent [~oppress] ~ 迫

촉 (觸) touch; stimulate

접촉*	a contact; a touch [contact~] 接~
촉감	the feel; the touch [~feeling] ~ 感
감촉	the feel; the touch [feeling~] 感 ~
촉각	feeler; antenna [~horn] ~ 角
촉매	catalyst [~go-between] ~ 媒

촌 ᵂ(村) village

농촌	agricultural village [agricultural~] 農 ~
어촌	fishing village [fishing~] 漁~
산촌	mountain village [mountain~] 山~
강촌	riverside village [river~] 江~
민속촌	folk village [folk customs~] 民俗~
촌·사람	country folk [~person] ~ K
촌놈	country bumpkin [~ fellow (vulgar)] ~ K
촌뜨기	country bumpkin [~person] ~ K
촌·닭	country bumpkin [~chicken] ~ K
촌티	rusticity; boorishness [~a smack] ~ K 촌티나다 look rustic
촌·스럽다	be boorish; be unrefined

촌 (寸) relation

삼촌 uncle (on father's side)
[three~] 三~
외삼촌 uncle
on mother's side

사촌 cousin (on father's side)
[four~] 四~
외사촌 cousin
on mother's side

총 ʷ(總) all; general

총계 the total (sum)
[~calculate] ~ 計

총합* the total (sum) [~unite] ~ 合

총수입 total income
[~income] ~ 收入

총액 total amount of money
[~amount of money] ~ 額

총.점 total score [~point] ~ 点

총결.산* final settlement of
accounts [~settlement
of accounts] ~ 決算

총괄* generalization;
summarizing [~include] ~ 括

총동원* general mobilization
[~mobilization] ~ 動員

총회 general meeting
[~meeting] ~ 會

총무 general affairs; manager
[~affairs] ~ 務

총장 president of a university
[~superior] ~ 長

총재 president of a political
party [~judge] ~ 裁

총각 unmarried man; bachelor
[~horn] ~ 角
총각김치 young radish
kimchi

총 ʷ(銃) gun

권총 pistol [fist~] 拳~

기관총 machine gun
[engine~] 機關~

다발총 Russian automatic rifle;
fast talking (slang)
[many shoot~] 多發~

물총 water pistol [water~] K~

총칼 gun and sword [~knife] ~ K

총알 bullet [~egg] ~ K

총탄 (rifle) bullet [~bullet] ~ 彈

총살* execution by shooting
[~kill] ~ 殺

총격전 gunfight
[~attack fight] ~ 擊戰

최 (最) the most

최고 the highest; the best
[~high] ~ 高
최고급 highest grade; first-rate
최고기온 highest temperature

최상 the best [~supreme] ~上
최상품 the best article
최상의 방법 the best way

최우수 the very best
[~excellence] ~ 優秀
최우수상 the highest award

최대 the largest; maximum
[~big] ~ 大
최대한 maximum

최소 the smallest; minimum
[~small] ~ 小
최소한 at least

최저 the lowest; minimum
[~low] ~ 低
최저기온 lowest temperature

최하 the lowest; the most
inferior [~below] ~ 下

최선 one's best [~good] ~ 善
최선을 다하다 do one's best

최악 the worst [~bad] ~ 惡
최악의 경우에는
if worst comes to worst

최초 the very first
[~beginning] ~ 初

최후 the last [~later] ~ 後

최종 the last; the end [~end] ~ 終
최종결.정* final decision

최신 the newest [~new] ~ 新
최신식 the newest style
최신유행* the latest fashion

최근 the latest; the most recent
[~recent] ~ 近

최 (催) urge

최면 hypnotism [~sleep] ~ 眠
최면걸다 hypnotize
최면술 hypnotism

최루탄 tear gas [~tears bullet] ~ 淚彈

개최* holding (a meeting)
[open~] 開~

주최* sponsorship [host~] 主~

추 (秋) autumn

춘추복 spring/autumn clothes
[spring~clothes] 春~服

추수* autumn harvest
[~harvest] ~ 收

추석 harvest full moon festival
on Aug. 15th by lunar
calendar [~evening] ~ 夕

추호도 (not) in the least
[~fuzz even] ~ 毫K

추파 amorous glance; ogle
[~wave] ~ 波

추 (追) follow; pursue

추종* following [~follow] ~ 從
추종자 follower
추종을 불허하다
be second to none

추격* chase; follow-up attack
[~attack] ~ 擊

추적* chasing; tracking
[~trace] ~ 跡

추월* passing (another car)
[~cross over] ~ 越

추구* pursuit [~seek] ~ 求

추억* reminiscence; memory
[~remember] ~ 憶

추모* cherishing the memory
of a deceased person
[~adore] ~ 慕

추가* adding; addition [~add] ~ 加

추신 postscript (P.S.)
[~extend] ~ 伸

추방* driving out; banishment
[~release] ~ 放

추 (推) push; infer

추진* propulsion; carrying
forward [~advance] ~ 進
추진력 driving force

추천* recommendation
[~recommend] ~ 薦
추천서 letter of
recommendation

추리* reasoning; inference
[~reason] ~ 理
추리소설 detective story

추산* estimate; calculation
[~calculate] ~ 算

추측* guess; conjecture
[~measure] ~ 測

추정* presumption; estimation
[~decide] ~ 定

추 (醜) ugly

추하다	be ugly; be indecent
추행*	ugly conduct; sexual assault [~act] ~ 行
추태	disgraceful behavior [~attitude] ~ 態
추문	scandal; ill fame [~hear] ~聞
추잡*	filthiness; indecency [~mixed] ~ 雜

추 (抽) extract

추출*	extraction [~come out] ~ 出
추첨*	drawing lots [~draw lots] ~ 籤
추상적	abstract [~image] ~ 象的

축 (祝) celebrate; congratulate

경축*	celebration [congratulate~] 慶 ~
자축*	self-celebration [self~] 自~
축배*	celebratory drink; toast [~cup] ~ 杯 축배를 들다 drink a toast
축하*	congratulation [~congratulate] ~ 賀
축가	song of congratulation [~song] ~ 歌
축사*	congratulatory speech [~speech] ~ 辭
축전	congratulatory telegram [~telegram] ~ 電 (<경축전보)
축의금	congratulatory money [~rite money] ~ 儀金
축복*	blessing [~blessing] ~ 福 축복받다 be blessed
축제*	festival [~rite] ~ 祭

축 (縮) shrink

수축*	shrinkage [bind~] 收~
축나다	diminish; fall short of; be reduced [~come out] ~ K
축소*	reduction [~small] ~ 小
단축*	shortening [short~] 短~
감축*	curtailing (the personnel) [decrease~] 減~
축도	reduced-size drawing; miniature copy [~drawing] ~ 圖
신축성	elasticity [stretch~nature] 伸 ~ 性
농축*	concentration; condensing [thickness~] 濃~
위축되다	being daunted; lose one's heart [wither~become] 萎 ~ K

축 ʷ(軸) axis

주축	main axis [main~] 主~
회전축	the axis of rotation [rotation~] 回轉~
축대	embankment [~tower] ~ 臺

축 (畜) livestock

가축	domestic animals [house~] 家~ 가축병원 veterinary hospital
목축*	cattle raising [raise~] 牧~
축산업	stockbreeding [~industry] ~ 産業

축 (蓄) store up

축적*	accumulation [~pile up] ~ 積
부정축재*	illegal profiteering [injustice~wealth] 不正~財

전축 record player; stereo [electricity~] 電~

축농·증 asthma; emphysema [~pus symptom] ~膿症

함축* implication [include~] 含~

출 (出) exit; come out; appear; produce; put forth

출구 an exit [~opening] ~口

출입* exit and entrance [~enter] ~入
출입구 exit and entrance

출국* departure from a country [~country] ~國

출발* departure [~depart] ~發

출·동* going out; mobilization [~move] ~動

외출* going out [outside~] 外~

출근* going to work [~work] ~勤

수출* export [transport~] 輸~

출·산* baby delivery [~produce] ~産

출·생* birth [~be born] ~生

출가* woman's getting married (and leaving home) [~house] ~家

가출* running away from home [house~] 家~

두문불출* confining oneself at home [close door not~] 杜門不~

출·장 business trip [~extend] ~張
출·장가다 go on a business trip

진출* advance; launching into [advance~] 進~

탈출* escape [escape~] 脫~

구출* rescuing; saving (a life) [rescue~] 救~

지출* expenditure; outlay [pay~] 支~

대출* lending out; loan [lend~] 貸~

출판* publication [~printing] ~版

배출* producing (scholars) [fellow members~] 輩~

출·신 a graduate; affiliation; origin [~person] ~身
출·신학교 alma mater; school one graduated from
군인출·신 former military man

출·제* making questions for an exam [~subject] ~題

출·세* success (in life); rising in the world [~world] ~世

특출하다 be outstanding; be prominent [special~] 特~

추출* extraction [extract~] 抽~

검출* (chemical) detection [inspect~] 檢~

색출* ferreting out (a criminal) [seek~] 索~

출혈* bleeding; sacrifices [~blood] ~血
내출혈* internal bleeding

호출* calling out; summons [call~] 呼~

출결 attendance and absence [~deficienct] ~缺

출·석* (school) attendance [~seat] ~席
출·석부 roster; attendance book

출마* running for election [~horse] ~馬

선출* electing [elect~] 選~

출.전* participating in an athletic contest [~fighting] ~ 戰

노출* exposure [expose~] 露~

출연* appearance on stage [~perform] ~ 演

연출* production; staging [perform~] 演~

출처 (information) origin; source [~place] ~ 處

제출* submitting; handing in [lift up~] 提~

충 (充) full

충족하다 be sufficient [~sufficient] ~足

충전* (battery) charge [~electricity] ~ 電

충분하다 be enough; be sufficient [~share] ~ 分

보충* supplementation [supplement~] 補~

충실하다 be substantial; be solid (in contents) [~reality] ~ 實

충당* appropriation; meeting (the demand) [~suitable] ~ 當

충혈되다 (eyes) be bloodshot [~blood become] ~ 血 K

충 (蟲) insect; worm

곤충 insect [insect~] 昆~
곤충채집* insect collecting

해충 harmful insect [harm~] 害~

병충해 damage by blight and harmful insects [disease~harm] 病~害

방충망 insectproof net [defend~net] 防~網

살충제 insecticide [kill~medicine] 殺~劑

기생충 parasitic worm [entrust live~] 寄生~

회충 roundworm [roundworm~] 蛔~

송충이 pine caterpillar [pine tree~] 松~ K

충치 decayed tooth; cavity [~tooth] ~齒

충 (忠) loyal

충성* loyalty; devotion [~sincerity] ~ 誠
과잉충성* excessive loyalty

충신 loyal subject [~subject] ~ 臣

충실하다 be faithful; be loyal [~genuine] ~ 實

충고* advice [~tell] 告

충 (衝) collision; rush into

충돌* collision [~collide] ~ 突

충격 a shock [~attack] ~ 擊

충동* instigation; impulse [~move] ~ 動
충동적 impulsive

취 (取) take; obtain

취하다 take (the position/a step); assume a posture
조치를 취하다 take measures
자세를 취하다 assume a posture

취득* attainment (of diploma, certificate, etc.) [~acquire] ~ 得

취재* selection of material; news gathering [~material] ~ 材

섭취*   intake [hold~] 攝~

취사선택*   adoption or rejection;
choice [~discard choice]
~捨選擇

취급*   treatment; handling
[~handle] ~ 扱
어린애 취급하다
treat (a person) like a child
취급주의*   Handle with care

취소*   cancellation [~dissolve] ~ 消

청취*   (radio) listening
[listen~] 聽~

취 (就)   take; complete

취업*   taking up a job;
employment [~job] ~業

취직*   getting a job [~post] ~職

취임*   assumption of office;
inauguration
[~be in charge] ~ 任

성취*   accomplishment;
realization [to complete~] 成~
성취감   sense of
accomplishment

취침*   going to bed [~sleep] ~寢

취 (醉)   intoxicated

취하다   get drunk

만취*   dead-drunkenness
[diffused~] 漫 ~

도취*   being intoxicated; being
in rapture [earthen jar~] 陶 ~
자기도취*   narcissism

마취*   anesthesia [paralysis~] 痲 ~

취 (趣)   hobby; tendency

취미   hobby; taste [~taste] ~ 味

취향   taste; liking [~to face] ~ 向

취지   purport; object
[~purport] ~ 旨

측 (側)   side

측면   the side; side surface
[~face] ~ 面

좌측   left side [left~] 左~

우측   right side [right~] 右~

측 (測)   measure

측량*   measuring; (land)
survey [~measure] ~ 量

측정*   measuring [~decide] ~ 定

예측*   pre-estimate
[beforehand~] 豫 ~

추측*   guess; conjecture
[infer~] 推 ~

억측*   random guess
[supposition~] 臆 ~

층 ʷ(層)   story; layer

단층   one-story (building)
[single~] 單 ~
단층집   one-story house

고층   high-rise (building)
[high~] 高 ~
고층건물   high-rise building
고층아파트
high-rise apartment

층계   stairs [~stairs] ~ 階

아래층   downstairs [lower~] K~

위층   upstairs [upper~] K~

계층   social stratum [rank~] 階 ~

하층   lower (social) class
[below~] 下 ~

고위**층**   persons holding high positions [high rank~] 高位~

부유**층**   wealthy class [wealth~] 富裕~

서민**층**   working class [common people~] 庶民~

중산**층**   middle class [middle produce~] 中産~

중간**층**   middle layers/class [middle~] 中間~

천**층**만**층**   countless varieties; innumerable ranks [thousand~ten thousand~] 千~萬~

치 (齒)   **tooth**

치아   tooth [~teeth] ~牙

치통   toothache [~pain] ~痛

충**치**   decayed tooth; cavity [insect~] 蟲~

치석   tartar on the teeth [~stone] ~石

칫솔   toothbrush [~brush] ~K

치약   toothpaste [~medicine] ~藥

치실   dental floss [~thread] ~K

치·과   dental office [~department] ~科

양**치**(질)*   brushing one's teeth [care~doing] 養~K

치떨리다   be infuriated; be sick of [~tremble] ~K

치 (治)   **treat; cure; govern**

치료*   medical treatment [~medical treatment] ~療

완**치***   complete cure [complete~] 完~

치유*   healing; cure [~cure] ~癒

만병통**치**약   cure-all [all diseases thoroughly~medicine] 萬病通 ~藥

불**치**.병   incurable disease [not~disease] 不~病

퇴**치***   extermination [retreat~] 退~

통**치***   rule; reign [govern~] 統~

정**치***   politics; government [politics~] 政~

치장*   embellishment; making fancy [~makeup] ~粧

이열**치**열   Like cures like. [with heat~heat] 以熱~熱

치 (置)   **to place**

위**치***   location [position~] 位~

대**치***   replacement [substitute~] 代~

배**치***   arrangement; placement [suitable~] 配~

설**치***   establishment; installation [establish~] 設~

장**치***   equipment; installation [decorate~] 裝~

비**치***   furnishing; equipping [prepare~] 備~

방**치***   leaving (things) neglected [release~] 放~

처**치***   disposal; getting rid of [manage~] 處~

도**치***   inversion [invert~] 倒~

치중하다   attach weight to; lay stress on [~weight] ~重

조**치***   measure; action [take action~] 措~ 조치를 취하다 take measures

유치장   police cell; detention house [detention~place] 留~場

치 (恥)   shameful

수치   shame; disgrace [shame~] 羞~
수치스럽다   be disgraceful

치욕   shame; disgrace [~disgrace] ~辱

치사하다   be shameful; be mean [~matter] ~事

염치   sense of shame [honest~] 廉~
염치없다   be shameless

치 (値)   value

수치   numerical value [number~] 數~

가치   value; worth [price~] 價~

값어치   worth (pron. = 가버치)
백원어치   a hundred won's worth of (goods)

치 (痴／癡) foolish; imbecile

바보천치   idiot [fool nature~] K 天~

백치   moron [clear~] 白~

음치   tone deafness; lack of musical ability [sound~] 音~

치정   foolish passion [~feeling] ~情

치한   molester of women [~base person] ~漢

칙 (則)   rule

규칙   rule; regulation [regulation~] 規~
규칙을 지키다   abide by rules

법칙   law; rule [law~] 法~

원칙   fundamental rule; general rule [origin~] 原~

반칙*   violation of rules; a foul (in sports) [opposite~] 反~

벌칙   penal regulations [punish~] 罰~

철칙   iron rule [iron~] 鐵~

친 (親)   friendly; parents

친구   friend [~oldtime] ~舊

친목   friendship; fraternization [~harmony] ~睦
친목회   social meeting

친절*   kindness [~earnest] ~切

친하다   (relationship) be close

절친*   be on the best terms (with) [earnest~] 切~

친근하다   be close; be familiar [~close] ~近
친근감   sense of closeness

친숙하다   be familiar; be well acquainted [~ripe] ~熟

양친   both parents (formal) [both~] 兩~

친부모   one's real parents [~parents] ~父母

친엄마   one's real mother [~mother] ~K

부친   one's father (formal) [father~] 父~

모친   one's mother (formal) [mother~] 母~

친정   married woman's parents' home [~yard] ~庭

친자식   one's real children [~children] ~子息

친형제	full brothers [~brothers] ~ 兄弟
친남매	real brother and sister [~brother and sister] ~ 男妹
친척	relatives; kinfolk [~relatives] ~ 戚

칠 ᵂ(七) seven(th)

칠월	July [~month] ~月
칠.순	being seventy years old [~ten years] ~ 旬
칠.전팔기*	never giving in to adversity [~upset eight rise] ~ 顚八起
칠면조	turkey [~face bird] ~ 面鳥

칠 ᵂ(漆) painting; smearing; black

색칠*	coloring; painting [color~] 色 ~
칠조심*	Wet Paint [~carefulness] ~ 操心
흙칠*	smearing with mud [soil~] K~
똥칠*	smearing dung; disgrace [feces~] K~ 얼굴에 똥칠하다 disgrace one's name
풀칠*	applying paste [paste~] K~
칠판	blackboard [~board] ~ 板
칠흑	pitch-dark (night) [~black] ~ 黑

침 (寢) sleep

침식	sleep and food; room and board [~food] ~ 食
동침*	sleeping together [together~] 同 ~

침낭	sleeping bag [~bag] ~ 囊
침실	bedroom [~room] ~ 室
침대	bed [~terrace] ~ 臺
취침*	going to bed [take~] 就 ~

침 (侵) invade

남침*	invasion of the South (Korea) [south~] 南 ~
침입*	invasion; trespass [~enter] ~ 入
침범*	invasion; encroachment [~offense] ~ 犯
침략*	invasion [~strategy] ~ 略
침해*	infringement [~harm] ~ 害

침 (沈) sink

침몰*	(boat) sinking [~sink] ~ 沒
침울하다	be dismal; be gloomy [~depressed] ~ 鬱
음침하다	be somber [dark~] 陰
침침하다	(light) be dim; (eyes) be blurry 어두침침하다 be dimly lit
침체*	stagnation; dullness [~obstructed] ~ 滯
침착하다	be composed; be self-possessed [~attach] ~ 着
침묵*	silence [~silent] ~ 默

침 (針) needle

피뢰침	lightning rod [avoid thunder~] 避雷 ~
초침	second hand [a second~] 秒~
분침	minute hand [a minute~] 分~
방침	plan; policy [method~] 方~

256

칭 (稱) praise; call

칭찬*   praise [~praise] ~ 讚

존칭*   honorific title [honor~] 尊~

명칭*   name; title [name~] 名~

호칭*   term of address [call~] 呼~

애칭   term of endearment [love~] 愛~

자칭*   self-styled; self-appointed [self~] 自~
천재라고 자칭하다
call oneself a genius

사칭*   assuming a false name [deceive~] 詐~

(지)칭하다   call; designate [to point~] 指~

ㅋ

쾌 (快) pleasant; refreshing

쾌감   pleasant feeling [~feeling] ~ 感

쾌락   pleasure; enjoyment [~pleasant] ~ 樂

유쾌하다   be pleasant; be cheerful [happy~] 愉~

불쾌하다   be unpleasant; be displeased [not~] 不~

통쾌하다   be thoroughly pleasant [intense~] 痛~

쾌활하다   be cheerful [~lively] ~ 活

쾌히   gladly; readily [~ -ly] ~ K
쾌히 승낙하다
readily consent

상쾌하다   be exhilarating; be refreshing [refreshing~] 爽 ~

쾌청하다   (weather) be refreshing and clear [~clear] ~ 晴

쾌적하다   (weather) be agreeable; be comfortable [~suitable] ~適

완쾌*   complete recovery [complete~] 完~

ㅌ

타 (他) other(s)

타국   foreign country; alien land [~country] ~ 國

타향   place away from home; strange land [~province] ~ 鄉

타살   homicide; murder [~kill] ~ 殺

타인   unrelated person; stranger [~person] ~人

배타적   exclusive (of others) [reject~] 排~的

기타   etc.; and so forth [they~] 其~

타 (打) hit

구타*   battery; assault [beat~] 毆~

타격   a shock; a blow [~strike] ~ 擊

타박상   bruise; contusion [~hit injure] ~ 撲傷

타자   (baseball) hitter [~person] ~ 者

안타   a hit (in baseball) [safe~] 安~

타자   typing [~characters] ~ 字

타작* threshing [~make] ~ 作

타도* overthrowing [~fall down] ~ 倒

타산적 calculating; selfish [~calculate] ~ 算的

타 (妥) reasonable

타당하다 be reasonable; be proper [~suitable] ~ 當
타당.성 propriety; validity

타협* a compromise [~harmony] ~ 協

타결* compromise; settlement [~result] ~ 結

탁 (卓) table

탁자 table [~thing] ~ 子

원탁 round table [round~] 圓 ~

식탁 dining table [eat~] 食 ~

탁구 table tennis [~ball] ~ 球

탁상공론* armchair theory [~above empty discuss] ~ 上空論

탁상시계 table-top clock [~above clock] ~ 上時計

탄 (彈) bullet; a spring

총탄 (rifle) bullet [gun~] 銃 ~

폭탄 bomb; bombshell [explode~] 爆 ~
시한폭탄 time bomb

최루탄 tear gas [urge tears~] 催淚 ~

규탄* impeachment; denunciation [impeach~] 糾 ~

지탄* censure; blame [to point~] 指 ~

탄압* oppression; suppression [~repress] ~ 壓

탄력 elasticity [~strength] ~ 力
탄력성 elasticity

탄 ʷ (炭) coal

석탄 coal [stone~] 石 ~

연탄 briquet [smelt~] 煉 ~

탄광 coal mine [~mine] ~ 鑛

탄소 carbon [~element] ~ 素

탄수화물 carbohydrate [~water change thing] ~ 水化物

탄 (歎) sigh; exclaim

통탄하다 lament bitterly; regret deeply [intense~] 痛 ~

한탄하다 lament; deplore [grudge~] 恨 ~

감탄하다 be struck with admiration [feeling~] 感 ~
감탄사 exclamation; interjection

탄 (誕) be born

탄생* birth [~be born] ~ 生

성탄절 Christmas day [saint~festival] 聖 ~ 節

석가탄신일 Buddha's birthday [Buddha~star day] 釋迦 ~ 辰日

탈 (脫) escape; take off

탈출* escape [~exit] ~ 出

탈영* desertion [~camp] ~ 營

탈.당* secession [~political party] ~ 黨

탈퇴* secession; withdrawal [~leave] ~ 退

이탈* secession; breakaway [leave~] 離 ~

ㅌ

탈피* breaking from (e.g., convention) [~skin] ~ 皮

탈·세* tax evasion [~tax] ~ 稅

탈락* being omitted; being eliminated [~omit] ~ 落

탈·선* derailment; aberration [~line] ~ 線

탈모 hair loss [~hair] ~ 毛

탈·색* discoloration; fading [~color] ~ 色

탈·수* dehydration [~water] ~ 水
탈·수기 machine for extracting water from clothes

탈·지면 absorbent cotton [~oil cotton] ~ 脂綿

탈의실 locker room; changing room [~clothes room] ~ 衣室

허**탈**하다 be atrophied; feel despondent [empty~] 虛~

소**탈**하다 be unceremonious; be informal [loose~] 疎~

탈 (奪) **deprive**

박**탈*** deprivation; forfeit [peel~] 剝~

강**탈*** extortion; robbery [force~] 强~

약**탈*** plunder [plunder~] 掠~

쟁**탈**전 a scramble (for the championship) [fight~fighting] 爭~戰

겁**탈*** rape [rape~] 劫~

탐 (探) **search; spy**

탐구* inquiry; study [~research] ~ 究

탐색* investigation; probe [~seek] ~ 索

탐지* detection [~know] ~ 知
거짓말 탐지기 lie detector

탐방* a visit; an interview [~visit] ~ 訪

탐험* exploration; expedition [~rough] ~ 險

탐정 detective [~spy] ~ 偵
탐정소설 detective story

탐 (貪) **covet**

탐하다 covet

탐내다 covet; be greedy for [~bring out] ~ K
돈을 탐내다
be greedy for money

탐나다 be covetous of; be desirable [~come out] ~ K
돈이 탐나다
be covetous of money

탐스럽다 be lovely; be appetizing

탐욕스럽다 be avaricious [~desire] ~ 慾

탕 ʷ(湯) **hot water; soup**

목욕**탕** bathhouse; bathing room [bathing~] 沐浴~

대중**탕** public bath [the public~] 大衆~

재**탕*** second brew; rehashing [again~] 再~

갈비**탕** beef rib soup [rib~] K~

매운**탕** pepper-pot soup [spicy hot~] K~

맹**탕** tasteless soup [plain~] K~

보신**탕** dog soup [supplement body~] 補身~

탕 (蕩) dissipation

방탕* dissipation; debauchery
[release~] 放 ~
허랑방탕하다 be dissolute;
be loose and profligate

탕진* dissipating (one's fortune)
[~entirely] ~ 盡
재산을 탕진하다
dissipate one's fortune

허탕 lost/fruitless labor
[empty~] 虛 ~
허탕치다 one's labor is lost

태 (太) greatest

태반 the most part; majority
[~half] ~ 半

태양 the sun [~sunlight] ~ 陽
태양열 solar energy

태평양 the Pacific Ocean
[~peaceful ocean] ~ 平洋

태극기 Korean flag
[~absolute flag] ~ 極旗

태 (泰) big

태산 tremendous thing
[~mountain] ~ 山
갈수록 태산 out of
the frying pan, into the fire
할 일이 태산같다
have so many things to do

태평이다 be easy-going;
be carefree [~peaceful] ~ 平

태연하다 be calm; be undisturbed
[~as such] ~ 然

태 (怠) lazy

나태하다 be lazy; be indolent
[indolent~] 懶 ~

권태기 stage of weariness
[lazy~period] 倦 ~ 期

태만* negligence; dereliction
[~arrogant] ~ 慢

태 (態) attitude; situation; form

태도 attitude; manner
[~degree] ~ 度

추태 disgraceful behavior
[ugly~] 醜 ~
추태부리다
behave disgracefully

태세 posture; preparedness
[~conditions] ~ 勢

상태 state; condition
[shape~] 狀 ~
정신상태 mental state
혼수상태 comatose condition

사태 situation; the state
of things [matters~] 事 ~

중태 serious condition (due
to an illness/injury)
[weighty~] 重 ~

형태 form; shape [shape~] 形 ~

태 (胎) pregnant (womb)

잉태* pregnancy; conception
[pregnant~] 孕 ~

낙태* abortion [omit~] 落 ~

태몽 dream that one is going to
get pregnant [~dream] ~ 夢

태교* prenatal care; fetal
education [~teach] ~ 教

태생 birth; origin [~be born] ~ 生
서울태생 Seoul-born

태아 embryo; fetus [~child] ~ 兒

태엽 spring (in a watch)
[~leaf] ~ 葉
태엽을 감다 wind a watch

택 (擇) **select**

택하다   choose; select

선택*   choice; option [select~] 選~
선택권 right of choice; option
취사선택하다
adopt or reject; choose

채택*   selection; adoption
[select~] 採~

양자택일* selecting one alternative;
choosing between the two
[both person~one] 兩者~一

택 (澤) **glossy; favor**

광택   luster; gloss [shine~] 光~

윤택하다   be abundant; be well-off
[enrich~] 潤~

혜택   a favor; benefit
[benefit~] 惠~
혜택을 입다
be a beneficiary of

덕택   indebtedness; thanks to
[virtue~] 德~
…덕택에 thanks to...
…덕택이다 I owe it to...

택 (宅) **residence**

주택   house; housing
[reside~] 住~
개인주택 private residence
연립주택 tenement house;
row houses

저택   residence; mansion
[residence~] 邸~

자택   private residence; one's
house (hon.) [self~] 自~

토 (土) **soil; land**

토질   soil quality
[~quality] ~質

점토   clay [sticky~] 粘~

토지   land; real estate [~place] ~地

국토   national land [nation~] 國~

향토   a country; one's native
land [province~] 鄉~

영토   territory [command~] 領~

농토   farmland [agricultural~] 農~

토대   foundation; groundwork
[~tower] ~臺

토박이   natives; aboriginals
[~inlaid thing] ~K
서울 토박이
Seoulite to the core

토성   Saturn [~star] ~星

토요일   Saturday
[~day of the week] ~曜日

토 (討) **discuss**

토론*   debate; discussion
[~discuss] ~論

토의*   debate; discussion
[~discuss] ~議

검토*   examination; scrutiny
[inspect~] 檢~

토 (吐) **vomit**

토하다   throw up; vomit

구토*   vomiting [vomit~] 嘔~

실토*   true confession; telling
the truth [reality~] 實~

통 (通) **go through; circulate;
communicate**

통과*   passing; passage
[~pass] ~過

통행*   passing; passage [~go] ~行
통행금지* suspension
of traffic; curfew
일방통행* one-way traffic

통로	passage; aisle [~road] ~ 路	불통	impassability; no communication [not~] 不~
통금	curfew [~prohibit] ~ 禁		전화가 불통이다 The phone is dead.
통관*	customs clearance [~customhouse] ~ 關		고집불통이다 be obstinate
통근*	commuting to office [~work] ~ 勤	통역*	interpreting [~translate] ~ 譯
통학*	commuting to school [~learning] ~ 學	신통하다	be marvelous; be extraordinary [god~] 神~
교통	traffic [exchange~] 交~	통장	bankbook; passbook [~accounts] ~ 帳
개통*	opening to traffic [open~] 開~		저금통장 savings passbook
직통*	through-traffic; direct communication [direct~] 直~	보통	(being) ordinary; common [ordinary~] 普~
간통*	adultery [adultery~] 姦~	**통 (痛)**	**pain; intense**
통고*	notification [~inform] ~ 告	통·증	ache; pain [~symptom] ~ 症
통보*	notification [~report] ~ 報	고통	pain; agony [suffering~] 苦 ~
통지*	notice; notification [~know] ~ 知		고통스럽다 be painful
	통지표 school report card	진통제	pain killer [suppress~medicine] 鎭 ~ 劑
통신*	correspondence; communication [~believe] ~ 信	두통	headache [head~] 頭 ~
	통신(사) news agency 통신판매* mail-order sale	치통	toothache [tooth~] 齒 ~
통하다	(air, electricity, etc.) circulate; communicate; understand (each other)	생리통	menstrual cramps [physiology~] 生理~
		복통	stomachache [abdomen~] 腹 ~
통풍*	ventilation [~wind] ~ 風 통풍이 잘되다 be well-ventilated	신경통	neuralgia [nerve~] 神經~
통속적	popular; nontechnical [~vulgar] ~ 俗 的	분통터지다	be greatly vexed [anger~explode] 憤 ~ K
소식통	well-informed sources; channel [news~] 消息~	통곡*	wailing [~cry] ~ 哭
의사소통*	mutual understanding [thought far apart~] 意思疏~	통탄하다	lament bitterly; regret deeply [~sigh] ~ 歎
통화*	telephone conversation [~talk] ~ 話	원통하다	be resentful; be lamentable [grieve~] 冤~
		통쾌하다	be thoroughly pleasant [~pleasant] ~ 快

통 (統) **govern; rule**

통치*	rule; reign [~govern] ~ 治
통솔*	command; leadership [~to lead] ~ 率
통제*	control; regulation [~suppress] ~ 制
대통령	president of a country [great~command] 大~領
통일*	unification; uniformity [~one] ~ 一
통합*	integration; merger [~unite] ~ 合
통계*	statistics [~calculate] ~ 計 통계내다 collect statistics (on)
계통	system; genealogy [connection~] 系~
혈통	blood; lineage [blood~] 血 ~
체통	dignity; respectability [body~] 體 ~
전통	tradition [transmit~] 傳~

통 ʷ(桶) **a can; box; tub**

쓰레기통	garbage can [garbage~] K~
휴지통	wastebasket [waste paper~] 休紙~
깡통	empty tin can; airhead (slang) [a can~] E~
물통	water container [water~] K~
통조림	canned food [~hard-boiled food] ~ K
밥통	boiled-rice container; a fool [boiled-rice~] K~
쌀통	(raw) rice box [rice~] K~
저금통	savings box; piggy bank [savings~] 貯金~

철통같다	(defense) be impregnable; be rigorously guarded [iron~be like] 鐵 ~ K

통 ʷ(筒) **tube; scale (of doing things)**

원통	cylinder [round~] 圓~
연통	stovepipe [smoke~] 煙 ~
필통	pencil case [pen~] 筆 ~
우체통	mailbox [mail post~] 郵遞~
통이 크다	do things in a big way [~big] ~ K

퇴 (退) **retreat; leave**

후퇴*	backing down; retreat [back~] 後~
사퇴*	resignation [resign~] 辭~
퇴직*	retirement [~post] ~ 職 정년퇴직* retirement at the official age 퇴직금 retirement allowance
은퇴*	retirement from a post; withdrawal from public life [hide~] 隱~
탈퇴*	secession; withdrawal [escape~] 脫 ~
퇴보*	retrogression [~step] ~ 步
퇴화*	degeneration; atrophy [~change] ~ 化
퇴짜	rejection [~thing] ~ K 퇴짜놓다 reject; brush off (a thing/person) 퇴짜맞다 get rejected
퇴치*	extermination [~govern] ~ 治
퇴원*	discharge from a hospital [~institution] ~ 院
퇴학	expulsion from school [~learning] ~ 學

자퇴*   voluntary withdrawing (from school) [self~] 自~

퇴근*   getting off work [~work] ~ 勤

퇴장*   leaving (the hall); exit; walkout [~place] ~ 場

조퇴*   getting off work/school earlier than usual [early~] 早~

투 (投) throw

투수   baseball pitcher [~hand] ~ 手

투표*   voting [~ticket] ~ 票
투표.권   right to vote

투서*   (sending an) anonymous letter [~writing] ~ 書

투고*   contributing an article [~manuscript] ~ 稿

투자*   investment [~funds] ~ 資

투입*   putting in; investing [~enter] ~入

투기*   speculation (in real estate) [~opportunity] ~ 機
투기꾼 speculator
부동산 투기*
speculation in real estate

투 (鬪) fight

전투*   combat; battle [fighting~] 戰~

격투*   grapple; fight [violent~] 激~

투쟁*   fighting; struggle [~fight] ~爭

권투*   boxing [fist~] 拳~
권투선수 boxer

투지   fighting spirit [~mind] ~ 志

투우사   bullfighter [~ bull soldier] ~ 牛士

투병*   fighting against a disease [~disease] ~ 病

건투를 빌다 hope one will do one's best [strong~pray] 健~ K

투 (透) transparent; permeate

투명하다   be transparent [~clear] ~ 明
불투명하다 be opaque

투철하다   (spirit) be penetrating; be thorough [~penetrate] ~ 徹

침투*   penetration; infiltration [soak~] 浸~

투 (套) wrapper; customary

외투   overcoat [outside~] 外~

봉투   envelope [sealed~] 封~
편지봉투 letter envelope
서류봉투 manila envelope

상투적   commonplace; hackneyed [usual~] 常~的

특 (特) special

특별하다   be special; be extraordinary [~special] ~ 別
특별대우* special treatment

특수하다   be special; be specific [~different] ~ 殊
특수효과 special effect

특혜   special benefit [~benefit] ~惠

특효   special efficacy [~effect] ~ 效
특효약 wonder drug

특색   specific character; characteristic [~color] ~ 色

특기　special skill; specialty [~skill] ~ 技
　　　주특기 main specialty

특실　special room [~room] ~ 室

특급　special express (train) [~fast] ~ 急

특매*　special sale [~sell] ~ 賣

특산품　special product; indigenous product [~produce article] ~ 産品

특제품　specially made goods [~product] ~ 製品

특집　special edition [~edit] ~ 輯

특보　special report [~report] ~ 報

특종　(news) scoop [~a kind] ~ 種

특히　especially [~ -ly] ~ K

특정*　specification; designated [~decide] ~ 定
　　　특정인 designated person

특대　outsize; extra large [~big] ~ 大

특성　distinctive quality; characteristic [~quality] ~ 性

특징　distinguishing feature; characteristic [~symptom] ~ 徵

특이하다　be unique [~different] ~ 異

독특하다　be unique [alone~] 獨 ~

특유하다　be peculiar [~exist] ~ 有

특출하다　be outstanding; be prominent [~come out] ~出

특권　privilege [~rights] ~ 權

특허*　a patent [~permit] ~ 許
　　　특허품 patented article

ㅍ

파 （破）　break

파괴*　destruction [~ruin] ~ 壞

파손*　damage; breakage [~damage] ~ 損

파편　broken piece; fragment [~piece] ~ 片

폭파*　blasting; blowing up [explode~] 爆 ~

파멸*　ruin; destruction [~destroy] ~ 滅

격파*　defeat; smash up [hit~] 擊 ~

파혼*　breaking off a marriage engagement [~marriage] ~ 婚

파산*　bankruptcy [~possession] ~ 産

파격적　exceptional [~rule] ~ 格的
　　　파격세일* exceptional sale

파렴치하다　be shameless [~sense of shame] ~ 廉恥

간파*　seeing through; grasping (a situation) [watch~] 看 ~

파 （波）　wave

파도　wave; billow [~wave] ~ 濤

한파　cold wave (weather) [cold~] 寒 ~

전파　electric wave [electricity~] 電 ~

인파　surging crowd; waves of people [person~] 人 ~

풍파　hardships; storm [wind~] 風 ~

파동	fluctuation; undulation; crisis [~move] ~ 動
파문	stir; sensation [~lines] ~ 紋 파문을 일으키다 create a stir/sensation
추파	amorous glance; ogle [autumn~] 秋~

파 (派) **branch**

종파	sect; denomination [sect~] 宗~
당파싸움	party dispute [political party~fight] 黨 ~ K
파생*	derivation [~be born] ~ 生
파견*	dispatch [~dispatch] ~ 遣
파출부	visiting housemaid [~come out woman] ~ 出婦
파출·소	police box [~come out place] ~ 出所

파 (罷) **cease**

파하다	finish; end
파업*	a strike; walkout [~business] ~ 業
파면*	dismissal [~pardon] ~ 免

판 (判) **judge**

판사	a judge [~matters] ~ 事 판검사 judges and public prosecutors
재판*	judgment; trial [judge~] 裁 ~
심판*	refereeing; a referee [judge~] 審 ~
판결*	judgment; decision of the court [~decide] ~ 決
판정*	decision; judgment [~decide] ~ 定

	판정을 내리다 pass judgment 판정승/패* a win/defeat on a decision
판단*	judgment [~stop] ~ 斷 판단기준 yardstick for judgment; standard of judgment
판별*	distinction; discernment [~separate] ~ 別
평판	reputation [evaluate~] 評 ~
판명되다	become clear; prove to be [~clear become] ~ 明 K

판 ʷ(板) **board; plank**

판자	wooden board; plank [~thing] ~ 子 판잣집 a shack
칠판	blackboard [black~] 漆 ~
빨래판	washboard [washing clothes~] K~
게시판	bulletin board [notice~] 揭示 ~
간판	signboard; credentials [watch~] 看 ~
전광판	electric signboard [electricity shine~] 電光 ~
주판	abacus; counting board [beads~] 珠 ~
빙판	icy road; icy place [ice~] 氷 ~
철판	iron plate; brazen-facedness [iron~] 鐵 ~

판 (版) **printing (board)**

출판*	publication [come out~] 出 ~
초판	first edition [first~] 初 ~
개정판	revised edition [revision~] 改訂 ~
원판	negative (film) [origin~] 原 ~

판화 woodblock print; etching [~drawing] ~ 畵

장판* floor cover [strong~] 壯 ~

판 (販) **sell**

판매* sale; selling [~sell] ~ 賣

시판* marketing; sale at a market [market~] 市 ~

판촉* sales promotion [~urge] ~促 판촉사원 employee for sales promotion

외판원 (travelling) salesperson [outside~member] 外 ~ 員

자판기 vending machine [automatic~machine] 自 ~ 機 (<자동판매기)

팔 ʷ(八) **eight**

삼팔선 the thirty-eighth parallel (dividing Korea) [three~line] 三 ~ 線

팔방 all directions; every side [~direction] ~ 方 사방팔방 all directions 팔방미인 beauty in every respect

팔·등신 well-proportioned figure [~equal body] ~ 等身

팔·자 destiny; fate [~character] ~ 字 팔·자가 세다 have a rough fate 걱정도 팔·자다 It's none of (your) business.

패 ʷ(牌) **badge; signboard; gang**

상패 medal [award~] 賞 ~

기념패 commemorative plate [commemoration~] 紀念 ~

문패 doorplate [door~] 門 ~

방패 a shield [defend~] 防 ~

깡패 gangster [gang~] E ~

패싸움 gang fight [~fighting] ~ K

패거리 mob ~ K

패 (敗) **lose; be defeated**

패하다 get defeated; lose

패배 a defeat [~be defeated] ~ 北 패배하다 be defeated

연패* consecutive defeats [connected~] 連~

승패 victory or defeat; outcome [win~] 勝~ 승패를 겨루다 contend for victory

참패* disastrous defeat [miserable~] 慘 ~

실패* failure [lose~] 失 ~

패자 loser [~person] ~ 者

편 ʷ(便) **side; convenient; means; mail**

한편 one side; on the one hand...and/but on the other hand; while [one~] K~

우리편 our side [our~] K~

상대편 the other person; counterpart [the other party~] 相對 ~

건너편 the opposite side (from where one is) [cross~] K~

반대편 the opposite side [the opposite~] 反對 ~

편들다 take sides with [~get in] ~ K

남편 husband [male~] 男 ~

여편네 — married woman; one's wife (vulgar) [female~] 女 ~ K

편하다 — be convenient; be comfortable

편리* — convenience [~benefit] ~ 利

간편하다 — be handy; be convenient [simple~] 簡 ~

편의 — convenience [~fitting] ~ 宜
편의상 for convenience sake

형편 — circumstances [shape~] 形 ~

불편* — discomfort; inconvenience [not~] 不~

편찮다 — be uncomfortable; be sick (hon.) [~not] ~ K

편안하다 — be comfortable; be peaceful [~peaceful] ~ 安

교통편 — facilities for transportation [traffic~] 交通 ~

우편 — mail [mail~] 郵~

편지 — letter [~paper] ~ 紙
편지지 letter paper
편지봉투 letter envelope

편 (編) weave; print

편집* — editing; compilation [~edit] ~ 輯

편곡* — (music) arrangement [~tune] ~ 曲

속편 — a sequel [sequel~] 續 ~

편입* — transfer (to another school) [~enter] ~ 入
편입생 transfer student

편찬* — compilation [~compile] ~ 纂

편 (篇) book

전편 — first volume; part I [front~] 前 ~

후편 — second/last volume [later~] 後 ~

장편 — long piece (writing) [long~] 長~
장편소설 long novel

단편 — short piece (writing) [short~] 短~
단편소설 short novel

옥편 — Chinese-Korean dictionary [gem~] 玉~

편 (偏) lean (toward)

편견 — biased view; prejudice [~opinion] ~見

편식* — unbalanced diet [~eat] ~ 食

편애* — being partial to; favoritism [~love] ~ 愛

편두통 — migraine [~headache] ~ 頭痛

편 (片) piece

파편 — broken piece; fragment [break~] 破~

단편적 — fragmentary; piecemeal [cut off~] 斷 ~ 的

편도 — one-way (ticket) [~way] ~ 道

평 (平) ordinary; even; peaceful

평범하다 — be commonplace; be ordinary [~ordinary] ~ 凡

평소 — ordinary times [~ordinary] ~ 素

평상시 — ordinary times; normally [~usual time] ~ 常時

평균* — average [~level] ~ 均

평상복 — everyday clothes [~usual clothes] ~ 常服

평일 — weekdays [~day] ~日

평면	a plane; a level [~surface] ~ 面		평·가*	evaluation; estimation [~value] ~ 價 과대평·가* overestimation 과소평·가* underestimation
평지	flat land [~place] ~ 地		평판	reputation [~judge] ~ 判
평평하다	be flat; be even		정평	public acknowledgment [decide~] 定~
평탄하다	be even; be smooth [~smooth] ~ 坦			
평영*	breast stroke [~swim] ~ 泳		**폐 (廢)**	**abolish(ed)**
평행*	parallel [~go] ~ 行 평행사변형 parallelogram		폐지*	abolition [~stop] ~ 止
평등*	equality; impartiality [~equal] ~ 等		철폐*	abolition (of a law); lifting (a ban) [remove~] 撤~
평준화*	equalization; leveling [~measure change] ~ 準化		폐품	waste article [~article] ~ 品
평방미터	square meter [~square meter] ~ 方 E		폐수	waste water [~water] ~ 水
공평하다	be fair; be just [official~] 公~ 불공평하다 be unfair		폐기물	waste matter [~abandon things] ~ 棄物
불평*	complaints [not~] 不~		폐차*	auto junking [~vehicle] ~ 車 폐차장 junkyard
평생	lifetime [~life] ~ 生		황폐하다	be desolate; be devastated [desolate~] 荒~
평서문	declarative sentence [~narrate writing] ~ 敍文		퇴폐적	corrupted; decadent [corrupt~] 頹~的
평화	peace [~peace] ~ 和			
태평이다	be easy-going; be carefree [big~] 泰~		**폐 ʷ (肺)**	**lung**
태평양	the Pacific Ocean [greatest~ocean] 太~洋		폐.병	lung disease [~disease] ~ 病
			폐결핵	pulmonary tuberculosis [~tuberculosis] ~ 結核
평 (評)	**criticize; comment**		폐렴	pneumonia [~inflammation] ~ 炎
평하다	criticize; comment on			
비평*	criticism; comment [criticize~] 批~		**폐 (閉)**	**to close**
평론*	criticism; review [~discuss] ~ 論		밀폐*	shutting tightly; sealing up [thorough~] 密~
호평*	favorable comment [good~] 好~		폐막식	closing ceremony (for a sporting event) [~curtain ceremony] ~ 幕式
혹평*	severe criticism [severe~] 酷~			

포 (捕) catch

체포* arresting [arrest~] 逮~

포로 prisoner of war; captive [~capture] ~ 虜

포착* capture; seizing (an opportunity) [~seize] ~ 捉

포수 (baseball) catcher [~hand] ~ 手

포 (包) wrap

포장* wrapping; packing [~pack] ~ 裝

소포 parcel; package [small~] 小~

포위* encirclement; beleaguerment [~circumference] ~ 圍

포함* inclusion [~include] ~ 含

포용하다 embrace; accept with magnanimity [~permit] ~ 容

포 (脯) dried slices of meat/fish

육포 beef jerky [meat~] 肉~

오징어포 dried cuttlefish [cuttlefish~] K~

대구포 dried codfish [codfish~] 大口~

쥐포 type of dried fish [mouse~] K ~

포 (抱) embrace

포옹* embrace; hug [~embrace] ~ 擁

포부 ambition; wishes [~carry] ~ 負

회포 one's heart; one's innermost thoughts [innermost desire~] 懷~

회포를 풀다 unburden oneself

포 (布) linen; notify

포목점 linen shop; drapery shop [~tree store] ~ 木店

포장마차 covered wagon bar [~curtain carriage] ~ 帳馬車

선포* proclamation [proclaim~] 宣~

포 ᵂ(砲) gun; cannon

대포 gun; cannon [big~] 大~

포수 hunter [~hand] ~ 手

포 (飽) full (from eating)

포식* eating one's fill; satiation [~eat] ~ 食

포화* saturation [~peace] ~ 和
포화상태 state of saturation

폭 (暴) cruel; suddenly

폭행* assault; violence [~act] ~ 行

폭력 violence [~strength] ~ 力

난폭하다 be rough; be violent [reckless~] 亂 ~

폭동 riot; rebellion [~move] ~ 動

폭설 heavy snowfall [~snow] ~雪

폭우 heavy rain; torrential rain [~rain] ~ 雨

폭풍 stormy wind [~wind] ~ 風

폭등* sudden rise (in price); skyrocketing [~go up] ~ 騰

폭락* (stock/price) sharp fall [~fall] ~ 落

폭로* disclosure; divulgence
[~expose] ~ 露

폭리 excessive profits
[~gain] ~ 利

폭(爆) explode

폭탄 bomb; bombshell
[~bullet] ~ 彈

폭파* blasting; blowing up
[~break] ~ 破

폭발* explosion; detonation
[~shoot] ~ 發
폭발적 explosive

폭격* bomb attack [~attack] ~擊

폭죽 firecracker [~bamboo] ~竹

폭소 burst of laughter
[~laugh] ~ 笑
폭소를 터뜨리다
burst into laughter

표 ᵂ(表) surface; manifest; chart

표면 surface [~surface] ~ 面

표지 (book) cover [~paper] ~ 紙

표나다 show signs [~come out] ~K

표하다 express; manifest
(one's feeling)

표시* indication; expression;
a sign [~manifest] ~ 示

표현* expression; manifestation
[~appear] ~ 現

표정 (facial) expression
[~feeling] ~ 情
무표정* lack of expression

대표* representation;
a representative
[substitute~] 代~

발표* announcement;
presentation [rise~] 發~

사표 letter of resignation
[resign~] 辭~

표창* official commendation
[~manifest] ~ 彰

표기* transcribing [~record] ~ 記

시간표 timetable [time~] 時間~

표구* mounting; framing
[~implement] ~ 具

표 ᵂ(票) ticket

차표 railroad/bus ticket
[vehicle~] 車~

버스표 bus ticket [bus~] E ~

비행기표 airline ticket
[airplane~] 飛行機~

왕복표 roundtrip ticket
[roundtrip~] 往復~

매표소 ticket office
[sell~place] 賣~所

이름표 name tag [name~] K~

번호표 number check
[number~] 番號~

꼬리표 (address) tag [tail~] K~

우표 (postage) stamp [mail~] 郵~

투표* voting [throw~] 投~
투표함 ballot box

개표* ballot counting [open~] 開~

수표 cheque [hand~] 手~
자기앞수표 cashier's cheque;
bank cheque

표 ᵂ(標) mark; sign(board)

표하다 mark (something)

표기* marking [~record] ~ 記

상표 trademark; brand
[trade~] 商~

271

물음표	question mark [question~] K~	비매품	articles not for sale [not sell~] 非賣~
따옴표	quotation mark [quoting~] K~	품목	a list of articles; item [~item] ~目
마침표	period [ending~] K~	폐품	waste article [abolished~] 廢~
화살표	arrow mark [arrow~] K~	품절	out of stock [~cut] ~切
별표*	asterisk [star~] K~	품귀	shortage of goods [~valuable] ~貴
목표*	aim; goal [eye~] 目~	필수품	necessities [surely essential~] 必需~
표어	slogan; motto [~words] ~語	용품	necessities; supplies [use~] 用~
표본	specimen; sample [~sample] ~本		일용품 daily necessities 학용품 school supplies 가정용품 household goods 사무용품 office supplies 전기용품 electric appliances
표준	standard; norm [~measure] ~準		
이정표	milestone [village route~] 里程~	귀중품	valuables [precious~] 貴重~
		소지품	one's belongings [possession~] 所持~
품 (品)	**article; goods; grade**	상품	prize; trophy [award~] 賞~
물품	goods; articles [things~] 物~	기념품	souvenir [commemoration~] 記念~
금품	money and goods [money~] 金~	유품	relic; article left by the deceased [bequeath~] 遺~
상품	goods; merchandise [trade~] 商~	부품	parts [part~] 部~ 자동차부품 auto parts
식품	foodstuffs; groceries [food~] 食~	비품	fixtures [prepare~] 備~
약품	drugs; medical supplies [medicine~] 藥~	품질	quality [~quality] ~質
화장품	cosmetics [makeup~] 化粧~	일품	(article of) top quality [first~] 一 ~
제품	manufactured goods; product [manufacture~] 製~ 신제품 new product 특제품 specially made goods 유제품 dairy product	품위	grace; dignity [~position] ~位
		품행	conduct; behavior [~act] ~行
유사품	an imitation (product) [similar~] 類似~		
특산품	special product; indigenous product [special produce~] 特産~	**풍 (風)**	**wind; customs; scenery**
		폭풍	stormy wind [cruel~] 暴~

풍랑	wind and waves [~wave] ~ 浪	풍 (豊)	**abundant**
돌풍	sudden gust of wind [sudden~] 突~	풍부하다	be abundant; be rich [~rich] ~ 富
풍파	hardships; storm [~wave] ~ 波	풍성하다	(harvest) be abundant [~prosper] ~ 盛
통풍*	ventilation [circulate~] 通~	풍년	year of good harvest [~year] ~ 年
환풍기	ventilation fan [exchange~machine] 換~機	풍요*	affluence [~abundant] ~ 饒 풍요롭다 be affluent
선풍기	mechanical fan [fan~machine] 扇~機	풍족하다	have plenty; be well off [~sufficient] ~ 足
병풍	folding screen (against a draft) [screen~] 屛~	풍만하다	be plump [~full] ~ 滿
풍차	windmill [~vehicle] ~ 車	피 (避)	**avoid; escape**
선풍	whirlwind [revolve~] 旋~ 선풍적 sensational 선풍을 일으키다 create a great sensation	피하다	avoid
		피서*	avoiding the heat of summer [~summer heat] ~ 暑 피서가다 go to a summer resort
풍선	(toy) balloon [~ship] ~ 船 풍선껌 bubble gum 고무풍선 rubber balloon	피임*	contraception [~pregnant] ~ 姙
풍금	reed organ [~lute] ~ 琴	기피*	evasion; shirking [shun~] 忌~
소풍	picnic; excursion [disperse~] 消~ 소풍가다 go on a picnic	회피*	evasion; shirking [turn~] 回~
허풍	big talk [empty~] 虛~ 허풍쟁이 braggart	피난*	refuge; evacuation [~difficulty] ~ 難
중풍	palsy; paralysis [middle~] 中~	대피*	taking shelter [wait~] 待~ 대피소 a shelter
풍속	customs; manners [~customs] ~ 俗	도피*	escape [escape~] 逃~ 현실도피* escape from reality
풍습	customs; manners [~practice] ~ 習	피신*	secret escape [~body] ~ 身
복고풍	revival of old fashions [restore old~] 復古~	피 (皮)	**skin**
풍기문란*	demoralization [~principle disorder] ~ 紀紊亂	피부	skin [~skin] ~ 膚 피부암 skin cancer 피부.병 skin disease
풍경	landscape [~scenery] ~ 景	피상적	superficial [~appearance] ~ 相的

철면**피**	brazen-facedness; shamelessness [iron face~] 鐵面~
탈**피**하다	breaking from (e.g., convention) [escape~] 脫~

피 (被) **suffer**

피해	damage; loss [~harm] ~害
피살되다	get killed [~kill become] ~ 殺 K
피고	defendant [~accuse] ~ 告

필 (必) **certainly; inevitably**

필시	certainly [~true] ~是
필히	surely [~ -ly] ~ K
필승	certain victory [~win] ~ 勝
필연적	inevitable [~as such] ~ 然的
필요*	necessity [~essential] ~ 要
필수	being required/essential [~necessary] ~須 필·수·과목 required subject 필·수조·건 necessary condition
필·수품	necessities [~essential article] ~ 需品
필·사적	desperate [~die] ~ 死的 필·사적으로 desperately

필 (筆) **pen; writing**

필기*	note taking [~record] ~ 記
연**필**	pencil [lead~] 鉛~ 연필꽂이 pencil stand
필통	pencil case [~tube] ~ 筒
분**필**	chalk [powder~] 粉 ~
수**필**	essay; miscellaneous writings [follow~] 隨 ~

명**필**	excellent handwriting [famous~] 名~
자**필**	one's own handwriting [self~] 自 ~

ㅎ

하 (下) **below; descend**

최**하**	the lowest; the most inferior [the most~] 最~
이**하**	not exceeding; under [from~] 以~ 이십세 이하 under 10 years old
영**하**	below zero (temp.) [zero~] 零~
부**하**	subordinate; underling [section~] 部 ~
하인	servant [~person] ~人
하층	lower (social) class [~layer] ~ 層
하류	downstream; low class [~stream] ~ 流
연**하**	junior in age [age~] 年 ~
저**하***	a decline (in quality, value, etc.); a drop [low~] 低~
인**하***	(price) lowering [pull~] 引~
급강**하***	sudden drop (in temp.) [fast descend~] 急降~
하행	(train) going down from Seoul [~go] ~ 行
하순	the last ten days of a month [~ten days] ~ 旬
하반신	lower half of the body [~half body] ~ 半身

하체	lower part of the body [~body] ~ 體	**은하수**	Milky Way; galaxy [silver~water] 銀~水

학 (學) learning; study

하수구	gutter; drain [~water opening] ~ 水口
하수도	sewage system [~waterway] ~ 水道
낙하산	parachute [fall~umbrella] 落~傘
하차*	getting out of a vehicle [~vehicle] ~ 車 승하차* getting in/out of a vehicle
하숙*	boarding; lodging [~lodge] ~ 宿
천하	the universe; the world [sky~] 天~
막상막하	neck and neck [not above not~] 莫上莫~
귀하	esquire (used on envelopes) [honorable~] 貴~

학문*	(the pursuit of) learning; studies [~inquire] ~ 問
학습*	studying; drilling [~study] ~ 習
학교	school [~school] ~ 校
학원	educational institution [~institution] ~ 院
대학	college [big~] 大~ 대학생 college student 대학교 university 대학원 graduate school
학부	undergraduate school [~section] ~ 部
학점	(college) credit [~point] ~ 點
학생	student [~student] ~ 生
학부모	parents of students [~parents] ~ 父母

하 (何) how; whatever

여하	how; how things are [similar~] 如~ 여하간 at any rate 여하튼 at any rate ...여하에 달려있다 depend on...
하여튼	anyway [~similar] ~ 如K
하여간	anyway [~similar between] ~ 如間
하등	(nothing) whatever [~rank] ~ 等 하등(의) 관계가 없다 have no relation whatever

장학금	scholarship [encourage~money] 獎~金 장학생 scholarship student
학자	scholar [~person] ~ 者
학장	college dean [~superior] ~ 長
학년	school year; grade [~year] ~ 年 일학년 first grade
학기	school semester [~term] ~期 일학기 first (spring) semester 이학기 second (fall) semester

하 (河) stream

하천	rivers; watercourses [~stream] ~ 川
운하	canal [transport~] 運~

방학*	school vacation [release~] 放~
개학*	beginning of school [begin~] 開~
입학*	admission into a school [enter~] 入~

퇴학 expulsion from school
[retreat~] 退~
퇴학시키다 expel
(a student) from school
퇴학당하다 be expelled
from school

정학 suspension from school
[stop~] 停~
무기정학당하다
be suspended from school
for an indefinite period

휴학* temporary absence
from school [rest~] 休~

통학* commuting to school
[go through~] 通~

전학* change of schools
[transfer~] 轉~

진학* continuing one's schooling
at the next level
[advance~] 進~

학용품 school supplies
[~supplies] ~用品

학비 school expenses
[~expense] ~費

문학 literature [writing~] 文~

신학 theology [god~] 神~
신학대학 theology school

심리학 psychology
[psychology~] 心理~
심리학자 psychologist

철학 philosophy [wisdom~] 哲~

수학 mathematics [number~] 數~

과학 science [science~] 科~
과학자 scientist

의학 medical science
[medical science~] 醫~

화학 chemistry [change~] 化~

학회 academic conference
[~meeting] ~會

학술 arts and sciences [~art] ~術

학 (虐) cruel

학대* maltreatment [~treat] ~待

학살* massacre [~kill] ~殺

한 (限) limit

한하다 limit; restrict

한도 a limit [~limit] ~度

한정* limitation; restriction
[~decide] ~定

제한* limitation; restriction
[suppress~] 制~

국한* localization; limitation
[position~] 局~

한없다 be unlimited [~not exist] ~ K

한껏 to the very limit
[~to the full extent] ~ K
한껏 먹다 eat one's fill

기한 time limit [period~] 期~

최대한 maximum
[the largest~] 最大~

최소한 minimum; at least
[the smallest~] 最小~

가능한 한 as far as possible
[possible~] 可能 K ~

무한하다 be infinite [no~] 無~

권한 rights; power [rights~] 權~

한사코 to the death; persistently
[~die] ~ 死 K

한 (漢) China; base person

한·자 Chinese character
[~character] ~字

한문 Chinese writing
[~writing] ~文

한약 Chinese medicine
[~medicine] ~藥

ㅎ

한방	Chinese medicine [~method] ~ 方
괴한	suspicious fellow [strange~] 怪~
치한	molester of women [foolish~] 痴~
문외한	outsider; layperson [door outside~] 門外~
한강	the Han River [~river] ~ 江

한 (韓) Korea(n)

한국	Korea [~country] ~國 한국어 Korean (language) 한국말 Korean (language) 대한민국 Republic of Korea
한글	Korean alphabet [~writing] ~ K
한반도	the Korean peninsula [~peninsula] ~半島
남한	South Korea [south~] 南~
북한	North Korea [north~] 北~
주한미군	U. S. armed forces stationed in Korea [stay~U. S. forces] 駐~美軍
한식	Korean food [~food] ~ 食
한영사전	Korean-English dictionary [~English dictionary] ~英辭典

한 (閑) leisure

한가하다	have leisure time [~leisure] ~暇
한산하다	be inactive; be slack (in traffic/trade) [~disperse] ~散
한적하다	be quiet and secluded [~quiet] ~寂
등한히하다	neglect; make light of [rank~] 等 ~ K

한 w(恨) grudge

원한	grudge; spite [grudge~] 怨~
한탄하다	lament; deplore [~sigh] ~歎
한없다	be gratified; have nothing to regret [~not exist] ~ K

한 (寒) cold

한파	cold wave (weather) [~wave] ~波
삼한사온	cycle of three cold and four warm days [three~four warm] 三~四溫
한심하다	be deplorable [~mind] ~心

할 (割) divide; cut

할.당*	allotment [~suitable] ~當
할부	installment [~pay] ~賦
분할*	division; partition [divide~] 分~
할애하다	share willingly; spare (time) [~love] ~愛
역할	role; part [role~] 役~
할.증	extra (charge) [~increase] ~增 (심야)할.증요금 (late night) surcharge
할인*	discount; reduction [~pull] ~引
할복*	disembowelment [~abdomen] ~腹

함 w(函) box

보석함	jewel box [jewelry~] 寶石~
투표함	ballot box [voting~] 投票~
사서함	post-office box [private writing~] 私書~

합 ᵂ(合) **unite; join; the total**

합하다	unite; combine
합치다	unite; combine
종**합***	synthesis; generalization [unite~] 綜~ 종합대학 university 종합병원 general hospital
합동*	combination; union [~together] ~同
통**합***	integration; merger [govern~] 統~
결**합***	union; cohesion [tie~] 結~ 재결합* reunion
합심하다	be united; be of one mind [~mind] ~心
단**합***	unity; solidarity [group~] 團~ 단합대회 a rally to strengthen unity
연**합***	union; alliance [association~] 聯~
총**합***	the total (sum) [all~] 總~
합계*	the total (sum) [~calculate] ~計
합산*	adding up [~calculate] ~算
합의*	mutual agreement [~wish] ~意
혼**합***	mixing; compounding [mix~] 混~
합금*	alloy; compound metal [~metal] ~金
화**합***	harmony; concord [harmony~] 和~
궁**합**	marital harmony as predicted by a fortune-teller [zodiac sign~] 宮~
융**합***	fusion; harmony [melt~] 融~
집**합***	gathering; a set [gather~] 集~
합석*	sitting together [~seat] ~席

합숙*	lodging together [~lodge] ~宿 합숙훈련* camp training
합승*	riding together; sharing a taxi [~ride] ~乘
합작*	joint work [~make] ~作
합주*	playing in concert [~play music] ~奏
합창*	singing together; chorus [~sing] ~唱
시**합***	a match; game [test~] 試~
합법적	lawful; legal [~law] ~法的
합리적	rational; reasonable [~reasoning] ~理的
합리화	rationalization [~reasoning change] ~理化
합격*	passing (an exam) [~category] ~格
합당하다	be suitable; be appropriate [~suitable] ~當
적**합**하다	be suitable; be fit (for) [suitable~] 適~
기**합**	concentration of spirit; disciplinary punishment [spirit~] 氣~

항 (抗) **resist**

저**항***	resistance; defiance [resist~] 抵~
반**항***	rebellion; defiance [opposite~] 反~
대**항***	counteraction; defiance [oppose~] 對~
항소*	an appeal to a higher court [~accuse] ~訴
항의*	protestation; remonstrance [~discuss] ~議
항생제	antibiotic [~life medicine] ~生劑

항암제	anticancer medicine [~cancer medicine] ~ 癌劑	**오해***	misunderstanding [mistake~] 誤~

항 (航) **sail; navigate**

항공	aviation [~sky] ~ 空
항로	(sea, air) route [~road] ~ 路
운항*	navigation; passage [transport~] 運~

항 (港) **port; harbor**

항구	port; harbor [~opening] ~ 口
부산항	Pusan harbor [Pusan~] 釜山~
공항	airport [sky~] 空~ 국제공항 international airport

항 (項) **item**

항목	item [~item] ~ 目
사항	items; matters [matters~] 事~
조항	articles and clauses; items [clause~] 條~

해 (解) **explain; solve; release**

해설*	explanation; commentary [~explain] ~ 說
해명*	elucidation; explanation [~clear] ~ 明
해석*	interpretation [~explain] ~ 釋
독해*	reading comprehension [read~] 讀 ~
이해*	understanding [reasoning~] 理~
양해*	understanding; consent [consent~] 諒~ 양해를 구하다 ask for consent

해독*	decoding; deciphering [~read] ~ 讀
해답	correct answer; solution [~answer] ~ 答
해결*	settlement (of a problem) [~decide] ~ 決
해소*	clearing up; solving [~dissolve] ~ 消 스트레스 해소* stress relief
분해*	decomposition [divide~] 分~
해부*	dissection [~cut] ~ 剖
해독제	antidote [~poison medicine] ~ 毒劑
해방*	liberation; emancipation [~release] ~ 放 여성해방 women's liberation
해고*	discharge; dismissal [~hire] ~雇 해고당하다 be dismissed
해약*	cancellation of a contract [~promise] ~ 約
해제*	cancellation; removal (of a ban) [~eliminate] ~ 除
해산*	(meeting) breaking up [~disperse] ~ 散
해체*	dismantling; dissolution [~body] ~ 體
해이하다	slacken up; relax [~loosen] ~ 弛
화해*	reconciliation; making up [harmony~] 和~

해 ᵂ (害) **harm**

해롭다	be harmful
해치다	injure; kill [~attack] ~ K
유해하다	be noxious [exist~] 有~ 유해식품 poisonous food

ㅎ

해충	harmful insect [~insect] ~ 蟲	해녀	woman diver (for seaweed, pearls, etc.) [~woman] ~ 女
손해	loss; damage [damage~] 損~		
수해	flood damage [water~] 水~	지중해	Mediterranean [earth middle~] 地中~
재해	calamity; disaster [calamity~] 災~		

핵 ᵂ(核) nucleus

피해 damage; loss [suffer~] 被~
피해자 victim
피해를 입다/주다
suffer/do damage

핵심	core; point [~heart] ~ 心
핵가족	nuclear family [~family] ~ 家族
핵무기	nuclear weapons [~weapon] ~ 武器

병충해 damage by blight and harmful insects [disease insect~] 病蟲~

살해*	murder; killing [kill~] 殺~
침해*	infringement [invade~] 侵~
방해*	disturbance; interruption [hinder~] 妨~ 방해되다 get in the way
저해*	hindrance; impediment [hinder~] 沮~
공해	public hazard; pollution [public~] 公~

행 (行) go; act

여행*	travel [travel~] 旅~
행선지	destination [~the first place] ~ 先地
운행*	(vehicle) running; operation [transport~] 運~
주행거리	mileage [run~distance] 走~距離
직행*	(vehicle) going nonstop [direct~] 直~
완행	(vehicle) going slow [slow~] 緩~
급행	an express (train) [fast~] 急~
상행	(train) going up toward Seoul [ascend~] 上~
하행	(train) going down from Seoul [descend~] 下~
통행*	passing; passage [go through~] 通~
행인	passerby [~person] ~ 人
행렬	parade; line [~line] ~ 列
행진*	march; parade [~advance] ~ 進

해 (海) sea; ocean

해외	overseas [~outside] ~ 外
해변	beach [~side] ~ 邊
해수욕장	beach for swimming [~water bathe place] ~ 水浴場
해안	coast [~shore] ~ 岸 동해안 the East Coast 서해안 the West Coast 남해안 the South Coast
해군	navy [~military] ~ 軍
해발	above sea level; elevation [~pull out] ~ 拔
해물	marine products [~things] ~ 物
해삼	sea cucumber [~ginseng] ~蔘
해초	seaweed [~grass] ~ 草

동행* going together; company [together~] 同 ~

일행 troupe; company [one~] 一~

미행* shadowing; tailing [tail~] 尾~

행방 whereabouts [~direction] ~方
행방불명
whereabouts unknown

진행* progress [advance~] 進~

평행* parallel [even~] 平~

행동* behavior; action [~move] ~動

수행* performing; carrying out [complete~] 遂~

행위 actions; conduct [~act] ~爲
부정행위* cheating; dishonest act

소행 one's actions; behavior [whatsoever~] 所~

품행 conduct; behavior [grade~] 品~

추행* ugly conduct; sexual assault [ugly~] 醜~

폭행* assault; violence [cruel~] 暴~

만행 brutality [barbarian~] 蠻~

실행* carrying out; practice [real~] 實~

시행* enforcing; putting in force [grant~] 施~

거행* carrying out; performing (a ceremony) [lift~] 擧~

이행* fulfillment (of a promise) [action~] 履~

행사 event; function [~matters] ~事

행정* administration [~govern] ~政

은행 bank [money~] 銀~

행 (幸) fortunate

행복* happiness [~blessing] ~福

행운 good luck [~luck] ~運
행운을 빌다 wish (one) good luck

다행* good fortune [many~] 多~
다행히 fortunately; luckily

불행* unhappiness; misfortune [not~] 不~
불행하게도 unfortunately

향 (向) to face

향하다 turn toward; aim at

방향 direction [direction~] 方~

남향 (house) southern exposure [south~] 南~

향상* elevation; improvement [~above] ~上

취향 taste; liking [tendency~] 趣~

의향 intention; inclination; willingness [wish~] 意~

경향 tendency; inclination [incline~] 傾~

동향 tendency; trend [move~] 動~

향 (鄕) province; hometown

향토 a country; one's native land [~land] ~土

고향 one's hometown [the past~] 故~

타향 place away from home; strange land [other~] 他~

향수 homesickness [~melancholy] ~愁

금의환향* returning home in glory [silk clothes return~] 錦衣還~

281

향 ʷ(香) **fragrant**

향기	fragrance [~air] ~ 氣 향기롭다　be fragrant 꽃향기　fragrance of a flower
향수	perfume [~water] ~ 水
방**향**제	air freshener [fragrant~medicine] 芳 ~ 劑
모기**향**	mosquito repellent stick/ coil [mosquito~] K~

허 (虛) **empty; unreal**

허공	a void [~sky] ~ 空
허사	vain attempt; failure [~business] ~ 事
허비*	waste [~use] ~ 費
허무*	nihility; futility [~nothing] ~ 無 허무주의　nihilism
허탈하다	be atrophied; feel despondent [~escape] ~ 脫
허.점	blind spot; loophole [~spot] ~ 点
허위	falsehood [~false] ~ 僞
허구	fiction [~compose] ~ 構
허풍	big talk [~wind] ~ 風 허풍치다/떨다　talk big
허약하다	be weak; be frail [~weak] ~ 弱
허기지다	be famished [~hunger become] ~ 飢 K
허세	false show of power; a bluff [~power] ~ 勢 허세부리다 make a show of power
허영	vanity; vainglory [~glory] ~ 榮

허례허식	vanity [~rites~decorate] ~ 禮 ~ 節
허황·되다	(dream) be wild; be chimerical [~desolate be] ~ 荒 K

허 (許) **permit**

허락*	permission; consent [~consent] ~ 諾
허용*	permission; allowance [~permit] ~ 容
허가*	permission; license [~alright] ~ 可 무허가　no permit; illegal
면**허**	license [pardon~] 免 ~ 운전면허　driver's license
특**허***	a patent [special~] 特 ~
허다하다	be numerous; be common [~many] ~ 多

헌 (獻) **offer**

헌신*	self-sacrifice; devotion [~body] ~ 身 헌신적　devotional
공**헌***	contribution; services [dedicate~] 貢 ~
헌혈*	blood donation [~blood] ~ 血
문**헌**	literature; (documentary) records [writing~] 文 ~

헌 (憲) **constitution**

헌.법	constitutional law [~law] ~ 法
제**헌**절	Constitution Day [decide~festival] 制 ~ 節
헌병	military police [~soldier] ~ 兵

험 (險) **rough**

험하다　be rugged; be rough

험난하다　be rough and difficult [~difficult] ~ 難

험악하다　(looks, weather) be threatening; be rough [~bad] ~ 惡

험상궂다　be rough; be savage-looking [~shape bad] ~ 狀 K

위험*　danger [dangerous~] 危~

모험*　adventure [risk~] 冒~

탐험*　exploration; expedition [search~] 探~

보험　insurance [protect~] 保~
생명보험　life insurance
자동차보험　car insurance

험담*　slanderous remark [~talk] ~ 談

험 (驗) **examine**

시험　exam; test [test~] 試~
시험보다　take an exam
시험하다　test; try out

수험생　student preparing for an entrance exam [receive~student] 受~生

실험*　experimentation [real~] 實~

경험*　experience [pass through~] 經~

체험*　personal experience [body~] 體~

혁 (革) **revolt; leather**

개혁*　reformation [amend~] 改~

혁신*　a reform; innovation [~new] ~ 新

혁명*　revolution [~command] ~ 命

혁대　leather belt [~belt] ~ 帶

현 (現) **appear; now; current**

실현*　realization; actualization [reality~] 實~

표현*　expression; manifestation [manifest~] 表~

현상　phenomenon [~representation] ~ 象

현상*　(film) developing [~image] ~ 像

현재　presently; present time [~be present] ~ 在

현대　present age; modern times [~generation] ~ 代
현대화　modernization

현실　reality [~reality] ~ 實

현직　present post; incumbent [~post] ~ 職

현장　the spot (of action) [~place] ~ 場

현지　the very spot [~place] ~ 地

현금　cash [~money] ~ 金

현찰　cash; bank notes [~document] ~ 札

혈 (血) **blood**

혈액　blood [~liquid] ~ 液
혈액형　blood type

혈관　blood vessel [~tube] ~ 管

혈.당　blood sugar [~sugar] ~ 糖

수혈*　blood transfusion [transport~] 輸~

헌혈*　blood donation [offer~] 獻~

혈.서　writing in blood [~writing] ~ 書

ㅎ

혈압 blood pressure
[~pressure] ~ 壓

빈혈 anemia [poor~] 貧~

충혈되다 (eyes) be bloodshot
[full~become] 充 ~ K

혈안이 되다 be frantic about (e.g.,
money) [~eye become] ~ 眼 K

출혈* bleeding; sacrifices
[come out~] 出~

지혈* stanching [stop~] 止~

혈기 hot blood; vitality
[~energy] ~ 氣

혈색 complexion; color
[~color] ~ 色

혈통 blood; lineage [~govern] ~統

혈연 blood relation [~affinity] ~緣

협 (協) **harmony; union**

협동* cooperation [~together] ~ 同
협동정신 cooperative spirit

협조* cooperation
[~harmonize] ~ 調
협조적 cooperative

협력* cooperation [~strength] ~力

농협 agricultural cooperative
union [agricultural industry~]
農~ (<농업협동조합)

협주곡 concerto
[~play-music tune] ~ 奏曲

타협* a compromise
[reasonable~] 妥~

협의* consultation; discussion
[~discuss] ~ 議

협상* negotiation [~trade] ~ 商

협회 association; league
[~meeting] ~ 會

협정 agreement; pact
[~decide] ~ 定

협 (脅) **threaten**

협박* a threat [~persecute] ~ 迫

위협* intimidation [stern~] 威~

형 (形) **shape; form**

형체 form; shape [~body] ~ 體

형태 form; shape [~form] ~ 態

원형 original form [origin~] 原~

원형 round shape [round~] 圓~

삼각형 triangle [three angle~] 三角~

체형 body shape; body type
[body~] 體~

기형 deformity [strange~] 奇~
기형아 deformed child

성형수술* plastic surgery
[make~operation] 成~手術

정형수술* orthopedic operation
[regulate~operation] 整~手術

형성* formation [~to complete] ~ 成

변형* transformation
[change~] 變~

인형 doll [person~] 人~

형식 formality [~ceremony] ~ 式
형식적 formal; perfunctory

형편 circumstances [~means] ~ 便
형편없다 be awful; be terrible

형용사 adjective
[~face words] ~ 容詞

형 w (型) **model; type**

모형 model; miniature
[pattern~] 模~

유형 type; pattern [a kind~] 類~

신형 new model [new~] 新~

284

구형 old-fashioned model [old~] 舊~

대형 big size; large model [big~] 大~

소형 small size; compact model [small~] 小~

혈액형 blood type [blood~] 血液~

유선형 streamline shape [streamline~] 流線~

전형적 typical [code~] 典~的

형 w(刑) **punishment; sentence**

형벌 (legal) punishment; penalty [~punish] ~ 罰

형.법 criminal law [~law] ~ 法

사형* death penalty [die~] 死~ 사형선고를 받다 be sentenced to death

교수형 punishment by hanging [hang head~] 絞首~

형무소 prison [~affairs place] ~ 務所

형사 (police) detective [~matters] ~ 事

형 w(兄) **elder brother**

형제 brothers/sisters [~junior] ~ 弟

형부 a female's elder sister's husband [~husband] ~ 夫

형수 a male's elder brother's wife [~elder brother's wife] ~ 嫂

매형 a male's elder sister's husband [sister~] 妹~

혜 (惠) **a favor; benefit**

혜택 a favor; benefit [~favor] ~ 澤 혜택을 입다 be benefited

은혜 a favor; indebtedness; obligation [favor~] 恩~

특혜 special benefit [special~] 特~

호 (好) **good; like**

호감 good feeling; favorable impression [~feeling] ~ 感

호의 goodwill; friendliness [~wish] ~ 意

호평* favorable comment [~comment] ~ 評

호전* favorable turn [~turn] ~ 轉

호황 prosperous condition [~state of affairs] ~ 況

호경기 business boom [~tone of the market] ~ 景氣

절호 the very best (chance) [absolute~] 絕~ 절호의 찬스 the best chance

호기.심 curiosity; inquisitiveness [~mysterious mind] ~ 奇心

기호 liking; taste [be fond of~] 嗜~

선호하다 prefer (over) [select~] 選~ 남아선호 preferring a son to a daughter

호 (呼) **call; exhale**

호출* calling out; summons [~come out] ~ 出

호칭* term of address [~call] ~ 稱

호응* response (to a request); acting in concert [~respond] ~ 應

ㅎ

환호*	a cheer; hurrah [cheer~] 歡~
호소*	an appeal; a petition [~tell] ~ 訴
호흡*	respiration [~inhale] ~ 吸

호 (護) protect; guard

보호*	protection [protect~] 保~
호위병	bodyguard [~guard soldier] ~ 衛兵
호신술	the art of self-defense [~body art] ~ 身術
옹호*	support; vindication [embrace~] 擁~
간호*	nursing; tending [take care~] 看~

호 (號) number; name

번호	number [number~] 番~
호.수	the number (of a house) [~number] ~ 數
기호	a sign; symbol [record~] 記~
신호*	a signal [believe~] 信~ 교통신호* traffic signal 신호등 signal light
암호	password [secret~] 暗~

호 (戶) family

호주	head of a family [~host] ~主
호적	family register [~record] ~籍
호구조사*	census taking [~mouth survey] ~ 口調查

혹 (惑) delude; bewitch; doubt

매혹적	captivating [attract~] 魅~的

유혹*	temptation; seduction [induce~] 誘~
현혹되다	be dazzled; be blinded [dizzy~become] 眩 ~ K
의혹	suspicion [doubt~] 疑~

혹 (酷) severe

혹독하다	be severe; be harsh [~poison] ~毒
혹평*	severe criticism [~criticize] ~ 評
혹사*	slave-driving; abuse [~employ] ~ 使 혹사당하다 be slave-driven
참혹하다	be pitiable; be miserable [miserable~] 慘~

혼 (婚) marriage

결혼*	marriage; wedding [tie~] 結~ 결혼식* wedding ceremony 연애결혼* love marriage 중매결혼* arranged marriage 국제결혼* international marriage
혼인*	marriage [~marriage] ~ 姻 혼인신고* report of marriage
신혼	new marriage [new~] 新~ 신혼부부 newlyweds 신혼여행* honeymoon
이혼*	divorce [leave~] 離~
재혼*	remarriage [again~] 再~
미혼	unmarried; single [no~] 未~
기혼	married [already~] 旣~
청혼*	proposal of marriage [request~] 請~
약혼*	(marriage) engagement [promise~] 約~ 약혼자 fiancé(e)

약혼식* engagement ceremony
약혼반지 engagement ring

파혼* breaking off a marriage engagement [break~] 破~

혼수 articles essential to a marriage [~essential] ~需

금혼식 golden wedding anniversary [gold~ceremony] 金~式

은혼식 silver wedding anniversary [silver~ceremony] 銀~式

혼 (混) mix; confused

혼동* confusion; mixing [~together] ~同
혼동되다 be confused

혼란* confusion; disorder; chaos [~chaos] ~亂

혼잡* congestion; disorder [~mixed] ~雜

혼합* mixing; compounding [~unite] ~合

혼선되다 (lines) be crossed [~line become] ~線 K

혼식* meal of mixed rice [~eat] ~食

혼방 mixed fabric [~weave] ~紡

혼 (昏) dusk

황혼 dusk; twilight [yellow~] 黃~

혼수상태 comatose condition [~sleep condition] ~睡 狀態

홍 (紅) red

주홍 bright orange color; scarlet [reddish~] 朱~

분홍색 pink color [powder~color] 粉~色

홍옥 Jonathan (apple) [~jade] ~玉

홍차 black tea [~tea] ~茶

홍당무 carrot [~China radish] ~唐 K

화 (化) change; -(iz)ation

변화* change [change~] 變~

진화* evolution [advance~] 進~

퇴화* degeneration; atrophy [retreat~] 退~

동화* assimilation [same~] 同~

강화* strengthening [strong~] 强~

미화* beautification; embellishment [beautiful~] 美~

악화* worsening; aggravation [bad~] 惡~

기계화* mechanization [machine~] 機械~

현대화* modernization [modern times~] 現代~

세계화 globalization [world~] 世界~

합리화* rationalization [unite reasoning~] 合理~

평준화* equalization; leveling [even measure~] 平準~

정화* purification [clean~] 淨~

문화 culture; civilization [writing~] 文~

화석 fossil [~stone] ~石

화학 chemistry [~study] ~學

화장* makeup [~makeup] ~粧

소화* digestion [dissolve~] 消~

화 (火)　fire; anger

화재　fire disaster [~calamity] ~ 災

진화*　putting out a fire
[suppress~] 鎭 ~

화로　brazier; fire pot [~stove] ~爐

화상　a burn [~scar] ~ 傷
화상을 입다 be burned

화염.병　Molotov cocktail
[~flame bottle] ~ 焰瓶

화장*　cremation [~funeral] ~ 葬

화산　volcano [~mountain] ~ 山

화력　thermal power [~power] ~力
화력발.전
steam power generation

화약　gunpowder [~medicine] ~ 藥

화나다　get angry [~come out] ~ K

화풀다　let go of anger [~solve] ~ K
화풀이* letting off steam;
venting one's wrath

울화　pent-up anger
[~grow thick] 鬱 ~
울화가 치밀다
feel a surge of anger

홧김에　in a fit of anger
[~on the impetus of] ~ K

성화*　vexation; irritation
[make~] 成 ~

화성　Mars [~star] ~ 星

화 (花)　flower

화초　flowering plants
[~grass] ~ 草

생화　real flower [living~] 生 ~

조화　artificial flower [make~] 造~

국화　chrysanthemum (flower)
[chrysanthemum~] 菊 ~

국화　national flower
[nation~] 國 ~

무궁화　Korean national flower;
the rose of Sharon
[eternity~] 無窮~

화분　flowerpot [~pot] ~ 盆

화병　vase [~jar] ~ 瓶

조화　floral condolences
[condole~] 弔~

화환　floral wreath; lei [~ring] ~環

화단　flower bed [~altar] ~ 壇

화원　flower shop [~garden] ~ 園

금상첨화　making still more
beautiful; making
something good better
[silk above add~] 錦上添~

화류계　pleasure quarters; geisha
world [~willow world] ~柳界

화 (畵)　picture; drawing

수채화　water-color painting
[water color~] 水彩 ~

유화　oil painting [oil~] 油~

판화　woodblock print; etching
[printing board~] 版 ~

정물화　still-life painting
[still thing~] 靜物~

풍경화　landscape painting
[landscape~] 風景~

도화지　drawing paper
[drawing~paper] 圖 ~ 紙

화선지　Chinese drawing paper
[~wide paper] ~ 宣紙

화가　painter; artist
[~specialist] ~ 家

화랑　gallery [~room] ~ 廊

만화　cartoon [diffused~] 漫~

영화　movie [cinema~] 映~

화면　screen [~surface] ~ 面

화 (話)　talk; story

회화* conversation [meeting~] 會 ~
영어회화* English conversation

대화* dialogue; conversation [opposite~] 對 ~

화술 conversational skill [~skill] ~ 術

화제 topic of a conversation [~subject] ~ 題

통화* telephone conversation [communicate~] 通 ~

전화* telephone; phone call [electricity~] 電 ~
전화걸다　make a call
전화끊다　hang up the phone
시내전화*　local call
시외전화*　long-distance call
국제전화*　international call
전화국　telephone company
전화기　telephone (instrument)
전화번호　telephone number
전화번호부　telephone directory

실화 true story [real~] 實 ~

신화 myth [god~] 神 ~

우화 fable; allegory [metaphor~] 寓 ~
이솝우화　Aesop's fables

동화 fairy tale; children's story [children~] 童 ~

화 (和)　harmony; peace

화합* harmony; concord [~unite] ~ 合

평화 peace [peaceful~] 平 ~

화목* peace; harmony [~harmony] ~ 睦

화해* reconciliation; making up [~solve] ~ 解

온화하다 be mild; be gentle [warm~] 溫 ~

완화* mitigation; ease [slow~] 緩 ~

중화* neutralization [middle~] 中 ~

포화* saturation [full stomach~] 飽 ~

화 (華)　splendid

화려하다 be splendid; be flashy; be dazzling [~beautiful] ~ 麗

화사하다 be luxurious; be splendid [~luxury] ~ 奢

호화롭다 be luxurious [great~] 豪 ~

번화하다 (street) be busy; be lively [prosper~] 繁 ~

화씨 fahrenheit [~clan] ~ 氏

화 (貨)　goods

화폐 money; currency [~money] ~ 幣

외화 foreign money [foreign~] 外 ~

미화 American money [America~] 美 ~

확 (確)　certain

확실하다 be certain; be sure [~real] ~ 實

정확하다 be accurate; be precise [right~] 正 ~

명확하다 be definite; be clear [clear~] 明 ~

확고하다 be firm; be adamant [~firm] ~ 固

확정* definite decision [~decide] ~ 定

확답* definite answer [~answer] ~ 答

확증* conclusive evidence [~evidence] ~ 證

확신*	firm belief; conviction [~believe] ~ 信
확인*	confirmation [~consent] ~ 認
확률	probability [~rate] ~ 率
확보*	securing; insuring [~protect] ~ 保

확 (擴) enlarge

확대*	enlargement [~big] ~ 大
확장*	extension; enlargement [~extend] ~ 張
확산*	spreading; dissemination [~disperse] ~ 散

환 (換) exchange

교환*	exchange [exchange~] 交~
환전*	money exchange [~money] ~ 錢
환율	exchange rate [~rate] ~ 率 (pron. = 환뉼)
환산*	conversion [~calculate] ~ 算
환기*	ventilation [~air] ~ 氣
환절기	transition between two seasons [~season period] ~ 節期
환장하다	go crazy; be out of one's mind [~intestine] ~ 腸

환 (歡) cheer(ful)

환영*	welcome; reception [~welcome] ~ 迎 환영회 welcome meeting 환영을 받다 be welcomed
환송*	farewell; send-off [~send] ~ 送
환성	a shout of joy [~voice] ~ 聲 환성을 올리다 shout for joy

환호*	a cheer; hurrah [~call] ~ 呼
환심	good graces; favor [~heart] ~ 心 환심을 사다 court (a person's) good graces
환락가	entertainment sections; pleasure resort [~pleasant street] ~ 樂街

환 (幻) illusion

환각제	hallucinogen [~perceive medicine] ~ 覺劑
환상	fantasy; illusion [~think] ~ 想
환멸	disillusionment [~destroy] ~ 滅 환멸을 느끼다 be disillusioned

환 (患) suffering; trouble

병환	sickness (hon.) [sickness~] 病~
질환	disease; ailment [ailment~] 疾~
환자	a patient [~person] ~ 者
환부	affected part [~part] ~ 部
후환	future trouble; evil consequence [later~] 後~ 후환을 두려워하다 fear future troubles

환 (還) return

반환*	return; giving back [return~] 返~
환불*	a refund [~pay] ~ 拂
환갑	one's sixtieth birthday [~the first] ~ 甲

활 (活) **live/lively**

활발하다 be lively; be active [~rise] ~發

활기 vigor; vitality [~energy] ~氣
활기를 띠다 be animated

활력 vitality; vital power [~strength] ~力
활력소 tonic
활력을 불어넣다 inject vigor

활·동* activity [~move] ~動

활약* (great) activity [~jump] ~躍

생활* life; living [life~] 生~

부활* resurrection [repeat~] 復~
부활·절 Easter

쾌활하다 be cheerful [pleasant~] 快~

활용* utilization; making the most of [~use] ~用

활·자 printing type; font [~character] ~字

활 (滑) **slippery**

윤활유 lubricating oil [luster~oil] 潤~油

원활하다 be smooth; be harmonious [round~] 圓~

활·주로 runway [~run road] ~走路

황 (黃) **yellow**

황금 gold; money [~gold] ~金

황인종 oriental race [~race] ~人種

황혼 dusk; twilight [~dusk] ~昏

황사현상 dust storm [~sand phenomenon] ~沙現象

황 (況) **situation**

근황 present situation [near~] 近~

상황 situation; circumstances [shape~] 狀~

경황 situation [scenery~] 景~
경황이 없다 have no time for

불황 (business) depression; slump [no~] 不~

호황 prosperous condition; brisk market [good~] 好~

성황 boom; success [prosper~] 盛~

황 (荒) **desolate**

황폐하다 be desolate; be devastated [~abolished] ~廢

황무지 wasteland [~wasteland place] ~蕪地

허황·되다 (dream) be wild; be chimerical [unreal~be] ~荒K

황당하다 be absurd; be nonsensical [~abrupt] ~唐

황 (皇) **emperor**

황제 emperor [~emperor] ~帝

황태자 crown prince [~greatest son] ~太子

교황 pope [religion~] 教~

황송하다 be awestruck; be grateful [~fear] ~悚

회 W(會) **meeting; gather**

총회 general meeting [general~] 總~

대회 large meeting; rally [big~] 大~

사회*	directing a meeting [hold office~] 司~ 사회자 chairperson; emcee 사회보다 chair (a meeting); emcee (a show)	회비	membership fee [~expense] ~費
회의*	conference; meeting [~discuss] ~議	사회	society [society~] 社~
학회	academic conference [study~] 學~	회사	company [~company] ~社
회관	assembly hall [~building] ~館 학생회관 student hall	회장	(committee) chairperson; (society) president [~superior] ~長
회화*	conversation [~talk] ~話	기회	opportunity; chance [opportunity~] 機~
회담*	parley; a talk [~talk] ~談	회계	finance; treasurer [~calculate] ~計 회계보다 serve as a treasurer

면회*   visiting; meeting [face~] 面~ 면회사절* no visitors

재회*   meeting again; reunion [again~] 再~

연회   banquet [banquet~] 宴~

회식*   dining together (in a group with coworkers) [~eat] ~食

야유회   picnic; outing [field outing~] 野遊~

음악회   concert [music~] 音樂~

망년회   year-end party [forget year~] 忘年~

청문회   (public) hearing [listen hear~] 聽聞~

국회   Congress [nation~] 國~ 국회의원 Congressman

교회   church [religion~] 敎~

협회   association; league [union~] 協~ 농구협회 basketball league

동창회   alumni association [schoolmate~] 同窓~

회원   member (of an association) [~member] ~員

회 (回) return; time

회전*   turning; rotation [~turn] ~轉 회전의자 swivel chair

회답*   a reply [~reply] ~答

회복*   recovery; restoration [~recover] ~復

만회*   retrieval; recovery [recover~] 挽~

회상*   reminiscing [~reflect] ~想

회피*   evasion; shirking [~avoid] ~避

회수*   withdrawal; retrieval [~collect] ~收

회.수   the number of times; frequency [~number] ~數 회수.권 commuter ticket; coupon ticket

(일)회전 (first) inning [first~fight] 一~戰

횡 (橫) across; unreasonable; unexpected

횡단*   crossing [~cut off] ~斷 횡단보도 crosswalk

횡령*   usurpation; embezzlement [~receive] ~領

ㅎ

횡포*	tyranny; high-handedness [~bad] ~ 暴 횡포부리다 tyrannize	후방	the rear (base) [~direction] ~ 方
횡설수설*	random talk; nonsense [~talk establish talk] ~ 說竪說	후퇴*	backing down; retreat [~retreat] ~ 退
횡재*	unexpected fortune; windfall [~property] ~ 財	후원*	support; backing [~help] ~ 援

효 (效) effect

효·과	effect [~result] ~ 果 효·과적 effective	후진국	backward country [~advance country] ~ 進國
즉효	immediate effect [immediate~] 即~	오후	P. M. [afternoon~] 午~
특효	special efficacy [special~] 特~	그후	after that; since then [that~] K~
효력	effect; validity [~power] ~ 力 효력이 있다 be effective	이후	from now on; thereafter [from~] 以~ 다섯시 이후 after 5 o'clock
유효하다	be valid; be effective [exist~] 有~	직후	immediately after [straight~] 直~
무효	invalidity [not~] 無~	식후	after meals [eat~] 食~
효율·적	efficient [~rate] ~ 率的	후식	dessert [~eat] ~ 食

효 ᵂ (孝) filial piety

		전후	before and after; in front of and behind; approximately [before~] 前~ 사십세 전후 about forty years old
효도*	filial duty [~principle] ~ 道	후년	the year after next [~year] ~ 年
효성	filial devotion [~sincerity] ~ 誠 효성이 지극하다 be devoted to one's parents	후천적	acquired; postnatal [~nature] ~ 天的
효녀	dutiful daughter [~female] ~ 女	후유·증	aftereffect (of a disease/ an injury); aftermath [~bequeath symptom] ~ 遺症
효자	dutiful son [~son] ~ 子 불효자 undutiful son	후불*	postpayment [~pay] ~ 拂
불효*	undutifulness to one's parents [no~] 不~	후환	future trouble; evil consequence [~trouble] ~ 患
		후세	future generation [~generation] ~ 世

후 (後) back; after; later

		후손	descendants [~descendant] ~ 孫
후문	back gate [~door] ~ 門	후임	successor (to a post) [~be in charge] ~ 任

ㅎ

후배	one's junior (in school) [~fellow member] ~ 輩	휴게실	a lounge [~rest room] ~ 憩室
최후	the last [the most~] 最~ 최후수단 last resort	휴가	(workers') vacation; time off [~leisure] ~ 暇
후자	the latter [~person] ~ 者	휴일	holiday [~day] ~日
후처	second wife [~wife] ~ 妻	연휴	consecutive holidays; long weekend [connected~] 連~
후편	second/last volume [~book] ~ 篇	휴교*	(temporary) closure of a school [~school] ~ 校
후반전	second half of a game [~half fighting] ~ 半戰	휴학*	temporary absence from school [~study] ~ 學
후회*	repentance; regret [~repent] ~ 悔	휴강*	(professor's) skipping a lecture [~lecture] ~ 講

훈 (訓) teach; admonish

훈련*	training; drill [~to train] ~ 鍊 맹훈련* intense training	휴직*	temporary rest from office [~office] ~ 職
교훈	precept; lesson [teach~] 敎~	휴업*	suspension of business [~business] ~ 業 금일휴업* closed for the day 임시휴업* temporarily closed
훈계*	admonition [~warn] ~ 戒		

휘 (揮) wield; direct

지휘*	conducting (orchestra); commanding [finger~] 指~	휴전*	armistice [~war] ~ 戰
발휘*	demonstration (of one's ability); manifestation [shoot~] 發~ 실력을 발휘하다 demonstrate one's ability	휴지	waste paper; toilet paper [~paper] ~ 紙
휘두르다	brandish; wield		

흉 (凶) evil; unlucky; ugly

휴 (休) rest

휴식*	a rest; a break [~rest] ~ 息	흉계	wicked scheme; evil plot [~plan] ~ 計
휴양*	a rest; recuperation [~care] ~ 養 휴양지 rest area; recreation center	음흉하다	be wicked and treacherous [dark~] 陰~
		흉악하다	(crime) be heinous; (looks) be unseemly [~evil] ~ 惡
휴게소	rest stop [~rest place] ~ 憩所	흉기	lethal weapon [~utensil] ~ 器
		흉년	year of bad harvest [~year] ~ 年
		흉하다	be ugly; be unsightly 보기 흉하다 be unsightly

흑 (黑) **black; dark**

흑백 black and white [~white] ~ 白

흑인 black person [~person] ~ 人

흑자 figures in black ink [~letter] ~ 字

암흑 darkness [dark~] 暗 ~

칠흑 pitch-dark [black~] 漆 ~
칠흑같은 밤 pitch-dark night

흑설탕 brown sugar [~sugar] ~雪糖

흑심 evil intention [~mind] ~ 心

흑막 something fishy [~curtain] ~ 幕

흡 (吸) **inhale**

호흡* respiration [exhale~] 呼~
인공호흡*
artificial respiration

흡연* smoking [~smoke] ~ 煙

흡수* absorption [~collect] ~ 收

흥 ʷ(興) **fun; prosper**

유흥 amusement; pleasure-
seeking [outing~] 遊~
유흥가 amusement center

흥겹다 be delightful; be fun
[~more than one can manage]
~K
흥겨운 시간 delightful time

흥나다 get merry [~come out] ~ K

흥분 excitement [~rouse] ~ 奮
흥분하다 get excited

흥미 an interest; an appeal
[~taste] ~ 味
흥미있다 be interesting

즉흥적 impromptu; improvised
[immediate~] 卽 ~ 的

흥하다 thrive; flourish

흥망 rise and fall [~perish] ~ 亡

문예부흥 renaissance
[art and learning again~]
文藝復~

희 (稀) **rare; scarce**

희귀하다 be rare [~precious] ~ 貴

희박하다 (chances) be slim; (air,
population) be sparse
[~thin] ~ 薄

희석* dilution; attenuation
[~release] ~ 釋

희미하다 be dim; be vague
[~tiny] ~ 微

희 (喜) **pleasure**

희노애락 joy, anger, sorrow,
and pleasure
[~anger sorrow pleasure]
~怒哀樂

희소식 good news [~news] ~ 消息

희극 comedy [~drama] ~ 劇

Roots
of
Native Korean
Origin

ㄱ

가 ᵂ   **end; edge**

가장자리   margin

눈·**가**   outer corner of the eye [eye~]

귓**가**   the rim of the ear [ear~]

바닷**가**   seaside [sea~]

길·**가**   roadside [road~]

강·**가**   riverside [river~] 江~

물·**가**   by the water [water~]

냇**가**   by the stream [stream~]

창·**가**   by the window [window~] 窓~

가게 ᵂ   **store**

생선·**가게**   raw-fish store [raw fish~] 生鮮~

과일·**가게**   fruit shop [fruit~]

구멍·**가게**   small store; hole-in-the-wall store [hole~]

가다 ᵂ   **go** (간 **modifier form**)

나**가다**   go out [come out~]

빠져나**가다**   escape; get away

빗나**가다**   go wide of the mark

들어**가다**   go in [enter~]

걸어**가다**   go on foot; walk [walk~]

올라**가다**   go up [rise~]

내려**가다**   go down [descend~]

건너**가다**   go across [to cross~]

지나**가다**   go past; pass by [pass~]

왔다**갔다**하다   come and go; walk back and forth [come~]

갔다오다   go and come back [go~]

돌아**가다**   go around; return; pass away [return~]

구경**가다**   go to see (the sights) [sightseeing~]

뛰어**가다**   run (to) [run~]

도망**가다**   run away; flee [fleeing~] 逃亡~

넘어**가다**   fall over; (sun) set; pass (to); be deceived [pass over~]

다녀**가다**   drop in and then go on [drop in~]

질러**가다**   take a short cut [shorten~]

훔쳐**가다**   steal away [steal~]

이사**가다**   move out [house moving~] 移徙~

시집**가다**   marry (a man) [husband's home~] 媤집~

장가**가다**   marry (a woman) [taking wife~]

오래**가다**   last long [long~]

간밤   last night [~night]

가락   **long slender object**

손·**가락**   finger [hand~]

발·**가락**   toe [foot~]

머리**카락**   a strand of hair [hair~]

가락국수   *udon* noodle [~noodle]

젓**가락**   chopstick [chopstick~] 나무젓가락 wooden chopstick

숟**가락**   spoon

ㄱ

가루 ᵂ   **powder**

가루약   powdered medicine [~medicine] ~ 藥

가루비누   powdered detergent [~soap]

고춧**가루**   red-pepper powder [pepper~]

후춧**가루**   black pepper [black pepper~]

빵·**가루**   bread crumbs [bread~]

밀·**가루**   flour [wheat~]

가르다 ᵂ   **split; divide**
(갈래 division; fork in the road)

갈라지다   split; branch off [~become]

갈랫길   forked road [~road]
(세)**갈**랫길   (three)-forked road

갈림.길   forked road; turning point [~road]

갈라서다   separate; divorce [~stand]

갈라놓다   cause to become estranged; put a barrier (between) [~put]

가리마   a part (in one's hair)
가리마타다   part one's hair

가만 ᵂ   **still; quietly**

가만히   still; quietly [~ -ly]

가만있다   keep still [~exist]

가만두다   leave as it is; leave alone [~leave]

가방 ᵂ   **bag**

가방끈   bag strap [~string]

손·**가방**   handbag [hand~]

책**가방**   book sack [book~] 冊~

서류**가방**   briefcase [document~] 書類~

여행·**가방**   suitcase [travel~] 旅行~

가슴 ᵂ   **breast; chest; heart**

젖**가슴**   breast [breast~]

앞**가슴**   chest [front~]

가슴둘레   bust; chest [~girth]

가시 ᵂ   **thorn; fish bone**

가시나무   thorny tree [~tree]

생선·**가시**   fish bone [raw fish~] 生鮮~

가시철망   barbed-wire barrier [~wire entanglement] ~ 鐵網

가죽 ᵂ   **leather; (animal) skin**

가죽제품   leather goods [~goods] ~ 製品

가죽구두   leather shoes [~shoes]

가죽잠바   leather jacket [~jumper] ~ E

가죽장갑   leather gloves [~gloves] ~ 掌匣

쇠**가죽**   cowskin [cow's~]

양**가죽**   sheepskin [sheep~] 羊~

뱀장어**가죽**   eelskin [eel~] 뱀 長魚~

통**가죽**   the whole skin of an animal [whole~]

가지   **a kind**

몇**가지**   how many kinds; several kinds [how many/several~]

여러**가지**   several kinds [several~]

각**가지**   various kinds [every~] 各~

가지가지   various kinds of

가지각색 various kinds of [~every color] ~ 各色

오만**가지** every sort and kind [fifty thousand~] 五万 ~

색색**가지** various colors of [color color~] 色色 ~

매한**가지** being much the same; making no difference [much one~]

마찬**가지** being much the same

갈비 ʷ **ribs**

갈비뼈 rib bone [~bone]

쇠**갈비** beef ribs [cow's~]

돼지**갈비** pork ribs [pig~]

갈비탕 beef-rib soup [~soup] ~ 湯

갈비찜 steamed rib [~steaming]

갈비씨 skinny person

감 ʷ **person/material suitable (for)**

사윗**감** suitable person for a son-in-law [son-in-law~]

대통령.**감** person who would make a good president [president~] 大統領 ~

장난.**감** toy [playing~]

옷**감** cloth; dress material [clothes~]

물.**감** dye; color [dyed color~]

뗄.**감** firewood [to burn~]

값 ʷ **price** (pron. = 갑)

집**값** price of a house [house~]

물건.**값** price of things [goods~] 物件 ~

쌀**값** price of rice [rice~]

책**값** price of books [book~] 冊 ~

옷**값** price of clothes [clothes~]

찻**값** price of tea/coffee [tea~] 茶 ~

방.**값** charge for a room [room~] 房 ~

술.**값** drink charge; drink money [liquor~]

외상.**값** tab; charge account [credit~]

값지다 be expensive; be valuable [~be]

헐.**값** dirt-cheap price [low price~] 歇 ~

값어치 worth; value [~worth] (pron. = 가버치)

같은**값**이면 other things being equal [same~if]

같다 ʷ **be the same; be like**

똑**같다** be exactly the same [exactly~] 똑같이 equally; evenly

새거**같다** be as good as new [new thing~]

꿈**같다** be dreamlike [dream~]

한결**같다** be constant; be consistent [one texture~]

같이 together ...같이 like...

개 ʷ **dog**

똥.**개** mongrel [shit~]

개집 kennel [~house]

개밥 dog food [~meal]

개고기 dog meat [~meat]

개자식	son of a bitch [~fellow]
개새끼	son of a bitch [~fellow (vulgar)]
개기름	(natural) grease on one's face [~oil]
개소리*	nonsense; stupid talk [~sound]
개꿈	meaningless dream [~dream]

개 — thing used for

날개	wing [fly~]
마개	lid [clog~]
덮개	a cover [cover~]
병따개	bottle opener [bottle open~] 瓶 따 ~
깔개	a mat; something to sit on [spread out~]
지우개	eraser [erase~]
베개	pillow [lay head on~]
이쑤시개	toothpick [tooth pick~]
귀후비개	ear cleaner [ear pick~]
부침개	pancake [griddle~]
아무개	a certain person; so-and-so [anybody~]

거 — thing (/것)

이거	this; this thing [this~]
저거	that; that thing [that~]
딴거	different thing; another one [~thing]
별거	rare thing [special~] 別~ 별거아니다 be no rare thing
새거	new thing [new~]

헌거	used thing [used~]
먹을·거	things to eat [to eat~]
마실·거	things to drink [to drink~]
단거	sweets [sweet~]
날거	raw stuff [raw~]
들·것	stretcher [to carry~]

거리 — material; makings

일·거리	piece of work [work~]
볼·거리	something to see [to see~]
구경·거리	object of interest; an attraction [sightseeing~]
웃음·거리	laughingstock [laughter~]
자랑·거리	source of pride; something to brag about [pride~]
걱정·거리	source of anxiety [anxiety~]
줄거리	stalk; outline [line~]

거리 ʷ — road; street

길·거리	street [road~]
삼거리	three-way junction [three~] 三 ~
사/네거리	intersection [four~] 四 /네 ~

거리다 ʷ — make (sound/movement)

두근거리다	throb; pit-a-pat [pit-a-pat~]
중얼거리다	mutter; murmur [murmuring~]
훌쩍거리다	sniffle [sniffling~]
흔들거리다	keep swaying/shaking [swaying~]

두리번**거리다** keep looking around

꼬불**거리다** wind; be curly [winding~]

끈적**거리다** be sticky [sticky~]

거품 ᵂ　**foam**

물**거품** water bubbles [water~]

비누**거품** soapsuds; lather [soap~]

맥주**거품** beer foam [beer~] 麥酒~

걱정 ᵂ　**worry; anxiety**

걱정하다 worry; be anxious over

걱정되다 feel uneasy; be worried about [~become]

걱정끼치다 cause (a person) anxiety [~cause]

한**걱정** big worry [extreme~]

돈**걱정*** financial worry [money~]

걱정.거리 source of anxiety [~makings]

건너다 ᵂ **to cross**

건너가다 go across [~go]

건너오다 come over [~come]

건너뛰다 jump across [~jump]

건널목 crosswalk [~neck]

건너편 the opposite side (from where one is) [~side] ~ 便

건너주다 hand over; give [~give]

걷다 ᵂ **to walk** (걸음 noun form)

걸어가다 go on foot; walk [~go]

걸음걸이 manner of walking

걸어다니다 walk about; commute on foot [~come and go]

뒷**걸음**질* stepping backward [back~doing]

한**걸음** one step [one~]
천릿길도 한걸음부터
A journey of a thousand miles starts with a single step.

발.**걸음*** pace; step [foot~]
발.걸음이 가볍다/무겁다
have light/leaden feet

헛**걸음*** a visit in vain; fruitless journey [vain~]

걸다 ᵂ　**hang; speak to** (걸이 **hanger**)

목**걸이** necklace [neck~]

귀**걸이** earring [ear~]

코**걸이** nose ring [nose~]

옷**걸이** clothes hanger [clothes~]

벽**걸이** wall tapestry [wall~] 壁~

턱**걸이*** chin-up [chin~]

문**걸다** lock the door [door~] 門~

목숨**걸다** stake one's life [life~]

말**걸다** address (a person) [speaking~]

전화**걸다** telephone (a person) [telephone~] 電話~

시비**걸다** provoke (a person) to quarrel [quarrel~] 是非~

걸리다 be hung; be caught; weigh (on one's mind); take (time); be afflicted with
돌에 걸리다 trip over a stone
경찰에 걸리다
be caught by a policeman
마음에 걸리다
weigh on one's mind
시간이 걸리다 take time
감기걸리다 catch a cold

검.다 ʷ　　be black　　(/까맣다)

검정색　　black (color) ~정 色

거무스름하다 be blackish [~-ish]

새까맣다　be jet black [vivid~]

까만색　　black (color) [~color] ~ 色

검둥이　　dark-skinned person; Negro [~person]

까매지다　get dark/tanned [~become]

까무잡잡하다 (skin) be darkish

깜깜하다　be pitch-dark
　　　　　깜깜이다　be ignorant (of)

까마아득하다 be remote [~remote]

겉 ʷ　　surface; outside

겉면　　surface side [~side] ~ 面

겉장　　front page; (book) cover [~sheet] ~ 張

겉봉　　outer envelope [~seal] ~ 封

겉껍질　outer cover/skin [~skin]

겉옷　　outer garment [~clothes]

겉모양　outer appearance [~shape] ~ 模樣

겉보기에는 outwardly [~looking]

겉멋　　superficial vanity [~show]

겉치레*　dressing up the outside [~embellishment]

겉치장*　dressing up the outside [~embellishment] ~ 治粧

겉절이*　vegetables pickled right before eating [~pickled vegetables]

수박겉핥기 having a smattering (of) [watermelon~licking] (pron. = 수박거탈끼)

겨울 ʷ　　winter

초겨울　early winter [beginning~] 初~

한겨울　midwinter [peak~]

겨울철　winter season [~season]

겨울옷　winter clothes [~clothes]

겨울.방학 (school) winter vacation [~vacation] ~ 放學

결　　in the midst of

꿈.결　　the midst of a dream; passing dream [dream~] 꿈.결에 듣다　hear while half asleep

잠.결　　in one's sleep; while asleep [sleep~] 잠.결에 듣다　hear while half asleep

얼떨.결　the confusion of the moment; moment of bewilderment

결 ʷ　　texture

살.결　　skin texture [skin~]

비단.결　silky texture [silk~]

나뭇결　wood texture [wood~]

한결같다　be constant; be consistent [one~be like]

겹 ʷ　　a fold; layer

한겹　　single fold [one~]

여러겹　several folds [several~]

겹겹이　in many layers

겹치다　lay one upon another; overlap; fall on 휴일이 일요일과 겹친다 The holiday falls on Sunday.

겹다 **be more than one can manage**

눈물**겹다** be moved to tears [tears~]
눈물겨운 tearful

힘**겹다** be beyond one's strength [strength~]

역**겹다** feel disgusted [contrary~] 逆~

지**겹다** be loathsome

흥**겹다** be delightful; be fun [fun~] 興~

곁 ʷ **side**

곁눈질* looking aside [~eye doing]

곁다리끼다 participate as an outsider [~leg insert]

곁들이다 garnish (with) [~let in]
고기에 야채를 곁들이다
garnish meat with vegetable

고기 ʷ **meat; live fish**

쇠**고기** beef [cow's~]

닭**고기** chicken meat [chicken~] (pron. = 다꼬기)

돼지**고기** pork [pig~]

고깃국 broth [~soup]

물·**고기** live fish [water~]

고기잡이* fishing [~catching]

고깃배 fishing boat [~boat]

고래 ʷ **whale**

고래잡이* whale fishing [~catching]

돌**고래** dolphin

술**고래** heavy drinker [liquor~]

고래고래 shouting
고래고래 소리
지르다 raise a shout

고리 ʷ **a ring; loop**

문·**고리** doorknob [door~] 門~

열·쇠**고리** key ring [key~]

고무 ʷ **rubber; eraser**

고뭇줄 elastic string; rubber band [~string]

고무밴드 rubber band [~band] ~ E

고무신 rubber shoes [~shoes]

고무장갑 rubber gloves [~gloves] ~ 掌匣

고무공 rubber ball [~ball]

고무풍선 rubber (toy) balloon [~balloon] ~ 風船

고추 ʷ **pepper**

빨간**고추** red pepper [red~]

파란**고추** green pepper [green~]

풋**고추** unripe (green) pepper [unripe~]

고추장 soypaste mixed with red peppers [~soy sauce] ~ 醬

고춧가루 red-pepper powder [~powder]

곧다 ʷ **be straight**

곧바로 straight; right away [~straight]

곧장 straight; right away

곧이**곧**대로 straightforwardly; frankly

곧이듣다   take (someone's word) seriously [~listen]

곧   soon; before long

곱하다 ʷ   **multiply**

곱셈*   multiplication (in math) [~calculation]

곱절   double; times
(두)곱절   (twice) as much/many

제곱*   (arithmetic) squaring

공 ʷ   **ball**

고무공   rubber ball [rubber~]

배구공   a volleyball [volleyball~] 排球~

농구공   a basketball [basketball~] 籠球~

축구공   soccer ball; a football [football~] 蹴球~

야구공   a baseball [baseball~] 野球~

탁구공   a Ping-Pong ball [Ping-Pong~] 卓球~

공놀이*   playing with a ball [~playing]

공차다   kick a ball [~kick]

공던지다   throw a ball [~throw]

공튀기다   bounce a ball [~bounce]

과일 ʷ   **fruit**

과일·바구니   fruit basket [~basket]

과일·가게   fruit store [~store]

과일장수   fruit seller [~seller]

풋과일   unripe fruit [unripe~]

햇과일   new crop of fruit [of the year~]

구경 ʷ   **(enjoyable) sight; sightseeing**

구경하다   see the sights; see (a play); look on

구경가다   go to see (the sights) [~go]
영화구경가다   go to a movie

구경·거리   object of interest; an attraction [~makings]

구경꾼   onlookers; spectators [~doer]

구기다 ʷ   **wrinkle; crumple**

구겨지다   get wrinkled/crumpled [~become]

구김·살   wrinkles; rumples [~arrow]

구깃구깃하다   be wrinkled/crumpled

구두 ʷ   **dress shoes**

가죽구두   leather shoes [leather~]

구두끈   shoestring [~string]

구두창   shoe sole [~shoe sole]

구둣굽   shoe heel [~a heel]
굽이 높은 구두   high-heeled shoes

뾰족구두   high heels [sharp-pointed~]

구둣주걱   shoehorn [~spatula]

구두약   shoe polish [~medicine] ~ 藥

구두닦이*   shoe polishing; shoeshine boy [~polishing]

구둣발   feet with shoes on [~foot]

구둣방   shoe store [~room] ~ 房

구두쇠   stingy person [~metal]

구름 ᵂ cloud
흰구름 white cloud [white~]
먹구름 black cloud [Chinese ink~]
비구름 rain cloud [rain~]
뭉게구름 cumulus cloud [fluffy~]
뜬구름 drifting cloud; evanescence (of life) [floating~]

구멍 ᵂ hole
단춧구멍 buttonhole [button~]
바늘·구멍 needle hole [needle~]
귓구멍 earhole [ear~]
콧구멍 nostril [nose~]
똥·구멍 anus [shit~]
구멍·가게 small store; hole-in-the-wall store [~store]

구석 ᵂ corner
방·구석 corner of a room; indoors [room~] 房 ~
구석구석 every nook and cranny
구석지다 be recessed [~be] 구석진 곳 a recess; nook

구이 ᵂ roasted/baked food (굽다 to roast/bake 군 modifier form)
구워먹다 bake and eat [~eat]
생선구이 * grilled fish [raw fish~] 生鮮 ~
장어구이 broiled eel [eel~] 長魚 ~
즉석구이 things grilled on the spot [on the spot~] 卽席 ~

양념구이 * food broiled with seasonings [seasonings~]
군밤 roasted chestnut [~chestnut]
군만두 toasted dumpling [~dumpling] ~ 饅頭
군고구마 baked sweet potatoes [~sweet potato]

국 ᵂ soup
국물 soup; broth [~water]
떡국 rice-cake soup [rice cake~] 떡만둣국 rice-cake and dumpling soup
해장·국 broth to chase a hangover [drinking to relieve a hangover~]
냉·국 cold soup [cold~] 冷 ~
미역국 seaweed soup [seaweed~] 미역국먹다 eat seaweed soup; fail an exam (slang)
김칫국 kimchi soup [kimchi~]

국수 ᵂ noodle
막국수 coarse noodle [rough~]
비빔국수 noodles mixed with assorted ingredients [mixing~]
가락국수 udon noodle [long slender object~]
칼국수 noodles cut with a kitchen knife [knife~]

군 extra; superfluous
군살 superfluous flesh; fat [~flesh]
군말 * uncalled-for remark [~talk]
군소리 * uncalled-for remark [~voice]

307

ㄱ

군침	excessive saliva [~saliva] 군침돌다 mouth waters
군더더기	excrescence; superfluous things
군식구	hanger-on [~family] ~ 食口
군것질*	eating/buying snacks between meals [~thing doing]

군데	**place**
한군데	one/same place [one~]
여러군데	several places [several~]
몇군데	how many places; several places [how many/several~]
군데군데	here and there; at places

귀 w	**ear; edge**
귀청	eardrum [~drum]
귓구멍	earhole [~hole]
귓가	the rim of the ear [~edge]
귀지	earwax
귀걸이	earring [~hanging object]
귀마개*	earmuff [~lid]
귀후비개	ear cleaner [~picker]
귀먹다	go deaf 가는귀먹다 get slightly deaf
귀머거리	deaf person
귓속말*	whispering; word in someone's ear [~inside talk]
귀띔하다	give a tip; hint
귀담아듣다	listen (to a person's words) attentively [~put in listen]

귀동냥*	knowledge picked up by keeping one's ears open [~begging]
잠.귀	sensitivity to sounds while asleep [sleep~] 잠.귀가 밝다 be a light sleeper
말.귀	understanding; ear for words [speaking~] 말.귀가 어둡다 be slow in understanding what one says 말.귀를 못 알아듣다 can't make out what one says
귀퉁이	corner; edge

그릇 w	**bowl; vessel**
밥그릇	rice bowl [rice~]
국그릇	soup bowl [soup~]
스텐그릇	stainless steel vessel [stainless steel~] E~
사기그릇	chinaware [chinaware~] 沙器~

그림 w	**picture; drawing** (그리다 to draw)
그림책	picture book [~book] ~ 冊
그림엽서	picture postcard [~postcard] ~ 葉書
그림물.감	paints; colors [~dye]
그림자	a shadow

글 w	**(a piece of) writing**
글쓰다	write (a story) [~write]
글씨	handwriting [~way of using something]
글.자	letter; character [~character] ~ 字
한글	Korean alphabet [great /Korean~]

글짓기*	composition [~composition]	시골.길	country road [countryside~]
글·재주	literary talent [~talent]	길·가	roadside [~edge]
		비탈.길	sloping road [a slope~]
금 ʷ	**line**	내리막길	downhill road [downhill~]
빗금	diagonal line	오르막길	uphill road [uphill~]
손·금	lines of the palm [hand~] 손·금보다 read someone's palm	눈.길	snowy road [snow~]
		빗길	rainy road [rain~]
눈·금	notch mark on a scale [eye~]	길·거리	street [~street]
		골목길	side street; lane [lane~]
금긋다	draw a line [~draw]	길모퉁이	street corner [~corner]
금가다	be cracked	철.길	railroad track [iron~] 鐵 ~
		지름.길	shortcut [diameter~]
기름 ʷ	**oil**	오솔.길	narrow path; lonely lane
콩기름	soybean oil [soybean~]	길눈	sense of direction [~eye] 길눈이 밝다/어둡다 have a good/poor sense of direction
옥수수기름	corn oil [corn~]		
참기름	sesame oil	눈.길	line of vision; one's gaze [eye~] 눈.길을 끌다 draw attention
들기름	wild sesame oil [perilla~]		
돼지기름	lard [pig~]		
식물.성기름	vegetable oil [vegetable property~] 植物性~	앞길	road ahead; future [ahead~]
		살.길	means to live [live~] 살.길을 찾다 seek a way to make a living
기름·기	oiliness; greasiness [~a touch] ~ 氣		
기름지다	(food/soil) be rich [~be]	길잡이	guide; waypost [~holder]
개기름	(natural) grease on one's face [dog~]	길다 ʷ	**be long** (긴 modifier form)
길 ʷ	**road**	길이	length 소매길이 sleeve length 치마길이 skirt length
찻길	roadway; driveway [vehicle~] 車 ~ 기찻길 railroad		
		길쭉하다	be longish [~have the property of]
한길	main road [big~]	길따랗다	be very long [~have the property of]
갈랫길	forked road [fork~]		
갈림.길	forked road; turning point [division~]	긴팔	long sleeve [~arm]
		긴소매	long sleeve [~sleeve]

긴바지   long pants [~pants]
긴치마   long skirt [~skirt]
긴머리   long hair [~hair]
긴말*   long talk [~talk]

김 ᵂ   **steam; breath**

입김   steam from breath [mouth~]

김나다   emit steam [~come out]

김빠지다   (beer) become stale; become dull [~leak out]

김새다   one's enthusiasm dies down (slang) [~leak]

김에   **on the impetus of; while**

술.김에   under the influence of alcohol [alcohol~]

홧김에   in a fit of anger [anger~] 火~

하는김에   while you are at it [doing~]

김치 ᵂ   **kimchi**

배추김치   cabbage kimchi [cabbage~]

물김치   juicy kimchi [water~]

열무김치   young radish kimchi [young radish~]

총각김치   young radish kimchi [bachelor~] 總角 ~

오이김치   cucumber kimchi [cucumber~]

날김치   raw/unaged kimchi [raw~]

신김치   sour/fermented kimchi [sour~]

김칫국   kimchi soup [~soup]

김치담그다   make kimchi [~pickle]

ㄲ

까맣다   be black (see 검.다)

깔다 ᵂ   **spread out; sit on**

깔개   mat; something to sit on [~thing used for]

깔고앉.다   sit on [~sit]

깔고뭉개다   sit on and mash; keep (a person) under one's thumb [~mash]

깔려죽다   be crushed to death [~die]

깔보다   look down on; slight [~see]

깜.박 ᵂ   **winking; twinkling**

깜.박거리다   blink (eyes); twinkle; flicker

깜.박이   turn signal [~thing]

깜.박하다   blink; twinkle; flicker; dim for a moment
깜.박깜.박*
blinking repeatedly
눈깜.박할·새   in a blink
정신이 깜.박하다   one's mind dims for a moment

깜.박잊다   slip one's mind for the moment [~forget]

깡   **chip**

감자깡   potato chip [potato~]

고구마깡   sweet potato chip [sweet potato~]

새우깡   shrimp chip [shrimp~]

양파깡   onion snack [onion~] 洋파 ~

깨 w	**sesame**
참깨	sesame
들깨	wild sesame [wild~]
깨소금	salted sesame [~salt] 깨소금맛 Serves one right.
깻잎	sesame leaf [~leaf] (pron.= 깬닙)
깨알	grain of sesame; something tiny [~grain] 깨알같다 be tiny (as a grain of sesame)
주근깨	freckles
껍질 w	**shell; skin**
겉껍질	outer cover; skin [outside~]
속껍질	inner layer of skin [inside~]
귤껍질	orange peel [orange~]
바나나껍질	banana peel [banana~]
사과껍질	skin of an apple [apple~]
달걀껍질	eggshell [egg~]
껏	**to the full extent of**
힘껏	to the utmost of one's strength [energy~]
정성껏	with utmost devotion [sincerity~] 精誠~
마음껏	to one's heart's content; to one's satisfaction [heart~]
한껏	to one's satisfaction [limit~] 限~
양껏	as much as one can (eat) [quantity~] 量~ 양껏 먹다 eat one's fill
실컷	one's fill; to one's heart's content 실컷 먹다 eat one's fill

실력껏	to the full extent of one's ability [real ability~] 實力~
여태껏	right up to now [till now~]
꼬다 w	**twist**
꼬부리다	bend 꼬부라지다 be bent
꼬불거리다	wind; be curly 꼬불꼬불* winding; zigzag
꽈배기	twisted things
비(비)꼬다	twist; give a sarcastic twist to one's words [rub~]
꼬리	tail
꼬집다	pinch [~pick]
꼬리 w	**tail**
쥐꼬리	rat tail; something small [rat~] 쥐꼬리만한 월급 small salary
꼬리곰탕	oxtail soup [~internals soup]
꼬리치다	wag its tail; act seductively [~wag]
꼬리밟히다	be caught in wrongdoing [~be stepped on] 꼬리가 길면 밟힌다 Misbehavior eventually catches up with one.
꼬리표	(address) tag [~ticket] ~ 標
꼴 w	**shape; form; appearance**
닮은꼴	similar figure [similar~]
사다리꼴	trapezoid [ladder~]
별꼴	obnoxious thing/person [special~] 別~ 별꼴이야! What an eyesore!
꼴불견	ugliness; unsightliness [~no see] ~ 不見

311

꼴좋다   Serves one right. [~good]

눈꼴사납다   be offensive to the eye;
               be an eyesore [eye~fierce]

꽁   **end**

꽁지   tail

꽁무니   tail; buttock
          꽁무니빼다 shrink back;
          chicken out

꽁초   cigarette butt

꽂이   **a stand; insertion**
         (꽂다 to insert)

책꽂이   bookstand [book~] 冊~

연필꽂이   pencil stand [pencil~] 鉛筆~

꽃꽂이*   flower arrangement
          [flower~]

꽃 ᵂ   **flower**

장미꽃   rose [rose~] 薔薇~

호박꽃   squash flower [squash~]

꽃잎   petal [~leaf] (pron. = 꼰닢)

꽃다발   bouquet; a bunch
          of flowers [~bunch]

꽃향기   scent of flowers
          [~scent] ~ 香氣

꽃병   flower vase [~bottle] ~ 瓶

꽃바구니   flower basket [~basket]

꽃밭   flower garden [~field]

꽃집   flower shop [~house]

꽃무늬   floral design [~design]

꽃꽂이*   flower arrangement
          [~insertion]

불꽃   flame; blaze [fire~]
          불꽃놀이* fireworks

꾸러기   **person who overdoes**
          (something); overindulger

잠꾸러기   sleepyhead [sleep~]

욕심꾸러기   greedy person
          [greed~] 慾心~

심술꾸러기   ill-natured person
          [ill nature~] 心術~

장난꾸러기   mischievous child
          [mischief~]

말썽꾸러기   troublemaker (child)
          [trouble~]

꾸미다 ᵂ   **decorate; fabricate**
          (꾸밈 noun form)

꾸밈없다   be unaffected; be natural
          [~not exist]

꾸며대다   cook up (a story) [~make]

꾸며내다   fabricate; cook up [~make]

꾼   **person occupied (with);**
          doer (of)

술꾼   (heavy) drinker; tippler
          [liquor~]

노름꾼   gambler [gambling~]

구경꾼   onlookers; spectators
          [sightseeing~]

일꾼   laborer; worker [work~]

짐꾼   porter; carrier [luggage~]

장사꾼   trader; merchant [trade~]

농사꾼   farmer [farming~] 農事~

낚시꾼   fisherman [fish hook~]

나무꾼   woodcutter [tree~]

꿀 ᵂ   **honey**

벌꿀   honey [bee~]

ㄲ

꿀물	honeyed water [~water]	끈끈이	sticky tape to catch insects
꿀맛	scrumptious taste [~taste]		

꿈 ᵂ **dream**
(꾸다 to dream)

꿈꾸다	dream (of) [~to dream]
꿈같다	be dreamlike [~be like]
개꿈	meaningless dream [dog~]
단꿈	sweet dream [sweet~]
꿈나라	dreamland; sleep [~country] 꿈나라로 가다 fall asleep
꿈.결	the midst of a dream; passing dream [~midst]

끈 ᵂ **string**

노끈	string; cord [string~]
가방끈	bag strap [bag~]
구두끈	shoestrings [dress shoes~]
운동화끈	sneaker strings [sneakers~] 運動靴~
끈매다	tie the strings [~tie]
끈풀다	untie the strings [~untie]

끈 **tenacious; sticky**

끈기	patience; tenacity [~spirit] ~ 氣 끈기있다 be tenacious
끈질기다	be persistent; be tenacious [~strong]
끈덕지다	be persistent 끈덕지게 persistently
끈끈하다	be sticky; be gluey
끈적거리다	be sticky 끈적끈적하다 be sticky

끌다 ᵂ **drag; pull; attract**

질질끌다	drag; drag on
끌어당기다	pull; draw [~pull]
이끌다	guide; lead
끌리다	be dragged; be attracted
끌어안.다	embrace tightly [~hold]
끌어들이다	draw into; let (someone/something) get involved [~let in]

끝 ᵂ **an end; the end**

맨끝	the very end [the very~]
끝까지	to the end [~to]
끝나다	come to an end; be over [~come out]
끝내다	put an end to; finish [~bring out]
끝내	to the very end; in the end 끝끝내 to the very end
끝장	an end; settlement 끝장나다 be brought to an end
끝으로	lastly; in conclusion [~-ly]
끝맺다	conclude; complete [~tie]
끝마치다	finish up (a job) [~finish]
끝마무리*	finishing touches [~finishing touches]
끝없다	be endless; be unlimited [~not exist]
혀끝	tip of the tongue [tongue~]
머리끝	ends of one's hair [hair~] 머리끝에서 발끝까지 from head to toe

끼다 ᵂ **gather; squeeze**

먼지끼다 become dusty [dust~]

때끼다 become dirty [dirt~]

구름끼다 be cloudy [cloud~]

안개끼다 fog up [fog~]

끼우다 put between; insert

끼어들다 edge into; wedge into [~enter]

끼어앉.다 squeeze to sit in [~sit]

껴안.다 embrace; hug [~hold]

팔짱끼다 fold one's arms [folding one's arms~]

껴입다 bundle up [~wear]

단추끼다 button up [button~]

끼치다 ᵂ **cause; give**

폐끼치다 trouble (a person) [trouble~] 弊~

걱정끼치다 worry (a person) [anxiety~]

소름끼치다 feel a chill creep over one [goose bumps~]

ㄴ

나다 ᵂ **come out**

나오다 come out; protrude [~come]

끝나다 come to an end [end~]

나가다 go out [~go]

나서다 leave; get out; put oneself forward [~stand]

떠나다 leave; depart

나타나다 appear

태어나다 be born

일어나다 get up; stand up; happen [rise~]

내다 bring out; put forth
내놓다 put out; expose
쫓아내다 drive out; expel
나타내다 indicate; manifest
드러내다 expose; reveal
화내다 show anger; get angry
겁내다 dread; fear
뽐내다 boast; show off
흉내내다 imitate; mimic
내다보다 look out/ahead
내기* a bet; a wager

겁나다 be scared [fear~] 怯~

화나다 get angry [anger~] 火~

열나다 become feverish; get angry [heat~] 熱~

잘나다 be handsome; be great (ironical) [nicely~]

못나다 be foolish; be ugly [not~]

생각나다 come to mind; be reminded of [thought~]

나라 ᵂ **country; world**

우리나라 our country [our~]

달나라 lunar world; moon [moon~]

꿈나라 dreamland; sleep [dream~]

하늘나라 Heaven [heaven~]

나무 ᵂ **tree**

나뭇잎 leaves of a tree [~leaf] (pron. = 나문닢)

나무그늘 the shade of a tree [~shade]

통나무 (whole) log; unsplit wood [whole~]

등나무	wisteria [rattan~] 藤~
나무토막	a chip of wood [~piece]
나무젓가락	wooden chopsticks [~chopsticks]
나무꾼	woodcutter [~doer]

나물 ʷ	**(seasoned) vegetables**
콩나물	soybean sprouts [bean~]
숙주나물	bean sprouts [bean sprouts~]
시금치나물	seasoned spinach [spinach~]
산나물	mountain vegetables [mountain~] 山~

날 ʷ	**day; time; weather**
오늘날	these days (formal) [today~]
지난날	old days [pass~]
옛날	old days [old~]
앞날	days ahead; future [ahead~]
날새다	(it) dawns; become hopeless (slang) [~dawn]
날마다	everyday; day after day [~every]
날로	day by day
나날이	day by day
날짜	date; day of the month
설날	New Year's Day [New Year's Day~]
복날	any one of the three dog days [dog days~] 伏~
어린이날	Children's Day [children~]
어버이날	Parents' Day [parents~]
백날	all the time [hundred~] 百~
날씨	weather [~condition]

날	**raw; bare**
날로	raw 날로 먹다 eat (something) raw
날거	raw stuff [~thing]
날계란	raw egg [~egg] ~ 鷄卵
날고기	raw meat [~meat]
날김치	raw/unaged kimchi [~kimchi]
날바닥	bare floor [~floor]
날밤새우다	stay up all night [~night stay up]
날도둑	barefaced swindler; shameless scoundrel [~thief]
날벼락	thunderbolt out of the blue sky [~thunder]

날 ʷ	**blade; edge**
칼날	blade of a knife [knife~]
면도날	razor blade [shaving~] 面刀~
콧날	bridge of the nose [nose~]

날다 ʷ	**fly**
날개	wing [~thing used for]
날리다	make fly; make famous; lose (a fortune) 홈런을 날리다 hit a homerun 이름을 날리다 win fame 재산을 날리다 lose a fortune
날쌔다	be quick; be nimble
날렵하다	be quick; be agile
날름	darting in and out; swiftly 혀를 날름 내밀다 put out one's tongue 날름 먹어치우다 eat up in a twinkle

날뛰다	jump up; go wild [~jump]		

날뛰다　jump up; go wild [~jump]

날치기*　snatching; snatcher [~hitting]

날림　a job done carelessly; slipshod thing

날씬하다　be slender

남 ʷ　**other people**

남의눈　others' attention [~'s eye]

남다르다　be peculiar; be different from others [~different]
남다르게 노력하다
work harder than others

남부끄럽다　be ashamed in front of others [~be ashamed]
남부끄럽지 않다 have nothing to be ashamed of

남부럽지않다　have no need to envy others [~envy not]

남몰래　in secret [~secretly]

남이야　none of your business

남.다 ʷ　**remain**

나머지　remainder; (as) a result of
당황한 나머지 all in a fluster

남기다　leave behind; let remain
남김없이 all; entirely

남아돌다　be in surplus [~circulate]

살아남.다　survive [live~]

낯 ʷ　**face**

낯두껍다　be thick-skinned; be brazen-faced [~thick]

낯가리다　(baby) be afraid of strangers [~discriminate]

낯뜨겁다　be ashamed [~hot]

낯간지럽다　be ashamed; be only too aware of one's own flattery [~ticklish]

낯이 없다　have no face; be ashamed of [~not exist]
볼 낯이 없다 be ashamed to face (a person)

낯익다　be familiar [~ripe]
(pron. = 난닉다)
낯익은 얼굴 familiar face

낯설다　be unfamiliar [~unripe]
낯선 얼굴 unfamiliar face

낱 ʷ　**each**

낱낱이　one by one; each and every one

낱개　a piece; individual piece
낱개로 팔다 sell by the piece

낱말　a word; each word [~word]

내　**smell**　(see 냄새)

냄새 ʷ　**smell**　(/내)

냄새나다　smell; emit odor [~come out]

냄새맡다　smell (something); sniff [~smell (something)]

향내　fragrant smell [incense~] 香~

술냄새　the smell of liquor [liquor~]

담배냄새　cigarette smell [cigarette~]

땀냄새　sweaty smell [sweat~]

암내　body odor

발냄새　foot odor [foot~]

방귀냄새　smell of flatulence [a fart~]

타는내　burning smell [burning~]

비린내　fishy smell [fishy~]

썩은내   rotten smell [rotten~]

노린내   fetid smell [fetid~]

구린내   foul smell [foul-smelling~]

지린내   smell of urine [urine-smelling~]

곰팡내   musty odor [mold~]

내리다 ᵂ **go down; get off**

내려가다   go down [~go]

내려오다   come down [~come]

내려놓다   put down [~put]

내려다보다   look down; overlook [~look]

내리치다   beat down; give a downward blow [~hit]

내리막   downhill

널 ᵂ   **a board; plank**

널빤지   a board

널찍하다   be quite wide; be spacious [~have the property of]

널따랗다   be quite wide; be spacious [~have the property of]

널리   widely

넓다 ᵂ   **be wide** (pron. = 널따)

넓이   width 넓이뛰기* broad jump

넓히다   widen

넓적하다   be broad and flat [~have the property of] (pron. = 넙저카다)

넓적다리   thigh [~leg] (pron. = 넙적다리)

넘다 ᵂ   **pass over; exceed**

넘치다   overflow; exceed

넘어지다   fall (over) [~become]

넘어뜨리다   throw down; throw (a person) to the ground [~cause]

넘어가다   fall over; pass (into); be deceived [~go] 속아넘어가다 be deceived

넘어오다   come over; vomit [~come] 넘어올 것 같다 feel like vomiting

넘기다   pass (the deadline); turn over (pages); pass through (a crisis)

넘겨주다   turn over; pass on [~give]

줄넘기*   rope jumping [rope~]

넘겨짚다   make (a random) guess [~guess]

넣다 ᵂ   **put in; fill**

집어넣다   put in [pick up~]

끼워넣다   put in; insert [squeeze~]

노래 ᵂ   **song**

노래하다   sing

콧노래*   humming [nose~]

노래방   karaoke room [~room] ~房

노래자랑*   singing contest [~boast]

노릇 ᵂ   **job; role**

선생노릇*   teaching job (derog.) [teacher~] 先生~

사위노릇*   son-in-law's role [son-in-law~]

며느리**노릇*** daughter-in-law's role
[daughter-in-law~]

놀다 ᵂ   **to play; relax**
(놀이 **noun form**
노는 **modifier form**)

놀이터   playground [~place]

놀리다   banter; tease

놀림   bantering; teasing
놀림.감   laughingstock
놀림받다   be made fun of

놀고먹다   lie around and eat [~eat]

노는날   holiday [~day]

노는시간   a recess; a break
(in school) [~time] ~ 時間

불꽃**놀이*** fireworks display
[fireworks~]

벚꽃**놀이*** cherry-blossom viewing
[cherry blossoms~]

돈**놀이***   money lending; usury
[money~]

놀아나다   take to fast living

놈   **fellow; bastard**

촌놈   country bumpkin
[village~] 村 ~

도둑놈   thief [thief~]

미친놈   crazy bastard [crazy~]

잡놈   bastard; son of a bitch
[mixed~] 雜 ~

높다 ᵂ   **be high**
(높은 **modifier form**)

높이   height; altitude;
(sound) pitch
높이뛰기*   high jump

높이   high(ly)
하늘높이   high up in the sky

높이다   make high; raise

높은자리   high position [~position]

높은사람   person of high position
[~person]

눈높다   aim high; have high
standards [eye~]

놓다 ᵂ   **put; release**

내놓다   put out; expose [take out~]

세워놓다   place on end [stand on end~]

놓아두다   put; leave (a thing/person)
alone [~put]

놓아주다   let go; release [~give]

놓치다   fail to catch; miss; drop

제쳐놓다   put aside [clear away~]

훼방놓다   interrupt; thwart
[interruption~] 毁謗 ~

마음놓다   set one's mind at ease;
relax [mind~]

한시름놓다   feel relieved
[great anxiety~]

말놓다   relax one's honorifics;
talk plainly [talk~]

눈 ᵂ   **eye**

눈깔   eye (vulgar)
눈깔사탕   toffee

눈.동자   pupil of the eye
[~pupil] ~ 瞳子

눈알   eyeball [~egg]

뜬눈   wide-awake eyes [open~]
뜬눈으로 밤을 새우다
stay wide-awake all night

눈.빛   eye color; expression
in one's eyes [~light]
눈.빛이 달라지다
change color

눈물	tears [~water]
눈썹	eyebrows 속눈썹 eyelashes
눈·살찌푸리다	knit one's brow; frown [~flesh frown]
눈·시울	the edge of the eyelid 눈·시울이 뜨거워지다 be moved to tears
눈·곱	mucous discharge from the eyes; modicum …(이)라곤 눈·곱만큼도 없다 have not an ounce of...
남의눈	others' attention [others'~]
눈·짓*	a wink; eye signal [~motion]
눈뜨다	open one's eyes; be awakened [~open]
보는눈	an eye (for) 보는눈이 있다 have an eye (for)
눈좋다	have good eyesight [~good]
눈나쁘다	have bad eyesight [~bad]
눈멀다	be/become blind [~go blind] 사랑에 눈이 멀다 be blind in the matter of love
눈이 삐다	have a blind spot (slang) [~sprain]
밤눈	night vision [night~]
눈·대중	measuring by eye [~rough estimate]
눈꼴사납다	be offensive to the eye; be an eyesore [~shape fierce]
눈부시다	be dazzling (to the eye); (development) be remarkable [~glaring]
눈깜짝할·사이에	in a blink [~blink interval]
눈흘기다	glare at [~look askance]
눈요기*	feasting one's eyes [~appeasing hunger] ~ 療飢
한눈팔다	let one's eyes wander [one~sell]
눈꼴시다	hate to see; be sick of [~shape sour]
눈·독들이다	keep one's eyes on; mark out [~poison put in]
눈앞	before one's eyes; immediate future [~front] 눈앞의 이익 immediate profit
눈감아주다	connive; overlook [~shut give]
길눈	sense of direction [road~]
눈치	tact; perceptiveness; slight indication of one's mental attitude 눈치없다 be tactless; have no sense 눈치 빠르다 be quick-witted 눈치보다/살피다 try to read one's mind 눈치채다 sense; get a hint
눈코뜰·새	없다 be very busy [~nose open time not exist]
눈높다	aim high; have high standards [~high]
눈·금	notch mark on a scale [~line]
눈 w	**snow**
첫눈	first snow of the season [first~]
흰눈	white snow [white~]
눈·길	snowy road [~road]
눈·사람	snowman [~person]
눈싸움	snowball fight [~fight]
눈사태	avalanche [~landslide] ~沙汰

ㄷ

눈보라   snowstorm
눈보라치다   snow drifts hard

함박눈   large flakes of snow [peony~]

늘다 ᵂ   **increase; improve**

늘어나다   grow longer; increase; stretch [~grow]

늘리다   increase; enlarge

늘어서다   form a line; line up [~stand]

늘어뜨리다   hang down; droop [~cause]

늘어놓다   arrange; spread out; enumerate [~put]

늘어지다   droop; be droopy [~become]

늦다 ᵂ   **be late**

밤늦게   late at night [night~]

늦잠   sleeping in [~sleep]
늦잠자다   sleep in

늦여름   late summer [~summer] (pron. = 는녀름)

늦더위   late summer heat [~heat]

늦어도   at the latest

한발늦다   fall a step behind; be late by a second [one step~]

늦추다   extend (the deadline); slow down (the speed)

니   **teeth/tooth**   (/이)

이(빨)   tooth

윗니   upper teeth [upper~]

아랫니   lower teeth [lower~]

앞니   front tooth [front~]

송곳니   canine tooth [awl~]

어금니   back tooth

사랑니   wisdom tooth [love~]

뻐드렁니   projecting front tooth; bucktooth [protruding~]

틀니   denture [frame~]

잇몸   (teeth) gums [~body]

톱니   teeth of a saw [a saw~]

님   **respected person**

부모님   parents [parents~] 父母~

선생님   teacher [teacher~] 先生~

교수님   professor [professor~] 教授~

하느님   God; the lord [heaven~] (<하늘님)

ㄷ

다가   **closer**

다가가다   go nearer; approach [~go]

다가오다   come nearer [~come]

다가서다   step up to; stand closer [~stand]

다가앉.다   sit closer [~sit] (pron. = 다가안따)

다니다 ᵂ   **drop in; go about; go to and from**

다녀가다   drop in and then go on [~go]

다녀오다   drop in and then come back [~come]

ㄷ

걸어**다니다** walk (about) [walk~]

뛰어**다니다** jump about;
rush about [run~]

돌아**다니다** go about; wander
about [go round~]

나**다니다** wander about [come out~]

쫓아**다니다** run about; dangle
after [chase~]

붙어**다니다** dangle about;
shadow [stick to~]

들고**다니다** carry about [carry~]

다랗다 **have the property of**

커**다랗다** be very big; be huge [big~]

길**따랗다** be rather long [long~]

널**따랗다** be rather wide;
be spacious [plank~]

좁**다랗다** be rather narrow [narrow~]

가느**다랗다** be very slender;
be fine [thin~]

굵.**다랗다** be rather thick [thick~]
(pron.= 국다라타)

다르다 ᵂ **be different**
(**다름** noun form)

달리 differently [~ly]

남**다르다** be peculiar; be different
from others [other people~]

별**다르다** be of a particular kind
[special~] 別~

색**다르다** be of a different cast;
be unique [color~] 色~

다름아니라 for no other reason
(than); just [~not]

다름없다 be the same [~not exist]

새거나 **다름없다**
be as good as new
다름없이 likewise; equally

다리 ᵂ **leg**

팔**다리** limbs [arm~]

무**다리** unshapely legs [radish~]

넓적**다리** thigh [flat~]
(pron.= 넙적다리)

키**다리** tall person; gangly
fellow [height~]

안짱**다리** knock-kneed person

꺽**다리** gangly fellow

책상**다리*** sitting on crossed legs
[desk~] 冊床~

양**다리**걸치다 try to have it both
ways; play both sides
[both~put on] 兩~

곁**다리**끼다 participate as an
outsider [side~insert]

다리 ᵂ **bridge**

돌**다리** stone bridge [stone~]

다리놓다 build a bridge; mediate
(between) [~put]

다리건너다 cross a bridge [~cross]

징검**다리** steppingstones

다리다 ᵂ **iron; press**
(**다림** noun form)

다림질* ironing [~doing]

다리미 an iron
다리미판 ironing board

다시 ᵂ **again**

다시한번 once again [~once] ~ 한 番

321

또다시	over again [again~]	단추 w	button
두번다시	again; second time [twice~] 두 番~ 두번다시 없는 기회 golden opportunity	소매단추	sleeve button [sleeve~]
		단춧구멍	buttonhole [~hole]
		단추달다	put on a button [~hang]
다시보다	have another look; come to have a better opinion of [~look]	단추풀다	unbutton [~untie]
		단추끼다	button (up) [~fasten]
다시말해서	in other words [~speaking]	똑딱단추	snap fastener [tap snap~]

다음 w　next; following

달 w　month; moon

다음.번	next time [~time] ~ 番	(한)달	(one) month [one~]
다음부터	from next time [~from]	이달	this month [this~]
다음날	next day [~day]	지난달	last month [pass~]
다음.주	next week [~week] ~ 週	다음.달	next month [next~]
다음에	next time	윤달	leap month [leap month~] 閏~
다음.사람	next person [~person]	보름.달	full moon [15 days~]
다음다음	the one after next 다음다음 일요일 the Sunday after next	반달	half moon [half~] 半~
		초생.달	new moon [newborn~] 初生~

닦이　polishing; washing

		달나라	lunar world; moon [~world]
구두닦이*	shoe polishing; shoeshine boy [shoes~]		
접시닦이*	dishwashing; dish washer (person) [dish~]		

달다 w　be sweet
　　　(단 modifier form)

단골 w　regular establishment; client

단골.손님	regular customer [~customer]	달짝지근하다	be rather sweet
단골술.집	one's regular drinking place [~drinking place]	단거	sweets [~thing]
		단맛	sweet taste [~taste]
단골식당	restaurant one goes to regularly [~restaurant] ~食堂	단무지	sweet radish [~radish]
		단팥	sweetened red bean [~red bean]
		단꿈	sweet dream [~dream]
		단잠	sound sleep [~sleep]

ㄷ

달다 ^w   **hang out; attach**

달리다   hang; dangle

매달다   hang up; tie oneself
down (to) [tie~]
매달리다   hang down
(from); cling to; entreat

달려있다   be hung; depend on [~exist]
...에 달려있다   depend on...

달라붙다   stick to; stand close to
[~stick]

닭 ^w   **chicken**
(pron. = 닥)

닭고기   chicken meat [~meat]

통닭   whole chicken [whole~]

암탉   hen [female~]

수탉   rooster [male~]

담배 ^w   **cigarette**

양.담배   American cigarette
[western~] 洋~

담뱃재   cigarette ashes [~ash]

담뱃불   cigarette light [~light]
담뱃불을 붙이다
light a cigarette

담배꽁초   cigarette butt [~butt]

담배냄새   cigarette smell [~smell]

담배피우다   smoke a cigarette
[~smoke]

담배끊다   quit smoking [~cut off]

줄담배   chain smoking [line~]

담뱃대   (smoking) pipe [~pole]

답다   **be like; be -ly**

여자답다   be womanly
[woman~] 女子~

남자답다   be manly [man~] 男子~

정답다   be affectionate; be friendly
[feeling~] 情~

당기다 ^w   **pull**

끌어당기다   pull; draw [drag~]

잡아당기다   pull; draw [grasp~]

앞당기다   advance (a date) [ahead~]

대 ^w   **pole; a stalk**

전봇대   electric pole
[telegram~] 電報~

막대기   stick of wood

빨.대   drinking straw [suck~]

담뱃대   (smoking) pipe [cigarette~]

뼈대   bone structure; frame
[bone~]

콧대   nose ridge; pride [nose~]

줏대   fixed principles; backbone
줏대가 없다 lack backbone

대다 ^w   **make; tell**

핑계대다   make an excuse [excuse~]

꾸며대다   cook up an excuse
[make up~]

둘러대다   employ subterfuges;
talk oneself out of
(difficulty) [put around~]

대로   **as; like**

멋대로   as one likes;
at one's pleasure [taste~]

마음대로   as one pleases [mind~]

뜻대로   as one wishes [intention~]

ㄷ

예정**대로**	as scheduled [schedule~] 豫定~
되는**대로**	at random; as it goes [become~]
제**대로**	as it should; properly [proper~]
그**대로**	as it is [it~]
될수있는**대로**	as...as possible 될수있는대로 빨리 as quickly as possible

대중 ^w **rough estimate**

대중잡다	make a rough estimate [~grasp]
손.**대중**	measuring by hand [hand~]
눈.**대중**	measuring by eye [eye~]
대중없다	there is no set way [~not exist]

댁 ^w **house (hon.); married woman**

시**댁**	one's husband's family/ house [husband's home~] 媤~
처갓**댁**	one's wife's family/ house [wife family~] 妻家~
선생님.**댁**	teacher's house [teacher respected person~] 先生님~
새**댁**	newly married woman [new~]

더 ^w **more**

좀**더**	little more; some more [little~]
더욱	more; all the more 더욱더 still more
더하다	be more; add up 더할나위 없다 be perfect; leave nothing to be desired

덧셈	addition (in math) [~calculation]
더구나	besides; moreover
더군다나	besides; moreover
덧붙이다	attach [~attach]
덧버선	outer socks [~Korean traditional socks]

더미 ^w **heap; pile**

쓰레깃**더미**	rubbish heap [rubbish~]
산.**더미**	mountain-high pile/stack [mountain~] 山~
잿**더미**	a lump of ash [ash~]

덜 ^w **less; incompletely**

덜하다	be less
덜익다	be unripe; be underdone [~ripe]
덜되다	(person) be no good; be not finished [~be finished]

덥다 ^w **be warm; be hot (더운 modifier form)**

무**덥다**	be sultry; be sweltering
더위	hot weather; heat 찌는더위 steaming heat 무더위 sultry heat 복더위 heatwave during the dog days
더운밥	warm rice [~rice]
더운물	hot/warm water [~water]

덩어리 ^w **lump; mass**

고깃**덩어리**	lump of meat [meat~]
흙**덩어리**	clod of earth [soil~] (pron.= 흑덩어리)
돌.**덩어리**	piece of stone [stone~]

핏**덩어리** blood clot [blood~]

금·**덩어리** gold nugget [gold~]

골칫**덩어리** troublesome fellow [headache~]

덮다 ᵂ **cover**

덮개 a cover [~thing used for]

덮밥 rice topped with X [~rice]

덮치다 throw (a thing) over; overlap one another 엎친데 덮친다 Misfortune never comes alone.

덮어두다 cover and leave; shut one's eyes (to); connive (at) [~leave]

덮어씌우다 cover (a thing) with; charge (a person) with blame [~cover]

덮어놓고 without giving any explanation [~put]

도둑 ᵂ **thief**

도둑놈 thief [~bastard]

좀·**도둑** petty thief [petty~]

날**도둑** barefaced swindler; shameless scoundrel [bare~]

도둑질* thievery [~doing]

돈 ᵂ **money**

종이**돈** paper money [paper~]

용·**돈** pocket money [use~] 用~

꾼**돈** borrowed money [borrowed~]

목**돈** sizable sum of money

푼·**돈** petty cash; paltry sum of money [penny~]

잔**돈** small change [small~]

거스름·**돈** change [give change~]

판·**돈** money set upon the gambling table [place~]

돈·지갑 wallet [~wallet] ~ 紙匣

돈문제 money matters [~matter] ~ 問題

돈걱정* financial worry [~worry]

돈·벌이* moneymaking [~earning]

돈놀이* moneylending; usury [~play]

돈맛 taste for money [~taste]

돈타령* talking about money all the time [~a kind of tune]

돈·벌레 money monger [~worm]

돋다 ᵂ **(sun) rise; (bud) shoot out; (pimple) break out**

돋보기 magnifying glass [~looking]

돋보이다 (appearance) look enhanced [~seem]

돋구다 heap up; stimulate (one's appetite)

북**돋우다** strengthen; stimulate 용기를 북돋우다 encourage

돌 ᵂ **stone**

돌멩이 a stone 돌멩이질* stone-throwing

돌솥 stone kettle [~kettle] 돌솥비빔밥 rice mixed with assorted ingredients in a stone kettle

맷**돌** grindstone

숫**돌** whetstone [pure~]

벽**돌** brick [brick~]

돌·덩어리	piece of stone [~lump]	며칠·동안	for several days [several days~]
조약돌	pebble	오랫동안	for a long time [long time~]
차돌	quartz; tough person	한동안	for a while [one~]
돌대가리	blockhead [~head (vulgar)]		

돌다 ^w   **turn round; circulate; spin**

돌아가다	go around; return; pass away [~go]
돌아오다	come back [~come]
돌아(다)보다	look back [~look]
돌이키다	retrieve
	돌이켜보다 look back upon
	돌이킬 수 없는 irrevocable
돌아다니다	go around; wander about [~go about]
돌려보내다	send back [~send]
돌아서다	turn around; turn one's back on [~stand]
빙빙돌다	spin round and round [round and round~]
돌려보다	pass (a book) around; read and pass on [~look]
돌라주다	hand round; distribute [~give]
돌리다	make (a thing) turn; pass round; deliver; attribute (a matter) to
따돌리다	leave (a person) out in the cold [exclude~]
	따돌림을 받다 be left out
빼돌리다	hide (a person/thing) away [pull out~]

동안   **interval; during**

그동안	during that time [that~]
잠깐·동안	for a little while [short time~]

되   **back; again**

되돌아가다	go back; return [~go back]
되찾다	regain; take back [~find]
되살리다	recall (one's memories) [~let alive]
되풀이*	doing over again
되묻다	ask in return [~ask]

되다 ^w   **be(come); be finished; will do**

헛되다	be futile [empty~]
속되다	be vulgar [vulgar~] 俗~
걱정되다	be worried about [worry~]
지연되다	be delayed [delay~] 遲延~
혼동되다	be confused [confusion~] 混同~
덜되다	(person) be no good; be not finished [less~]
버릇되다	grow into a habit [habit~]
안되다	feel sorry (for); must not do; does not work [not~]
잘되다	go well [well~]
말되다	make sense; stand to reason [words~]
되는대로	at random; as it goes [~as]
되도록	as...as possible
	되도록 빨리 as soon as possible
될수있는대로	as...as possible

돼지 ᵂ **pig**

돼지고기 pork [~meat]

돼지기름 lard [~oil]

돼지우리 pigsty [~pen]

멧돼지 wild boar [mountain~]

돼지저금통 piggy bank [~savings box]

돼지코 turned-up nose [~nose]

두다 ᵂ **put; leave**

놓아두다 put; leave [put~]

가만두다 leave alone; leave as it is [quietly~]

그냥두다 leave alone; leave as it is [as it is~]

내버려두다 leave alone; neglect [throw away~]

두고가다 go leaving behind [~go]

두고오다 come leaving behind; forget [~come]

쌓아두다 heap up [pile up~]

덮어두다 cover and leave; shut one's eyes (to); connive (at) [cover~]

두르다 ᵂ **put around; engirdle**

둘러서다 stand in a circle [~stand]

둘러앉.다 sit in a circle [~sit]

둘러싸다 enclose; surround [~wrap]
둘러싸이다 be surrounded

둘러쓰다 wear around [~wear]

둘러메다 fling (a thing) around one's shoulder [~carry]

둘러보다 look around [~look]

두리번거리다 keep looking around

두루 all around; far and wide

두루마리 a roll of paper

둘레 girth; circumference
가슴둘레 bust
허리둘레 waist measure

테두리 border; edge [rim~]

변두리 outskirts (of a town) [edge~] 邊~

둘러엎다 overturn [~turn upside down]

둘러대다 employ subterfuges; talk oneself out of (difficulty) [~make]

둥이 **person**

흰둥이 white person (derog.) [white~]

깜둥이 black person; Negro (derog.) [black~]

귀염둥이 child who is beloved by all [affection~]

바람둥이 a flirt; philanderer [fickleness~]

뒤 ᵂ **back; later**

뒷면 reverse side [~side] ~ 面

뒷문 back gate [~door] ~ 門

뒷골목 back alley [~alley]

뒤꿈치 heel [~heel]

뒷굽 heel of a shoe [~heel]

뒤통수 back of the head

뒷받침* backing; supporting [~support]

뒷바라지* looking after; helping from behind [~looking after]

뒷모습 appearance from behind [~appearance] ~ 模襲

뒤돌아보다 look back [~look back]

뒤떨어지다 fall behind [~fall]
시대에 뒤떨어지다
be behind the times

뒤지다 fall behind [~become]

뒷걸음질* stepping backward
[~walking doing]
뒷걸음질치다
step backward

뒤쫓다 follow up; run after
[~chase]

뒤를 잇다 follow; succeed (someone)
[~connect]

뒤를 밟다 shadow; follow [~step on]

뒷조사* secret investigation
[~investigation] ~ 調査

맨뒤 the very end [the very~]

뒷정리* arrangements for
the end; cleaning up
[~arrangement] ~ 整理

뒤늦게 too late; belatedly [~late]

뒤처리* after-measure;
settlement (of an affair)
[~disposal] ~ 處理

뒷일 later happenings; the rest
[~matter] (pron. = 뒨닐)

뒷맛 aftertaste [~taste]

뒤탈 later trouble [~trouble]

뒷말 idle discussion after
something is over [~talk]

뒤집다 turn the other way;
turn over [~pick]
뒤집히다 be turned
inside out; be overturned

뒷짐지다 fold one's hands behind
one's back [~baggage carry]

앞뒤 back and forth; sequence
[front~]

앞뒤가 맞지 않다
be inconsistent

뒤집어쓰다 pull (a thing) over one's
head; be covered (with);
take (blame) upon oneself
[~pick wear]
뒤집어씌우다 cover
(a thing) with; put (the blame)
on (a person)

뒤 **mingled**

뒤섞이다 be jumbled up; be
intermingled [~be mixed]

뒤범벅 mess; hodgepodge
[~hodgepodge]

뒤엉키다 get tangled [~get tangled]

뒤죽박죽 topsy-turvy; jumbled up

뒤바뀌다 be taken the wrong way;
be switched [~be changed]

뒤적거리다 rummage; fumble;
browse through (a book)

뒤엎다 overturn; overthrow
[~turn upside down]

뒤지다 search; rummage

뒤흔들다 shake hard; disturb
[~shake]

듣다 ʷ **hear**

들리다 can hear; be heard

곧이듣다 take (someone's word)
seriously [straightforwardly~]

엿듣다 listen secretly; eavesdrop

알아듣다 understand (by hearing)
[know~]

들 ʷ **field; wild**

들판 a plain; field [~place]

들.짐승 wild animal [~animal]

들기름   wild sesame oil [~oil]

들국화   wild chrysanthemum [~chrysanthemum] ~ 菊花

들   **intensely**

들끓다   be crowded with; be infested with [~boil]

들볶다   annoy; torment [~pester]

들쑤시다   dig up; rummage out [~prickle]

들다 ᵂ   **enter; become; cost**

들어가다   enter; go in [~go]

드나들다   go/come in and out; frequent

들락날락하다   go in and out frequently

병들다   fall sick [illness~] 病~

감기들다   catch a cold [a cold~] 感氣~

멍들다   get bruised [a bruise~]

들쭉날쭉하다   be jagged

잠들다   fall asleep [sleep~]

철들다   become possessed with discretion [sense~]

길들다   become tame; get a polish

정들다   grow fond (of); become attached [affection~] 情~

줄어들다   shrink; decrease [decrease~]

물들다   dye; be dyed [dye~]

힘들다   be tough; be difficult [energy~]

들키다   be found out; be caught (in the act of doing)

편들다   side with [side~] 便~

들이다   let in; put in
- 끌어들이다   drag into
- 받아들이다   accept; receive
- 들여다보다   look in
- 들여놓다   bring in; buy in
- 들이치다   (rain) drive into
- 길들이다   tame; give a polish
- 물들이다   dye

들다 ᵂ   **carry; lift**

들고다니다   carry about [~go about]

들어올리다   lift up [~raise]

받들다   uphold; hold (a person) in reverence [prop~]

손들다   raise a hand; give in; be floored [hand~]

들치기*   (shop) lifting; (shop) lifter [~attacking]

들창코   turned-up nose [~window nose] ~ 窓코

들추다   disclose; expose
잘못을 들추다
expose a person's fault

들뜨다   grow restless; (one's mind) wanders [~float]

예를 들다   give an example [example~] 例를 ~

등 ᵂ   **the back**

등허리   back and waist [~waist]

등돌리다   turn one's back [~turn]

발·등   top of the foot [foot~]
발·등의 불   most urgent matter

손·등   back of the hand [hand~]

ㄸ

따르다 ᵂ **follow**

따라가다 follow; go with [~go]

따라오다 follow; come with [~come]

따라다니다 follow around; dangle after [~go about]

따라잡다 overtake; catch up with [~catch]

따라서 accordingly; according to; along
경우에 따라서
according to circumstances
해변을 따라서 걷다
walk along the beach

딴 **different; separate**

딴거 different thing; another one [~thing]

딴사람 different person; someone else [~person]

딴생각* different thought; ulterior motive [~thought]

딴판 a completely different situation [~situation]
생각했던 것과 딴판이다
be quite different from what one thought

딴데 somewhere else; other place [~place]

딴청하다 do (something) irrelevant; not pay attention

딴말* irrelevant remark; double tongue [~talk]

딴소리* irrelevant remark; double tongue [~talk]

딸 ᵂ **daughter**

맏딸 eldest daughter [first~]

큰딸 eldest daughter [big~]

첫딸 first-born daughter [first~]

둘째딸 second daughter [second~]

막내딸 youngest daughter [lastborn~]

외동딸 only daughter [only~]

땀 ᵂ **sweat**

땀나다 sweat; perspire [~come out]

땀흘리다 sweat; perspire profusely [~drop]

땀.방울 beads of sweat [~a drop]

땀냄새 sweaty smell [~smell]

진땀 sweat of anxiety; sticky sweat [thick~] 津~
진땀빼다 have a hard time

식은땀 cold sweat [cooled off~]

땀띠 heat rash

땅 ᵂ **the ground; land**

땅.바닥 bare ground [~floor]

땅.굴 tunnel; underground passage [~tunnel] ~ 窟

땅.볼 (baseball) grounder [~ball] ~ E

땅콩 peanuts [~bean]

때 ᵂ **time; opportunity**

점심때 lunch time [lunch~]

저녁때 evening time [evening~]

제때 right time [proper~]

한때 one time [one~]

때때로   from time to time

때로는   sometimes

때마침   at the right moment; timely [~just in time]

한창때   the prime (of one's life) [the peak~]

때아닌   untimely [~not]

때를 만나다   time is in one's favor; get a chance [~meet]

때 ʷ   **dirt**

때묻다   be stained with dirt [~be stained]

기름때   oil stain [oil~]

때밀이   scrubbers at a public bath [~scrubber]

떡 ʷ   **rice cake**

찰떡   sticky rice cake [sticky~]

가래떡   long and slender rice cake [long round chunk~]

고사떡   rice cake offered to spirits [offering to spirits~] 告祀~

시루떡   steamed rice cake [earthenware steamer~]

모찌떡   *mochi* rice cake [*mochi*~]

떡국   rice-cake soup [~soup]

떡볶이*   broiled dish of sliced rice cake [~panbroil]

떡하다   make rice cakes

떨다 ʷ   **remove; shake off** (떨이 noun form)

떨어내다   shake off [~take out]

떨어지다   fall; be apart; fail (an exam); (clothes/ shoes) be worn out; run out of [~become]
뒤떨어지다   fall behind
정떨어지다   get disaffected

떨어뜨리다   drop; debase; reject (a candidate) [~cause]

재떨이   ashtray [ash~]

떨이   clearance goods

떨다   **do; display**

아양떨다   flirt; flatter [coquetry~]

엄살떨다   exaggerate pain [exaggeration of pain~]

방정떨다   act frivolously [frivolity~]

떼 ʷ   **group; swarm**

떼지어   in groups

떼거리   group; swarm

개미떼   a swarm of ants [ant~]

물.고기떼   a school of fish [live fish~]

떼죽음*   mass death [~death]

떼다   **detach; pull off**

떼어놓다   pull apart; separate [~put]

손떼다   wash one's hands (of) [hand~]

떼어먹다   renege (on one's debt/bill) [~eat]

시치미떼다   play the innocent; pretend not to know [feigning innocence~]

잡아떼다   pull apart; deny with an innocent face; feign ignorance [hold~]

또 w   **also; again**

또한   besides; also

또다시   over again [~again]

또는   or (else)

똑   **just; exactly**

똑바로   straight; upright [~straight]

똑같다   be exactly the same [~same]
똑같이 equally; evenly

똑똑하다   (pronunciation) be clear; be smart; be bright

똥 w   **shit**

똥.구멍   anus [~hole]

똥.개   mongrel [~dog]

똥.값   dirt-cheap price [~price]

똥차   night-soil wagon; ramshackle car [~car] ~ 車

똥.배   potbelly [~belly]

똥칠*   smearing dung; disgrace [~smearing] ~ 漆

별똥   meteorite [star~]

뚜껑 w   **lid; cap**

병뚜껑   bottle cap [bottle~] 瓶 ~

만년필뚜껑   cap of a fountain pen [fountain pen~] 萬年筆 ~

남비뚜껑   potlid [pot~]

뛰다 w   **run; jump**
(뜀 noun form)

뛰어오다   come running [~come]

뛰어가다   run (to) [~go]

뛰어나가다   run forward/out [~go out]

뜀뛰기*   running; jumping

뜀박질*   running; jumping

뛰어내리다   jump down [~get down]

뛰어넘다   jump over [~pass over]

뛰어다니다   jump about; rush about [~go about]

뛰어들다   jump in [~enter]

날뛰다   jump up; go wild [fly~]

뛰놀다   romp; gambol [~play]

뜨기   **person**

촌뜨기   country bumpkin [countryside~] 村~

시골뜨기   country bumpkin [countryside~]

사팔뜨기   squint-eyed person [squint~]

칠뜨기   moron [seven~] 七~

뜨다 w   **float**
(뜬 modifier form)

떠다니다   float (about) [~go about]

떠오르다   rise to the surface; occur to (one) [~rise]

뜬구름   drifting cloud; evanescence (of life) [~cloud]

떠내려가다   be swept away (by the stream) [~go down]

떠돌다   roam; (rumor) get about [~go round]
떠돌이 vagabond

뜬소문   groundless rumor [~rumor] ~ 所聞

들뜨다   grow restless; (one's mind) wanders [lift~]

뜨리다　cause; let

깨뜨리다　break; smash [break~]

망가뜨리다　put out of shape;
　　　　　break; mar

빠뜨리다　drop (a thing) into; plunge
　　　　　(a person) into difficulties;
　　　　　omit [fall into/be omitted~]

떨어뜨리다　drop; debase; reject
　　　　　(a candidate) [shake off~]

넘어뜨리다　throw down; throw
　　　　　(a person) to the ground
　　　　　[pass over~]

쓰러뜨리다　throw down; knock
　　　　　(a person) down

뜻 ᵂ　　**intention; mind; meaning**

뜻하다　intend; plan

뜻대로　as one wishes [~as]
　　　　뜻대로 되다　turn out
　　　　just as one wished

뜻밖　being contrary to one's
　　　expectation; a surprise
　　　[~outside]

뜻이 맞다　be like-minded [~agree]

뜻있는　meaningful [~existing]
　　　　(pron.= 뜨딘는)

말뜻　meaning of words [words~]

속뜻　inner meaning [inside~]

띠 ᵂ　　**belt**

머리띠　hairband [hair~]

허리띠　waistband [waist~]

ㅁ

마다　　every

날마다　every day [day~]

해마다　every year [year~]

곳곳마다　in place after place;
　　　　　everywhere
　　　　　[place after place~]

집집마다　each and every house
　　　　　[house house~]

마르다 ᵂ　**dry (up); become thin**

말라붙다　dry (up) [~stick]

바싹마르다　be dried up completely;
　　　　　be very skinny [parching~]

말리다　make dry

마른안주　dried meat/fish or peanuts
　　　　　eaten with alcohol
　　　　　[~side dish for alcohol] ~按酒

마른행주　dry dish towel [~dish towel]

목마르다　be thirsty [throat~]

말라죽다　wither; be blighted [~die]

마음 ᵂ　　**mind; heart**

마음씨　a turn of mind; nature
　　　　[~the use of]

마음가짐　mental attitude [~carrying]

한마음　one mind; one accord
　　　　[one~]

딴마음　any other intention;
　　　　ulterior motive [different~]

마음먹다　make up one's mind;
　　　　　intend to

마음놓다   set one's mind at ease;
relax [~leave]

마음내키다   feel inclined (to do);
be in the mood (for doing)
[~incline]
마음내키지 않다 be reluctant

마음.속   deep inside one's heart
[~inside]

마음에 들다 be to one's liking;
be satisfactory [~enter]

마음껏   to one's heart's content;
to one's satisfaction
[~to the full extent of]

마음대로   as one likes [~as]

마음잡다   get a grip on oneself
[~hold]

마음든든하다 feel secure [~secure]

마음졸이다   be nervous; be anxious
(about) [~be nervous]

마주 ʷ   **face to face; opposite**
(see 맞)

막   **last**

마지막   the last

막판   last round;
last moment [~scene]

막내   the lastborn
막내딸 youngest daughter
막내아들   youngest son

막차   last bus/train
[~vehicle] ~ 車

막바지   the very end; last moment

막상   ultimately; when you
get down to it
쉬워보이지만 막상하려면
어렵다 (It) looks easy
but is difficult when one
comes to do it.

막다른   dead-end
막다른 골목 dead-end road

막   **rough**

막노동*   rough work; chore [~labor]

막일*   rough work; chore
[~work] (pron. = 망닐)

막말*   blunt remark;
rough talk [~talk]
막말로 to put it bluntly

막국수   coarse noodle [~noodle]

막장   soybean paste mixed
with assorted ingredients
[~soy sauce] ~ 醬

막걸리   unstrained rice wine

막다 ʷ   **clog; block**

막히다   be clogged; be held up
숨막히다 be choked
기막히다 be dumbfounded;
be flabbergasted
차가 막히다
(traffic) be held up

가로막다   block (a passage);
interrupt (one's talking)
[across~]

틀어막다   stop up (a hole/one's
mouth) [twist~]

마개   lid [~thing used for]

칸막이   compartment; booth
[space~] 間~

막아내다   ward off

맏   **firstborn; first**

맏딸   eldest daughter [~daughter]

맏아들   eldest son [~son]

맏며느리   the wife of one's eldest son
[~daughter in law]

맏이   the eldest

말 ^w	**language; talking**	낱말	a word; each word [each~]
한국말*	the Korean language [Korea~] 韓國~	참말	truth; true remark [truth~]
서울말*	Seoul speech [Seoul~]	정말	truth; true remark [right~] 正~
표준말*	standard language [standard~] 標準~	거짓말*	a lie [falsehood~]
존댓말*	honorific speech [respectful treat~] 尊待~	머릿말	preface [head~]
반말*	impolite speech; neutral style of speech [half~] 半~	말·소리	voice [~sound]
귓속말*	whispering; word in one's ear [ear inside~]	인삿말	greeting; welcoming address [greeting~] 人事~
말투	one's way of talking [~style]	말다툼*	wrangle; dispute [~fight]
말씨	manner of speaking; mode of expression [~the use of]	말이 통하다	make oneself understood [~communicate] ~이通
말·버릇	manner of speaking [~habit]	말되다	make sense; stand to reason [~become] 말안되다 make no sense
말솜씨	ability to speak; eloquence [~skill]	잔말*	useless talk; small complaints [small~]
말·재주	ability to speak; eloquence [~talent]	뒷말*	idle discussion after something is over [later~]
말·주변	ability to speak; eloquence [~resourcefulness]	딴말*	irrelevant remark; double tongue [different~]
말대답*	back talk [~reply] ~對答	두말하다	be double-tongued; say anything further [two~] 두말없이 without saying anything further; without any complaint
말참견*	interference; putting in a word [~interference] ~參見		
말장난*	playing with words [~play]	말많다	be talkative [~much]
옛말	old saying [old~]	말없다	be taciturn [~not exist]
말씀*	word; speech (hon.)	말걸다	address (a person) [~speak to]
빈말*	empty words [empty~]		
바른말*	right word; straight talk [righteous~]	말꺼내다	broach a subject [~take out]
아무말	any word [any~] 아무말도 없이 without a word	말더듬.다	stammer; stutter [~fumble]
		말.귀	good ear for words [~ear]
		말문이 막히다	be struck dumb [~door clogged] ~門이

335

맛 ^w	**taste**
단맛	sweet taste [sweet~]
짠맛	salty taste [salty~]
신맛	sour taste [sour~]
쓴맛	bitter taste [bitter~]
매운맛	spicy hot taste [hot~]
꿀맛	scrumptious taste [honey~]
뒷맛	aftertaste [after~]
맛있다	be tasty [~exist]
맛없다	be untasty [~not exist]
입맛	appetite; one's palate [mouth~]
맛소금	seasoned salt [~salt]
밥맛	taste of rice; appetite [rice~]
돈맛	taste for money [money~]
살맛	joy of living [live~] 살맛이 안나다 find no joy in life
맛을 보여주다	teach (a person) a lesson [~show]
깨소금맛	Serves one right. [sesame salt~]
맛살	crab/clam meat [~flesh]
맞	**face to face; opposite; mutually** (/마주)
마주보다	face each other [~look]
마주앉.다	sit face to face [~sit]
마주서다	stand face to face [~stand]
맞서다	confront; stand against [~stand]
맞대다	bring into contact with each other; sit face to face with [~touch]

맞대면*	face-to-face meeting [~facing] ~ 對面
맞은편	the opposite side (from where one is) [~side]~은 便
맞담배피우다	smoke together with another person face to face [~cigarette smoke]
맞절*	mutual bowing [~bow]
맞바람	cross ventilation [~wind]
맞붙다	stick together; grapple with [~stick]
맞장구치다	chime in (with a person); echo another's words [~drum hit]
맞벌이*	working together for a living; dual income [~earning]
맞선	interview with a view to marriage [~marriage meeting] 맞선보다 have an interview with a prospective spouse
맞먹다	be a match for; be equivalent to
맞바꾸다	exchange one thing for another [~exchange]
마주치다	run across (a person); (eyes) meet [~bump]
맞다 ^w	**meet; receive**
맞이하다	meet; welcome; greet 새해를 맞이하다 greet the New Year
마중나가다	go out to meet/greet (a person) [~go out]
바람맞다	be stood up [wind~]
비맞다	get rained on [rain~]

매**맞다**	be beaten; be flogged [whip~]	**맨**손	empty hands [~hand]
얻어**맞다**	receive a blow; be beaten [get~]	**맨**정신	sober mind [~mind]
야단**맞다**	get a scolding; catch it [scolding~] 惹端 ~	**맨**밥	rice without any side dishes [~rice]
퇴짜**맞다**	be spurned; be rejected [rejection~] 退 짜 ~	**맹**	**plain**
딱지**맞다**	be spurned [rejection~]	**맹**물	plain water [~water]
도둑**맞다**	have (something) stolen [thief~]	**맹**탕	tasteless soup [~soup] ~ 湯
맞다 ᵂ	**be correct; agree; fit**	**맹**맛	plain taste [~taste]
맞아떨어지다	tally; be correct [~tally with]	**맹**추	blockhead; dullard
들어**맞다**	(guess) be right; prove right	**맹**꽁이	birdbrain; idiot
맞히다	guess right; hit (the mark)	**머리** ᵂ	**head; hair**
맞추다	put together; fit; adjust 입**맞추다** kiss (a person) 비위**맞추다** make oneself agreeable to (a person) **맞춤**.법 rules of spelling; orthography	대**머리**	bald head
		머리쓰다	use one's head [~use]
		머리아프다	have a headache [~ache]
		머릿말	preface [~words]
		머리좋다	be bright [~good]
		머리나쁘다	be dull-brained [~bad]
		긴**머리**	long hair [long~]
맨	**most; the very**	짧은**머리**	short hair [short~]
맨먼저	at the very first [~first]	단발**머리**	bobbed hair [bobbed hair~] 斷髮~
맨처음	at the very first [~first]	흰**머리**	grey hair [white~]
맨끝	the very end [~end]	검은**머리**	black hair [black~]
맨뒤	the very end [~back]	노랑**머리**	blond hair; westerner [yellow~]
맨나중	the very last [~later]	곱슬**머리**	(naturally) curly hair [curly~]
맨밑	the very bottom [~bottom]	생**머리**	natural hair (vs. permed hair) [raw~] 生~
맨앞	the very front [~front]	파마**머리**	permed hair [permanent~] E~
맨	**bare; unprotected**	**머리**카락	a strand of hair [~long slender object]
맨발	bare feet [~feet]		
맨주먹	bare fists [~fist]		

앞**머리**	bangs [front~]
머리띠	hairband [~band]
머리핀	hairpin [~pin] ~ E
머리빗다	comb one's hair [~comb]
머리감.다	wash one's hair [~wash]
머리기르다	let one's hair grow long [~grow]
머리·자르다	get a haircut [~cut]
머리깎다	get a haircut [~cut]
머리다듬.다	get a hair trim [~trim]
머리땋다	braid one's hair [~braid]

먹 ʷ	**Chinese ink**
먹물	Chinese ink [~water]
먹칠*	smearing with ink; tarnishing (one's reputation) [~painting] ~ 漆
먹구름	black cloud [~cloud]

먹다 ʷ	**eat; suffer; make**
밥**먹**다	have one's meal [rice~]
씹어**먹**다	eat by chewing [chew~]
빨아**먹**다	eat by sucking [suck~]
나눠**먹**다	share (something to eat) [divide~]
얻어**먹**다	get free food [gain~]
먹이	food (for animals); prey
먹음직스럽다	be delicious looking; be appetizing
먹자판	orgy of eating [~let's scene]
먹히다	get eaten

좀**먹**다	be moth-eaten; get destroyed little by little from within [moth~]
벌레**먹**다	be worm-eaten; be decayed [worm~]
먹이다	feed; bribe; inflict (on a person) 젖**먹**이다 breastfeed 돈**먹**이다 bribe (a person) 욕**먹**이다 cause a person to be reviled
구워**먹**다	bake and eat [bake~]
잡아**먹**다	slaughter and eat [catch~]
놀고**먹**다	lie around and eat [play~]
까**먹**다	peel and eat; use up (money); forget [peel~]
먹고살다	make one's living [~live]
잊어**먹**다	forget [forget~]
부려**먹**다	slave drive [drive~]
욕**먹**다	be reviled; be spoken ill of [abuse~] 辱~
떼어**먹**다	renege (on one's debt/bill) [detach~]
겁**먹**다	get scared [fear~] 怯~
애**먹**다	have a hard time [trouble~]
골탕**먹**다	have a bad time of it; be taken in [great injury~]
나이**먹**다	get older [age~]
더위**먹**다	be ill from the heat [heat~]
마음**먹**다	make up one's mind; intend to [mind~]

멀다 ʷ	**be far** (**먼** modifier form)
멀리	far; distantly [~~ly] **멀**리하다 keep away (from)
먼데	far-off place [~place]

먼길	a long way; long journey [~way]	멋(도)모르고	without knowing anything [~even not knowing]

먼길　a long way; long journey [~way]

먼친척　distant relatives [~relatives] ~ 親戚

멀어지다　become distant [~become]

멀지않아　before long [~not]

멀미 ʷ　**(motion) sickness**

차**멀미**＊　car sickness [vehicle~] 車 ~

배**멀미**＊　seasickness [boat~]

멀미약　medicine for (motion) sickness [~medicine] ~ 藥

사람**멀미**＊　fear of crowds [people~]

멋 ʷ　**a show; relish; taste**

멋으로　for show

겉**멋**　superficial vanity [outside~]

멋내다　spruce up [~display]

멋부리다　spruce up; fancy up [~show off]

멋쟁이　stylish person [~person noted for]

멋대로＊　at one's pleasure; waywardly [~as]

제**멋**　one's own taste [self~] 제멋대로　as one pleases

멋있다　be charming; be tasteful [~exist]

멋없다　be tasteless; be uninteresting [~not exist]

멋적다　feel awkward; be embarrassed [~little]

멋지다　be nice; be stylish [~become]

멋(도)모르고　without knowing anything [~even not knowing]

모 ʷ　**edge; angle**

세**모**　triangle [three~]

네**모**　quadrangle [four~]

모나다　be angular [~come out]

모기 ʷ　**mosquito**

모기약　mosquito poison [~medicine] ~ 藥

모기장　mosquito net [~net] ~ 帳

모기향　mosquito coil/stick [~fragrance] ~ 香

모르다 ʷ　**not know**

모른체하다　pretend not to know [~pretend]

몰라보다　fail to recognize [~see]

생판**모르**는　utterly unfamiliar [utterly~] 生板~

어딘지**모르**게　in some way; without knowing why

왠지**모르**게　for some reason one cannot figure out

나도**모르**게　in spite of myself

목 ʷ　**neck; throat**

목구멍　throat; windpipe [~hole]

목소리　voice [~voice]

목청　vocal chords [~membrane]

목숨　life; breath of life [~breath] 목숨걸다　risk one's life

목마르다　be thirsty [~dry]

339

목쉬다	become hoarse [~hoarse]	몸소	personally; in person
목잠기다	become hoarse [~sink]	홀몸이 아니다	be pregnant [single~not]
목메다	be choked [~choke]	잇몸	(teeth) gums [teeth~]
목덜미	nape; back of the neck [~back]		

못   **not; cannot**

목걸이	necklace [~hanger]
목도리	neckcloth; muffler
손목	wrist [hand~]
발목	ankle [feet~]
길목	bottleneck in a road [road~]
건널목	crosswalk [to cross~]

몸 ʷ   **body**

몸뚱이	body
온몸	whole body [whole~]
몸.집	body; frame; bulk [~house]
몸통	trunk; the bulk of one's body [~trunk]
알몸	naked body [egg~]
몸무게	body weight [~weight]
몸매	one's figure; shape [~shape]
몸조심*	taking care of oneself [~taking care] ~ 操心
몸조리*	care of health [~care of health] ~ 調理
몸달다	be all hot and bothered; fidget [~fret]
몸부림*	kicking and screaming; struggle [~wield]
몸.짓*	gesture [~gesture]
몸살	general fatigue from overwork

못나다	be foolish; be ugly [~come out]
못되다	be inside of; be evil [~become] 한달이 못되다 be inside of a month
못마땅하다	be unsatisfactory [~satisfactory]
못본체하다	pretend not to see [~see pretend]
못생기다	be ugly; be bad looking [~form]
못쓰다	be unusable; be no good [~use]
못하다	be not so good as; cannot 못(하)지 않다 be not inferior to
못살게굴다	tease; torment [~live act]

무게 ʷ   **weight**

몸무게	body weight [body~]
무게를 달다	weigh (a thing) [~weigh]
무게중심	center of gravity [~weight center] ~ 重心
무게가 있다	have dignity [~exist]

무늬 ʷ   **design**

꽃무늬	floral design [flower~]
줄무늬	stripes [stripe~]
얼룩무늬	dappled design [dappled~]

무르다 ^w **take back; get/give a refund**

물러나다 withdraw; resign [~come out]

물러앉.다 draw one's seat back [~sit]

물러가다 retreat; withdraw; be gone [~go]

물러서다 step back; retreat [~stand]

물러주다 give a refund [~give]

무 ^w **radish**

열무 young radish

단무지 pickled sweet radish [sweet~]

무말랭이 dried radish slices [~dried thing]

홍당무 carrot [red Chinese~] 紅唐~

무다리 unshapely legs [~leg]

물 ^w **water**

물·기 moisture; dampness [~spirit] ~ 氣

찬물 cold water [cold~]

더운물 hot water [hot~]

약숫물 mineral water [medicine water~] 藥水~

흙탕물 muddy water [muddy water~]

구정물 used dirty water

비눗물 soapy water [soap~]

수돗물 tap water [waterway~] 水道~

샘물 spring water [spring~]

우물 a well

강물 river water [river~] 江 ~

민물 freshwater

소금물 saltwater [salt~]

바닷물 ocean water [ocean~]

밀물 high tide [push~]

썰물 low tide

물바다 a sea of water [~sea]

낙숫물 raindrops from the eaves [drop water~] 落水~

물통 water bottle; bucket [~can] ~ 桶

물총 water pistol [~gun] ~ 銃

물안경 goggles [~glasses] ~ 眼鏡

눈물 tears [eye~]
눈물나다 shed tears

콧물 snot [nose~]

진물 ooze from a sore [thick~]

물약 liquid medicine [~medicine] ~ 藥

물냉면 noodle in cold soup [~cold noodle] ~ 冷麵

물·고기 live fish [~live fish]

물·개 otter [~dog]

물·집 blister [~house]

미끄럽다 ^w **be slippery**

미끈미끈하다 be slippery

미끄러지다 slide; slip

미끄럼 sliding
미끄럼타다 have a slide
미끄럼틀 a slide

미꾸라지 mudfish; loach

ㅂ

밑 ^w **bottom**

맨**밑**   the very bottom [very~]

밑바닥   bottom; lowest stratum [~bottom]

밑창   sole of a shoe; bottom piece [~sole]

밑줄   an underline [~line] 밑줄치다 underline

밑바탕   groundwork; foundation [~base]

밑받침   underlay; under-support [~support]

밑거름   base manure; fertilizer [~fertilizer]

밑천   principal (money) [~cloth]

밑지다   lose on the cost price

ㅂ

바가지^w **(gourd) dipper; overcharging**

물.**바가지**   water dipper [water~]

탈.**바가지**   mask (made with a gourd) [mask~]

바가지긁다   nag (at one's husband) [~scratch]

바가지요금   excessive price [~charge] ~ 料金

바가지쓰다   be overcharged; be ripped off [~put on] 바가지씌우다 overcharge; rip off

바구니^w **basket**

꽃**바구니**   flower basket [flower~]

과일.**바구니**   fruit basket [fruit~]

장.**바구니**   shopping basket [market~] 場~

틈**바구니**   narrow space; squeezed place [space~]

바깥 ^w **outside**   (/밖)

바깥쪽   outside; exterior side [~side]

바깥공기   outside air [~air] ~ 空氣

창**밖**   outside the window [window~] 窓~

안**팎**   inside and outside [inside~]

그**밖**에   other than that; in addition

뜻**밖**   being unexpected; a surprise [mind~]

바꾸다 ^w **change; exchange**

바꿔입다   change (clothes) [~wear]

바뀌다   be changed; be switched

맞**바꾸**다   exchange one thing for another [mutually~]

바늘 ^w **needle; hands of a clock**

바느질   sewing [~doing]

바늘.구멍   needle hole [~hole]

바늘방석   bed of nails [~cushion] ~ 方席

시계**바늘**   hands of a clock [clock~] 時計~

작은**바늘**   short hand of a clock [small~]

큰**바늘**   long hand of a clock [big~]

바다 ᵂ   **sea**

물**바다**   a sea of water [water~]

겨울.**바다**   winter sea [winter~]

바닷물   seawater [~water]

바닷가   seashore; beach [~edge]

바다낚시*   sea fishing [~fishing]

바닥 ᵂ   **floor; bottom**

방.**바닥**   floor (of a room) [room~] 房~

마룻**바닥**   surface (of a wooden floor) [wooden floor~]

날**바닥**   bare floor [bare~]

땅.**바닥**   bare ground [ground~]

길.**바닥**   roadbed [road~]

손.**바닥**   palm [hand~]

혓**바닥**   (the flat of the) tongue [tongue~]

발.**바닥**   sole of the foot [foot~]

신발.**바닥**   sole of a shoe [shoes~]

밑**바닥**   bottom; lowest stratum [bottom~]

바닥나다   be used up; be out of stock [~come out]

바람 ᵂ   **wind; fickleness**

바람불다   be windy [~blow]

바닷바람   wind from the ocean [ocean~]

찬**바람**   cold wind [cold~]

봄.**바람**   spring wind [spring~]

꽃샘**바람**   cold wind in early spring [flower jealousy~]

맞**바람**   cross ventilation [facing~]

바람개비   pinwheel [~piece of wood]

바람맞다   be stood up [~receive]
바람맞히다
stand (a person) up

바람나다   keep fast company; have an affair [~come out]

바람피우다   play the wanton; have an affair [~play]

바람둥이   playboy; philanderer [~person]

바람·기   philanderer spirit; wantonness [~spirit] ~氣

바르다 ᵂ   **be straight; be right**
(**바로** straight; correctly; right)

똑**바르다**   be straight; be upright [exactly~]
똑**바로** straight; upright

올**바르다**   be upright; be honest
올**바로** uprightly; honestly

곧**바로**   straight; right away [soon~]

바로밑에   right under [~under]

바로옆에   right next to [~next to]

바로잡다   straighten; rectify [~hold]

바지 ᵂ   **pants**

나팔**바지**   bell-bottom pants [bugle~]

긴**바지**   long pants [long~]

짧은**바지**   shorts [short~]

반**바지**   shorts [half~] 半~

청**바지**   blue jeans [blue~] 靑~

바짓단   hem on pants [~hem]

바지주머니   trouser pocket [~pocket]

쫄**바지**   leggings

바퀴 ᵂ **wheel; a turn**

앞바퀴 front wheel [front~]

뒷바퀴 rear wheel [back~]

톱니바퀴 toothed wheel [sawtooth~]

한바퀴돌다 make the rounds (of) [one~turn]

바탕 ᵂ **ground; nature**

밑바탕 ground; base [bottom~]

본바탕 intrinsic nature [origin~] 本~

바탕색 background color [~color] ~色

박이 **inlaid thing**

점박이 spotted animal [spot~] 點~

붙박이 fixture; built-in furniture [attach~] 붙박이장 built-in closet

토박이 natives; aboriginals [land~] 土~

밖 ᵂ **outside** (see 바깥)

받다 ᵂ **receive**

벌받다 suffer punishment [punishment~] 罰~

주고받다 give and take [give~]

물려받다 inherit [shift~]

의심받다 incur suspicion [suspicion~] 疑心~

인정받다 receive recognition [recognition~] 認定~

받아쓰다 take down from dictation [~write]

받아들이다 accept; receive [~let in]

발 ᵂ **foot; step**

손발 hands and feet [hand~]

앞발 paw; forefoot [front~]

뒷발 hind foot [back~]

맨발 bare foot [bare~]

구둣발 feet with shoes on [shoes~]

마당발 wide foot [yard~]

발·바닥 sole of the foot [~bottom]

발·등 top of the foot [~the back]

발·가락 toe [~long slender object]

발목 ankle [~neck]

발·뒤꿈치 heel [~heel]

발톱 toenail [~a saw]

발·자국 footprint [~trace]

발·소리 sound of footsteps [~sound]

발야구* foot baseball [~baseball] ~野球

발장구 flutter kick [~drum] 발장구치다 kick (in water)

발버둥치다 (kick and) struggle

발·걸음 a pace; a step [~walking]

한발늦다 fall a step behind; be late by a second [one~late]

신발 footwear [shoes~]

목발* a crutch [wood~] 木~

세발자전거 tricycle [three~bicycle] 세 ~自轉車

발이 넓다 have wide feet; have a large number of social connections [~wide]

발벗고 나서다 throw oneself into (a matter) with enthusiasm [~take off go forward]

발끊다 cease to visit [~cut off]

발뺌*   finding a way to avoid blame; wriggling out [~taking out]

오리발내밀다   have the nerve to feign innocence [duck~thrust out]

밤 w   **night**

오늘.밤   tonight [today~]

어젯밤   last night [yesterday~]

간밤   last night [gone~]

밤낮   night and day; all the time [~day]

한밤.중   middle of the night [peak~middle] 한 ~中

밤늦게   late at night [~late]

밤새   during the night; overnight [~interval] 밤새껏 all night through

밤새(우)다   stay up all night [~dawn] 밤새도록 all night through 밤샘* staying up all night

밤.거리   street at night [~street]

밤.길   a walk at night [~road]

밤차   night train [~vehicle] ~車

밤.배   night boat [~boat]

밤낚시*   night fishing [~fishing]

밤일*   night work; night shift [~work] (pron. = 밤닐)

밤참   late-night snack

밤눈   night vision [~eye]

밤.손님   night prowler; burglar [~guest]

밥 w   **cooked rice; livelihood**

쌀밥   white rice [raw rice~]

잡곡밥   mixed rice [mixed cereal~] 雜穀~

보리밥   rice mixed with barley [barley~] 꽁보리밥 cooked barley

콩밥   rice mixed with beans [bean~]

오곡밥   five-grain rice [five grain~] 五穀~

비빔밥   rice mixed with assorted ingredients [mixing~] 산채비빔밥 rice mixed with mountain-grown vegetables

김밥   sushi

초밥   Japanese-style vinegared rice delicacies [vinegar~] 醋~

볶음밥   fried rice [frying~]

덮밥   rice topped with *X* [cover~] 계란덮밥 rice topped with scrambled eggs 새우덮밥 rice topped with deep-fried prawns

밥풀   grains of boiled rice (used as paste/starch) [~paste]

찬밥   cold rice; person who gets cool treatment (slang) [cold~]

더운밥   warm rice [warm~]

밥그릇   rice bowl [~bowl]

밥솥   rice kettle [~kettle] 전기밥솥 electric rice-cooker 압력밥솥 pressure cooker

밥통   boiled rice container; a fool [~box] ~桶 전기밥통 electric rice-warmer

밥맛   taste of rice; appetite [~taste]

밥상   (foldable) eating table [~table] ~床

개밥   dog food [dog~]

밥벌이*	breadwinning; job [~earning]		똥.배	potbelly [shit~]
밥줄	means of livelihood [~string] 밥줄 끊어지다 lose one's job		물.배차다	have a water-filled stomach [water~be filled]
			배꼽	navel; belly button
			배짱	boldness; guts

방울 ᵂ **drop**

빗**방울**	raindrop [rain~]
눈물.**방울**	teardrop [tears~]
물.**방울**	water drop [water~]
이슬.**방울**	dewdrop [dew~]
땀.**방울**	beads of sweat [sweat~]

밭 ᵂ **dry field**

논밭	rice paddies and dry fields [rice paddy~]
딸기**밭**	strawberry field [strawberry~]
포도**밭**	vineyard [grapes~] 葡萄~
풀**밭**	grass field [grass~]
꽃**밭**	flower garden [flower~]

배 ᵂ **abdomen; belly**

배부르다	have a full stomach [~be full]
배고프다	feel hungry [~be hungry]
배탈	stomach trouble [~trouble] 배탈나다 have stomach trouble
배아프다	have a stomach ache; be jealous 배아파하다 be jealous (of another's success)
배나오다	develop a potbelly; be potbellied [~protrude]

배 ᵂ **ship**

밤.배	night boat [night~]
고깃배	fishing boat [live fish~]
뱃고동	boat whistle [~whistle]
뱃사공	boatman [~boatman] ~ 沙工
배멀미*	seasickness [~sickness]

배추 ᵂ **cabbage**

통배추	whole cabbage [whole~]
배추김치	cabbage kimchi [~kimchi]
양배추	western cabbage [western~] 洋~

뱀 ᵂ **snake**

도마뱀	lizard
뱀장어	eel [~eel] ~ 長魚

뱅이 **person with undesired characteristic**

게으름뱅이	lazybones [laziness~]
가난뱅이	very poor person [poverty~]
주정뱅이	drunken brawler; a bad drunk [drunken rowdiness~]
앉은뱅이	cripple who is wholly deprived of the use of his/her legs [sit~]

버릇 ^w **habit; etiquette**

손.**버릇**　any habitual action
of the hands;
thievish habit [hand~]
손.버릇이 나쁘다
be light-fingered

말.**버릇**　manner of speaking
[talking~]
말.버릇이 고약하다
be rude in speech

술.**버릇**　drinking habit [liquor~]
술.버릇이 나쁘다
be a bad drunk

잠.**버릇**　sleeping habit [sleep~]

버릇없다　be ill-mannered; be rude
[~not exist]

버릇하다　get accustomed to

버릇되다　become a habit [~become]

버리다 ^w **throw away;
do completely**
(**버림** noun form)

내**버리**다　throw away [take out~]

벗어**버리**다　take off; throw off
[take off~]

잘라**버리**다　cut away [cut~]

버림받다　be deserted [~receive]

가**버리**다　go away [go~]

떠나**버리**다　go away; leave [leave~]

써**버리**다　use up [use~]

먹어**버리**다　eat up [eat~]

타**버리**다　be burnt to ashes [burn~]

잊어**버리**다　(completely) forget
[forget ~]

잃어**버리**다　lose (a thing/one's way)
[lose~]

벌레 ^w **worm**

바퀴**벌레**　cockroach [cockroach~]

벌레먹다　be worm-eaten;
be decayed [~eat]

책**벌레**　bookworm [book~] 冊 ~

공부**벌레**　nerd; keener
[studying~] 工夫~

일.**벌레**　workaholic [work~]

돈.**벌레**　money maniac [money~]

벗다 ^w **take off**

벗기다　undress (a person); peel
벗겨지다　come off

벗어버리다　take off; throw off
[~throw away]

발가**벗**다　strip oneself naked [red~]

헐**벗**다　be in need of clothes;
be shabbily clothed
[be worn-out~]
헐벗고 굶주리다
be hungry and cold

벗어나다　get out of (difficulties);
deviate (from) [~come out]
가난에서 벗어나다
overcome poverty
눈에 벗어나다　fall under
(someone's) displeasure
예의에 벗어나다
get against etiquette

벙어리 ^w **a mute**

반**벙어리**　a half-mute; stammerer
[half~] 半~

벙어리장갑　mittens [~gloves] ~ 掌匣

벙어리저금통　piggy bank
[~saving box] ~ 貯金桶

ㅂ

벼락 ʷ	**thunderbolt; thunder**
벼락치다	thunderbolt strikes [~strike]
벼락맞다	be struck by thunder [~receive]
날벼락	sudden calamity [raw~] 청천하늘에 날벼락 sudden calamity out of the blue
벼락부자	overnight millionaire; nouveau riche [~rich person] ~ 富者
벼락공부*	cramming (for an exam) [~studying] ~工夫
벼락치기*	hasty preparation
물벼락	pouring water (on a person) suddenly [water~]

별 ʷ	**star**
별표	asterisk [~mark] ~ 票
별·빛	starlight [~light]
별·자리	constellation [~place]
별똥	meteorite [~shit]

보	**person manifesting a particular characteristic**
먹보	eating machine [eat~]
잠·보	sleepyhead [sleep~]
울보	crybaby [cry~]
겁보	coward [cowardice~] 怯~
털보	scraggly person [hair~]
뚱보	fat person [fat~]
바보	a fool; idiot
곰보	person with a pockmarked face

보내다 ʷ	**send**
심부름보내다	send (a person) on an errand [errand~]
돌려보내다	send back [turn~]
내보내다	let out; send out [take out~]

보다	**see; look**
보이다	be seen; seem; show 쉬워보이다 seem easy 보여주다 let (a person) see; show
얼핏보다	have a quick glance
쳐다보다	look upward; stare (at)
바라보다	look at; gaze (at)
째려보다	give a severe look
노려보다	glare at [glare~]
돌아보다	look back [turn~]
알아보다	make inquiries; recognize [know~]
몰라보다	fail to recognize [do not know~]
잘못보다	mistake X for Y; misjudge [wrong~]
내다보다	look out; look ahead [take out~]
들여다보다	look in; peep in [let in~]
얕보다	look down on; slight [low~]
깔보다	look down on; slight [sit on~]
지켜보다	watch intently [watch~]
엿보다	steal a glance; watch for (a chance)
볼만하다	be worth seeing [~be worth]
볼·거리	things to see [~material]

348

ㅂ

보기	illustration; way of looking at things 돋보기 magnifying glass 내가 보기에 from my point of view
두고보다	wait and see [leave~]
보나마나	undoubtedly; in all probability
볼품없다	have a bad appearance; make a poor show [~looks not exist]
볼썽사납다	be ungainly
보는눈이 있다	have an eye (for) [~eye exist]
흉보다	speak ill of; backbite [flaw~]
손해보다	suffer a loss [loss~] 損害~
재미보다	enjoy oneself [fun~]
물어보다	ask [ask~]
여쭤보다	ask (hon.) [ask~]
집보다	housesit [house~]
돌보다	look after [turn~]
손보다	see to it that there are no defects; touch up; beat (someone) (slang) [hand~]
장보다	go shopping [market~] 場~
볼일	things to do; business [~matter] (pron.= 볼릴) 급한 볼일 urgent business
볼.장다보다	have done with (a thing); be ruined

보다 try (something)

먹어보다	try out (food) [eat~]
해보다	try doing; give it a try [do~]
만져보다	try touching; feel [touch~]
신어보다	try (shoes) on [wear shoes~]

입어보다	try (clothes) on [wear clothes~]

볶다 w **panbroil; stirfry; pester**
(**볶음/볶이 noun form**)

볶음밥	fried rice [~rice]
떡볶이*	broiled dish of sliced rice cake [rice cake~]
오징어볶음	stir-fried squid [squid~]
들볶다	annoy; torment hard [intensely~]

부리다 **display**

멋부리다	spruce up; fancy up [a show~]
심술부리다	act cross [ill-nature~] 心術~
재주부리다	exercise one's talent; perform a trick [talent~]
말썽부리다	cause trouble [trouble~]
꾀부리다	shirk (one's duty) with a phony excuse; resort to wiles [wile~]

불 w **fire; light**

불.길	flames [~road]
불꽃	flame; fireworks [~flower] 불꽃놀이* fireworks display
산.불	forest fire [mountain~] 山~
불티	sparks of fire [~particle] 불티나게 팔리다 sell like hot cakes
불.덩어리	fireball; person with high fever [~lump]
불나다	fire break out [~come out]
불지르다	set on fire [~set fire]

불붙이다 set alight; light up [~light]

불조심* precaution against fire [~precaution] ~ 操心

불자동차 fire engine [~automobile] ~ 自動車

불장난* playing with fire [~playing]

불씨 coal kindling to make a fire; cause [~seed]

불볕더위 sweltering heat [~sun heat]

불쬐다 warm oneself at the fire [~take warmth]

불끈하다 flare up (in anger)

등.불 light; lamp [lamp~] 燈 ~

전깃불 electric light [electricity~] 電氣~

촛불 candlelight [candle~]

불켜다 turn on the light [~turn on]

불끄다 turn off the light [~turn off]

불나가다 light is out [~go out]

붙다 ʷ stick (to)
(붙임 noun form)

달라붙다 cling to

들러붙다 cling to

붙이다 attach (one thing to another); paste
말붙이다 speak to; address
싸움붙이다 make (persons) quarrel

붙잡다 seize; grasp [~catch]
붙잡히다 be seized

붙들다 catch; take hold of [~hold]

붙어다니다 dangle about [~go about]

붙임.성 sociability; affability [~nature] ~임 性

불박이 fixture; built-in furniture [~inlaid thing]

얼어붙다 be completely frozen [freeze~]

말라붙다 be completely dried-out [dry~]

비 ʷ rain

비바람 rain and wind; storm [~wind]
비바람치다 be stormy

눈비 snow and rain [snow~]

비오다 to rain [~come]

비맞다 get rained on [~receive]

빗물 rainwater [~water]

빗방울 raindrops [~drop]

이슬비 misty rain [dew~]

부슬비 sprinkling rain

가랑비 drizzle

빗소리 the sound of rain [~sound]

빗속 the midst of rain [~inside]

빗줄기 streaks of rain [~trunk]

빗발치듯 in streaks

비옷 raincoat [~clothes]

빗길 rainy road [~road]

비누 ʷ soap

세숫비누 facial soap [washing up~] 洗手 ~

빨랫비누 laundry soap [washing clothes~]

가루비누 powdered detergent [powder~]

비누거품 soapsuds; lather [~foam]

비눗물 soapy water [~water]

ㅃ

비누질*	soaping [~doing]
비눗갑	soap case [~case] ~ 匣
비비다 ʷ	**rub; mix** (비빔 noun form)
비빔밥	rice mixed with assorted ingredients [~rice]
비빔국수	noodles mixed with assorted ingredients [~noodles]
비빔냉면	cold noodles mixed with assorted ingredients [~cold noodles] ~ 冷麵
비(비)꼬다	twist; give a sarcastic twist to one's words [~twist]
빈 ʷ	**empty** (비다 to be empty)
빈병	empty bottle [~bottle] ~ 瓶
빈방	empty room [~room] ~ 房
빈속	empty stomach [~inside]
빈자리	vacant seat; room [~seat]
빈차	empty taxi [~vehicle] ~ 車
빈손으로	empty-handed [~hand]
빈말	empty words; lip homage [~words]
빈틈없다	leave no space; be shrewd [~opening not exist]
빈털터리	person who is broke [~person with empty pockets]
빗 ʷ	**a comb**
빗다	to comb
머리빗	a comb [hair~]
참빗	fine-tooth comb
빗질*	combing [~doing]

빚 ʷ	**debt**
빚지다	get into debt [~become]
빚내다	borrow money [~take out]
빚장이	moneylender; creditor [~doer]
빛 ʷ	**light; color**
빛나다	shine [~come out]
빛내다	make (a thing) shine; bring glory to [~bring out]
달.빛	moonlight [moon~]
별.빛	starlight [star~]
햇빛	sunlight [sun~]
빛을 보다	see the light of day; be brought to light [~see]
빛깔	color
눈.빛	eye color; expression in one's eyes [eye~]
얼굴.빛	complexion; countenance [face~]

ㅃ

빠지다	**utterly**
낡아**빠지다**	be well-worn [wear out~]
썩어**빠지다**	be rotten to the core [rotten~]
흔해**빠지다**	be everywhere [common~]
게을러**빠지다**	be thoroughly lazy [lazy~]
약아**빠지다**	be rascally shrewd [shrewd~]

351

빨다 w   **suck**

빨아먹다 eat by sucking [~eat]

빨아들이다 suck in; absorb [~let in]

빨.대 drinking straw [~rod]

빨래 w   **washing (clothes)**
(빨다 to wash clothes)

빨래하다 wash clothes

손빨래* washing by hand [hand~]

빨랫비누 laundry soap [~soap]

빨래판 washboard [~board] ~ 板

빨랫줄 clothesline [~line]

빵 w   **bread**

식빵 (plain) bread; table bread [food~] 食~

보리빵 barley bread [barley~]

옥수수빵 corn bread [corn~]

마늘빵 garlic bread [garlic~]

크림빵 cream bun [cream~] E~

팥빵 red-bean bun [red bean~]

찐빵 steamed bread [steamed~]

호빵 steamed bread

빵·가루 bread crumbs [~powder]

빵.집 bakery [~house]

빼다 w   **pull out; subtract**

빼내다 pull out; take out [~take out]

빼먹다 pull out and eat; leave out; cut (a class) [~eat]

빼앗다 take (by force); deprive (a person) of (a thing) [~take away]

빠뜨리다 drop (a thing) into; miss out; leave out [~cause]

빼돌리다 hide (a person/thing) away [~turn]

뺄.셈 subtraction (in math) [~calculation]

빠지다 fall into; indulge in; be omitted; come off [~become]

빠짐없이 without omission; thoroughly [~without]

뻔하다   **be almost**

늦을뻔하다 be almost late [late~]

죽을뻔하다 be nearly dead [die~]

넘어질뻔하다 almost fall over [fall over~]

잊어버릴뻔하다 almost forget [completely forget~]

뼈 w   **bone**

갈비뼈 rib bone [ribs~]

뼈대 bone structure [~rod]
뼈대가 굵다 be large-boned

뼈다귀 a piece of bone

통뼈 someone special (slang) [whole~]

뼈저리다 pierce one's heart/bone [~sore]
뼈저리게 느끼다 feel keenly

뼈빠지다 be painstaking [~come off]
뼈빠지게 일하다
work one's guts out

ㅅ

뿌리 ᵂ   root

뿌리깊다   be deep rooted [~deep]

뿌리뽑다   root out; eradicate [~pluck]

뿌리치다   shake oneself free from (a grasp); shake off (a person's hand, temptation, etc.) [~remove]

사람 ᵂ   person

새**사람**   reborn person [new~]

딴**사람**   different person; changed person [different~]

집**사람**   one's wife [house~]

눈·**사람**   snowman [snow~]

생**사람**잡다 accuse an innocent person [raw~arrest] 生~

사랑 ᵂ   love

사랑스럽다 be lovable; be lovely

참**사랑**   true love [true~]

첫**사랑**   first love [first~]

옛**사랑**   bygone love [old~]

풋**사랑**   puppy love [unripe~]

짝**사랑***   one-sided love; unrequited love [one side~]

사랑싸움* love quarrel [~fighting]

사랑니   wisdom teeth [~teeth]

살 ᵂ   flesh; skin

군**살**   superfluous flesh; fat [superfluous~]

멱**살**   flesh of the throat [throat~]
멱**살**을 잡다
grab (a person's) throat

눈·**살**찌푸리다 knit one's brow; frown [eye~frown]

살·점   a piece of flesh [~spot] ~ 點

살·덩어리 lump of flesh [~lump]

살코기   lean meat; red meat [~meat]

맛**살**   crab meat; clam meat [taste~]

살찌다   gain weight [~grow fat]

살빠지다 lose weight [~come off]

살빼다   work off surplus fat [~take out]

살·색   flesh color; natural color [~color] ~ 色
살·색 스타킹
natural-colored stockings

살·결   skin texture [~texture]

살·갗   surface of the skin

살 ᵂ   an arrow; a force like an arrow

화**살**   an arrow
화**살**표 arrow mark

햇**살**   sunbeams [sun~]

물·**살**   current of water [water~]
물·**살**이 세다
The current is strong.

구김·**살**   wrinkles; rumples [wrinkles~]

주름·**살**   wrinkles [wrinkles~]

살	**discomfort; fatigue**
몸살	general fatigue (from overwork) [body~]
엄살*	exaggeration of pain

살다 w	**live** (삶이 noun form)
삶	life; existence
살아생전	one's lifetime [~lifetime] ~이生前
살아나다	revive; come back to life [~become]
살아남.다	survive [~remain]
살리다	let live; make the most of 살려주다 save; spare (a person's life)
시집살이*	living with one's husband's parents [husband's home~] 媤집~
타향살이*	living away from home [place away from home~] 他鄉~
살림*	livelihood; housekeeping
징역살이*	serving one's term of imprisonment [imprisonment~] 懲役~
살.길	means to live [~way]
살맛	joy of living [~taste]
살판나다	strike it rich; come into a fortune [~situation become]
하루살이	short-lived insect; an ephemeral [one day~]

삼아	**for (the sake of); as**
재미삼아	partly out of sport [fun~]
장난삼아	for fun [play~]
시험삼아	as a trial [trial~] 試驗~
자랑삼아	boastfully [boast~]

새	**new**
새로	newly [~-ly]
새롭다	be new; be fresh
새거	new thing [~thing]
새해	New Year [~year]
새색시	newly married woman [~bride]
새댁	newly married woman [~married woman] ~ 宅
새사람	reborn person [~person]
새출발*	fresh start [~start] ~ 出發
새살림*	new home [~livelihood]
새싹	a shoot; bud [~bud]
새벽	daybreak; dawn

새	**interval; space**
밤새	overnight [night~]
요새	these days [near at hand~]
눈깜짝할·새	in a blink [eye blink~]
어느새	before one is aware [which~]
새치기*	cutting in (line) [~attacking]

새 w	**bird**
철·새	migratory bird [season~]
참새	sparrow
새소리	birdcall [~sound]
새장	birdcage [~cage] ~ 欌

ㅅ

새   **vivid; deep; intense**

새빨갛다   be vivid red; be brazen;
             be downright [~red]
             새빨간 거짓말   downright lie

새파랗다   be vivid blue [~blue]

새하얗다   be white as snow [~white]

새까맣다   be jet black [~black]

새끼 ᵂ   **baby (animal); brat**

새끼고양이   kitten [~cat]

새끼강아지   puppy [~puppy]

새끼발·가락   little toe [~toe]

새끼손·가락   little finger [~finger]

개새끼   son of a bitch [dog~]

새우 ᵂ   **shrimp**

새우젓   tiny salted shrimps
          [~pickled fish]

새우튀김   shrimp tempura [~tempura]

왕새우   prawn [king~] 王 ~

새우덮밥   rice topped with
          deep-fried prawns
          [~rice topped with *X*]

새우깡   shrimp chips [~chip]

새우잠   sleeping all curled up
          [~sleep]

서다 ᵂ   **stand (as)**

일어서다   stand up [rise~]

줄서다   stand in a line [line~]

늘어서다   form a line [increase~]

맞서다   confront; stand against
          [face to face~]

세우다   make (a thing) stand;
          establish; lay (a plan);
          bring (a car) to a halt
          앞세우다   give priority to;
          set (a person) at the head

앞서다   go first; precede [front~]

나서다   leave; get out; put oneself
          forward [come out~]

중매서다   serve as a matchmaker
          [matchmaking~] 仲媒~

들러리서다   serve as a best
          man/bridesmaid
          [best man/bridesmaid~]

세다 ᵂ   **be strong**

드세다   be strong and rough

고집세다   be stubborn
          [stubbornness~] 固執~

억세다   be tough; be brawny
          [tough~]

셈 ᵂ   **calculation**
          (세다 to calculate)

덧셈*   addition (in math) [add~]

뺄·셈*   subtraction (in math)
          [subtract~]

곱셈*   multiplication (in math)
          [multiply~]

나눗셈*   division (in math)
          [divide~]

속셈   mental calculation;
          ulterior motive [inside~]

소금 ᵂ   **salt**

소금물   salt water [~water]

깨소금   salted sesame [sesame~]

맛소금   seasoned salt [taste~]

소리 ᵂ	sound; voice		속 ᵂ	the inside
소리나다	make a sound [~come out]		속옷	underwear [~clothes]
빗소리	sound of rain [rain~]		속치마	underskirt; slip [~skirt]
찻소리	sound of cars [vehicle~] 車~		속껍질	inner layer of skin [~skin]
새소리	birdcall [bird~]		속눈썹	eyelashes [~eyebrow]
말·소리	voice; talking sound [talk~]		빈속	empty stomach [empty~]
목소리	voice [throat~]		속뜻	inner meaning [~meaning]
콧소리	nasal voice [nose~]		속사정	private circumstances [~circumstances] ~ 事情
큰소리	a yell; big talk [big~] 큰소리치다 yell at (a person); talk big		속마음	innermost feelings [~mind]
소리지르다	shout; yell [~yell]		마음·속	bottom of one's heart [heart~]
잔소리*	useless talk; nagging [small~]		속셈	mental calculation; ulterior motive [~calculation]
헛소리*	silly talk; nonsense; baloney [empty~]		속보이다	give oneself away; disclose one's intention [~be seen]
군소리*	uncalled-for remark [superfluous~]		속상하다	be distressed; be annoyed [~hurt] ~ 傷
딴소리*	irrelevant remark; double tongue [different~]		꿍꿍이속	secret design; underlying motive
별소리	absurd remark [special~] 別~		실·속	substance; real content [real~] 實~
끽소리	even one word of protest [squeak~] 끽소리 못하다 can't say a thing		속속들이	thoroughly; inside out
			빗속	the midst of rain [rain~]
소매 ᵂ	sleeve		손 ᵂ	hand
긴소매	long sleeve [long~]		양손	both hands [both~] 兩~
짧은소매	short sleeve [short~]		빈손으로	empty-handed [empty~]
반소매	short sleeve [half~] 半~		손·가락	finger [~long slender object] 새끼손·가락 little finger 손·가락질* pointing one's finger (at); scorning
소매치기*	a pickpocket; pick-pocketing [~attack]		손·바닥	palm [~bottom]

손·금 lines of the palm [~line]

손목 wrist [~neck]

손톱 fingernail [~a saw]
손톱깎이 nail clipper

손뼉치다 clap one's hands

손꼽다 count on one's fingers
[~count]
손꼽아 기다리다 look
forward to; be counting on

손잡다 hold one's hand; cooperate
(with) [~hold]

손·짓* motion of the hand;
a signal [~motion]

손대다 touch; start [~touch]

손들다 raise one's hand; throw up
one's hand [~raise]

손떼다 wash one's hands of;
[~remove]

손빨래* washing by hand
[~washing clothes]

손수 with one's own hands;
personally

일·손 helping hands [work~]
일·손이 모자라다
be short of hands

손잡이 a handle; a knob [~holder]

손이 크다 be big-handed;
be generous [~big]

손·재주 hand skill; dexterity [~skill]

손·버릇 any habitual action of
the hands; thievish habit
[~habit]

손·수건 handkerchief [~towel] ~手巾

손·거울 hand glass [~mirror]

손·가방 handbag [~bag]

손·전등 flashlight [~lamp] ~ 電燈

손쓰다 take measures [~use]

손보다 see to it that there are no
defects; touch up; beat
(someone) (slang) [~see]

손질* care; trimming
[~act of doing]

손찌검* hitting; beating

손쉽다 be easy; be simple [~easy]

솔 w a brush

칫솔 toothbrush [tooth~] 齒 ~

구둣솔 shoe brush [dress shoes~]

옷솔 clothes brush [clothes~]

솔질* brushing (clothes/shoes)
[~act of doing]

솜 w cotton(ball)

약솜 surgical cotton
[medicine~] 藥~

화장솜 cosmetic puffs
[makeup~] 化粧 ~

솜털 fluff; down [~hair]

솜이불 quilt; comforter [~quilt]
(pron. = 솜니불)

솜사탕 cotton candy
[~candy] ~ 砂糖

송이 cluster; bunch

꽃송이 a blossom; a flower
[flower~]

포도송이 bunch of grapes
[grapes~] 葡萄~

(한)송이 (one) bunch of fruit;
(one) flower [one~]

밤송이 rough, prickly covering
on a chestnut [chestnut~]

쇠 ʷ   **metal**

쇳덩어리   a lump of metal [~lump]

열쇠   key [open~]
       열쇠꾸러미 a bunch of keys

자물쇠   a lock

구두쇠   stingy person [shoes~]

술 ʷ   **liquor; alcohol**

술집   drinking house; bar
       [~house]

술잔   liquor glass [~glass] ~ 盞

술안주   side dish for drinking
       [~side dish for drinking] ~按酒

술냄새   the smell of liquor [~smell]

술꾼   (heavy) drinker; tippler
       [~person occupied with]

술고래   heavy drinker; drunkard
       [~whale]

술취하다   get drunk [~get drunk] ~ 醉

술깨다   sober up [~wake up]

술주정*   misconduct caused by
       liquor; drunken rowdiness
       [~drunken rowdiness] ~ 酒酊

술끊다   quit drinking [~cut off]

술이·세다   have strong resistance to
       alcohol [~strong]

술이 약하다   have weak resistance
       to alcohol [~weak] ~이弱

숨 ʷ   **breath**

숨쉬다   breathe [~breathe]

한숨   a breath; a pause [one~]
       한숨돌리다 catch
       one's breath; breathe easy
       한숨자다 take a nap

한숨   a sigh; deep breath [big~]
       한숨쉬다 sigh

단숨에   in a single breath
       [single~] 單~

숨죽이다   hold one's breath [~kill]

숨차다   be out of breath [~full]

숨막히다   be suffocated [~be blocked]

숨가쁘다   be gasping [~gasp]

숨넘어가다   breathe one's last; die
       [~go over]

목숨   life [neck~]

숫   **pure; innocent**

숫기   innocent openness
       [~spirit] ~ 氣

숫처녀   immaculate virgin
       [~virgin] ~ 處女

숫총각   innocent bachelor
       [~bachelor] ~ 總角

숫돌   whetstone [~stone]

스럽다   **be; give the impression of**

촌스럽다   be boorish; be unrefined
       [countryside~] 村~

복스럽다   be (chubby and)
       prosperous looking
       [blessing~] 福~

사랑스럽다   be lovable; be lovely
       [love~]

변덕스럽다   be capricious
       [caprice~] 變德~

의심스럽다   be doubtful; be dubious
       [doubt~] 疑心~

부담스럽다   be burdensome
       [burden~] 負擔~

스름하다 **be X-ish; be slightly colored**

거무스름하다 be blackish [black~]

불그스름하다 be reddish [red~]

노르스름하다 be yellowish [yellow~]

푸르스름하다 be deep-bluish/greenish [blue/green~]

파르스름하다 be bluish/greenish [blue/green~]

신 w **footwear; shoes**

신발   footwear; shoes [~foot]
신발신.다   put on shoes
신발벗다   take off shoes

고무신   rubber shoes [rubber~]

짚신   straw shoes [straw~]

신.장   shoe cabinet [~cabinet] ~ 欌

실 w **thread**

실바늘   needle and thread [~needle]

치실   dental floss [teeth~] 齒~

털실   woolen yarn [wool~]

실패   a flat piece of wood for winding thread

ㅆ

싸움 w **fighting**
(**싸우다 to fight**)

싸움하다   fight

눈**싸움***   snowball fight [snow~]

패**싸움***   gang fight [gang~] 牌~

사랑**싸움***   love quarrel [love~]

부부**싸움***   a quarrel between husband and wife [husband and wife~]

싸움걸다   pick a fight [~hang]

싸움말리다   stop other people's quarrel [~stop]

싸움붙이다   make (persons) quarrel [~paste]

쌀 w **uncooked rice**

쌀밥   white rice [~cooked rice]

찹쌀   *mochi* rice

좁쌀   hulled millet; petty person

보리쌀   barley [barley~]

쌀.값   price of rice [~price]

쓰다 w **to use**

써버리다   use up [~completely]

써먹다   make use of [~eat]

쓰이다   be used

쓸.데   usefulness; purpose [~place]
쓸.데없이   unnecessarily

쓸모   use; usefulness
쓸모없다   be useless

애쓰다   endeavor; make efforts [pains~]

힘쓰다   endeavor; make efforts [energy~]

신경쓰다   mind; worry [nerve~] 神經~

손쓰다   take measures [hand~]

ㅇ

쓰다 w   **write**

받아**쓰다** take down from dictation
[receive~]
받아쓰기* dictation

띄어**쓰다** write leaving space
(between the words)
[leave space~]
띄어쓰기* spacing words

갈겨**쓰다** scrawl; scribble [hit~]

쓸다 w   **sweep**

쓸어내다 sweep out [~take out]

쓸어버리다 sweep away [~take away]

쓰레기 garbage
쓰레기차 garbage truck
쓰레기통 garbage can

쓰레받기 dustpan [~receiving]

씨   **the use of; condition**

말**씨** manner of speaking; mode
of expression [speaking~]

글**씨** handwriting [writing~]

솜**씨** skill; dexterity
음식솜씨 cooking skill

날**씨** weather [day~]

마음**씨** a turn of mind; nature
[mind~]

씨 w   **seed**

씨앗 seeds

수박**씨** watermelon seeds
[watermelon~]

사과**씨** apple pips [apple~] 沙果~

복숭아**씨** peach pits [peach~]

불**씨** kindling coal to make
a fire; cause [fire~]

아들 w   **son**

큰**아들** eldest son [big~]

맏**아들** eldest son [first~]

첫**아들** first-born son [first~]
(pron. = 처다들)

둘째**아들** second son [second~]

막내**아들** youngest son [lastborn~]

아래 w   **lower part**

아래쪽 lower part/direction
[~direction]

아래층 downstairs [~a story] ~ 層

아랫니 lower teeth [~teeth]

아랫배 belly; abdomen [~abdomen]

아랫도리 lower part of the body;
lower garments

아랫사람 one's junior; subordinate
[~person]

손**아래** one's junior [hand~]

아무   **any; anyone; nobody**

아무말 any word [~words]
아무말 없이
without (saying) a word

아무일 something; anything;
nothing [~matter]
오늘 아무일 없었다
Nothing happened today.

아무데 anywhere [~place]

아무때 any time [~time]

아무짝 any place; any use [~side]
아무짝에도 쓸모없다
be of no use whatsoever

아무런	any sort of 아무런 이유도 없이 without any reason
아무리	no matter how 아무리 돈이 많아도 no matter how rich (a person) may be 아무리 생각해도 in all probability
아무래도	by any means; in any way; in every respect
아무러면	(not) in any way; whatever it is 아무러면 그럴 수 있을까 It is not at all likely. 옷이야 아무러면 어때 It doesn't matter what you wear.
아무렇게나	any which way; at random
아무개	a certain person; so-and-so [~thing used for]
안 w	**the interior; inside**
안쪽	the inside [~side]
안팎	inside and outside [~outside]
안.주머니	inside pocket [~pocket]
집안	family; household; inside the house [house~]
안.방	main living room [~room] ~ 房
아내	one's wife
안짱다리	knock-kneed person
안.다 w	**hold**
껴안.다	embrace; hug [squeeze~]
끌어안.다	embrace tightly [pull~]
안기다	be embraced

앉.다 w	**sit** (pron.= 안따)
마주앉.다	sit face to face [facing~]
둘러앉.다	sit in a circle [put around~]
끼어앉.다	squeeze to sit in [squeeze~]
주저앉.다	plop down; collapse
앉을.자리	place to sit [~place]
앉은뱅이	a cripple who is wholly deprived of the use of his/her legs [~person with an undesired characteristic]
앉은키	one's height when seated [~height]
가라앉.다	sink; subside
알 w	**egg; small round object**
생선알	fish egg [raw fish~] 生鮮~
알짜	the best thing; the essence [~thing]
알통	biceps [~bulk]
알몸	naked body [~body]
눈알	eyeball [eye~]
안경알	spectacle lens [glasses~] 眼鏡~
총알	bullet [gun~] 銃~
콩알	bean; something small [bean~]
깨알	grain of sesame; something tiny [sesame~]
모래알	grain of sand [sand~]
알맹이	kernel; substance
알갱이	granule
알약	tablet (medicine) [~medicine] ~ 藥

ㅇ

알다 ^w   **know**

아는체하다 pretend to know
[~pretend]

알리다 inform; notify
알려지다 become
(well) known

알아보다 make inquiries; recognize
[~look]

알아듣다 understand (by hearing)
[~hear]

알아주다 understand; acknowledge
[~do something for]

알아내다 find out [~bring out]

알아맞히다 guess right [~guess right]

알아차리다 realize in advance;
become aware of [~prepare]

알아서하다   do as one thinks fit

앞 ^w   **the front; ahead**

맨앞 the very front [the very~]

역전앞 (plaza) in front of a train
station [station front~] 驛前~

앞문 front door [~door] ~ 門

앞자리 front seat [~seat]

앞마당 front yard [~yard]

앞바퀴 front wheel [~wheel]

앞니 front tooth [~tooth]

앞가슴 breast [~breast]

앞머리 bangs [~hair]

앞치마 apron [~skirt]

앞뒤 back and forth; sequence
[~back]
앞뒤가 맞지 않다
be inconsistent

눈앞 before one's eyes;
immediate future [eye~]

코앞 under one's nose;
immediate future [nose~]
코앞에 닥치다 be imminent

앞길 road ahead; future [~road]

앞날 days ahead; future [~day]

앞일 things to come; future
[~matter] (pron. = 암닐)

앞당기다 advance (a date); make
(anything) earlier [~pull]

앞두다 have (something)
ahead [~put]

앞지르다 get ahead of (another)
[~shorten]

앞서다 go first; precede [~stand]
앞서 previously; before
앞장서다 lead;
stand at the head

앞세우다 give priority to; set
(a person) at the head
[~make (a thing) stand]

애 ^w   **bowels; pains**

애타다 be anxious; be worried
[~burn]
애태우다 worry (a person)

애쓰다 endeavor; make efforts
[~use]

애먹다 have much trouble [~suffer]

애처롭다 be pitiful

애꿎다 be to be pitied [~ill]
애꿎은 사람
blameless person

애 ^w   **baby; inexperienced; first**

애기 baby

애늙은이 precocious child
[~old person]

애호박 young squash [~squash]

362

애송이	greenhorn
애초	the very first time; the outset 애초의 계획 original plan

어리다 ᵂ **be very young; be childish**

어린시절	childhood [~days] ~ 時節
어린애	baby; child [~baby]
어린이	child; children 어린이날 Children's Day
어리광	child's winning ways 어리광떨다/부리다 play the baby

억 **tough**

억척	(person) being tough 억척스럽다 be tough
억세다	be tough; be brawny [~strong]
억지	stubbornness; unreasonableness 억지로 by force; against one's will 억지부리다 persist stubbornly
억수	pouring rain 비가 억수같이 오다 rain cats and dogs

언제 ᵂ **when; whenever**

언제든지	whenever [~ever]
언제부터	since when [~from]
언제까지	until when [~until]
언젠가	some time; one time
언제나	always

얼룩 ᵂ **stain; spot**

얼룩지다	become stained [~become]
얼룩무늬	dappled design [~design]
얼룩덜룩*	being dappled
얼룩말	zebra [~horse]

얼음 ᵂ **ice**
(얼다 to freeze)

얼음물	ice water [~water]
얼음판	icy ground [~place]
살얼음	thin ice 살얼음판 touchy situation

없다 ᵂ **not exist** (pron.= 업다)

없애다	get rid of
없어지다	be lost; disappear [~become]
없이	without; lacking
틀림없다	be infallible; there is no doubt (that) [being wrong/difference~] 틀림없이 without fail; surely
다름없다	be the same; be not different [difference~]
소용없다	be useless; be needless [use~] 所用~
쓸모없다	be useless [usefulness~]
상관없다	have nothing to do with [correlation~] 相關~
재수없다	be unlucky [luck~] 財數~
정신없다	be distracted; be absent-minded [mind~] 精神~

여러 **several; many**

여러해	several years [~year]
여러번	several times [~repeat] ~ 番

여러가지	various kinds [~a kind]
여러분	ladies and gentleman; everybody [~esteemed person]
여럿	several (people)
여름 ᵂ	**summer**
여름철	summer season [~season]
초여름	early summer [beginning~] 初~
한여름	midsummer [the peak~]
여름옷	summer clothes [~clothes]
여름학교	summer school [~school] ~ 學校
여름.방학	(school) summer vacation [~vacation] ~ 放學
여름타다	be susceptible to summer heat [~be susceptible to]
옆 ᵂ	**side**
옆집	adjacent house; next door [~house]
옆자리	seat next to (a person) [~seat]
옆모습	side of the face; profile [~appearance] ~ 模襲
옆구리	the side; the flank
옛	**old; ancient**
옛날	old days [~day] 옛날이야기 old story
옛말	old saying [~saying]
옛친구	old friend [~friend] ~ 親舊
옛추억	memory of old days [~memory] ~ 追憶
옛사랑	bygone love [~love]

옛일	bygones; past event [~matter] (pron. = 옌닐)
옛모습	trace; vestige [~appearance] ~ 模襲
오다 ᵂ	**come**
나오다	come out [come out~]
걸어오다	come on foot [walk~]
뛰어오다	come running [run~]
달려오다	come running [run~]
내려오다	come down [descend~]
올라오다	come up [rise~]
들어오다	come in [enter~]
다가오다	come closer; draw near [closer~]
다녀오다	drop in and then come back [drop in~]
가져오다	bring [have~]
오락가락하다 come and go; wander 비가 오락가락하다 rain off and on 정신이 오락가락하다 One's mind strays.	
오나가나	always; everywhere you turn
오는	coming; next 오는 토요일 next Saturday
오래	**long; for a long time**
오랫동안	for a long time [~during]
오래전에	long ago [~ago] ~ 前에
오래가다	last long [~go]
오래걸리다	take (much) time [~take]
오래간만	a long time (since) 오래간만이에요 Long time no see.

오르다 ^w go up; rise

올라가다 go up; rise [~go]

올라오다 come up [~come]

올리다 raise

오르내리다 go up and down [~go down]

약오르다 be exasperated; be provoked
약올리다 provoke (a person)

오른 the right

오른쪽 right side [~side]
오른쪽 눈 right eye

오른손 right hand [~hand]

오른발 right foot [~foot]

오른팔 right arm [~arm]

온 all; whole

온몸 whole body [~body]

온세상 all the world [~world] ~世上

온종일 all day [~all day] ~ 終日

온집안 whole family; all over the house [~inside the house]

온통 entirely; all over

온갖 every; all sorts of
온갖 수단 every possible means

올 this year

올해 this year [~year]

올·봄 this spring [~spring]

올여름 this summer [~summer]
(pron. = 올려름)

올·가을 this fall [~fall]

올·겨울 this winter [~winter]

옷 ^w clothes

옷장 wardrobe cabinet; closet [~cabinet] ~ 欌

옷감 cloth; dress material [~material]

옷걸이 (clothes) hanger [~hanger]

속옷 underwear [inside~]

겉옷 outer garment [outside~]
(pron.= 거돗)

잠옷 sleeping garment [sleeping~]

털옷 fur clothes [woolen~]

겨울옷 winter clothes [winter~]

여름옷 summer clothes [summer~]

비옷 raincoat [rain~]

외 only; isolated

외아들 only son [~son]

외동딸 only daughter [~daughter]

외롭다 be lonely
외로움 loneliness

외토리 isolated/lonely person

외딴 isolated; out-of-the-way
외딴섬 solitary island

왼 left

왼쪽 left side [~side]
왼쪽 눈 left eye

왼손 left hand [~hand]
왼손잡이 left-handed person

왼발 left foot [~foot]

왼팔 left arm [~arm]

o

요	**near at hand**
요기	right here
요새	these days [~interval]
요즈음	these days [~time]
요전	just recently; last time [~before] ~ 前
울다 ʷ	**cry**
울보	crybaby [~person]
울.상	tearful face [~face] ~ 相
울음	crying 울음을 터뜨리다 burst into tears
울리다	make (a person) cry
웃다 ʷ	**laugh** (**웃**음 noun form)
웃기다	make (a person) laugh 웃기는 사람 ridiculous person
우습다	be funny; be ridiculous
웃을일	laughing matter [~matter] 웃을일이 아니다 It is no laughing matter.
비**웃**다	laugh at; deride
웃음.거리	laughingstock [~makings]
코**웃**음치다	sneer [nose~do]
눈**웃**음치다	smile with one's eyes [eye~do]
쓴**웃**음짓다	smile a bitter smile [bitter~make]
함박**웃**음	big smile [peony~]
위 ʷ	**upside; upper part**
위쪽	upper part; direction [~side]
위층	upstairs [~story] ~ 層
윗니	upper teeth [~teeth]
윗도리	upper part of the body; upper clothes
윗물	water in the upper part of a stream [~water] 윗물이 맑아야 아랫물이 맑다 A servant is only as honest as his master.
손**위**	one's senior [hand~]
윗사람	one's senior; superior [~person]
웃어른	one's elders [~older person] (pron.= 우더른)
유리 ʷ	**glass**
유리병	glass bottle [~bottle] ~ 瓶
유리잔	a glass [~glass] ~ 盞
유리창	glass window [~window] ~ 窓
시계**유리**	watch crystal [watch~] 時計~
이 ʷ	**teeth/tooth** (see **니**)
이름 ʷ	**name**
이름표	name tag [~ticket] ~ 票
이름있는	famous [~existing]
이름나다	become famous [~come out]
일 ʷ	**work; matter**
일·자리	job; position [~place]
일·거리	piece of work [~material]
부엌**일***	kitchen work [kitchen~] (pron.= 부엉닐)
집안**일***	housework [house inside~] (pron.= 집안닐)

큰일	great undertaking; great trouble [big~]
일꾼	laborer; worker [~doer]
일터	the place where one works [~place]
일손	helping hands [~hand]
일.벌레	workaholic [~worm]
잔일	sundry small matters [small~] (pron. = 잔닐)
별일	particular thing [special~] 別~(pron.=별릴)
앞일	things to come; future [ahead~] (pron. = 암닐)
옛일	bygones; past event [old~] (pron. = 옌닐)
지난일	bygone matters [pass by~] (pron. = 지난닐)
헛일	useless work; vain effort [vain~] (pron. = 헌닐)
웃을일	laughing matter [~matter] (pron. = 우슬릴)

입 ᵂ	**mouth**
입천장	roof of the mouth [~ceiling] ~ 天障
입술	lips
입가심*	taking away the aftertaste from one's mouth [~rinsing]
입김	steam from breath [~steam]
입맛	appetite [~taste]
입맛다시다	smack one's lips [~taste smack]
입맞추다	kiss (a person) [~put together]
입이 가볍다	be a blabbermouth [~be light]
입이 무겁다	be reticent [~be heavy]

입방아찧다	nag; gossip [~mill grain]
입덧*	morning sickness

잇다 ᵂ	**connect; succeed (to)**
이어지다	be connected; be continued [~become]
잇따르다	follow one after another [~follow] 잇따라 in succession
이어받다	inherit [~receive]
이어서	next; in the next place

있다 ᵂ	**exist**
멋있다	be charming; be tasteful [taste~]
맛있다	be tasty [taste~]
가만있다	keep still [quietly~]
달려있다	be hung; depend on [hang~]

잎 ᵂ	**leaf**
잎사귀	leaf
나뭇잎	leaves of a tree [tree~] (pron. = 나문닢)
꽃잎	petal [flower~] (pron. = 끈닢)

ㅈ

자국 ᵂ	**mark; trace**
자국나다	get marked [~come out]
눈물·자국	traces of tears [tears~]
이빨·자국	tooth-marks [teeth~]
발·자국	footprint [foot~]

ㅈ

자랑 ᵂ　pride; boast

자랑스럽다　be proud

자랑·거리　source of pride; something to brag about [~material]

자랑하다　boast about

자랑삼아　boastfully [~for the sake of]

돈자랑*　boast of one's wealth [money~]

힘자랑*　boast of one's physical strength [strength~]

노래자랑*　singing contest [song~]

자리 ᵂ　seat; place; position

앞자리　front seat [front~]

뒷자리　back seat [back~]

옆자리　seat next to (a person) [side~]

앉을·자리　place to sit [to sit~]

제자리　proper place; original place [proper/one's own~] 제자리걸음* marking time

잠·자리　sleeping place; bed [sleep~]

일·자리　job; position [work~]

취직자리　job; position [employment~] 就職~

높은자리　high position [high~]

자리나다　a job/seat opens [~come out]

별·자리　constellation [star~]

가장자리　margin

보금자리　nest

자루 ᵂ　handle (of a tool)

칼·자루　handle of a knife [knife~]

빗자루　broomstick [broom~]

잔　small; fine (잘다 to be small/fine)

잔글씨　small letters [~letters]

잔돈　small change [~money]

잔말*　useless talk; small complaints [~talk]

잔소리*　useless talk; nagging [~voice]

잔일*　sundry small matters [~matter] (pron. = 잔닐)

잔심부름*　sundry errands [~errand]

잔병　constant slight sickness [~sickness] ~ 病

잔털　fine hairs [~hair]

잔주름　fine wrinkles [~wrinkle]

잘　well; nicely

잘하다　do well

잘되다　go well [~become]

잘생기다　be handsome [~form]

잘나다　be handsome; be great (ironical) [~come out] 잘난체하다 put on airs

잘살다　live in opulence [~live]

잘못*　fault; mistake; wrongly [~not]

잠 ᵂ　sleep (자다 to sleep)

잠자다　to sleep

잠들다　fall asleep [~come in]

잠깨다　wake up from sleeping [~wake up]

자나깨나　awake or asleep [~awake]

밤·잠　night sleep [night~]

낮**잠**	a (midday) nap [daytime~]
단**잠**	sweet sleep [sweet~]
선**잠**	light sleep; catnap [underdone~]
새우**잠**	sleeping all curled up [shrimp~]
잠꾸러기	sleepyhead [~overindulger]
잠.버릇	sleeping habit [~habit]
잠투정*	baby's peevishness before or after sleep [~growling]
잠.결	in one's sleep; while asleep [~in the midst of]
잠.귀	sensitivity to sounds while asleep [~ear]
잠꼬대*	talking in one's sleep
잠옷	sleeping garment; pajama [~clothes]
잠·자리	sleeping place; bed [~place]
자**장**가	lullaby
잠자코	without a word; silently

잡다 ᵂ	**hold; catch** (**잡**이 noun form)
붙**잡**다	seize; grasp [stick~]
골라**잡**다	select; take (as one's choice) [select~]
잡아먹다	slaughter and eat [~eat]
걷**잡**다	hold; stop [take away~] 걷**잡**을 수 없다 be out of control
바로**잡**다	straighten; rectify [straight~]
손**잡**다	hold one's hand; cooperate (with) [hand~]
손**잡**이	a handle; a knob [hand~]
잡아당기다	pull; draw [~pull]

왼손**잡**이	left-handed person [left hand~]
양손**잡**이	ambidextrous person [both hands~] 兩 손 ~
길**잡**이	guide; waypost [road~]
잡아떼다	pull apart; deny with an innocent face; feign ignorance [~pull off]
흠**잡**다	find fault with [flaw~]

장난 ᵂ	**play; mischief**
장난치다	play; do mischief [~do]
불**장**난*	playing with fire [fire~]
물**장**난*	dabbling in water [water~]
흙**장**난*	playing in the dirt [soil~] (pron. = 흑장난)
말**장**난*	playing with words [words~]
장난.감	toy [~material]
장난·기	playfulness; mischievousness [~spirit] ~ 氣

장수	**peddler; seller**
꽃**장**수	flower seller [flower~]
과일**장**수	fruit seller [fruit~]
생선**장**수	fishmonger [raw fish~] 生鮮 ~

장이/**쟁**이	**professional/habitual doer (of)**
점**장**이	fortune-teller [fortune-telling~] 占 ~
중매**장**이	matchmaker [matchmaking~] 仲媒~
빚**장**이	moneylender; creditor [debt ~]

고집쟁이	stubborn person [stubbornness~] 固執~
욕심쟁이	greedy person [greed~] 慾心~
심술쟁이	ill-natured person [ill nature~] 心術~
변덕쟁이	capricious person [caprice~] 變德~
허풍쟁이	braggart [big talk~] 虛風~
수다쟁이	chatterbox [chattering~]
거짓말쟁이	liar [lie~]
멋쟁이	stylish person [style~]
겁쟁이	coward [cowardice~] 怯~

재 w **ash**

담뱃재	cigarette ashes [cigarette~]
재떨이	ash tray [~remover]
잿더미	a lump of ash [~pile]
연탄·재	used briquet [briquet~] 煉炭~

젖 w **milk; breasts**

젖소	milk cow [~cow]
젖병	nursing bottle [~bottle] ~ 瓶
젖가슴	breasts [~breast]
젖꼭지	nipples [~nipple]
젖먹이다	nurse (a baby) [~feed]
젖떼다	wean a baby [~detach]

접시 w **plate; saucer**

종이접시	paper plate [paper~]
접시닦이*	dish washing; dish washer (person) [~washing]
비행접시	flying saucer [flying~] 飛行~

젓 **pickled fish**

젓갈	pickled seafood
새우젓	pickled shrimp [shrimp~]
조개젓	pickled clam [clam~]
명란젓	salted pollack caviar [spawn of a pollack~] 明卵~

제 **one's own; proper**

제멋대로	as one pleases; in one's own way [~at one's pleasure]
제대로	as it should; properly [~as]
제때	right time [~time]
제시간	proper time [~time] ~ 時間 제시간에 on time
제철	right season [~season]
제자리	proper place; original place [~place]
제정신	sanity; right mind [~mind] ~ 精神 제정신이 아니다 not be in one's right mind

조림 **hard-boiled (food)** **(조리다 to boil down)**

통조림	canned food [can~] 桶~
장조림	beef boiled in soy sauce [soy sauce~] 醬~
감자조림	potato sautéed in soy sauce [potato ~]
두부조림	tofu sautéed in soy sauce [tofu~]

종이 w **paper**

색종이	colored paper [color~] 色~
종이돈	paper money [~money]
종이컵	paper cup [~cup] ~ E

종이접시　paper plate [~plate]

종이학　paper crane [~crane] ~ 鶴

종이비행기　paper airplane
[~airplane] ~ 飛行機

주걱 ᵂ　**spatula**

밥주걱　rice scoop [rice~]

구둣주걱　shoehorn [shoes~]

주걱턱　turned-up chin [~chin]

주다 ᵂ　**give; do as a favor (for)**

건네주다　hand over; give [to cross~]

물려주다　hand over; bequeath
[shift~]

주어진　given
주어진 시간　the time given

해주다　do as a favor (for) [do~]

보여주다　let (a person) see; show
[show~]

사주다　buy (for) [buy~]

도와주다　help with [help~]

물어주다　pay (for); reimburse [pay~]

갖다주다　bring (as a favor) [carry~]

알아주다　understand; acknowledge
[know~]

바래다주다　see (a person to a
place); escort [escort~]

주름 ᵂ　**wrinkles; pleats**

주름.살　wrinkles [~arrow]

잔주름　fine wrinkles [small~]

주름치마　pleated skirt [~skirt]

주머니 ᵂ　**a pocket**

호주머니　pocket

안.주머니　inside pocket [inside~]

속주머니　inside pocket [inside~]

뒷주머니　back pocket [back~]

바지주머니　trouser pocket [pants~]

주먹 ᵂ　**fist**

맨주먹　bare fists [bare~]

주먹질*　fisticuffs [~act of doing]

주먹밥　rice ball [~rice]

주먹구구　finger-counting;
rule of thumb
[~multiplication rules] ~ 九九

죽다 ᵂ　**die**

얼어죽다　be frozen to death [freeze~]

굶어죽다　be starved to death [starve~]

말라죽다　wither; be blighted [dry up~]

죽이다　kill
때려죽이다　beat to death

죽는소리*　poor mouth
[~sound]

죽어라하고　desperately;
as hard as one can

줄 ᵂ　**string; line**

밧줄　a rope

거미줄　spider's web [spider~]
거미줄치다　weave a web

전깃줄　electric wire
[electricity~] 電氣~

빨랫줄　clothesline [laundry~]

고뭇줄　elastic string; rubber band
[rubber~]

ㅈ

줄넘·기*	ropeskipping [~skipping]
줄타기*	tightrope walking [~ride]
줄다리기*	tug-of-war
줄무늬	stripes [~design]
밑줄	an underline [bottom~] 밑줄치다 underline
줄서다	stand in a line [~stand]
줄줄이	in row upon row
힘.줄	tendon; vein [energy~]
줄기	trunk; stalk 빗줄기 streaks of rain
줄거리	stalk; outline [~makings]
핏줄	blood vessel; blood relationship [blood~]
연줄	pull; connections [affinity~] 緣~
줄곧	all the way; continually

쥐 ʷ	**rat; mouse**
쥐꼬리	rat tail; something small [~tail]
쥐약	rat poison [~medicine] ~ 藥
쥐구멍	rathole [~hole] 쥐구멍에도 볕들 날 있다 Every dog has his day.
쥐덫	mousetrap [~a trap]
생쥐	mouse 물에 빠진 생쥐 someone who is drenched to the skin
박쥐	a bat
다람쥐	squirrel
쥐포	type of dried fish [~dried slices of meat] ~ 脯
쥐죽은듯하다	be as quiet as a mouse [~dead as if]

지나다 ʷ	**pass (by)** (지난 modifier form)
지내다	pass; spend (time)
지난날	bygone days [~day]
지난일	bygone matters [~matter] (pron. = 지난닐)
지난번	last time [~number] ~ 番
지난주	last week [~week] ~ 週
지난달	last month [~month]
지나가다	go past; pass by [~go]
지나오다	come through; pass by [~come]
지나치다	go too far; overdo (it); pass by 지나치게 excessively

지다	**become; be**
달라지다	become different; change [different~]
추워지다	grow cold [cold~]
더워지다	grow hot [hot~]
늦어지다	be delayed [late~]
가까와지다	become close [close~]
멀어지다	grow distant; become estranged [far~]
없어지다	be lost; disappear [not exist~]
사라지다	disappear; vanish
떨어지다	fall; be apart; fail (an exam); (clothes, shoes) be worn out; run out of [shake off~]
넘어지다	fall (over) [pass over~]
쓰러지다	fall down; collapse
뒤지다	fall behind [back~]

벗겨지다   come off; be taken off [take off~]

구겨지다   be wrinkled [crumple~]

알려지다   become (well) known [let know~]

구석지다   be recessed [corner~]

기름지다   (food/soil) be rich [oil~]

값지다   be expensive; be valuable [price~] (pron.= 갑지다)

지다 ᵂ   **carry on one's shoulder**

책임지다   take responsibility [responsibility~] 責任~

빚지다   get into debt [dedt~]

신세지다   be indebted [indebtedness~]

지붕 ᵂ   **roof**

기와지붕   tiled roof [tile~]

초가지붕   thatched roof [thatched house~] 草家~

양철지붕   tin roof [tinned sheet~] 洋鐵~

직하다   **having the property of**

큼직하다   be quite big [bigness~]

널찍하다   be quite wide; be spacious [a board~]

바람직하다   be desirable [desire~]

믿음직하다   be reliable [belief~]

듬직하다   be weighty; be dignified

진   **muddy; wet** (질다 to be muddy/wet)

진흙   mud; clay [~soil]

진창   muddy spot

진눈깨비   sleet

질   **the act of doing**

양치질*   brushing one's teeth [brushing one's teeth~] 養齒~

비누질*   soaping [soap~]

다림질*   ironing [ironing~]

가위질*   cutting with scissors [scissors~]

바느질*   sewing [needle~] (<바늘질)

칼질*   cutting with a knife [knife~]

부채질*   fanning [hand fan~] 불난데 부채질하다 add oil to the fire

걸레질*   wiping; mopping [dustcloth~]

돌멩이질*   stone-throwing [a stone~]

저울질*   weighing; comparing [a scale~]

낚시질*   fishing [fish hook~]

채찍질*   whipping; urging on [a whip~]

도둑질*   stealing [thief~]

곁눈질*   looking aside [side eye~]

발·길질*   a kick; kicking [a kick~]

손·가락질*   pointing one's finger at; scorning [finger~]

손질*   care; trimming [hand~]

구역질   nausea [nausea~]

딸꾹질*   hiccupping

군것질*   eating/buying snacks between meals [superfluous things~]

숨바꼭질*   hide-and-seek

짐 ᵂ   **baggage; burden**

이삿짐   house-moving baggage [house-moving~] 移徙~

짐싸다	pack up [~pack]	집다 w	**pick up**
짐꾼	porter; carrier [~person occupied with]	집어가다	take (away) [~go]
짐스럽다	be burdensome	집어치우다	put away [~put away]
		집어먹다	pick up and eat [~eat] 손으로 집어먹다 eat with one's fingers

집 w **house; home**

집어넣다 put in; stuff [~put in]

집집마다	each and every house [~~every]	집게	tongs; tweezers 쪽집게 tweezers
초가집	thatched house [grass house~] 草家~	꼬집다	pinch [twist~]
기와집	tile-roofed house [tile~]		

짓 **an act of behavior; motion**

하숙집	boarding house [boarding~] 下宿~	나쁜짓*	bad conduct [bad~]
옆집	next door [side~]	미친짓*	act of insanity; foolish behavior [insane~]
집들이*	housewarming	짓궂다	be annoying; be mischievous [~bad]
집세	rent for a house [~rent] ~ 貰	몸짓*	gesture [body~]
집주인	landlord [~owner] ~ 主人	손짓*	motion of the hand; a signal [hand~] 손짓발짓* motion of the hand and foot; every possible gesture
집안	family; household; inside the house [~inside] 집안일* housework 집안식구 family members		
집사람	one's wife [~person]	눈짓*	a wink; eye signal [eye~]
시집	one's husband's family/ house [husband's home~] 媤~		
처갓집	one's wife's family/ house [wife's home~] 妻家~		

ㅉ

꽃집	flower shop [flower~]		
찻집	coffee shop; tea house [tea~] 茶~	짜	**thing; person**
안경집	glasses case [glasses~] 眼鏡~	진짜	genuine article [genuine~] 眞~
두꺼비집	fuse box [toad~]	가짜	imitation; spurious article [false~] 假~
물집	blister [water~]	알짜	the best thing; the essence [egg~]

공짜	a thing obtained without cost; free (of charge) [empty~] 空~	남쪽	southern side [south~] 南~
괴짜	eccentric person [strange~] 怪~	북쪽	northern side [north~] 北~
퇴짜	rejection; brushing off [retreat~] 退~	오른쪽	right side [right~]
		왼쪽	left side [left~]

짝 ᵂ　the mate; one side

쪽　side; direction

짝맞다　match with another one [~agree]
　　짝맞추다　match two things; make a match

짝짓다　make a match; pair [~make]

단짝　inseparable buddy; shadow [single~] 單~

짝수　even number [~number] ~ 數

짝이 없다　be matchless; be incomparable [~not exist]
　멍청하기 짝이없다
　be stupid beyond measure

짝짝이　unmatched pair

짝사랑*　unrequited love [~love]

아무짝　any place; any use [any~]
　아무짝에도 쓸모없다
　It is of no use whatsoever.

짧은 ᵂ　short
　(짧.다　to be short)
　(pron.= 짤따)

짧은머리　short hair [~hair]

짧은치마　miniskirt [~skirt]

짧은바지　shorts [~pants]

짧은소매　short sleeve [~sleeve]

짧은팔　short sleeve [~arm]

쪽　side; direction

동쪽　eastern side [east~] 東~

서쪽　western side [west~] 西~

양쪽　both sides; both parties [both~] 兩~

안쪽　the inside [inside~]

바깥쪽　the outside; exterior side [outside~]

아래쪽　lower part/direction [lower part~]

위쪽　upper part/direction [upper part~]

쫓다 ᵂ　drive away; chase

쫓아내다　drive out; expel [~take out]

쫓아버리다　drive (a person) away; send off [~throw away]

내쫓다　kick out; expel [take out~]

뒤쫓다　follow up; run after [after~]

쫓기다　be chased

쫓아가다　go in pursuit; catch up with [~go]

쫓아오다　come in pursuit; catch up with [~come]

쫓아다니다　run about; dangle after [~go about]

찌개 ᵂ　pot stew

김치찌개　kimchi stew [kimchi~]

된장찌개　soybean-paste stew [soybean paste~]

생선찌개　fish stew [raw fish~] 生鮮~

찾아가다 go to see; visit [~go]

찾아오다 come to see; visit [~come]

차다 ʷ   **be cold**
          (찬 modifier form)

찬물   cold water [~water]

찬밥   cold rice; person who gets
          cool treatment (slang) [~rice]

찬바람   cold wind [~wind]

기차다   be dumbfounded;
          be stunning [spirit~] 氣~
          기가 차서 말이 안나오다
          be struck speechless
          기찬 미인 a stunning beauty

척/체하다 **pretend; make believe**

아는척하다 pretend to know; act
            knowing [know~]

모르는척하다 pretend not to know
              [not know~]

못본척하다 pretend not to see;
            overlook [not see~]

잘난척하다 assume airs [be great~]

철 ʷ   **season**

사철   four seasons; all the year
          round [four~] 四~

봄철   spring season [spring~]

여름철   summer season [summer~]

가을철   fall season [fall~]

겨울철   winter season [winter~]

장마철   rainy season [rainy spell~]

제철   right season [proper~]

철·새   migratory bird [~bird]

찰   **sticky**

찰밥   sticky rice [~rice]

찰떡   rice cake made of
          sticky rice [~rice cake]

찰거머리   sticky leech; persistently
          sticky person [~leech]

찰흙   clay [~soil] (pron. = 찰흑)

참   **true; genuine**

참되다   be true; be genuine

참사랑   true love [~love]

참말   true remark [~words]

참으로   truly [~-ly]

첫   **the first; new**

첫째   the first
          첫번째 the first time

첫날   first day [~day]
          첫날.밤 wedding night

첫해   first year [~year]

첫돌   first birthday of a baby
          [~anniversary]

찾다 ʷ   **search; find**

찾아헤매다 search about
            [~roam about]

찾아주다   find (a thing) for
          (someone) [~give]

되찾다   regain; take back [again~]

첫딸   first-born daughter
          [~daughter]

첫아들   first-born son [~son]
          (pron. = 처다들)

첫차 first bus/train
[~vehicle] ~ 車

첫눈 first snow of the season
[~snow]

첫눈 first sight [~eye]
첫눈에 반하다
be smitten at first sight

첫사랑 first love [~love]

첫인상 first impression
[~impression] ~ 印象
(pron. = 처딘상)

첫마디 first word; opening
remark [~a word]

첫발 first step; start [~step]
첫발을 내딛다
take the first step

첫솜씨 first try; first attempt
[~skill]

치다 ᵂ **hit; attack**
(치기 noun form)

치이다 be run over; be hit
차에 치이다
be run over by a car

박치기* butting one's head against

부딪치다 bump (into/against) [hit~]

마주치다 run across (a person);
(eyes) meet [mutually~]

손뼉치다 clap one's hands
[palm of the hand~]

박수치다 clap; applaud
[clapping~] 拍手~

내리치다 give a downward blow;
beat down [go down~]

쳐들어가다 invade; raid [~go in]

소매치기* a pickpocket; pick-
pocketing [sleeve~]

날치기* snatching; snatcher [fly~]

새치기* cutting in (line) [a space~]

벼락치기* hasty preparation [thunder~]

치마 ᵂ **skirt**

속치마 underskirt; slip [inside~]

긴치마 long skirt [long~]

짧은치마 miniskirt [short~]

행주치마 apron [dish cloth~]

앞치마 apron [front~]

치우다 ᵂ **put away; clean up;**
do completely

집어치우다 put away [pick up~]

해치우다 finish up; kill [do~]

먹어치우다 eat up all [eat~]

팔아치우다 sell off; dispose [sell~]

침 ᵂ **saliva**

침뱉다 spit [~spit]

군침 excessive saliva
[superfluous~]
군침흘리다 drool

침넘어가다 mouth waters [~go over]

침튀기다 sputter [~spatter]

침흘리다 drivel [~spill]

가래침 phlegm

ㅋ

칼 w   **knife**

조각칼   carving knife
[carving~] 彫刻~

부엌칼   kitchen knife [kitchen~]

식칼   kitchen knife [food~] 食~

창칼   small knife

칼날   blade of a knife [~blade]

칼·자루   handle of a knife [~handle]

칼국수   noodles cut with
a kitchen knife [~noodle]

면도칼   razor [shaving~] 面刀~

칼질*   cutting with a knife [~doing]

코 w   **nose**

콧구멍   nostril [~hole]

콧날   bridge of the nose [~blade]

콧대   nose ridge; pride [~a stalk]
콧대가 높다
be puffed up with pride
콧대를 꺾다
humble (a person)

돼지코   turned-up nose [pig~]

들창코   turned-up nose
[lift window~] 들 窓~

콧물   snot [~water]

코딱지   dried mucus from the
nose; nose wax [~scab]

코피   blood from the nose
[~blood]
코피나다   have a nosebleed

코감기   nasal cold [~a cold]

코풀다   blow one's nose [~loosen]

코흘리다   snivel; drivel [~spill]

콧수염   mustache [~beard] ~ 鬚髥

콧소리   nasal voice [~voice]

콧노래*   humming [~song]

코골다   snore [~snore]

코웃음치다   sneer [~laughter do]

코방귀뀌다   pooh-pooh; snort [~fart]

코앞   under one's nose;
immediate future [~front]

코끼리   elephant

콤하다   **be X-ish;**
be slightly flavored

새콤하다   be sourish

시큼하다   be sourish [sour~]

달콤하다   be sweetish [sweet~]

매콤하다   be somewhat spicy [spicy~]

콩 w   **bean**

콩나물   bean sprouts [~vegetable]
콩나물·국   bean-sprout soup
콩나물밥   rice cooked
with bean sprouts
콩나물교실
overcrowded classrooms

콩·국   soybean soup [~soup]

콩밥   rice mixed with beans [~rice]
콩밥먹다   eat bean-mixed rice;
serve a prison term

콩장   beans sautéed in soy sauce
[~soy sauce] ~ 醬

콩기름   soybean oil [~oil]

콩알   bean; something small
[~small round object]
콩알만하다   be very small
간이 콩알만해지다
have one's heart in one's mouth

땅콩	peanut [ground~]
완두콩	pea
강남콩	kidney bean

큰 w **big**
(크다 to be big)

커다랗다	be very big; be huge [~have the property of]
큰길	main road [~road]
큰돈	large sum of money [~money]
큰소리*	a yell; big talk [~voice]
큰일	great undertaking; great trouble [~matter]
큰탈나다	be in big trouble [~trouble come out]
큰딸	eldest daughter [~daughter]
큰아들	eldest son [~son]
큰절*	deep bow [~a bow]
큰코다치다	have a bitter experience [~nose injure]

키 **one's height**

키순	order of height [~order] ~ 順
앉은키	one's height when seated [sit~]
키다리	tall person; gangly fellow [~leg]

ㅌ

터 w **site; place**

일터	one's place of work [work~]
낚시터	fishing place [fishing~]
놀이터	playground [playing~]
약수터	mineral spring resort [mineral water~] 藥水~
흉터	a scar [a scar~]

턱 w **chin**

턱수염	beard [~mustache] ~ 鬚髥
턱걸이*	chin-up [~hanging]
주걱턱	turned-up chin [spatula~]

털 w **wool; fur; hair**

털실	woolen yarn [~thread]
털옷	fur/woolen clothes [~clothes]
털모자	fur hat; woolen cap [~hat] ~ 帽子
털장갑	fur/woolen gloves [~gloves] ~ 掌匣
털보	hairy person [~person]
잔털	fine hair [fine~]
솜털	downy hair [cotton~]
털끝	the end of a hair; a bit [~end] 털끝만큼도 (not) in the least
깃털	a feather [a feather~]

털다 ^w   **shake off; to empty; rob**

털리다   get shaken off; get emptied; get robbed

털어놓다   empty out; confide in [~put]

털어먹다   run through (one's fortune) [~eat]

빈털터리   person who is broke

테 ^w   **a rim**

테두리   border; rim

금테   gold rim [gold~] 金~ 금테안경 gold-rimmed glasses

뿔테   plastic rim [horn~]

안경테   glasses frame [glasses~] 眼鏡~

통 ^w   **whole; bulk**

통째로   all; whole 통째로 먹다 eat (something) whole

온통   entirely; wholly [whole~]

통닭   whole chicken [~chicken] (pron. = 통닥)

통팥   whole (unsplit) red beans [~red bean]

통나무   whole log; unsplit wood [~wood]

통가죽   the whole skin of an animal [~animal skin]

통틀어   all told; altogether

알통   biceps [egg~]

통뼈   someone special (slang) [~bone]

통통하다   be plump; be chubby

투성이   **covered all over with**

피투성이   all bloody [blood~]

흙투성이   all muddy [soil~] (pron. = 흑투성이)

땀투성이   all sweaty [sweat~]

먼지투성이   full of dust [dust~]

거짓말투성이   pack of lies [lie~]

튀다 ^w   **bounce; be spattered**

튀어나오다   protrude; stick out [~come out]

튀기다   spatter; fry

튀김   deep-fried food; tempura
야채튀김 vegetable tempura
새우튀김 shrimp tempura
감자튀김 french fries
고구마튀김 sweet-potato fries
오징어튀김 squid tempura

틀 ^w   **frame; pattern; machine**

창틀   window frame [window~] 窓~

사진틀   picture frame [picture~] 寫眞~

틀니   denture [~tooth]

틀에 박히다 fall into a groove; be conventional [~get stuck]

재봉틀   sewing machine [sewing~] 裁縫~

미끄럼틀   a slide [sliding~]

틀다 ^w   **twist; turn on**

비틀다   twist

틀어막다   stop up (a hole/one's mouth) [~block]

틀어박히다   closet oneself in [~get stuck]

틈 w · a crack; time

문틈	crack in the door [door~] 門~
빈틈없다	leave no space; be shrewd [empty~not exist]
틈바구니	narrow space; squeezed place
틈이 없다	have no room/time (for) [~not exist]
틈나다	come to have time [~come out]
틈틈이	in spare moments
어느틈에	before one knows it [which~]

티 w · a smack; particle

티나다	have a smack of
부티나다	look rich [wealth~come out] 富~
빈티나다	look poor [poor~come out] 貧~
촌티	rusticity; boorishness [countryside~] 村~
불티	sparks of fire [fire~] 불티나게 팔리다 sell like hot cakes

ㅍ

파리 w · a fly

파리약	fly poison [~medicine] ~藥
파리채	fly swatter [~a whip]
파리목숨	ephemeral existence [~life]

판 w · place; scene; situation

들판	a plain; field [field~]
(한)복판	the very middle; center 길 한복판 middle of the road
얼음판	icy ground [ice~]
노름판	gambling place [gambling~]
판돈	money set upon the gambling table [~money]
판국	state of affairs; situation [~circumstances] ~局
딴판	a completely different situation [different~]
먹자판	orgy of eating [let's eat~]
싸움판	fighting scene [fighting~]
난장판	chaotic scene [chaotic place~] 亂場~
살판나다	strike it rich; come into a fortune [live~come out]
막판	last round; last moment [last~]

팔 w · an arm

오른팔	right arm [right~]
왼팔	left arm [left~]
팔목	wrist [~neck] 팔목시계 wristwatch
팔찌*	bracelet
팔걸이	arm rest [~hanger]
팔씨름*	arm wrestling [~wrestling]
팔베개*	arm used as a pillow [~pillow]
팔짱	folding one's arms 팔짱끼다 fold one's arms; be arm in arm

ㅎ

긴팔   long sleeve [long~]

짧은팔   short sleeve [short~]

팔 w   **red bean**

통팔   whole (unsplit) red bean [whole~]

단팔   sweetened red bean [sweet~]
단팥빵 red bean bun

팥빙수   shaved ice with red beans [~shaved ice] ~ 氷水

풀 w   **paste; starch**

풀칠*   applying paste [~painting] ~ 漆

고무풀   mucilage [rubber~]

밥풀   grains of boiled rice (used as paste/starch) [rice~]

풀먹이다   starch (one's clothes) [~feed]

풀죽다   lose one's starch/spunk [~die]

풋   **unripe**

풋고추   unripe green pepper [~pepper]

풋사랑   puppy love [~love]

풋나기   inexperienced person

풋과일   unripe fruit [~fruit]

피 w   **blood**

피나다   bleed [~come out]

피투성이   all bloody [~all covered with]

코피   nose blood [nose~]

핏줄   blood vessel; blood relationship [~line]

피땀   blood and sweat [~sweat]
피땀흘려 번 돈 money earned by the sweat of one's brow

피눈물   bitter tears; tears of agony [~tears]

ㅎ

하늘 w   **sky; heaven**

하늘.색   sky blue (color) [~color] ~ 色

하늘나라   heaven [~world]

하느님   God; the lord [~respected person]

하루 w   **one day**

하루종일   all day [~all day]

하루하루   day by day

초하루   first day of a month [beginning~] 初~

하루아침에   overnight [~in the morning]

하루살이   short-lived insect; an ephemeral [~living]

하룻강아지   (one-day-old) puppy [~puppy]
하룻강아지 범 무서운 줄 모른다 Fools rush in where angels fear to tread.

382

ㅎ

한	**one; the same**	**한**	**the peak; the extreme; big**

한가지	one kind [~a kind]
한군데	one/same place [~place]
한마디	single word [~a word]
한때	one time [~time]
한마음	one mind; one accord [~mind]
한통·속	one and the same group; fellow conspirators [~bulk inside]
한꺼번에	at one time; all together
한편	one side; on the one hand...and/but on the other hand; while [~side] ~ 便
한동안	for a while [~during]
한나절	half a day [~half a day]
한바탕	a round; a bout [~a bout]
한시도	even for a moment [~time even] ~ 時도
한평생	one's whole life [~lifetime] ~ 平生
한눈에	at a glance [~eye]
한가닥	a ray (of hope) [~a piece]
한눈팔다	let one's eyes wander [~eye sell]
한잠자다	sleep a wink [~sleep]
한숨자다	sleep a wink [~breath sleep]
한숨돌리다	breathe easy; catch one's breath [~breath pause]
한푼없다	be penniless [~penny not exist]
한결같다	be constant; be consistent [~texture same]
한층	much more [~layer] ~ 層
한턱	a treat 한턱내다 treat (a person)

한창	the peak; prime 한창때 prime of one's life
한물가다	be past one's prime
한가운데	the very middle; center [~the middle]
한복판	the very middle; center [~the middle]
한여름	midsummer [~summer] (pron. = 한녀름)
한겨울	midwinter [~winter]
한낮	high noon; midday [~daytime]
한밤·중	dead of the night [~middle of the night] ~밤 中
한숨	a sigh; deep breath [~breath]
한걱정	big worry; great anxiety [~worry]
한시름놓다	feel relieved [~worry release]
한길	main road [~road]

해 w	**year**
올해	this year [this year~]
새해	New Year [new~]
첫해	first year [first~]
여러해	several years [several~]
해마다	every year [~every]
햇수	the number of years [~number] ~ 數
햇과일	new crop of fruit [~fruit]

해 w	**sun**
해돋이	sunrise [~rise]
햇빛	sunshine; sunlight [~light]

햇볕 (heat of) the sun [~heat of the sun]
햇볕에 타다 be sun tanned

햇살 sunbeams [~beam]

허 empty; vain

허전하다 feel empty

허술하다 be loose; be careless

헛소리* silly talk; nonsense; baloney [~voice]

허튼소리* idle talk; absurd remark

헛소문 groundless rumor [~rumor] ~ 所聞

헛수고* wasted efforts; fruitless labor [~efforts]

헛일* useless work; vain effort [~work] (pron. = 헌닐)

헛걸음* visit in vain; fruitless journey [~walking]

허탕치다 do something in vain; make a fruitless labor

헛되다 be vain; be futile

헛다리짚다 fall short of one's expectation; guess wrong [~leg touch]

헛디디다 misstep [~step on]

허수아비 scarecrow

허깨비 hallucination; phantom

허리 ᵂ waist

허리띠 waistband [~band]

허리둘레 waist measure [~circumference]

개미허리 slim waist [ant~]

헌 used; old

헌거 used thing [~thing]

헌책 used book [~book] ~ 冊
헌책방 used-book store

헌차 used car [~vehicle] ~ 車

헌옷 used/old clothes [~clothes]

홀 single

홀로 single; alone [~-ly]

홀수 odd number [~number] ~ 數

홀아비 widower [~father]

홀가분하다 feel light; feel unencumbered

홀몸이 아니다 be pregnant [~body not]

흉 ᵂ scar; flaw

흉터 scar [~place]

흉보다 speak ill of; backbite [~see]

흉잡다 find fault with [~catch]
흉잡히다 be found fault with

흙 ᵂ soil (pron. = 흑)

진흙 mud [muddy~]

찰흙 clay [sticky~]

흙덩어리 a clod of earth [~lump]

흙투성이 all muddy [~covered all over with]

흙탕 muddy spot
흙탕물 muddy water

흙장난* playing with dirt [~play]

흰	white (**희다** to be white)	**힘** w	**physical strength; energy**
흰색	white color [~color] ~ 色	**힘·세다**	be physically strong [~strong]
흰눈	white snow [~snow]	**힘차다**	be full of strength; be energetic [~full]
흰옷	white clothes [~clothes]	**힘껏**	with all one's might [~to the full extent of]
흰장갑	white gloves [~gloves] ~ 掌匣	**힘자랑***	boast of one's strength [~boast]
흰구름	white cloud [~cloud]	**힘들다**	be tough; be difficult [~cost] **힘들이다** put in efforts
흰설탕	white sugar [~sugar] ~ 雪糖	**힘쓰다**	endeavor; make efforts [~use]
흰자	white (of an egg/the eye)	**힘겹다**	be beyond one's strength [~be more than one can manage]
흰머리	grey hair [~hair]	**힘없이**	feebly; dejectedly [~without]
		힘·줄	tendon; vein [~string]

Index

Studies from
the Center for Korean Studies

Studies on Korea: A Scholar's Guide, edited by Han-Kyo Kim. 1980.

Korean Communism, 1945–1980: A Reference Guide to the Political System, by Dae-Sook Suh. 1981.

Korea and the United States: A Century of Cooperation, edited by Youngnok Koo and Dae-Sook Suh. 1984.

The Reluctant Crusade: American Foreign Policy in Korea, 1941–1950, by James I. Matray. 1985.

The Korean Frontier in America: Immigration to Hawaii, 1896–1910, by Wayne Patterson. 1988.

Korean-American Relations: Documents Pertaining to the Far Eastern Diplomacy of the United States. Volume III. *The Period of Diminishing Influence, 1896–1905,* edited and with an introduction by Scott S. Burnett. 1989.

Diplomacy of Asymmetry: Korean-American Relations to 1910, by Jongsuk Chay. 1990.

South Korea's Minjung Movement: The Culture and Politics of Dissidence, edited by Kenneth M. Wells. 1995.

Handbook of Korean Vocabulary: A Resource for Word Recognition and Comprehension, by Miho Choo and William O'Grady. 1996.